A Nation of
Counterfeiters

A Nation of Counterfeiters

CAPITALISTS, CON MEN,
AND THE MAKING OF
THE UNITED STATES

STEPHEN MIHM

HARVARD UNIVERSITY PRESS
Cambridge, Massachusetts
London, England

First Harvard University Press paperback edition, 2009.

Publication of this book has been supported through the generous provisions of the Maurice and Lula Bradley Smith Memorial Fund.

Figures 1, 13, 14, 15, 23, and 26 are used, with permission, from Q. David Bowers, *Obsolete Paper Money Issued by Banks in the United States, 1782–1866*, copyright © 2006 Whitman Publishing, LLC. All Rights Reserved.

Portions of Chapter 1 appeared previously as "The Alchemy of the Self: Stephen Burroughs and the Counterfeit Economy of the Early Republic," *Early American Studies* 2 (Spring 2004): 123–159. The material appears here by permission of the McNeil Center for Early American Studies and the University of Pennsylvania Press.

Library of Congress Cataloging-in-Publication Data

Mihm, Stephen, 1968–
A nation of counterfeiters : capitalists, con men, and the making of
the United States / Stephen Mihm.
p.   cm.
Includes bibliographical references and index.
ISBN 978-0-674-02657-5 (cloth : alk. paper)
ISBN 978-0-674-03244-6 (pbk.)
1. Bank notes—Forgeries—United States.   2. Banks and banking—United States.
3. Counterfeits and counterfeiting—United States.   I. Title.
HG336.U5M54   2007
332.10973'09034—dc22   2007009741

For Silas

CONTENTS

ILLUSTRATIONS

A Nation of
Counterfeiters

Confidence and the Currency

Few of us question the slips of green paper that come and go in our wallets, purses, and pockets. While we may obsess over how much money we have, we do not scrutinize the notes themselves: in fact, many of us cannot remember (without looking) which scenes or secular saints go with which denomination. Our ignorance is a testament to just how secure we feel about the nation's currency. The money is in our hands and is universally accepted at face value: that is all we need to know.

It was not always so. In the years between the Revolution and the Civil War, money inspired not careless faith and trust, but nagging doubt and scrutiny. Most money in circulation during these years originated not with the national government, but with sometimes shaky private banks. This right to make money—literally—was a privilege that bankers acquired when they obtained a corporate charter from one of the individual states. After depositing bonds or other assets with a state government, a bank could commission an engraver to design and print so-called bank notes, colorful slips of paper that pledged to pay an

FIGURE 1. Bank notes from the late eighteenth and early nineteenth centuries lacked the elaborate designs and fine engraving that became commonplace by the 1830s. *Courtesy, Q. David Bowers.*

equivalent amount of gold or silver coin—what was called specie—if presented for redemption at the bank, and which entered into circulation as the bank issued loans, transferred money, paid its debts, and conducted its day-to-day business. The principal capitalists of the emerging market economy, banks and bankers underwrote enterprise while providing a medium of exchange—even if the notes they issued were not legal tender.

Though only a few banks issued notes in the 1790s, close to two hundred did by 1815, and by 1830, the number had climbed to 321. Ten years later, the number of banks jumped again, to 711, and after dipping in the early 1840s, skyrocketed upward. To complicate matters further, other state-chartered corporations—insurance companies, railroads, import and export firms, and canal companies—also issued notes at this time, as did numerous unchartered bankers and merchants operating in defiance of the law. By the 1850s, with so many entities commissioning bank notes of their own design (and in denominations, sizes, and colors of their choosing), the money supply became a great confluence of more than ten thousand different kinds of paper that continually changed hands, baffled the uninitiated, and fluctuated in value according to the whims of the market. Thousands of different kinds of gold, silver, and copper coins issued by foreign governments and domestic merchants complicated the mix.[1]

Such a multifarious monetary system was not what the framers of the Constitution had intended. In very clear language, the document they drafted gave the federal government the right to coin money. The states, by contrast, could not, and were also denied the privilege of issuing paper money, or "bills of credit." Even so, state-chartered banks ended up supplying most of the money in circulation, claiming that if the states could not issue paper money, they could nonetheless bestow that right on the corporations they chartered. Not everyone bought this dubious legal argument, but there were pragmatic reasons for letting the banks alone: there was never enough gold or silver coin in circulation to meet the demand for money. An obvious alternative was to have the federal government supply a uniform paper currency, and Congress chartered two national banks that did just that in the first few decades of the country's existence. Nonetheless, neither institution gained exclusive control over the paper money supply, and both fell victim to politics and neglect. By the 1830s, the state-chartered banks operated free of federal control or oversight.[2]

While many editorialists and economic theorists lamented this state of affairs, it was a novelist who painted one of the more disturbing portraits of this confusing system of currency and the capitalist society it both symbolized and sustained. By the time he began writing *The Confidence Man*, Herman Melville had already receded from public view, a victim of his resistance to the demands of the popular literary market. The novel, which arrived in bookstores during the financial panic of 1857—when most of the nation's banks stopped honoring their notes—was a parable of the market economy and the paradoxical forces that kept it alive. Set aboard a steamboat drifting down the Mississippi on April Fools' Day, the novel followed a shape-shifting imposter who appears in various guises—a patent medicine salesman, a seller of stock in a coal company, a representative of an employment agency—and engages passengers in abstruse discussions about human nature, trust, charity, and confidence. These tête-à-têtes inevitably end with him asking his victim for "confidence" in the form of a donation, purchase, cash advance, or loan. Some hesitate, but most accede to the confidence man's request. Money changes hands, the confidence man changes his appearance, and the cycle begins anew. He operates with impunity, for Melville's "ship of fools" has no captain, no officers of the law, not even the semblance of a community. The boat, "though always full of strangers," nevertheless "continually . . . adds to, or replaces them with strangers still more strange."[3]

The final scene dwells on the confidence man watching an older gentleman as he looks over some bank notes received in St. Louis. Wanting to know if they are "all right," the man turns to a publication called a "counterfeit detector," and lays the bills before it. After a lengthy examination, he declares that one bill "looks to be a three dollar bill on the Vicksburgh Trust and Insurance Banking Company," but hesitates, noting that "the Detector says, among fifty other things, that, if a good bill, it must have, thickened here and there into the substance of the paper, little wavy spots of red . . . being made by the lint of a red silk handkerchief stirred upon the paper-maker's vat—the paper being made to order for the company." But he cannot find the telltale red marks: the note has circulated too much and has become worn. Desperate to unequivocally classify the note as genuine or counterfeit, the elderly man enters a spiral of uncertainty. "I don't know, I don't know . . . there's so many marks of all sorts to go by, it makes it . . . kind of uncertain." The old man—whether because of his failing eyesight or a more metaphorical blindness—never determines whether the bill is counterfeit or not, and the novel ends on this note of uncertainty.[4]

The scene comes close to capturing how difficult it became to determine the authenticity and value of money by the 1850s. How could a person reliably distinguish between the real and the counterfeit, between the "all right" and the outright fake? Could secret signs embedded in the bill offer a reliable marker of authenticity? Failing that, could some other authority—a so-called counterfeit detector—delineate the line between the solid and the spurious by initiating readers into the cabalistic secrets of the currency? Or might it be better to take the money at face value, whether counterfeit or not? These dilemmas intensified over the first half of the nineteenth century. When only a few banks issued notes, it was relatively easy to remember the different designs, and detecting counterfeit notes—at least poorly made ones—remained a relatively simple task. But as the decades passed, and the market economy extended to the most remote corners of the new nation, bank notes drifted ever farther from the institutions that issued them, making it increasingly difficult to decipher these monetary hieroglyphs, much less spot a counterfeit. "There are very few persons, if any, in the United States," concluded one commentator in the early 1860s, "who can truthfully declare their ability to detect at a glance any fraudulent paper money . . . In spite of all precautions," he observed, "every merchant has his pile of counterfeit money, and his hourly fear of having it increased."[5]

It staggers the imagination to comprehend the extent and ubiquity of counterfeiting during the first half of the nineteenth century. "We seem about to become liable to be called *a nation of counterfeiters!*" predicted Hezekiah Niles in 1818. Niles, whose *Weekly Register* was the premier financial publication of the day, looked with horror at the proliferation of fraudulent paper. "Counterfeiters and false bank notes are so common, that forgery seems to have lost its criminality in the minds of many." Just how common the problem had become was hard to quantify, but most agreed that it had reached remarkable levels by the early 1800s. "The whole country was deluged with counterfeit money," recalled John Neal of his childhood as an apprentice storekeeper in Maine. "Ten per cent . . . of all that was in circulation was absolutely worthless; being either counterfeit, or the floating issue of broken banks." Subsequent estimates echo such figures, though in times of financial distress or in regions where counterfeiting was particularly rife, observers believed that counterfeits and other kinds of fraudulent bills accounted for as much as half of the paper money in circulation. Such figures may better reflect anxiety about counterfeiting than the actual number of counterfeits, but even conservative estimates suggest that the problem was hardly a trifling one. So pervasive had counterfeiting become by the 1830s that enterprising publishers began issuing

FIGURE 2. Though most counterfeits remained in circulation, a handful of conscientious banks stamped or even branded bogus notes to prevent their continued use. *Courtesy, National Numismatic Collection, Smithsonian Institution.*

"counterfeit detectors" like the one that Melville's character consulted. Close to eighty such publications flourished in the antebellum era, testament to the growing number of fraudulent notes.[6]

Counterfeits proliferated, but so too did the very categories of counterfeit money, which assumed guises beyond mere imitations. Counterfeiters exploited people's unfamiliarity with the currency by issuing "spurious notes" that bore no resemblance whatsoever to the genuine article. Others produced notes with their title, locality, or denomination erased and a new version put in its place—so-called altered or raised notes. Still others dropped all pretense of authenticity and arrogated the privilege of banking, producing notes that sounded plausible—the Merchants' Bank of Utica, for instance—but which existed only within the counterfeit economy. Such notes, while deemed counterfeit, blurred imperceptibly into yet another category of fraud, that is, the notes of wildcat banks—institutions founded by unscrupulous financiers in remote areas for the express purpose of making it difficult, if not impossible, for the notes to be exchanged for gold and silver. For most people, the proliferation of these overlapping categories of real and imagined fraud made the task of sorting out the genuine from the counterfeit next to impossible.[7]

Even the notes of legitimate banks might migrate into counterfeit territory in the wake of economic distress or panic. Hezekiah Niles claimed not to "see any real difference, in point of fact, between a set of *bank directors,* who make and issue notes for 5, 10, or 100 dollars, which are not worth the money stated on the face of them, which they deliberately promise to pay with a previous resolution not to pay, and a gang of fair, open, *honest* counterfeiters. One *speculates* by law, and the other against the law; but both are speculators and have [a] unity of interest." Casting his eyes over a pile of bills scattered on his desk, Niles observed that "some of them are called *genuine* and a few pronounced to be *counterfeits.* But the latter are just as valuable as the former—and it seems impossible to draw a distinction between them; their *intention* and *effect* being the same." Such comparisons swiftly gained credibility. Nearly two decades later, former president John Quincy Adams watched the nation's banks suspend specie payments in the wake of the panic of 1837. The only difference between a bank director and a counterfeiter, he opined, was that the counterfeiter gave "evidence of superior skill and superior modesty. It requires more talent to sign another man's name than one's own and the counterfeiter does at least his work in the dark, while the suspenders of specie payments [are] brazen in the face of day, and laugh at the victims and dupes, who have put faith in their promises."[8]

The rhetoric and reality of banking and counterfeiting raised unsettling questions about the foundations of the capitalist system that flourished from the late eighteenth century onward. Bank notes, which put the "capital" in capitalism, were nothing more than glorified IOUs, "promises to pay" that legally entitled the bearer to present the note at the issuing institution and receive the face value in specie. Put differently, bank notes represented both wealth and debt. Notes consequently circulated at a value relative to the perception that the bank could redeem its promises, and notes passed "below par" (below face value) if a consensus developed that the bank had insufficient assets on hand to meet its obligations. Of course, few banks had sufficient specie in their vaults to redeem all their promises. As one critic observed, paper money was nothing more than "*credit*-money, or *confidence*-money," resting as it did on a "*promise to pay*, which, by universal understanding, is meant to signify a promise to pay *on condition of not being required to do so.*" Most banks had many more notes in circulation than specie on hand to meet their obligations. Counterfeiting, then, was only part of a much larger problem. Notes might be genuine, but the bank that issued them might be unable—or unwilling—to redeem them.[9]

These twin threats—bad notes and bad banks—varied in importance depending on how they affected that most important asset of paper money: its ability to be passed to someone else. This led to some unusual distinctions. As one detective later reminisced, "It was a popular remark among men of business at this time that they preferred a good counterfeit on a solid bank to any genuine bill upon [a] shyster institution." Beyond testifying to a perennial shortage of commercial ethics, such practices acknowledged that distinctions between counterfeit money and real money had yet to coalesce. Whether a note was counterfeit or not, or whether the bank that issued it could ultimately make good on its promise to pay, mattered little at the moment money changed hands—that is, when someone else took the bank note because he or she felt confident they could find another person who would accept it. As John Neal recalled, "In *our* establishment, all such moneys, whether counterfeit, or only questionable, were always put back into the till"—to await an appropriate, if unsuspecting, customer. Value, then, was not something inert, something inherent in the note itself, the way that gold in a coin was thought to have an intrinsic value. Far from it: value was something that materialized and became tangible when the note was exchanged, when one person put confidence in the note of another. Only then, at that instant, would an intrinsically worthless piece of paper come to mean something more.[10]

Counterfeiters grasped this essential truth, which applied not only to bank notes, but also to the emergent market economy as a whole. Confidence was the engine of economic growth, the mysterious sentiment that permitted a country poor in specie but rich in promises to create something from nothing. "Confidence is the indispensable basis of all sorts of business transactions," claims Melville's rogue at one point. "Without it, commerce between man and man, as between country and country, would, like a watch, run down and stop." Counterfeiters, arguably the most ubiquitous and sophisticated of all confidence men, likewise understood that confidence was fragile, incapable of withstanding close scrutiny. Anyone who looked too carefully at what stood behind a bill would destroy it, just like the farmer in the fairy tale who, in trying to find out how the goose laid golden eggs, killed the priceless bird. Bills could function whether counterfeit or not, so long as they entered into circulation with enough trust on the part of the person receiving them. At its core, capitalism was little more than a confidence game. As long as confidence flourished, even the most far-fetched speculations could get off the ground, wealth would increase, and bank notes—the very pieces of paper that made it all possible—would circulate.[11]

The challenge of playing that game intensified with the rapid rise of an expansive commercial society in the eighteenth century. Each person's fate was increasingly tied to individuals and institutions that he or she did not know and could not comprehend. New paper instruments—bills of exchange and bills of credit—functioned as proxies for distant financial forces. While the proliferation of paper was well under way in the colonial era, it moved with startling speed in the early republic. The bank notes that began circulating in this era were an expression of a new organization of society, for they enabled a far greater level of economic anonymity than other forms of money in use at this time: personal checks drawn on bank accounts; drafts, which were checks drawn on individuals instead of banks; book credits, which permitted individuals to settle accounts periodically rather than exchange cash on a daily basis; and promissory notes, a person's promise to pay a specified sum on a future date. Unlike bank notes, these instruments worked best at enabling transactions between individuals who already knew each other. Strangers rarely passed checks to other strangers; nor could they write out a draft, claim a book credit, or issue a promissory note on someone unfamiliar with their creditworthiness. All of these pieces of paper rested on the trust and confidence of familiars: farmers and merchants who settled accounts in the spring and fall; businessmen borrowing money from others in a tight-knit community of commerce; wholesalers purchasing goods from a trusted importer. Financial transactions involving these devices all rested on the personal ties within circles of known and long-standing associates and rarely circulated beyond them.[12]

Bank notes were different. They originated with often distant corporations, entered into the streams of commerce, and floated far away from the legal abstractions that had issued them. Anyone could use them; their worth did not depend on the assets of the individual who presented them, but on confidence in corporate fortunes. Strangers could use them when transacting business with other strangers, and bank notes thus became the preferred payment in retail transactions, where individuals who had never met and might never meet again could do business. And it was in this newly anonymous setting that the counterfeiter, like all confidence men, made his money. Presenting a bank note at a shop, liquor den, or store, the counterfeiter implicitly raised questions that cut to the core contradictions of an emergent commercial society—a society where commodities, currency, reputations, and flesh-and-blood people increasingly floated free of custom, tradition, and place. In this atmosphere of swift and dizzying change, how could one have confidence in bank notes tendered by a stranger? How could one have confidence in the paper promises of a strange bank? The counterfeiter symbolized the perceived perils of an increasingly mobile, anonymous society, one in which credit slipped the bounds of individual reputation and drifted out into the wider world. Value in this system did not rest, as it does today, on something that could maintain the illusion of operating outside the day-to-day market economy, such as the nation-state. Rather, value disappeared into an endless series of private hands, each issuing paper promises dependent on yet more paper promises.[13]

Both counterfeiters and capitalists thrived within this system, and to a certain extent, the story of one is the story of the other. As the federal government abdicated its constitutional authority over the currency, and the right to make money became ever more dispersed, counterfeiters and capitalists flourished together. Every bank note had its counterfeit counterpart, so that two economies emerged simultaneously, mirror images of each other. As Hezekiah Niles and John Quincy Adams recognized, both bankers and counterfeiters issued bills or notes with little or nothing in the way of assets backing their promises to pay, and both drew their energy from the same boundless faith that slips of paper could, with the elixir of confidence, take the place of gold and silver coin. And yet the similarity went deeper. To the "legitimate" business community, counterfeiters lurked about like a company of ghostly doubles. Many merchants and financial writers referred to counterfeiters as "bankers" or "capitalists," a tacit acknowledgment that these criminals conducted their affairs with a comparable level of sophistication. Counterfeiters fashioned elaborate schemes for producing and distributing counterfeit notes, building a vast shadow economy similar in scope and scale to more orthodox avenues of making money. "So systematic, indeed, has this nefarious traffic become of late," complained the editors of the *National Police Gazette* in 1849, "that the great dealers execute orders for the town and country with the same method and regularity, as manufacturers in fair branches of trade."[14]

Players in this illicit economy employed many of the same technologies, people, and practices as conventional capitalists did. The same advances in bank note engraving that promised to provide protection from counterfeit notes instead opened the floodgates to new and dangerous frauds. The same skilled (but struggling) artisans who engraved notes on behalf of the banks also moonlighted as counterfeiters. The same dies and plates used to print genuine notes ended up in the hands of counterfeiters. The same laborers who eked out marginal wages in the mills and factories of the capitalist class supplemented their income with counterfeit money. And the same "counterfeit detectors" published to assist the unwary became useful tools for passing counterfeit notes. Even those charged with policing the economy worked both sides of the fence, lending a hand to the very counterfeiters they were supposed to prosecute. In all of this, the border between the real and the counterfeit became blurry, and the counterfeiter and his minions became ghosts in the machine of American capitalism, simultaneously reflecting and questioning the values that lay behind the unrestrained pursuit of profit.

Not that capitalists and counterfeiters operated with impunity. A host of laws and regulations sought to restrain both legitimate and illegitimate commerce. But such codes, largely instituted and (imperfectly) enforced on a local level, did little to regulate either legal or illegal commercial transactions that stretched beyond village or city jurisdictions, state lines, or even national boundaries. Whatever their intent, laws had rather limited bearing on either the corporations that issued bank notes or the counterfeiters who imitated them. Only in the most established and financially conservative portions of the country did regulatory regimes enjoy a measure of success. Otherwise, money makers of all stripes operated with minimal oversight, especially in areas of the country where institutional authority was weak or ineffectual: the rough-and-tumble world of the frontier, the burgeoning urban underworlds, even the steamboats plying the western rivers that for Melville symbolized the anonymity and anarchy of the modern marketplace.[15]

And yet the system worked. For all the counterfeit bank bills, raised and altered notes, and dubious currency in circulation, the United States was hardly held back by these illicit additions to the money supply. Between the Revolution and the Civil War, the nation's economy grew by leaps and bounds, expanding at a clip not seen since. Perhaps, in a nation poor in gold and silver but rich in promise, counterfeit notes and their close cousins helped meet the growing desire for credit and capital. Indeed, all the invidious comparisons between bankers and counterfeiters hinted at a deeper truth. This was a country whose inhabitants desperately needed and wanted money to make their dreams a reality, and where the banks fell short, counterfeiters proved more than willing to pick up the slack. Many people in the business of banking viewed counterfeiting as a small price to pay for a system of money creation governed not by the edicts of a central bank or the fiscal arm of the state, but by insatiable private demand for credit in the form of bank notes.

What follows is a chronicle of counterfeiting, but it is more broadly the story of those bank notes and what they represented. Throughout this period, bank notes symbolized the dramatic economic transformation taking place. Entrepreneurs borrowed money in the form of bank notes; factory owners paid wages in bank notes; farmers who took their crops to market accepted payment in bank notes. They were markers of the market revolution; they were capitalism incarnate.[16] But the brand of capitalism symbolized by bank notes reveals a very different economic ethos than the one Max Weber identified in his classic treatise on the "spirit of capitalism." It is not the plodding, methodical, gradual pursuit of wealth that unfolds in the succeeding pages; instead, the history of bank notes, both real and counterfeit, captures the get-rich-quick scheme, the confidence game, and the mania for speculation that obsessed Melville and the nation during this era. This alchemical vision of wealth creation—the magical transformation of flimsy paper

into concrete capital—is part of the hidden history of the nation's economic development, and to see the counterfeit economy is to gain a
glimpse of that spirit. After all, the activities of banking, counterfeiting,
and speculative capitalism coexisted on a continuum. As Hezekiah
Niles observed, if "the *Daemon of Avarice* [was] the author of modern
banking," so too was "banking the fountain of counterfeiting." Or as
the *Working Man's Advocate* lamented, observing the proliferation of
both banks and counterfeiters, "'Make money, honestly, if you can, but
at all events, *make* money,' seems to be the rule of the present day; for
there is scarcely a section of the country to which we turn where we
will not see some people industriously *making* money."[17]

If the story of counterfeiting is the story of the confidence game that
is at the heart of speculative capitalism, it is also the story of people.
Economic history too often traffics in numbers more than names, and
the history of counterfeiting is nothing if not a tale of legendary individuals, outsized personalities, and curious characters who exploited
the ethical ambiguities of a market-driven society to survive and thrive
at this time. Long before the outlaws of the late nineteenth century
seized the popular imagination, tales of individual counterfeiters became the scrim through which people experiencing the market revolution could perceive and project their hopes, fears, anxieties, envy, and
admiration. Counterfeiters' reputations could easily accommodate this
range of sentiments because they reflected the capitalist ethos of making money while hijacking the totems of an emergent market economy.
That the boundary between the counterfeit and the real, between federal sovereignty and state sovereignty, between criminals and bankers,
was so murky and ill-defined only made the persona of the counterfeiter all the more capable of encompassing such contradictory impulses.[18]

The counterfeiters whose enterprises are the focus of this book did not observe boundaries of individual and political identity; nor did they have much respect for geographical boundaries. Like the bank notes they imitated, they floated free of their original moorings, roaming across state and national borders with remarkable ease. From the wilds of the border region between Vermont and Canada to the gullies and caves of the Western Reserve; from the rum shops and oyster cellars of New York City to the rough-and-tumble society of the Mississippi River Valley; and even farther west, to the gold fields of California, counterfeiters drifted to the external and internal margins of the nation, where they could operate with relative impunity, free from the threat of organized law enforcement and the disapproval of communities in more established regions of the country. The succeeding chapters illuminate their stories, as well as track those who tried—and more often than not, failed—to put an end to illicit money making: bounty hunters, bankers, engravers, detectives, and even the publishers of the "counterfeit detectors" that Melville satirized. Throughout this history of counterfeiting and counterfeits, particular attention has been paid to authenticity, and the words uncovered in the historical record—whether written in a letter, transcribed in the course of taking a deposition, or spoken in the halls of a legislature—have been reproduced here in their original format, complete with misspellings and archaic punctuation.

If the story of counterfeiting necessarily traverses the nation's more remote borders, boundaries, and far-flung corners, it is also the story of our nation at that time, for debates over counterfeiting, currency, and capitalism repeatedly raised unanswered questions about national identity, and indeed, about whether this was really a nation at all. Those questions boiled down to a simple choice. Should the nation control the currency, or should the right to print and mint money belong to the very capitalists who wanted it most? Those questions originated in the eighteenth century, when the individual colonies first flouted imperial authority by printing their own money. And while the federal constitution attempted to reassert centralized control, matters turned out otherwise. Consequently, every note of a state-chartered bank struck economic nationalists as a nagging reminder of the federal government's abdication of its right to regulate; every counterfeit seemed to flout the authority of the nation-state. At times, the country seemed less a coherent whole than a collection of self-interested strivers united only in their restless ambition, their hatred of monopoly, and their love of lucre.

Indeed, during this era the country itself was as much a counterfeit as the money that circulated within its borders. Like the promises to pay that adorned bank notes, there was little substance to the nation's claims of sovereignty over the individual states. Whether or not the federal government held the upper hand over the state governments was an unresolved and bitterly contested question for at least the first seventy years of the nation's existence. Whether the issue was the War of 1812, tariffs on manufactured goods, or most important, the looming question of slavery, the nation was beset from threats to its continued existence from within and without, and the idea of a permanent, enduring union existed more on paper than in practice. This was especially true when it came to monetary matters, over which the federal government exercised next to no control for much of this period. Though economic nationalists repeatedly tried to rein in private money making of all kinds, they would have to wait until the conflagration of the Civil War before the interests of the currency and the country became irrevocably intertwined.

Over the course of that conflict, a reinvigorated federal government banned the issue of notes by state-chartered banks and other corporations, and replaced them with a common national currency founded on an almost mystical faith in the credit of the country. Confidence in the currency no longer rested on the diffuse and almost infinite number of variables that governed the values of privately issued bank notes. Rather, it depended on faith in a new abstraction—the nation—that transcended both the market economy and the individuals and corporations constituting it. As a consequence, counterfeiting went from being a nuisance to being a threat to national sovereignty and sanctity. In response, the government founded a national police force that extirpated the counterfeit economy and the uncertainties that accompanied it. A modern nation and a genuine currency emerged from the ashes of the Civil War, and faith in one became synonymous with confidence in the other, an equivalence that has intensified and solidified in the succeeding century and a half.

That prospect was unimaginable at the time Melville published his parable of the market economy. To visit the world he knew and experience its contradictions and ambiguities is to venture into a strange domain where shadows turn to substance, appearances become realities, and whispers of confidence transmute worthless pieces of paper into gleaming gold. It is a world that has disappeared, yet its spirit lives on in other incarnations, be they speculative bubbles, stock market gambles, or myriad get-rich schemes. We may no longer scrutinize the money that passes through our hands, but the great confidence game of capitalism is alive and well.

ONE

Bordering on Alchemy

L egend has it that in the spring of 1806, a caravan of twenty or so men mounted on horseback threaded their way across "the lines," the contested borderland separating Vermont and Canada. No ordinary group of travelers, they probably moved by night along a rutted dirt road, concealed beneath stands of maple and birch trees. Possibly it was a clear night; if so, moonlight may have bathed the band each time they crossed a clearing in the forest. Their apparent leader would have cast the longest shadow: he was a tall man who no doubt carried a menacing array of weaponry—a brace of pistols, perhaps, or at the very least, a rifle and knife. When the road opened into a farmer's field a few miles north of the border, he and his men likely dismounted before making their way on foot toward a cluster of outbuildings and barns that circled a stone house a short distance away.

An innocent observer could be forgiven for thinking that a band of brigands was loose, bent on making mischief in a region already infamous for its lawlessness. But this company of men, led by legendary

Vermont sheriff Mike Barron, had crossed the boundary lines on business of a more law-abiding nature. The farm belonged to the notorious Stephen Burroughs, a man whom Barron's biographer aptly described as "a most shrewd and accomplished villain . . . especially in the business of manufacturing and issuing counterfeit currency." It was in this unusual line of work that Burroughs achieved lasting fame, and tales of his prowess as a counterfeiter—and his demonstrated ability to escape the most vigilant captors—circulated as widely as the bogus bank notes he issued.[1]

Accounts of what happened next contradict one another. According to Barron's biographer, the sheriff and his men stormed the house and rushed upstairs. As they burst into the counterfeiter's room, Burroughs drew a pistol from beneath his pillow, only to have it struck from his hand as Barron and his men overpowered and bound him. In the "clearer light of morning," Burroughs recognized his captor—they had crossed paths previously—and entreated him to unbind his arms. "Colonel Mike," he supposedly said, "you are a gentleman, and so am I; unbind my arms, and I give you my word of honor that I will be entirely subject to your orders." Burroughs, who was by all accounts "kind, courteous, and gentlemanly in his appearance and manners," had a way of getting what he wanted, and the sheriff succumbed to his charms— only to turn around a few moments later and find that Burroughs was aiming another pistol at him. The counterfeiter pulled the trigger, but according to one source, "no report followed. It had missed fire!" Wresting the gun from him, Barron asked Burroughs what he had meant to do. "I meant to shoot you," Burroughs replied, honest for once.[2]

Did events unfold in such dramatic fashion? Possibly, though this was neither the first nor the last time that Burroughs had pulled the trigger of a pistol, only to have it mysteriously misfire. He may have been a criminal, but as this same account conceded, he was "skilled not in . . . deeds of violence and blood, but in diverting tricks of deception." Tales of cold-blooded attempted murder collide with the reality that he never wounded or killed another person. Possibly the exaggerations of Burroughs's villainy aimed to ensure that his life would not appear too attractive to impressionable readers. Like the condemned prisoners of the colonial era who warned the crowd gathered below the gallows not to follow in their footsteps, it was thought important that Burroughs's life instruct, not inspire. As Barron's biographer duly noted upon relating this anecdote of Burroughs's arrest, the infamous counterfeiter repented in later years, and was "said to have been in the habit of giving good advice to young men, telling them not to do as he had done, for he had found the way of the transgressor to be hard."[3]

Perhaps. Whatever happened that morning, contrition was the last thing on Burroughs's mind as the sheriff marched him to Montreal under armed guard and handed him over to British authorities. "These distinguished heroes returned home to their own country," recalled Burroughs thirty years later, his pen dripping with sarcasm. His captors, he complained, "published in their periodicals, a flaming account of this brilliant and dauntless expedition!!!" Indeed, he continued, "the exultation of the Romans on the death of Hannibal was in no proportion to the triumph of the Americans at this wonderful display of courage and *sagacity* performed by their *illustrious* citizens." But did everyone join the jubilation when they received the tidings that "Stephen Burroughs, of money-making memory" had finally fallen into the clutches of the law? For all the infamy attached to his reputation— the word "notorious" invariably appeared before his name, like some grim honorific—Burroughs enjoyed a measure of secret admiration, even awe. He was, in the words of many a newspaper, a "celebrated character," and the "first consul of bank bill counterfeiters." His best-

selling memoirs, published in 1798, chronicled a long and successful career as a con man, seducer, and counterfeiter, and cemented his burgeoning reputation as a trickster and folk hero who invariably outwit-
ted the wealthy and the powerful. He proved an appealing figure,
despite (or because) of his roguery, and as tales of his exploits spread in
print and by word of mouth, Burroughs became the first outlaw—but
by no means the last—to capture in equal measure his country's careful
condemnation and its reluctant respect.[4]

As Burroughs languished in prison facing the prospect of ignomini-
ous deportation or death, he managed yet once more to live up to the
expectations of both his detractors and admirers. One morning late in
November, shortly before his trial was to begin, his jailer found the
door to Burroughs's cell ajar and the famed counterfeiter missing. An
alarm was raised, and a substantial reward offered, but Burroughs had
vanished. A local sheriff brought in to investigate could only conclude that Burroughs had procured a false key, freed himself from his
cell, walked down the corridor of the jail, and surmounted the final
barrier—a door secured by an iron bar—with the help of his son, who
then ushered his father to freedom. The sheriff believed that Burroughs would flee the country, but the counterfeiter did no such thing.[5]
"Money-making" was his destiny, and he returned once more to the
wilds of what is now Quebec, where he would continue to ply his trade
for several more years, furnishing the United States with yet more
counterfeit money—and simultaneously exasperating and entertaining
the new nation with more stories of his deceptions, inventions, and
imitations.

Why did Burroughs evoke such a contradictory welter of reactions?
On some deep and disturbing level, Burroughs embodied the profound
economic and social dislocations of the post-Revolutionary era; he represented both the promise and the peril of an emergent market econ-

omy. His adult years spanned a tumultuous period in which the rigid hierarchies of colonial times finally dissolved, replaced by the more fluid social order of a democratic commercial society. Self-fashioning and self-advancement slowly became a viable way of life for a growing number of white men, and Burroughs, who counterfeited with equal ease both bank notes and identities, symbolized this new ethos.[6] Indeed, in a society increasingly focused on the pursuit of easy wealth, Burroughs appeared to both his critics and his admirers as an extreme incarnation of the self-made man, one who thrived in a society where identity was increasingly malleable and imitable and where capitalism and counterfeiting could coexist as two sides of the same coin.

This conflation of categories accompanied the rise of note-issuing banks in the late eighteenth century. Like the colonial governments of Burroughs's youth, which issued paper money to provide a circulating medium for their specie-poor economies, the state-chartered banks of the new nation skirted legal barriers to pump credit into the economy. The successful circulation of these bills depended on what seemed, at the time, an almost magical belief that bank notes constituted wealth, that paper could pass as gold. Burroughs, it appeared to many, simply carried these acts of alchemy one step further, issuing imitations from his own "bank." Tales of his exploits soon spread, and Burroughs became the real and imagined source of every counterfeit note in circulation. In the process, he embodied the common spirit animating the conventional and illicit pursuit of wealth in the post-Revolutionary era, a time when the right to "make money"—literally and figuratively—went from being a privilege of the few to a franchise of the many, and the distinction between bankers and men like Burroughs became hard to discern.

In Burroughs's case, the confusing contours of the border between crime and capitalism found a corollary in the boundaries of the nation itself. Burroughs did not ply his trade within the United States, but instead commenced counterfeiting in the highly contested region separating the United States and Canada. As a border region, it proved resistant to the usual mechanisms of state control, especially those of a fledgling nation like the United States. Though the framers of the Constitution had envisioned a strong national government, the United States did little at this stage to protect the currency and the country from the counterfeiters who lurked on its margins. Burroughs thus came to symbolize not only the conflation of capitalism and counterfeiting, but also the limits of American economic and political authority. Worse, his much-publicized depredations inspired a host of imitators, all of whom helped make counterfeiting an integral part of economic life in the early republic. If some of his successors cultivated equally outsized reputations, Burroughs remained in popular folklore the quintessential counterfeiter. He was the original against which all imitators would be weighed, measured, and valued.

The Promise of Paper

Despite his reputation, Burroughs was hardly the first to forge an identity, much less a piece of currency. Con men and counterfeiters had long thrived in England amid the dissolution of feudal structures of authority and the rise of a more anonymous commercial society. These criminal subcultures took root in the future United States not along after the first settlers arrived.[7] Nonetheless, it was not until the late seventeenth century that counterfeiters began plying their trade on a grand scale, churning out a steady stream of bogus coins made of pewter and debased gold and silver. Though successful, the signal achievement of this first generation of homegrown criminals was not the manufacture of false coin, but the printing of fraudulent paper money. Counterfeiters had plenty of opportunities to hone this particular branch of their craft during the eighteenth century, for the colonists led not only the mother country but also the rest of Europe in discovering the virtues and vices of paper currency. Indeed, by the time Burroughs was born, the impulse to substitute extrinsic confidence in paper currency for the intrinsic virtues of gold and silver was already well established in the colonies, arguably more so than any other place in the world.

Americans' faith in paper currency, though, was less a choice than a necessity. As the colonists who first arrived on the shores of the future United States discovered, the land contained little in the way of precious metals, in contrast to the more established colonies of Latin America. While a motley assortment of Spanish pieces of eight, Portuguese reales, and British coins and copper tokens circulated in America, most such currency did not linger long in colonial coffers, but returned overseas to pay for much-needed finished goods. A persistent trade imbalance, and the popularity of mercantilist economic philosophy, which equated the accumulation of specie with national wealth, only increased the likelihood that gold and silver in the colonies would eventually end up in the mother country. What little coin remained in America often disappeared into hoards or into the melting pots of jewelers, silversmiths, and goldsmiths, where it could be put to more profitable use.[8]

In the absence of sufficient specie, the need for a circulating medium remained. Book credits and barter could only go so far in facilitating economic exchange. Particularly in the growing seaport cities, merchants needed something a bit more fungible than a cow, a bolt of cloth, or a peck of grain when they paid for goods or settled debts. Colonial governments consequently sanctioned a host of commodity monies beginning in the early seventeenth century. Tobacco, iron nails, and animal pelts all served as crude currencies, with a legislative fiat setting up equivalence between the commodity and a specified number of shillings or pennies. Though such makeshift monies circulated, they proved an unreliable store or measure of value, because their prices fluctuated far more than precious metals did. Wampum, strings of clam shell beads that could be traded with the Indians for pelts, proved a better substitute for specie. First adopted by the Dutch and then by the English, wampum nonetheless fell victim to overproduction, counterfeiting, and the growing scarcity of beaver. One by one, the colonies revoked its legal tender status by the end of the seventeenth century.[9]

The Massachusetts Bay Colony took the lead in formulating solutions to the currency shortage. It issued the first colonial coinage in 1652, a series of substandard coins made from low-grade Spanish silver gathered from illegal trade in the Caribbean. Imperial authorities put a stop to the mint in 1682, but this did not curtail the colony's experimentation. Eight years later, in the midst of the imperial conflicts between Britain and France, Massachusetts struggled to find a way to fund its contribution to the war effort. The solution—issuing "bills of credit" that would circulate as money—marked a radical departure in monetary practice. Though printed to pay for soldiers and supplies, the preamble to the law justified the move by citing "the present poverty and calamities of the country, and through a scarcity of money, the want of an adequate measure of commerce." War or no war, the colonies would have a circulating medium, one that could be used to pay private debts and public taxes, and grease the wheels of commerce. This was the first government-backed bank in the Western world to issue public notes, but it was hardly the last: the Massachusetts colony resorted to successive issues of paper money, as did almost every other colony in the future United States. All these issues ostensibly originated as attempts to shoulder (or defer) the burden of waging imperial

FIGURE 3. Crudely engraved and easily counterfeited, despite the warning on the face of the bill, notes like this circulated far beyond the colony that issued them. *Courtesy, National Numismatic Collection, Smithsonian Institution.*

wars, but did as much to pump credit into the economy. The colonies lacked the customary forms of capital, but could make do with slips of paper that passed from hand to hand, affirming a common confidence in future prosperity.[10]

The gradual adoption of different forms of paper money on both sides of the ocean—first by Massachusetts, then by the Bank of England a few years later, and eventually by all the colonies—marked a sea change in thinking about the nature of monetary value. An earlier tradition of economic thought held that gold and silver were the only source of value: immutable, intrinsic, absolute, transcendent. This "bullionist" view maintained that precious metals, which predated the rise of civil society, necessarily existed beyond the realm of government and human agency. John Locke was perhaps the most eloquent defender of this position, though he held that only silver, not gold, constituted "real" money. In contrast to bullionist thinking, an emergent liberal tradition saw money as a commodity, responsive to economic supply and demand, as well as to the interventions of banks and governments. In other words, because the value of money derived from extrinsic forces, a surrogate for gold and silver such as paper could do the job just as well. While Locke's belief in the intrinsic value of money continued to attract adherents well into the nineteenth and even twentieth centuries, the future belonged to paper currency. Indeed, though during the first three centuries of paper money there lingered an attachment to the illusion that specie stood behind its promises, experience demonstrated otherwise. In reality, the value of paper money depended ultimately on the confidence that participants in the market economy accorded it.[11]

There was in all of this a hint of the magical, or at the very least, magic by other means. In fact, some of the very first proposals for issuing paper currency originated with a coterie of Puritan intellectuals who had a double obsession with money and magic. Samuel Hartlib, a scientist active in the founding of the Royal Society, was the center of this group. He wrote on economic matters and believed that an increase in money would lead to an increase in economic activity. "The more there is of money in any Nation, the quicker also must all those wayes be, wherein money is ordinarily imployed." Hartlib and the circle of thinkers around him—including George Starkey and John Winthrop Jr. in Massachusetts—pursued extensive studies in alchemy in the hopes of increasing the stock of money. While eventually frustrated in their ambitions, these men eventually settled on paper money as a roundabout means of achieving the alchemical effect. A 1652 pamphlet on bank currency authored by a member of the Hartlib circle made the connection explicit, likening such money to "the Elixir or Philosopher's Stone."[12]

That paper money could function as a proxy for alchemy did not escape the detractors of the new money, either. In 1714, in the midst of debates over currency in Massachusetts, Paul Dudley accused the proponents of paper money of creating value out of thin air. "If this be not the *Philosopher's Stone,*" he charged, "there is no such thing in the world." The twinning of magic and money achieved an even more enduring and infamous association the following year, when the new regent of France, Philippe d'Orléans, faced with a dire financial crisis, summoned a number of alchemists to his court in the hopes they could manufacture artificial gold. According to legend, he dismissed them upon the arrival of a Scottish gambler named John Law, who proposed a more modern solution to his woes: the creation of a bank that would issue paper money backed by lands owned by the state. Law superintended the creation of two note-issuing institutions whose paper promises were ultimately backed by the promised discovery of gold in America's Mississippi River Valley. Eventually, confidence in Law and his creations collapsed and the currency ceased to circulate.[13]

But if France and most of Europe remained skeptical of paper currency, seeing in its associations with alchemy and magic the potential for mischief and evil, the future United States remained enamored of its promise. For every critic like Paul Dudley, there was someone like John Wise, who wrote in support of a "land bank" the year after Law's scheme collapsed. Arguing that this bank's paper would fuel economic growth, Wise claimed that "we carry as much of the *Lapis Aurificus* or *Philosophers Stone* in our heads, and can turn other matter into Silver and Gold by the Power of thought as soon as any other People, or else

I must own I have not yet Learnt the Character of my Country." Prescient words, indeed: from that time forward, the colonies of the future United States enthusiastically embraced paper money to solve shortages of specie and to stimulate trade. Though paper money would gain many adherents in the pre-Revolutionary period, none came close in influence to Benjamin Franklin, whose writings on paper money ushered in some of the most successful experiments in turning paper into gold.[14]

Franklin made the case in a pamphlet published in 1729, where he laid out arguments that would surface again and again in the coming years. "Those who are Lovers of Trade, and delight to see Manufactures encouraged, will be for having a large Addition to our Currency," Franklin wrote. "For they very well know, that People will have little Heart to advance Money in Trade, when what they can get is scarce sufficient to purchase Necessaries." Like Law before him, Franklin proposed that paper currency be backed by mortgages of property, or what he called "Coined Land," though he had no illusions about finding gold beneath the soil. In a piece published a month before his pamphlet appeared, Franklin counseled his readers with an anecdote of a gentleman farmer leaving his son a plantation with the claim that "I have found a considerable Quantity of Gold by Digging there; thee mayst do the same. But Thee must carefully observe this, *Never to dig more than Plow-deep!*" The fortuitous discovery of hidden gold would not attract confidence in the currency; only the steady application of labor and industry could perform that feat. So-called land banks like the one envisioned by Franklin enjoyed considerable success throughout the colonial era, operating under the auspices of the individual colonies.[15]

Nonetheless, most of the paper money in circulation originated directly with colonial governments in the manner of the original issue of Massachusetts. Such money seemed to appear out of thin air, flowing off the presses with little in the way of hard assets backing these promises to pay. The colonial assemblies generally conferred legal tender status on these bills of credit, always for the payment of public taxes, less frequently for the payment of private debts. Given the sobriety with which Franklin approached the subject of money, it is appropriate that of all the colonial issues of paper currency, those of his native Pennsylvania (and to a lesser extent, several other mid-Atlantic colonies) proved most reliable. In these places, paper money did work: through prudent management and a good dose of economic growth, these colonial governments managed to keep one step ahead of their obligations. Confidence in these bills of credit (many of them printed by Franklin himself) rarely wavered. By contrast, the fiscal legerdemain of several of the other colonies proved disastrous. Some colonial governments turned to the printing presses to avoid imposing additional tax burdens, often redeeming one issue of bills with another, and it was not long before the excessive demands made on the colonists' fiscal faith led to the collapse of the monetary covenant. In Massachusetts, the paper currency eventually depreciated to a fifth of its face value, while Burroughs's native New Hampshire emitted vast quantities of bills relative to its population, leading at least one contemporary to characterize the colony as "always inclinable to a depreciating fraudulent currency." The worst offender, though, turned out to be Rhode Island, which ultimately redeemed its copious emissions at only a tiny fraction of their original value.[16]

With each of the colonies issuing notes in denominations, sizes, and patterns of their own choosing (and with reputations ranging from solid to suspect), and with a dizzying variety of foreign coins in circulation as well (additional attempts by the colonies to mint coins enjoyed little success), by the mid-eighteenth century the monetary system of the future United States was considered anarchic and unstable. Though the British made feeble attempts at imposing some order throughout the colonies, attempts to regulate the money supply did not become serious until 1740, when two short-lived land banks of dubious promise commenced operation in Massachusetts. Parliament moved swiftly to curtail what it called "a Scheme for Supplying a pretended Want of Medium in Trade"—that is, a plan to set up a land bank. The imperial authorities put a stop to these particular schemes, but the colonies went on emitting paper currency, despite the passage of laws in 1751 and 1764 aimed at stopping the practice. The crackdown stirred discontent: as Franklin explained to Parliament in 1767, much of the colonies' ill will was a response to "the prohibition of making paper money among themselves."[17]

Even if the imperial authorities had succeeded in throttling the colonies' impulse to "make money," enterprising criminals would have supplied a circulating medium. Initially, counterfeiters restricted themselves to imitating the various Spanish and English coins in circulation, drawing on criminal expertise honed in England, which was home to sophisticated gangs of coiners. But enterprising forgers also began engraving counterfeit plates and imitating paper money not long after Massachusetts issued its first paper money. Many of these individuals, like their successors in the nineteenth century, came from the ranks of former convicts and petty criminals, while a handful could boast more distinguished pedigrees. The aristocratic John Potter of Rhode Island, for example, was charged with the task of signing that colony's genuine currency, but used his position and knowledge to issue—and sign—well-crafted imitations. Though apprehended, he escaped having his ears cropped (a customary punishment) by paying thousands of pounds' worth of gold dust into the colonial treasury.[18]

Counterfeiters like John Potter and Stephen Burroughs enjoyed advantages denied their brethren on the other side of the Atlantic. In

Britain, as in Europe generally, counterfeiting—particularly the forgery of coins or notes of the state or its adjuncts—constituted a treasonable act, punishable by death without benefit of clergy. From the sixteenth century onward, a steady parade of counterfeiters, coiners, and "utterers" of counterfeit coin and paper went to the gallows in England. It was, as one historian has aptly put it, the use of the "death penalty as monetary policy." In the colonies, by contrast, even if some high-profile criminals ended up dangling at the end of a hangman's noose, most counterfeiters evaded punishment, thanks to the relative weakness of state authority, the absence of a policing apparatus, and even the lack of secure jails. But the ease with which counterfeiters plied their trade stemmed from ambivalence on the part of the colonists: most did not view counterfeiting as a threat so much as a harmless activity, if not a beneficial one. Counterfeiters, after all, did a public service by increasing the amount of money in circulation in a part of the world where the demand for money invariably outstripped the supply. Like their successors in the nineteenth century, counterfeiters stirred appreciation as much as anger.[19]

A host of other factors contributed to the impunity with which counterfeiters operated, and foreshadowed many of the same problems that would plague law enforcement officials by the time Burroughs and his ilk commenced operations. One, organized gangs of counterfeiters often operated beyond the geographical boundaries of the colonies. A curious loophole in imperial laws meant that it was perfectly legal to counterfeit colonial bills of credit in Ireland as well as England itself. Likewise, counterfeiters operating in one colony often enjoyed relative immunity in the event they fled to another colony, though laws passed after the mid-eighteenth century attempted to limit such evasion. Even then, the authorities in one of the future states might refuse to cooperate with another. In the unlikely event of a conviction, many counterfeiters secured pardons from governors who recognized that responsibility for the families of these men and women would fall on already burdened local communities. Despite the grim promise that adorned many bills—"To Counterfeit is Death"—counterfeiters operated with relative impunity in the future United States.[20]

Roguery and Revolution

Burroughs's early years are well documented, thanks to his *Memoirs*, parts of which began appearing in the late 1790s. It is a remarkable work, akin to Benjamin Franklin's *Autobiography*, but far more literary—and far more cynical. Like Franklin's narrative, it relates the story of a self-made man who exploits the growing fluidity of eighteenth-century society to make his way in the world. Burroughs grew up in the shadow of his father, a prominent Presbyterian theologian who served as a minister in Coventry, New Hampshire. The son did not follow his father's calling, much less his example. Burroughs recalled that he was "the terror of the people where I lived, and all were very unanimous in declaring, that Stephen Burroughs was the worst boy in town, and those who could get him whipped were most worthy of esteem." Fond of pranks, Burroughs attended Dartmouth, "where he was courted by lovers of wild college-fun on the one hand, and suspected and watched on the other." After more practical jokes, he quit school and soon shipped out on a privateer during the Revolution, obtaining passage by impersonating a physician.[21]

That first false identity, like so many that followed, derived from Burroughs's inclination to see life in theatrical terms. He recalled, for example, how his father "let me loose on the broad theater of the world, to act my part according to my abilities." The fascination with artifice was not his alone: there was a growing obsession throughout

FIGURE 4. Portrait of a confidence man: posing as a distinguished member of the clergy was but the beginning of a career built on pretense and fraud. *Courtesy, Library Company of Philadelphia.*

the colonial period with deceit and imposture, concerns that coincided with challenges posed to the conventional social order by religious ferment, Revolutionary politics, and the spread of market capitalism. Like the beneficiaries of these other trends, Burroughs spoke the language of social mobility. Democracy became a powerful force in the closing decades of the eighteenth century. New possibilities emerged for middling white men like Burroughs; they could now become architects of their own destiny, instead of remaining mired in inherited roles and obligations. It followed that social roles, like theatrical parts, could be assumed and abandoned at will.[22]

Burroughs pursued this logic further than most of his contemporaries. After returning home to New Hampshire after his stint on the privateer, he cast around for other means of support, at which time he managed to get himself excommunicated from the Dartmouth Church of Christ (allegedly for violating commandments three and eight—misusing the name of God and stealing). Burroughs took appropriate revenge by impersonating a minister. As he related the tale many years later, he stole a number of his father's sermons and headed 150 miles down the Connecticut River. After auditioning in several towns under an assumed name, he obtained a position in Pelham, Massachusetts. Several successful sermons later, Burroughs's imposture was unmasked, and he found himself cornered in a barn by an angry mob. In Burroughs's version of events, some bystanders asked his pursuers why they sought to punish him. After all, hadn't he preached well? Reluctantly, the mob answered that he had. "Well," said the bystander, "why need you make any difficulty? He preached well—you paid him well—all parties were satisfied . . . What signifies what he called his name? A name does no good nor hurt, as to the matter of his doctrine." Deflated, the angry mob dispersed and Burroughs escaped—or so he claimed. Whether true or not, the episode afforded him a subtle way to defend a new code of conduct that he returned to again and again. It suffved that the sermons appealed and that they provided spiritual nourishment; the confidence the villagers put in him did not depend on intrinsic qualifications or theological assets. It was a lesson with considerable relevance for his experiments with money.[23]

Around the time Burroughs was preaching in Pelham, he and an associate learned that an alchemist named Philips had set up shop in New Salem, offering to divulge (for a price) the secret of turning copper into silver. Burroughs recalled that his associate, a man to whom he gave the pseudonym Lysander, "appeared to entertain the highest confidence in the business." Whether Lysander was an actual individual or an incarnation of Burroughs's criminal alter ego is difficult to determine. The choice of the name was striking. Lysander was the Spartan general who brought home enormous amounts of gold and silver plundered from the Athenians during the Peloponnesian War. Flooded with precious metals, the Spartans abandoned their more modest iron coinage and developed a corrupt taste for wealth and luxury. So, too, did Burroughs after visiting Philips and seeing a demonstration of the transmutation of copper into silver. "I felt all the confidence in the business which was possible to feel on any subject," Burroughs recalled after returning home. "I saw, in my own imagination, my fortune certainly made."[24]

Burroughs was soon disappointed: Philips deceived him along with many other men in nearby towns, borrowing money to underwrite his experiments and absconding with the funds. Among those who fell victim to Philips's con was Glazier Wheeler, a skilled counterfeiter of coin. According to Burroughs, Lysander, still entranced with the prospect of easy wealth, proposed that they embrace the next best thing to alchemy, and join forces with Wheeler. Burroughs had some misgivings, but Lysander (or Burroughs's criminal conscience) dispelled his fears with clever argumentation. "Money," Lysander said, "of itself, is of no consequence, only as we, by mutual agreement, annex to it a nominal value, as the representation of property. Anything else might answer the same purpose, equally with silver and gold, should mankind only agree to consider it as such, and carry that agreement into execution in their dealings with each other. We find this verified by fact," added Lysander, "by those bills of credit which are in circulation through the world." These slips of paper, he observed, "are good for nothing; but the moment mankind agree to put a value on them, as representing property, they become of as great consequence as silver and gold, and no one is injured by receiving a small insignificant piece of paper for a hundred bushels of wheat."[25]

Lysander based his observations on practical experience, for the colonists had embraced paper money far earlier and more enthusiastically than their counterparts in Europe. The lesson of all this paper money was obvious—at least to Lysander. As he explained to Burroughs, "The only thing necessary to make a matter valuable, is to induce the world to deem it so; and let that esteem be raised by any means whatever, yet the value is the same, and no one becomes injured by receiving it at the valuation." Counterfeiting was an extension of this logic: it likewise required others to deem something valuable that had no intrinsic, objective value. That Lysander and Burroughs came to this conclusion after their failed investment in alchemy was appropriate. The alchemical quest for riches was disappearing at this very time, replaced by other means of creating value out of thin air. Paper money was one such surrogate for alchemy. Counterfeiting was another, and Glazier Wheeler embodied the common spirit animating both pursuits. An artisan skilled in the alchemical arts of metallurgy and chemistry, he had long directed a gang in New Hampshire that manufactured and distributed bogus coin throughout the colonies.[26]

Whatever the risks of counterfeiting, Burroughs became convinced by Lysander's arguments. More to the point, he recalled, in what became a common refrain in his *Memoirs*, "the mania of wealth had taken strong possession of our minds, and we listened with eagerness to her calls." Taking some counterfeit coin from Wheeler, Burroughs tried to pass it at an apothecary in Springfield, Massachusetts, only to be immediately arrested and committed to trial. He represented himself before the court in what from all accounts was an entertaining performance, but again his reputation hurt him. As he related the story in his *Memoirs*, the prosecutor cited his impersonation of a minister as evidence of his iniquity. Burroughs lamented that the jurist claimed "I had been a counterfeiter not only of the coin of the country, but had likewise counterfeited a name, a character, a calling: all of which seemed to communicate this idea to the world, that I had given a loose to the practice of every enormity; that my wickedness had at length found me out." The court found Burroughs and Wheeler guilty and sentenced both to three years hard labor on Castle Island, a fortress-like prison in Boston harbor.[27]

Burroughs made many attempts to break out of jail, including one rather spectacular escape by boat that ended in his recapture a day later. He finally emerged several years later to a very different world than the one he had left behind. When he had passed counterfeit coin in the mid-1780s, Massachusetts was in the midst of a postwar economic slump. Farmers suffered more than most: many owed money but lacked the hard currency to make their payments. Money was scarce, and the state constitution, which forbade the use of paper currency and gave no protection to debtors, exacerbated matters, as did a new law requiring that taxes be paid in coin. Gold and silver became extraordinarily rare, much as Burroughs's friend Lysander acknowledged when he justified counterfeiting on the grounds that "an undue scarcity of cash now prevails [and] whoever contributes, really, to increase the quantity of cash, does not only himself, but likewise the community, an essential benefit." As in colonial times, demand for money outstripped supply, though counterfeiters were happy to make up the difference.[28]

If Burroughs and Lysander failed in their attempts to increase the quantity of cash, so did Daniel Shays, the Massachusetts farmer who led an insurrection to bring some relief to the specie-starved farmers. The revolt failed, but focused attention on political reform, particularly among the economic and social elite who met in 1787 to discuss changes to the Articles of Confederation. After considerable debate, they jettisoned the Articles altogether and instead drafted a blueprint for a much stronger central government: the Constitution. That document, which was debated and sent to the colonies for ratification just before Burroughs emerged from prison in 1788, reflected the hard-money bias of the individuals who framed it. It granted to Congress the power to regulate interstate and foreign commerce, mint coin, and regulate the money supply. Significantly, it was forbidden for individual states to "emit Bills of Credit [or] make anything but Gold or Silver Coin a Tender in Payment of Debts." This was another way of saying, however ambiguously, that paper money should not have a place in the nation's circulating medium.[29]

The aversion to paper stemmed from the fact that both Congress and the individual state governments had printed vast quantities of worthless paper money to underwrite their debts both during and after the Revolution. The Continental Congress became especially infamous for its irredeemable wartime issues, known as "continentals," which over the course of the war lost almost all their value, thanks in part to counterfeits issued by the British. A popular phrase at the time, "not worth a continental," summed up the failure of these issues and the poor reputation of paper money generally. While there was initially a clause in the Constitution that permitted the federal government to issue notes, it was quickly eliminated, one delegate recalled, to "shut and bar the door against paper money." This fear was widely shared. As another argued, retaining the right to issue paper "would be as alarming as the mark of the Beast in Revelations." It would be better, another urged, to "reject the whole plan than retain the three words 'and emit bills.'"[30]

While many of the framers wished to keep paper money out of circulation, this proved impractical. There was no way that the specie-poor United States could conduct all of its business in the gold and silver coin preferred by the more developed economies of Europe. Bank notes solved the problem. The Continental Congress had already chartered the first note-issuing bank in 1782 (the Bank of North America) and after the war's end, several state-chartered banks emerged as well, one in each of the major cities on the eastern seaboard. These early institutions enjoyed a reputation for conservative management, and did not issue bank notes in excess of their specie reserves. They operated as practical monopolies, making loans and doing business with an elite sliver of society. These were joined in 1791 by the Bank of the United States, chartered by the U.S. Congress. The brainchild of Alexander Hamilton, it was modeled on the Bank of England and designed to assist in the collection of federal taxes and the administration of public finances. It also provided a market for the national debt, because subscribers had to pay for shares using federal securities. It was chartered over the strong opposition of the antifederalists, who criticized it as monopolistic.[31]

The antifederalists need not have worried. The number of note-issuing banks grew from five to more than three hundred in the quarter-century after the chartering of the Bank of the United States. Many of these banks, moreover, differed from those favored by conservative financiers like Hamilton. They tended to represent a more aggressive, entrepreneurial, risk-taking segment of society, many of whom harbored antifederalist sympathies. The banks they established did more than simply receive money and store it; they created it, too. "For each dollar paid in by the stockholders," one historian of banking has written, "the banks lent two, three, four, or five. The more sanguine part of the people were happy to have it so, no matter if they did not understand how it could be." Many of these loans took the form of bank notes. That these banks had far more notes in circulation than specie in their vaults was a lesson many would learn the hard way in the succeeding decades. But for now, few people bothered to inquire too deeply into the arcana of fractional-reserve banking, capital requirements, and specie ratios. Confidence in the promise of future profit was enough for most converts to banks and banking.[32]

As the years passed, it became increasingly easy to obtain a bank charter from well-placed friends in state legislatures. In time, this tactic permitted most every special interest or class to have its own bank: tradesmen, merchants, mechanics, farmers, and others. Even individual states chartered banks—the Bank of Vermont, for example—to serve their needs. Like Hamilton's Bank of the United States, these institutions functioned as adjuncts to the state governments by absorbing state debts, or bonds, in the process of capitalization. But whatever their origin or motive, all of these new banks had one thing in common: they issued bank notes. These slips of paper, adorned with the name of the bank, denomination, and some kind of vignette, or ornamental design, look crude by today's standards, and could be easily counterfeited. The federal government, which did not charter these banks, had little interest or control over their issues, and ceded the problem to the individual states.[33]

When Burroughs left prison in the fall of 1788, he stood on the cusp of these developments, and over the course of the next decade he wandered about the new nation, marrying his cousin, Sally Davis, and working as a schoolteacher in Massachusetts before falling afoul of authorities, this time for allegedly seducing his female students. After yet another escape from prison (this time successful) and a stint teaching school on Long Island, Burroughs fled to Georgia, taking a job as a tutor, only to be drawn to a financial mania that gripped the region. In 1795, the state legislature sold millions of acres in the Yazoo River watershed, precipitating what Burroughs described as a "rage for land speculation." Though a few speculators started the frenzy, eventually "all were seized with the mania of rushing suddenly into immense wealth, and the most nefarious schemes were put in practice to defraud a credulous world with the idea of becoming interested in the excellent soil of the Georgia lands." Burroughs, characteristically enough, joined the stampede, for "it offered to my imagination the animating prospect of speedy affluence." Working as a surveyor, Burroughs got himself hired by none other than Philadelphia financier Robert Morris, who eventually charged him with the task of voyaging beyond the western frontier in order to establish a fur trade with the Indians.[34]

It was not to be. "Mr. Morris," wrote Burroughs, "by a concatenation of the most astounding incidents, became embarrassed, notwithstanding his immense property and unequaled fiscal abilities," and confidence in the scheme collapsed. Morris ended up in debtors' prison thanks to his speculative investments in land; Burroughs, who had lent the financier money, lost it all when a crooked lawyer sold his property without his consent, pocketed the money, and fled the country. Laid low by someone more conniving than himself, he returned home to his father's house. The next few years he spent writing his memoirs and pondering his next act of self-invention.[35]

The Banker

On several occasions in his *Memoirs*, Burroughs complained of the notoriety that had attached to his name over the course of his life. "When mankind had once formed an unfavorable opinion," he observed of his own dubious reputation, "it was hard to eradicate such an idea, even by the most pointed evidence." Perhaps tired of his fame, which began to assume a life of its own after the publication of his autobiography, Burroughs eventually left the United States altogether, moving to what is now Quebec and settling in the township of Stanstead, just north of the Vermont border. According to his own account, he arrived there in 1799, settling on a small river that drained into Lake Massawippi. Burroughs cleared the land and built several mills that harnessed the power of the nearby falls. There was some question as to whether the land had already been claimed by someone else, but otherwise Burroughs stayed out of trouble. Had this been the end of it, his reputation would have been confined to the misdeeds of his memoirs. But Burroughs, it seems, had acquired a thirst for making money, as an appendix to an 1804 edition of his life story made clear. "For several years he gave great encouragement to his friends, that he might still be a useful member of society," it was reported. "But, alas! how have their hopes been blasted! Common fame says, that several of his last years have been assiduously employed in counterfeiting bills of the various banks of the United States."[36]

It was thanks to such exploits that Burroughs went from a mildly notorious figure to a larger-than-life outlaw, a threat to the nation's fledgling economy as well as an embodiment of the growing impulse to make money at any cost. Such fears and anxieties were exaggerated, but they testified to Burroughs's growing status in the popular imagination. Forged notes, wherever they appeared, were attributed to him, and he soon became in many minds the fountainhead of the counterfeit economy. That he never documented his doings in Canada in the detail that he related his earlier life only encouraged further speculation, and Burroughs soon found that his reputation outstripped his actual exploits. It helped that the region to which he relocated appealed to romantic sensibilities. "Stephen Burroughs was supposed to have his manufactory of counterfeit money somewhere in the recesses of those mountains," recalled one novelist some years later. "It was a wilderness then . . . It heard then the nightly scream of the panther; the growl of the bear; the bark of the wolf." This was not too far from the truth: though the French had claimed the region just north of Vermont when they established trading posts at Quebec in 1608 and Montreal in 1642, few people settled there because it had minimal access to water and no roads. That it was the hunting ground of the Iroquois did not make it any more inviting.[37]

When the British assumed control of New France with the Treaty of Paris in 1763, they did not institute any radical changes in the provinces of Upper and Lower Canada (later renamed Ontario and Quebec, respectively, according to their positions along the north-flowing St. Lawrence River). Then, after the Revolution, they opened the area to settlement. Because all newcomers had to bear the cost of surveying subdivisions and of obtaining royal patents, wealthier Loyalists tended to be among the first permanent settlers. They set up small villages in the different tracts of land along the frontier, settling in places like Stanbridge, Dunham, and Stanstead. Many people arrived after Vermont's leaders, who had contemplated joining Lower Canada, opted instead to throw their lot in with the new nation to the south. Still, while Loyalists and their sympathizers numbered among the first settlers of the region that became known as the Eastern Townships, many subsequent settlers, Burroughs included, had no reason for being there aside from easy access to land. As one historian of the region wrote in the mid-nineteenth century, "Others came in, who could only be regarded in the light of unavoidable evils, being of that irresponsible ill-regulated class who 'neither feared God, nor regarded man.'"[38]

Border regions tend to attract fugitives from justice, but the stretch of frontier between Vermont and Canada offered more than the usual inducements for those seeking refuge from authorities in either country. Access to the townships was next to impossible, because there were no reliable roads connecting the region to any of the major cities of Lower Canada. Even as late as the 1830s, a survey of the roads near the border succinctly described them as "very rugged, broken, and otherwise bad." This made finding fugitives, much less bringing them to trial, extraordinarily difficult. That most criminal cases had to be tried before the Court of King's Bench in distant Montreal did not help matters, nor did the absence of any kind of police force, a scarcity of magistrates and justices of the peace, a continual clash between competing legal systems, and a number of Loyalists who had little love or respect for the laws of the United States. The federal government could do little to control criminal activity originating in the townships, for it possessed minimal authority over the region. It lacked an extradition treaty with Lower Canada, and an ongoing territorial dispute between Britain and the United States made the actual location of the border a matter of personal opinion. (In a testament to this ambiguity, settlers referred to the boundary as "the lines.")[39]

The townships became a classic borderland, an area where the conflicting loyalties of the residents, the isolation of the settlements, and the unusual mix of cultures and jurisdictions made for a breakdown in authority that worried British administrators of the region. Indeed, the settlers of Lower Canada looked less to the imperial authorities than to their counterparts south of the border, with whom they forged strong commercial and criminal ties. Communities in northwestern Vermont, for example, exported timber and potash northward, along with a stream of cheap smuggled goods: tea, silks, cotton fabrics, china, and other portable items. Until the early 1800s, this trade was very much a one-sided affair, with little in the way of contraband goods flowing south. Things remained that way until Stephen Burroughs arrived. He had something to sell the Americans to the south, something that had not been part of the normal ebb and flow of commerce—until now.[40]

It is unclear when, exactly, Burroughs produced his first notes. Popular lore in the townships holds that the first night Burroughs arrived in Lower Canada, he purchased a lot of gilt buttons wrapped in tissue paper, upon which he printed counterfeits of the Bank of Haverhill, New Hampshire. This bank, however, did not go into business until after Burroughs arrived, and the incident, however suggestive, is probably apocryphal. But within a few years, reports of counterfeit notes in the neighborhood of Stanstead aroused suspicions. These were confirmed in September 1805, when Sheriff Mike Barron arrested Samuel Spring and Russell Underwood in Barre, Vermont, for having in their possession a variety of counterfeit notes on banks in New Hampshire, Maine, Connecticut, and Rhode Island. During the trial, it came out that Spring was an "old offender and partner with the notorious Stephen Burroughs, in the Canada manufactory." This was one of the first public acknowledgments that Burroughs, who was well-known throughout the country thanks to his *Memoirs,* had begun another life in crime beyond the reach of the usual authorities.[41]

The conviction of Spring, as well as others associated with Burroughs, did not stem the tide of counterfeits that now began to flow from Burroughs's twin manufactories: one in Stanstead and another in the township of Shipton to the north. As news of Burroughs's doings spread, a number of state-chartered banks—most prominently the Coos Bank of Haverhill, New Hampshire—banded together to underwrite Barron's well-publicized raid across the Vermont border. Notably, private "citizens," not official government representatives, initiated this movement to arrest Burroughs. Neither the states nor the federal government had the resources to mount a campaign against Burroughs or any other counterfeiter, particularly a campaign that entailed international diplomacy. In what would remain a common practice well into the nineteenth century, private bounty hunters moved into the enforcement void. Often corrupt, such men resorted to tactics of dubious legality, hauling fugitives across state and national lines in violation of local laws. In Burroughs's case, Barron crossed into Canada with the blessing of another reward seeker, a local justice of the peace named Oliver Barker, to whom Barron transferred custody of Burroughs. The counterfeiter complained many years later that while Barker acted as a "legal agent" for the crown, he nonetheless "had a double duty to perform, one of *honor* for his original master, another of *profit* for the U. States; and as money has a great influence in human affairs, he chose, in this instance, to sacrifice honor at the shrine of Plutus."[42]

How, exactly, someone like Barker managed to get Burroughs committed to jail in Montreal remains unclear. While the newspapers of New England opined that Burroughs would be transported or hanged for his offenses, this was far too optimistic. As the wily counterfeiter doubtless knew, however draconian the laws might be when it came to the counterfeiting of British currency, there were no laws against counterfeiting foreign bank notes. Obscure banks chartered by the now independent British colonies did not fall within the compass of the existing statutes, even if those same notes circulated north of the border. Burroughs quickly posted bail in advance of having the case dismissed, but the indefatigable Barker managed to have him recommitted once more on misdemeanor and theft charges. The counterfeiter made his well-publicized flight from the Montreal jail shortly thereafter with the blessing, Burroughs intimated many years later, of high-level authorities in the imperial government unsympathetic to American banks. "His dexterity at escaping from a halter," observed one newspaper in the wake of these events, "appears to be no less than his adroitness at deserving one."[43]

Other observers tacitly applauded Burroughs the trickster, at the same time they mocked the banks he imitated. One widely reprinted article lampooned the events of that year by casting Burroughs in the role of just another banker. The piece opened with an observation that Burroughs "has carried on the *banking business* on a large scale," and noted that the counterfeiter had cut into the profits of the banks of New England. In turn, "the Yankees, being so hard run upon by Mr. Burroughs, determined to try the strength of that gentleman's *banking house.*" His competitors, this article reported, "went forthwith to his bank, and after sacking it of the *specie capital,* proceeded to . . . an inventory of his valuables." And what did they find? Counterfeit notes on various banks in the United States. Putting words in Burroughs's mouth, they had the counterfeiter make a speech to these "rival bankers." "Gentlemen, this is the most unpleasant day in my whole life. To be ruined by an ill-advised *extension of banking speculations* is enough to disturb the repose of a man of my Christian temper." The counterfeit money, Burroughs insisted, was a bank deposit of his elderly mother, who had obtained the notes while speculating in securities. "She always had an itch for speculation," Burroughs was made to say. "It is owing to her that I am now a ruined man. I told her this banking was a *'hazard-ous business.'*"[44]

This burlesque, with its peculiar conflation of banking and counterfeiting, spoke to the unease that many felt about the proliferation of paper money. What was the difference between a capitalist banker and a criminal counterfeiter? There were differences, to be sure, but not to the extent many people would have preferred. Both trafficked in confidence, and by making Burroughs into a banker, writers like this one captured the ambiguities of an economy based on very little in the way of "real" money. And to have the counterfeiter decry the business of banking and speculation only made this little bit of satire all the more amusing to readers skeptical of banks and bank notes. Some may have condemned Burroughs, but others found him a caricature of the entire business of banking and money making, someone whose criminal behavior implicitly called into question the legitimacy of the entire capitalist enterprise.

Burroughs managed to escape prosecution in this instance, as he did on a number of occasions. His skill at outwitting his pursuers had much to do with his many allies in the townships. As one traveler to the region later explained, "Burroughs made himself popular by several acts of publick utility in Stanstead," including building a twenty-mile-long road that enabled farmers to sell their produce. That he had also cared for several residents during a smallpox epidemic a few years earlier no doubt endeared him to the local community. As Burroughs's popularity grew, he could trade the security of isolation for the watchful eyes of his neighbors, many of whom embraced the opportunity to participate in the counterfeit economy, and protected and harbored him when the need arose. Oliver Barker later recalled that his own attempts to arrest Burroughs met with resistance from sympathetic locals, if not members of his gang. According to Barker, Burroughs es-

caped from his clutches in March 1807 thanks to the "exertions &
vigilance of his numerous accomplices," one of whom attempted—as
usual, without success—to shoot the bounty hunter when he visited
Stanstead.[45]

Political considerations may have played a role as well in Burroughs's
uncanny ability to escape prosecution. This was a region settled by
Loyalists, and few of the inhabitants respected the United States, much
less its banks. Even the local authorities had mixed feelings on the
subject, as is evident from a petition submitted by the local magistrates in the wake of the failed attempt to arrest Burroughs in the
spring of 1807, at which time Barker ransacked Burroughs's residence
in Stanstead, confiscating many of his possessions and stealing some
$53,000 in cash—or so the aging counterfeiter alleged many years later.
For his part, Barker claimed the raid had broken up the remnants of
"Burroughs' old company." Local authorities sympathetic to Burroughs
were not impressed. Citing the "reprehensible" conduct of Barker, these
men complained that their colleague "in his official capacity has been
hired (not to use a harsher term) and paid by sundry of the Banks of
the United States" to assist in prosecuting "the Notorious Stephen
Burroughs and his confederates." Worse, they noted that Barker had
called U.S. citizens into the province and "authorized them as constables and assistants," and with them behaved "in an overbearing, tumultuous, and even riotous manner greatly to the Annoyance of his Majesty's peaceable good subjects." Most damning of all, Barker had not
delivered the plates and notes seized from Burroughs to the imperial
authorities, as would have been expected, but had "taken them to the
Banks of the United States, and there received his payment, or reward,
as stipulated between them." Their message was clear: while Burroughs
may have been "notorious," these transgressions of the colony's political
sovereignty should not be tolerated.[46]

Despite Barker's best efforts, Burroughs remained at large, and the lack of laws against counterfeiting made prosecution a difficult affair. Meanwhile, the bogus bills continued to stream south, and individuals arrested as far away as Connecticut and Pennsylvania were accused of being in league with Burroughs, whose reputation by this time had spread far beyond northern New England. Newspaper accounts from this period give the impression that Burroughs had a monopoly on the counterfeiting trade in Lower Canada, though Barker's own testimony suggests that several allied gangs had commenced operations as well. Unfortunately, the details are difficult to reconstruct, because the relevant court records have long been destroyed. Still, from what little remains, it appears that Burroughs had hired some skilled engravers to produce the bogus plates, and handled much of the printing himself. Other family members—his sons, especially—worked with him, or served as couriers to deliver the counterfeit money throughout the United States. Some accounts alleged that his wife and daughter were also involved, though these claims are more difficult to substantiate. Burroughs, one newspaper asserted, had a wife "with all the accomplishments, address and spirit to carry on his intrigues and iniquity; and a large family of children . . . some of whom are said to be equally expert with the father in the science of 'dressing up vice in the garb of virtue.'"[47]

Evidence of the growing sophistication of Burroughs's ring surfaced around this time, after yet more raids by Barker. According to a newspaper report, one of Burroughs's accomplices, a man named Remington, visited a paper mill in Montreal with an unusual request. "He told us he wanted about twenty reams, of as many different kinds as we could make," related a witness, and "he shewed bills of more than fifty different kinds, which he said he wanted paper to suit them all." The paper maker agreed, but notified the authorities. "We found that

Burroughs was the head of the business," reported the paper maker, who later learned that the counterfeiters anticipated needing one hundred reams of paper in the coming year. There was no limit to their ambitions: as this same witness claimed, Remington told him that "after trying New York a spell," they planned on turning their attention to the banks in "old Massachusetts." But the counterfeiters never made it to Massachusetts: Barker arrested Remington and several others in late September, catching them in the act of stamping five-dollar notes on the Farmers' Bank of New York. Subsequent arrests confirmed that Burroughs was masterminding much of the illicit "banking" conducted north of the border. Petitions for pardon filed by Burroughs's imprisoned associates at this time cast him as a charismatic figure with a silver tongue. One spoke of Burroughs's "peculiar seductive language," with which the counterfeiter painted "the most flattering, though visionary prospects of acquiring sudden wealth." The fictive Lysander and the real-life Burroughs had become one and the same.[48]

Burroughs's reputation now began to assume a life of its own, thanks in part to the many pirated—or counterfeited—versions of his *Memoirs* circulating in the United States. He delighted in the notoriety, using his fame to poke fun at his foes in the banking establishment. But until the spring of 1809, Burroughs had little opportunity to draw a parallel between his own activities and those of his more respectable counterparts. That changed with the implosion of the infamous Farmers Exchange Bank of Gloucester, based in Rhode Island, a state with a long-standing reputation for monetary mischief. Incorporated in 1804 by an imaginative financier named Andrew Dexter, the Farmers Exchange Bank was to the United States what John Law's Banque Royale had been to France. By putting notes into circulation hundreds of miles away from where they could be redeemed, Dexter played a consummate shell game, dodging redemption for many months until the entire scheme collapsed in March of 1807. The auditors who picked over the carcass of Dexter's creation discovered that the institution had close to a million dollars in outstanding bank notes, and a mere forty-five dollars in specie available to redeem them.[49]

Burroughs kept abreast of the falling fortunes of Dexter's bank, and found the opportunity to weigh in on the crisis irresistible. He wrote a letter to Samuel Gilbert and Thomas Dean, two bank note brokers associated with Dexter who, in addition to their service to the fallen financier, published a guide to the counterfeit notes emanating from Burroughs's workshops. The letter began on a tone of mock seriousness. "Gentleman, Having seen your 'Only sure guide to bank Bills,' and admiring your kind labors for the public weal . . . I have enclosed and forwarded to your Exchange Office, a bill on the Shipton Bank." Noting that this bank, of which he was the principal stockholder, "has very recently commenced its operation," Burroughs requested that they "give the public the earliest notice should spurious bills of that Bank be discovered to be in circulation." Alluding to the recent troubles of the Exchange Bank (whose discredited notes had sunk below counterfeit money in the public's estimation), Burroughs slyly ridiculed the logic of intrinsic value. "Such is the depravity of man, and such the success of counterfeiting," he wrote, "that I lately observed in one of your newspapers, that patent *buck wheat pancakes* had been so exactly counterfeited . . . that none except the Officers of the *Pancake Exchange* could distinguish them from the originals!!!" Burroughs enclosed a satirical bank note that mocked the efforts of the banking community to send him to the gallows or a penal colony. It depicted "a figure of an Ourang Outang from whose mouth issued a label with these words: *'Death or Botany Bay, ha, ha, ha!'*"[50]

These and other pranks only added to Burroughs's burgeoning reputation as a folk hero. Accounts of his exploits began to acquire the kind of details that, even if utterly fabricated, testified to the growing respect for his remarkable ability to defeat his more powerful foes through a mixture of ingenuity and artifice. For example, when officers of the law showed up at his bank note manufactory in Shipton, Burroughs was supposed to have "immediately put on his snow-shoes, forward end behind, and went away, leaving the appearance of tracks toward his house, while he was going from it." This may have been Burroughs's own invention, or as this account suggested, the idea may have been a variation on "Virgil's description of Cacus, the son of Vulcan whom Hercules slew, who drew his stolen cattle into his cave backwards to deceive his pursuers." The evocation of classical mythology was telling: Burroughs had become, like other folk heroes, a larger-than-life figure—and in this case, was deemed responsible for every counterfeit in circulation. A number of popular editions of his *Memoirs* published at this time only cemented his reputation. So, too, did the news that Burroughs, captured in an ambush orchestrated by Oliver Barker, had managed to escape yet again.[51]

Burroughs's career mirrored the final dissolution of the colonial architecture of authority, and its replacement by a more raucous and individualistic expression of political and economic power. Growing numbers of upstart entrepreneurs claimed the right to "make money" in both senses of the phrase. They founded banks, issuing paper money as a means of underwriting their speculations outside the sort of established financial circles represented by the Boston banking establishment. In his attacks (rhetorical or otherwise) on this older order, Burroughs enjoyed a certain kinship with a new breed of self-made political and economic entrepreneurs with whom he shared a scorn of prerogative and inherited rights. Burroughs said as much in the first page of his *Memoirs* when he wrote, "I am so far a republican, that I consider a man's merit to rest entirely with himself, without any regard to family, blood, or connection." Or as one newspaper observed at this time, "Burroughs was always an advocate of the equalizing doctrines."[52]

Few of Burroughs's distant cousins, the Jeffersonian Republicans, showed much interest in prosecuting him—in part because politicians of this mold had little desire to expand the policing powers of the nation-state. They in fact distrusted centralized authority, which may account for why the federal government did so little to prevent, prosecute, or punish counterfeiting of any sort in the years after 1800. Even imitations of the coins issued by the national mint went unchecked and unpunished. Congress instead ceded responsibility for counterfeiting to the individual state legislatures, few of which showed much initiative in combating the problem. One notable exception was Vermont, which was still dominated by the Federalists just as Burroughs's exploits began to attract considerable attention. Late in the fall of 1808, the governor dispatched an emissary to lobby the provincial legislature of Lower Canada to pass laws against the counterfeiting of U.S. bank notes. It was not surprising that of all the states, Vermont took the lead in addressing the problem. Not only did most of the counterfeit notes pass through the state on their way to various destinations throughout the country, but Vermont also had a special relationship with Canada. It relied heavily on Canadian markets for its goods, and many families had relatives on both sides of the border. Thanks in part to these ties, the legislature of Lower Canada acceded to the request, finally passing a law that made the counterfeiting of foreign bank notes a crime, though not a capital offense.[53]

Burroughs was not unaware of these developments. After his last escape, he had relocated to his lair in the less-settled township of Shipton, farther from the border with Vermont. There he learned of the pending legislation. Seeing the writing on the wall, he quickly submitted a petition to the governor. In it he reviewed the charges against him, which included counterfeiting the notes of banks in the United States; persuading someone to pass counterfeit coin; escaping from the common jail of Montreal; and last but not least, stealing an ox, a crime that potentially carried the death penalty. Burroughs admitted that he had "made impressions representing the Bank notes or bills in circulation in the United States," but correctly claimed that at the time he did so, it "was not injurious to this Province or to Great Britain, and that he was not in any manner contravening the Laws of the same." Moreover, he claimed that upon hearing that the parliament was considering criminalizing the very thing that he had been doing, he had quit the business, burning the notes in his possession and destroying his printing press. He dismissed the other charges as "calumnious imputations," being the product of "machinations entered into by the agents of several of the Banks of the United States with divers persons within this Province." Finally, he conceded that he had broken out of jail, but pointed out with his usual fondness for legal niceties that he had walked out without "any breaking or the use of force or violence," making it a much less objectionable crime. On these grounds he requested clemency, arguing that he had otherwise led an honorable life, "making agricultural improvements on several very extensive Farms."[54]

Burroughs was eventually tried in the provincial city of Trois-Rivières, though not before turning the tables on Oliver Barker by having the bounty hunter arrested on bogus charges. Barker eventually walked free, however, and Burroughs did not. In 1811, as Burroughs awaited sentencing, American newspapers predicted that he would finally "meet the punishment he has so much laughed at, 'death or Botany Bay.'" The court opted for Botany Bay, but in typical fashion, Burroughs escaped deportation; after he offered substantial bonds for his future good conduct, Governor Craig pardoned him. Not that the former counterfeiter stayed entirely out of trouble. With the outbreak of war between Britain and the United States the following year, the border region between the two countries erupted in fighting, and Burroughs, mindful of the need to prove his loyalty to the British—and tempted by the promise of what he called "a handsome provision"—began performing "secret services" on behalf of the royal authorities. By his own account, he helped forestall a mutiny among some troops quartered near his home in Shipton, and worked as a spy, collecting military intelligence that proved critical in one of the battles fought on the frontier.[55]

As a result of his spying, Burroughs was thrown in prison and accused, he later claimed, of working as a double agent. The charges may well have been true, but he escaped prosecution once more. This time, however, events seemed to have conspired against him. His son Edward, who had been arrested several years back while traveling to Vermont as a wholesaler of counterfeit money, cut off contact with his father, establishing himself at Trois-Rivières as—*sacre bleu!*—a chore-boy for the chief justice of the provincial court. Shortly after this, Burroughs lost title to his farms in lawsuits that contested his right to the land in Shipton and Stanstead. Finding himself once again without money, Burroughs moved what was left of his family to Trois-Rivières, where he worked as a schoolteacher and a tutor and, as one wag later put it, "'took up the business of being a respectable man!' and well and honorably did he follow that business, as his many friends—enemies he had none—who were long his neighbors, will all cheerfully testify."[56]

It may have helped that Burroughs apparently became a devout Catholic in the 1810s, most likely inspired by his wife, a long-time convert. Catholicism, he wrote in a letter published in 1815, was a religion of "consequence, importance, and beauty" that put to shame the "horrid absurdities" of his father's Calvinism. His daughter, Sally, likewise converted, despite having only a few years earlier been rumored to

FIGURE 5. The counterfeiter as respectable citizen: this portrait of Burroughs was painted toward the end of his life, most likely in the early 1830s. *Courtesy, Maurice O'Bready Collection, Sherbrooke Historical Society, Quebec.*

have been supporting herself "in stile *[sic]* and elegance by the simple business of signing the [counterfeit] bills, in which art she arrived to great perfection." She embraced the new faith with fervor, entering the Ursuline Convent in Trois-Rivières as a cloistered nun, eventually becoming the mother superior of that institution.[57] Burroughs himself became more pious in his later years, taking up the cause of the French Catholics who were his neighbors, and performing a variety of benevolent acts. Rumors circulated in the United States that he had become a "high dignitary in that Church, and accumulated wealth . . . chiefly in pardoning sins and granting absolution and acts of indulgence," but accounts of his behavior from the 1820s onward suggest that for once Burroughs had truly reformed, even if his conversion constituted a final act of rebellion against his father. One visitor in 1839 reported that Burroughs spent his days reading and writing in a room "hung round with copies, or originals" (the writer, appropriately enough, could not tell which was which) "of the master-pieces of some of the distinguished painters of Christian life and suffering, and every thing about him indicated very convincingly the genuineness of his repentance and reformation." After spending most of his adult life adopting and discarding guises in a caricature of the Protestant self-made man, Burroughs apparently took some refuge in his new faith. Perhaps it offered solidity, stability—and after a life spent playing the counterfeit, the promise of redemption.[58]

Stephen Burroughs died in 1840, but many of his characteristics surfaced in the self-made men who succeeded him. Some made their money in banking; others took up counterfeiting. All thrived in the increasingly freewheeling culture of capitalism in the new nation, and all exploited the federal government's powerlessness to advance their own agendas. Bankers did so by arrogating the money-making function, securing sanction to do so from state legislatures, while the counterfeiters who followed Burroughs looked to the margins of the nation-state to pursue their vocation, exploiting the country's vague and confusing physical and cultural borders. All these capitalists, whether operating within the confines of the law or not, had one thing in common: a growing confidence that their notes might pass as good as gold, regardless of how little substance stood behind them. As one critic of banking wrote around this time, a growing number of "practical men" now realized that so long as "confidence continued, a bank really required no more specie than it would be called upon to pay in aid of those enterprizes, in which bank bills would not answer; and that a capital almost entirely fictitious, might go into operation, as securely, and more profitably, than one bottomed on actual and deposited funds." It was an observation that the swelling ranks of confidence men—be they bankers or counterfeiters—would soon turn to profitable ends.[59]

Cogniac Street Capitalism

V isit the town cemetery in the tiny village of Bakersfield, Vermont, and one stone stands out from the rest.
It belongs to Seneca Paige, whose lengthy epitaph puts
to shame the more modest messages of his neighbors. The inscription
begins conventionally enough, noting his birth in 1788 and death in
1856. A New Englander by birth, he nonetheless lived in Lower Canada "for nearly 40 years," and became sufficiently well established that
he "represented [his] county in the Provincial Parliament." More intriguing still, Paige predicts that "his loss will be felt by many. Particularly by the poor. He was truly the poor man's friend." Lest we walk
away worried about Paige's fate in the afterlife, he closes by noting that
he "converted to God in this town in 1833," joining the Methodist
church "in which communion he died."[1]

At first glance, this curious missive seems an innocent instance of
someone giving his legacy a posthumous polish. But in Seneca Paige's
case, a more vigorous scrubbing would have been needed to erase his
reputation among his contemporaries as "the greatest devil in all the

Canadas, Stephen Burroughs not excepted." Paige was a counterfeiter, and a rather successful one at that. His "manufactory" stood at the center of a far-reaching web of engravers, wholesalers, retailers, and "passers" who together constituted an emerging capitalist underworld. One contemporary, marveling at the growing complexity of the market in counterfeits governed by men like Paige, observed that "this counterfeiting traffic . . . as with honest mercantile business, has all its branches, and descends from the wholesale to the retail venders, and generally ends in the hands of the poorest and most simple individuals."[2] So perhaps Paige was a "poor man's friend," if by that he meant getting rich selling counterfeit money to people who had trouble getting hold of the genuine article.

That Paige's sprawling empire had its headquarters on the indeterminate line between the United States and Canada was no accident. Despite the passage of laws criminalizing counterfeiting, the region remained as it had been in Stephen Burroughs's time: a place of continual contest between different markets, nations, and legal systems. While the British authorities made sporadic attempts to suppress the counterfeit trade thriving in the interstices of the two nations, tensions with their former colony, the conflicted and ever-changing loyalties of the townships' residents, and the rugged, isolated terrain of the area frustrated efforts to enforce the law well into the 1830s.[3] Officials from the United States had even less power over the region, because they lacked a presence on the contested border and could neither compel the return of fugitives nor rely on the cooperation of their British counterparts. As a consequence, the townships quickly became the home of a class of criminals for whom the border between the real and counterfeit was as vague as the one separating them from the nation to the south.

If the tale of Stephen Burroughs reveals the counterfeiter's *mentalité*, the story of his successors yields a far grittier glimpse of the inner workings of the counterfeit economy as it developed in the opening decades of the nineteenth century. Although it was based in the small village of Dunham, Quebec, that economy stretched southward to encompass most of the cities and towns of the United States, drawing up a vast number of players in a web of illicit exchange. The notes circulating within this shadow economy followed the same paths to buyers and sellers that more conventional commodities did: the canals, roads, and rivers of an expanding commercial society. Likewise, the various dealers and engravers who bought and sold counterfeits managed their affairs in a manner not so different from their more legitimate counterparts, extending credit, selling on commission, and keeping rudimentary accounts with a growing number of peripatetic wholesalers, distributors, and retailers. It would not be an exaggeration to call these criminals capitalists, even if their idea of making money was more literal-minded than the bankers whose notes they imitated.

To watch the emergence of the counterfeit economy north of the border is to glimpse—in a mirror, dimly—the emergence of a freewheeling capitalist economy in the new nation to the south. The sounds of industry emanating from new factories underwritten with bank notes echoed in the clank of the counterfeit printing press; the scribble of pen and ink in the counting house blurred imperceptibly into the forged signatures scrawled across a bogus bill; the iron laws of supply and demand that governed the movements of ordinary commodities applied no less stringently to the prices at which counterfeit money could be bought and sold. Capitalists and counterfeiters thrived together in the early republic, and for every new bank note symbolizing a confidence in capitalism, there was a ghostly double born in the village here. Like their genuine counterparts, these notes passed from hand to hand, sometimes vexing, occasionally perplexing, but almost always feeding a market economy whose participants hungered for a means of exchange.

Koniackers and Kings

Most every class of criminals develops its own argot, and counterfeiters were no exception. They had slang terms for their profession and their stock in trade, words that seem puzzling to us today. No one, for example, still calls a counterfeiter a "koniacker." One of the first to explain the term was William Coffey, who in 1823 wrote an exposé of prison life where he observed that "counterfeit money is called, among Sharpers, by the slang name of COGNIAC." In New York City alone, he reported, "there are *sixteen* wholesale dealers, pursuing different occupations, who have steady customers, to whom they sell, at a regular per centage, their *imported* Cogniac," and who maintained, Coffey reported, a "regular chain of communication, extending directly through the most populous parts of the State of New York, and onward to the Canadian line." Koniackers, coniackers, cogniac: it makes sense if you look at old maps of the township of Dunham, the epicenter of the counterfeit economy in the early nineteenth century. Branching out from what was once the main street of the village is a tiny road that snakes up into the hills. Both on maps, as well as in many secret circles in Canada and the United States, this dirt road was called "Cogniac Street."[4]

It is not known who gave the road its name: the counterfeiters, the customers, or someone else. It is a picturesque if somewhat windswept place today, lined with fields, patches of forest, apple orchards, and the occasional squat stone house. As modest as it looks now, for some twenty years this was the cradle of counterfeiting in North America, a

FIGURE 6. Still a dirt road today, Cogniac Street is lined with fields and remnants of the original farm buildings from the early nineteenth century. *Photograph from the author's collection.*

reputation its inhabitants did not bother to hide. Fitch Reed, a minister who was stationed in nearby St. Armand in the 1820s, recalled the "settlement known as *Coniac Street*—'Coniac' being a vulgar name for counterfeit money. I was told that every family in that place was concerned in the production of spurious bank-bills." Noting that he often saw "the engraver of their plates, and the scribe who filled up the bills" at his meetings, Reed claimed that "the greater part of the counterfeit bank-bills circulating at that time in the United States . . . were manufactured in this region."[5]

Cogniac Street began flourishing around the time that Stephen Burroughs faded from the scene and a number of colorful characters, all men, came to be associated with the "Canada Counterfeiting Company," as one newspaper dubbed the business. These included Seneca Paige; an illiterate farmer named Ebenezer Gleason, whose many sons served in the counterfeiting workshops; William Crane, a skilled engraver with a penchant for brandishing a sword cane when provoked;

an embittered refugee from a Loyalist family named Thomas Adams Lewis; Benjamin Moses and Reuben Moses, brothers with lengthy criminal records; and the virtuoso engraver Lyman Parkes, whose imitations outshone the genuine notes he counterfeited. Of the principals, Seneca Paige probably arrived first, when his father moved the family to Bakersfield, Vermont, a few miles south of Dunham. He most likely spent some time in the townships to the north, where at least one of his brothers purchased land. Another source suggests that he kept a livery stable in Boston for some time. Unlike Stephen Burroughs, Paige remains a ghostly figure. He left behind no memoirs, no portraits, no confessions. A single newspaper article from 1812 described him as a "tall, slender young man, of light or fair complexion [who] stutters or stammers in his speech."[6]

This was hardly the portrait of a criminal mastermind, but in Paige's case, appearances could deceive. He first surfaced in the United States in 1809 while working as a distributor for a gang of counterfeiters, perhaps for Burroughs himself. Arrested in New Jersey with close to $25,000 worth of bogus notes, he somehow managed to escape prosecution and continued to travel back and forth between Canada and the United States. He was arrested once more in New York City in the spring of 1811 after passing a counterfeit note. It came out during his questioning that he had come to town to testify on behalf of a suspected dealer in counterfeit money, suggesting that Paige, too, may have been in the city on similar business. Whatever the reason, he managed to secure an acquittal (the first of many) and returned to St. Armand that summer. Paige apparently brought some bank note paper with him, for in July of the same year the local authorities charged him with intending to use it to counterfeit "foreign" bank notes. Hauled to Montreal to face charges, Paige posted bail, then failed to appear when it came time to face trial two months later. Subsequent attempts to find

Paige also came up empty-handed. This was not too surprising: whatever the threat posed by the new laws, the distance from Montreal, the minimal police presence, and the abundance of hiding places in the region's caves, swamps, and forests all conspired to make the townships an ideal place to escape prosecution. But Paige was not one to take chances. In the fall of 1811 he returned to New York City and spent the winter there, taking refuge from his pursuers and, perhaps, from the harsh winters that often gripped the Canadian townships.[7]

What little remains of the police records from New York City during this period suggests that Paige remained there for a couple of years, spending his days associating with suspected dealers in counterfeit money. He may well have been cultivating future contacts for himself, or taking orders for his associates back in Canada, several of whom had continued production, perhaps heartened by the rising tensions between Britain and the United States that culminated in the War of 1812. Some measure of his success can be gauged from the fact that a host of banks cobbled together the unprecedented sum of $1,000 for information leading to his arrest and conviction. The reward had the desired effect: Paige was captured not long afterward in New York City and escorted to Baltimore to face trial. Paige nonetheless managed to wriggle free by cutting a deal with local authorities, volunteering information about his confederates in exchange for freedom. On May 13, 1812, he sat down and directed his interlocutors to search the house of an associate back in Canada, claiming that the man possessed no fewer than twenty-four counterfeit bank note plates.[8]

Paige's timing could not have been better. The United States declared war on Britain the following month, and invaded Canada later that year. Whatever cooperative efforts already under way between the two nations collapsed, and Paige disappeared from custody around this time, at little cost to himself or his confederates. In theory, the conflict should have ushered in a period of peace for the community of Cogniac Street, but matters turned out otherwise. War or no war, imperial officers prosecuted the "koniackers" anyway, possibly because bank notes from the United States continued to circulate as the common currency in the region or because bank officers from New England maintained informal ties with law enforcement officials north of the border despite the outbreak of war. Whoever initiated the prosecution, the case yielded a detailed portrait of the counterfeiting community at Dunham, along with a revealing character sketch of Thomas Adams Lewis (known by most simply as Adams), an engraver who became one of Seneca Paige's closest associates.

According to surviving accounts, sometime in late February of 1813, a local citizen working on behalf of banks in the United States filed counterfeiting charges against Thomas Adams Lewis, Joel Hill, and Daniel Blasdell. Joseph Powell, one of the few justices of the peace in St. Armand, drew up a warrant for their arrest and quickly deputized several citizens, as was the custom in a region with little in the way of law enforcement. One of those impressed into service, Abraham Welch, later testified that they all bundled into a sleigh and made the trek over the snow to Dunham, a few miles north. There they surrounded the house of Adams and Hill, taking both men prisoner. "There was found certain tools for the purpose of engraving," Welch reported, along with some scrap copper, but no plates for printing counterfeit notes. Welch accused Hill of hiding the plates, but Hill shrugged off the accusation, telling him "he had not any for the making of army bills and if he had any others they would not find them." Taking Hill and Adams prisoner, the group then went to Daniel Blasdell's house, also in Dunham, where they found a chest containing a "great Quantity of Bills on different Banks of the United States some of which were signed and some not." The party then returned to St.

Armand with their prisoners, in preparation for taking them to Montreal for trial.[9]

The first to confess was Daniel Blasdell, who on the sleigh ride back to St. Armand told Welch that he had been the one who had signed the bills. In a formal confession made a few days later, Blasdell testified that in the summer of 1812, Joel Hill had approached him and asked him to "sign off bank bills upon some of the banks of the United States." He agreed, and a short time later went with Hill deep into the woods, about a mile from Hill's house, where they struck off considerable quantities of notes on various banks using counterfeit plates. They then returned, and Blasdell forged signatures on the bills for a set fee: two dollars genuine money for every hundred bills he completed. Hill, he recalled, promised him that in the future "he should be entitled to a share of the bills that might thereafter be made." That Hill had hired Blasdell was not unusual. Every bank note, whether genuine or counterfeit, bore the signature of the corporation's president and cashier as a testament of its authenticity. Artisanal engravers like Hill and Adams tended to be illiterate or have relatively poor penmanship, so they hired people like Blasdell to copy the handwriting off a genuine note and fill in any dates or numbers.[10]

Hill and Adams may have had deficient handwriting, but they seem to have been adept at the art of engraving. Both were skilled craftsmen; the previous year Adams testified to being "by trade a wheelwright & engraver" who also repaired clocks, while Hill claimed to be a blacksmith. Moreover, a witness called in the case reported that he had overheard Hill and Adams discuss their plans for engraving plates some three years before, and that Adams had bragged he "was a good Engraver." According to other accounts, Hill and Adams pursued their craft in secrecy, stashing their copper plates and tools in different hiding places and printing their counterfeits in the woods at least a mile from their homes. This was the pattern of things to come: engravers would work at home or in some outbuilding on the plates, which could easily be concealed if a magistrate came to the door. When it came time to manufacture the notes, the counterfeiters retreated deep into the forest, and worked in the cave or hut that held their press and paper. The process may seem crude, but producing counterfeits at this time did not require a great deal of training or special equipment. Bank notes lacked the elaborate designs that would become standard in later years, and counterfeiters had only to imitate a few simple vignettes.[11]

While awaiting a hearing, Adams wrote a letter to the local magistrate, asking him to set bail as low as possible, and offering a defense of his actions that betrayed a complicated set of motives for his money making. No doubt aware that the Americans had just scored a major victory in the Battle of York, Adams professed shock that the government would "throw such Calamities on my family for no other Crime than my ingraving plates on the United States." This was a nation, he reminded the magistrate, which was an "Enemy of his Majesty." And as he had already told the men who arrested him, he had not counterfeited army bills, the paper scrip that the imperial government was using to pay its troops. He had only counterfeited the notes of banks in an enemy nation, which he had a poor opinion of anyway. In halting and half-literate sentences, he wrote: "I well remember how my father was treated by the government of Rode island because he only said that taking up arms against great britton was like children rising up against their parents . . . for saying that and refusing to take up arms," he lamented, "they harassed him . . . and took his property."[12]

But as much as Adams spilled out his hatred for the former colonists, he reserved his strongest words for the banks of the United States, which he accused of "villainy and treachery" because of a clash back in 1806. Adams, who back then was probably working for Stephen

Burroughs, had been lured over the border by bounty hunters in order to face counterfeiting charges. In his letter to McCord, Adams claimed that these same agents had paid a resident sixty dollars to assist with the operation. Adams's accusations were probably true: several magistrates wrote to the provincial government shortly after Adams's abduction to complain that Stephen Burroughs's arch-rival, Oliver Barker, had by "deception" enticed Adams across the contested border ("the lines") in order to put him in the clutches of the banks whose notes he had counterfeited. Barker himself admitted as much several years later, testifying that he had been sent by none other than the directors of the Farmers Exchange Bank of Gloucester, whose fiscal chicanery would eventually earn their bank a reputation comparable to a counterfeiter's. But in those earlier days, when the bank still enjoyed a reputation for solidity and sobriety, it funded the arrest of Adams, a mission Barker accomplished with his customary disregard of laws governing state and national sovereignty (though Adams managed to escape jail after being convicted).[13]

The kidnapping did little to raise Adams's estimation of the United States or its banks. "After getting clear from them by trial," he related, "I returned to Canada and have ever since been an Enemy to that government and to their Banking System." It is not apparent, however, what came first—his habit of counterfeiting or his hatred of banks in the United States—for much of the rest of the letter was a furious screed against the monetary confidence game that lay at the heart of the American economy. "Their banking system is a private Speculation," he wrote, complaining that the Americans issued "their bills when they pleas and Brake when they pleas & they Swindle their Subjects out of their just due." In a rhetorical flourish, he lumped together the bankers and the government of the United States, calling them a "corporation of Speculators" who had once before "cheated their Soldiers out of their Just due by paper money and they will do the Same now again . . . who ever lives to See this war over will find it so."[14]

Was Adams playing to his audience or speaking from experience? He did not bother to go into detail about his family's persecution during the Revolution, making it difficult to fit his inflamed rhetoric into a larger life story. Yet it is easy to imagine how a sequence of events—the abuse his father endured, the appropriation of the family property, and the economic collapse that accompanied the Revolution—all combined to give Adams a pathological hatred of both the United States and its peculiar dependency on paper money. Not that he was alone in his opinions about banks and bank notes: no less of an authority than John Adams (no relation to our counterfeiter) took an equally dim view, contending that "every dollar of a bank bill that is issued beyond the quantity of gold and silver in the vaults represents nothing and is therefore a cheat upon somebody." This was especially true at the time Adams the counterfeiter wrote his letter. In 1811, Congress failed to renew the charter for the First Bank of the United States, which had been keeping many of the state-chartered banks in check. With this stabilizing influence gone, the number of note-issuing banks tripled in the 1810s. Many of these new institutions proved less than reputable, refusing to redeem their notes for specie and eventually failing in the financial panic at the end of the decade. In what became a common comparison, one critic writing at this time likened bankers to counterfeiters, claiming that "the whole sum of bank notes are a deception; they are false and counterfeit—and that majority in legislatures who have authorized them, a band of mercenary swindlers." Banking bred hypocrisy, the writer argued. After all, how could the laws send a counterfeiter "to the state-prison for life," but permit a banker "to fabricate millions with impunity"?[15]

It was against this deteriorating financial situation that a pair of local justices of the peace interrogated Adams two years later regarding new charges of counterfeiting the notes of banks in the United States. "I have thirty plates, of different banks of the United States," he declared, but added, "I am not such a fool, as to deliver them to you, or any one else. These bills on the table," he said, gesturing toward the counterfeits spread out before him, "are *true bills*, made at my bank. And if the United States will give me Two Thousand dollars, I will promise to make no more plates or bills against their banks. They have made peace," he observed, "but I am yet at war with them." My bank, their banks: Adams fashioned a world where his imitations would bear witness to the perfidy of paper money and the bankers who issued it. In claiming the mantle of the banker, Adams was not trying to elevate himself to the level of a reputable financier. Rather he was arguing, as many critics did at this time, that a banker was nothing more than a counterfeiter in disguise, and paper money, whatever the source, was unworthy of confidence.[16]

The counterfeiters of the region, even if they lacked the political leanings of Adams, shared his disdain for authority. Adams and his confederates who lived on Cogniac Street paid little attention to governments of any kind, and recognized no laws save their own. It would have been a difficult way of life to maintain elsewhere, but the townships were a special place. Montreal, the closest center of imperial power, was several days away, and the few proxies of state authority— magistrates, justices of the peace—struggled to maintain order in a region that harbored counterfeiters, thieves, murderers, and other fugitives from justice.[17] As early as 1803, a local magistrate lamented that the "tranquility of the new settlements" had been dangerously disturbed "by the arrival of a class of profligate and unprincipled men" who moved to the townships "conceiving they might follow their evil course with less danger of detection." This became a common refrain, and every year the townships' more law-abiding citizens would petition the colonial authorities for help, as did one supplicant who complained in 1821 of the "influx of a transitory and immoral class, liberated from the Gaols of the neighboring States, smuggling or escaping from their creditors, or the pursuit of the Laws of their Country." Yet other residents—many of them former Loyalists—looked the other way when counterfeiters like Adams preyed on banks in the hated United States.[18]

As the townships' reputation for lawlessness spread, local officials made sporadic attempts to assert control, but met with little success. In a typical incident one evening in 1818, a group of rioters began carousing in the neighborhood of a bailiff named Ephraim Knight. As he later relayed the story, Knight stepped up to the crowd and "commanded the Peace in the King's Name," but was immediately surrounded and clubbed "unmercifully in such a way that he lay sick for several Days afterwards." A similar episode transpired only a few months later, when a mob assembled on the bridge in the same town, fired off guns, and proclaimed "the street was theirs and that they meant to keep it, and that no man should pass." Slow to learn, Knight again stepped into the fray and "commanded the peace in his Majesty's name," only to have his listeners begin "beating him with clubs" before "knock[ing] him off the bridge into a small brook," where the mob "continued beating him while lying in the water until a party came out of the house and took him from them."[19]

The violence of these episodes notwithstanding, there is something rather quaint about an officer of the law like Knight wading into a confrontation armed with nothing beyond his authority to speak for the interests of a distant monarch. But for many years, this was the only weapon that bailiffs and magistrates had at their disposal. Such performances of authority rarely worked, no matter how artfully delivered. Around the same time as the assault on Knight, for example, the Court of King's Bench in Montreal sent an officer named Parker out to the townships to arrest a suspected counterfeiter. By his own account, this officer of the law traveled several days through wild terrain, equipped with nothing to substantiate his mission beyond an arrest warrant. After locating his quarry, he marched up and "put his hand on the shoulder" of the suspect and said, "I arrest you in his Majesty's name." The counterfeiter, Parker reported with some incredulity, turned around and "demanded by what authority!" A bit flummoxed, Parker showed him the warrant, but his intended prisoner allegedly said "that was no authority and he would not go unless compelled by force." Parker tried to command the bystanders to assist him (also in the king's name), but they laughed at him, and one warned him that he would receive "a damned licking before he left the place" if he continued his efforts. Parker decided to cut his losses, and returned empty-handed.[20]

Parker's superiors ascribed his failure to "personal timidity," but William Felton, a local property owner, defended him in a letter to Montreal. "No man who knows these people and their manners can believe them incapable of conveying a threat in a manner which, while it is short of actual violence, is not the less serious and menacing to a person who knows how atrocious and unprincipled they are." This may have been an oblique reference to the beatings of Knight the previous year, or it may have been a more general acknowledgment of the willingness of counterfeiters and their allies to back up their threats. Counterfeiters often burned down the homes of individuals who initiated prosecutions, or fended off teams of officers with guns, clubs, axes, and pitchforks. Many counterfeiters also showed themselves willing to mount rescue attempts if officers seized their confederates. In one instance, several citizens served an arrest warrant on a counterfeiter named John Little, tied him up, and set out with their prisoner on a sleigh for Montreal. According to the lead officer, no sooner had the team gone more than a mile "when he saw 5 hostile men on horseback brandishing their arms," one of whom rode up in front of the sleigh, cocked a pistol at him, and said, "Stop or die."[21]

Few counterfeiters resorted to such extreme measures. There was a far simpler solution, if a little inconvenient: go to Montreal, post bail, and return home to Cogniac Street and begin counterfeiting anew. This is exactly what Thomas Adams Lewis did after his last encounter with the authorities in 1816, and in his case, as with others like it, the authorities failed to follow up, frustrated by the time and expense of capturing the suspect yet again. The few times that cases went to court, the counterfeiters always escaped prosecution, thanks to the efforts of their defense attorney, who was especially skilled at having indictments quashed outright.[22] Only in those rare instances when counterfeiters extended their efforts to the Bank of Canada or the Bank of Montreal (a capital offense) did authorities have some success. Counterfeiters who restricted their imitations to the notes of banks south of the border had little to fear.[23]

Seneca Paige eventually drifted back to Cogniac Street after extricating himself from the clutches of the Baltimore authorities—and after making a well-publicized escape from a Wilkesbarre jail three years later. By at least one account, he entered into an alliance with Thomas Adams Lewis and several other borderline bankers: Elijah Hurd, Ebenezer Gleason, and Joseph Brace. According to one witness a few years later, these individuals "conducted the counterfeiting business in company and . . . received an equal proportion of the profits arising thereupon." Despite this show of equality, each played a different role. Paige, for example, handled orders and sales while Adams and Hurd engraved the plates. A similar collective had also coalesced by this time around a former carpenter turned engraver named William Crane, who had ties to the Wing family, another of the criminal dynasties of Cogniac Street. Crane, one of the more talented engravers working at this time, became something of a mentor to succeeding generations of counterfeiters. Over the next twenty years, the two companies that coalesced around Paige and Crane engaged in a desperate battle for a larger share of the market in counterfeit notes, enacting the same struggle between monopoly and competition that preoccupied legitimate commerce around this time.[24]

Relations between the two gangs of counterfeiters soured sometime in 1818. The reasons remain obscure. Perhaps Crane's talents put Paige and Adams at a disadvantage when competing for the customers who visited Cogniac Street; maybe Crane wanted to monopolize the trade for himself. Whatever the reason, the resulting tangle of treachery and deception enmeshed officers of the law from both Canada and the United States in a contretemps that accomplished little, save to demonstrate that counterfeiters befriended their enemies and betrayed their friends (though not their families) with bewildering ease. Like some caricature of *homo economicus,* counterfeiters embraced self-interest to guide their motives and movements, no matter how damaging the consequences. Counterfeiters as a class acquired a reputation for shape-shifting, forging and abandoning partnerships with equanimity, constantly adapting to the needs of the moment, never remaining in one place or personality for long. They crossed, double-crossed, and otherwise deceived one another with little provocation. While their propensity for internecine struggle left them open to infiltration, translating those conflicts into convictions proved next to impossible. If anything, law enforcement officers who tried to navigate the criminal economy inevitably ended up becoming the unwitting instruments of one gang or another.

The events of 1818 offered a remarkable demonstration of the power of counterfeiters to exploit the law to their own advantage. A local magistrate, Leon Lalanne, launched a series of raids. In a succession of intrigues too convoluted to narrate in detail, local counterfeiters Turner Wing and William Crane, who sought to "engross the whole of the trade to themselves," directed the magistrate to prosecute their rivals on Cogniac Street. Lalanne eventually realized his mistake, and tried to arrest Crane, who by this time was busy at work churning out a new batch of counterfeits. "I sent a party thither," he reported, but Crane was prepared for him: "he barred every aperture in the walls of his house, & swore he would shoot every one that would attempt to enter." Stymied, Lalanne watched as Crane blew a trumpet and fired three guns, which was "the signal for the mustering of his associates who flew to his aid." Soon after, several men—members of the Wing family—materialized out of the forest, "threatened to kill whoever would approach," and then went up to the windows and carried away all the incriminating materials on horseback.[25]

In the end, Lalanne was left with nothing, as he himself admitted in this last report on the subject. The only positive aspect of his encounter was his assessment of the code of conduct among the counterfeiters in his district. "They are a divided family," he observed, "and if they are properly managed, they will ruin each other sooner than any foolish & inefficient provincial statute could if they were united." And with that, Lalanne concluded his narrative, complaining, "I have been harassed these six days & nights by thieves & coniackers. My clock strikes two A.M.," he observed, and "my eyes . . . permit me not to see." He signed off and sent the letter, receiving a reply a couple weeks later from Thomas McCord, the chief magistrate of Montreal. McCord agreed that the whole affair could have been better managed, and in an allusion to Crane's treachery, conceded that the government had "been made tools by one set to annoy another." He also added, in a pessimistic aside, that he thought nothing could be done until the legislature made counterfeiting a capital crime. As for Crane, he encouraged Lalanne to "drive him out of your neighborhood," but reminded him that "we have no funds to carry on these prosecutions and therefore will not employ people we cannot pay." The colonial government, McCord reminded Lalanne, had already registered "enormous expense" in getting people to and from Montreal to testify as witnesses and could not continue doing so.[26]

McCord's letter testified to the extraordinary obstacles in the way of prosecuting counterfeiters operating in the townships. While local officials like Lalanne could initiate proceedings against counterfeiters, they rarely turned the counterfeiters' ever-shifting alliances to any advantage. If captured, counterfeiters could always post bail and return to the townships or, in special cases, slip across the border to the United States. There, one writer would later recall, they could "snap their fingers in the faces of the pursuers, who, for lack of an extradition treaty, dared not pursue them beyond their own jurisdiction." This is what William Crane eventually did sometime after his last encounter with Lalanne, and settled just over the border in Vermont, where he commenced operations once again. As for the counterfeiters who remained behind, the 1820s proved to be a rather prosperous decade. Thanks to Seneca Paige, who assumed a leadership role, Cogniac Street became the leading supplier of counterfeit money throughout the United States. By the 1830s, an extensive network of wholesalers, distributors, and dealers looked to Paige and his confederates to supply them with money.[27]

Paige, who adopted the outward guise of a respectable merchant, running his country store and speculating in lumber and real estate, worked diligently to defend Cogniac Street's competitive edge. Toward that end, Paige recruited skilled engravers, enabling the gang to keep pace with the intricate notes that banks commissioned to frustrate counterfeiters. The influx of outside talent did not go unnoticed. In the spring of 1824, for instance, a self-proclaimed member of the "Anti-Coniack Club" wrote to a newspaper in Vermont, reporting on Paige's movements. This and several other letters sent by the same individual are difficult to interpret, in part because the writer, perhaps fearful of a libel suit, rarely referred to anyone by name. Seneca Paige, for example, was described as a "man . . . whose Sir name is P. and his Christian name is very similar to that which Druggists give to a certain root." This same correspondent was a bit more specific about the new hire, noting that Paige had "employed a first-rate sculptor from the United States, (a dishonest devil no doubt) to come into Canada and there in a den prepared for him 'by the devil and his angels,' to engrave for him a quantity of plates on the different banks of the United States. The name of the engraver is by some said to be Parks."[28]

This missive offered the first hard evidence that Paige had secured the talents of Lyman Parkes, one of the most accomplished criminal engravers of his day. Much of what is known about Parkes comes from the *National Police Gazette*, which some years later published a biography that turned him into a tragic hero, a brilliant mechanic seduced from the path of righteousness by a cabal of counterfeiters—a "victim of his own genius." According to this didactic account, Parkes was born in a small town in western Massachusetts. He demonstrated considerable artistic talent, and his parents apprenticed him to learn the craft of carving headstones. Parkes, however, "was ambitious, and a secret, burning pride, which is the natural offspring of an aspiring mind, made him look forward hopefully to a better destiny than that of a mere chiseller of formal characters, and monotonous outlines upon monumental marble." Bored, he took up the study of chemistry, specifically the study of acids, and "attracted . . . by numerous accounts of ingenious counterfeits and alterations of bank notes, by certain subtle fluids, he amused

himself by experimenting in the same science." These endeavors naturally led him to take up the craft of engraving, which he "conquered . . .
with the same masterly facility that had marked every other effort of
his skill."[29]

In keeping with this sentimental portrait, the downfall of Parkes
came at the hands of others less scrupulous than himself. According to
the *National Police Gazette*, Parkes worked as both an engraver and
carver of gravestones, married at age twenty-two, and achieved some
measure of prosperity. This same account claimed that Parkes's wife
died not long after, leaving him with a daughter. The tragedy left him
"desolate," and Parkes "neglected his business, secluded himself in the
house, and sunk into a profound misanthropy." Somehow—and here
his biographer was curiously vague—Parkes met Smith Davis, a distributor working for the Cogniac Street gang. Davis, cast as a diabolical
figure by the *National Police Gazette*, approached Parkes while posing as
the cashier of a Boston bank, and asked him to engrave a bank note
plate. Parkes did the job so well that Davis commissioned him to do
another plate, and then another. In an intricate maneuver, Davis next
arranged a trap for Parkes, hiring accomplices to pose as constables and
arrest the two men. After staging an "escape," he persuaded Parkes to
flee with him to Cogniac Street. "The Devil and Smith Davis had triumphed," the *National Police Gazette* reported, and Parkes thus "became a great counterfeiter, and consequently a great rogue." It was a
compelling story: the innocent man drawn into a life of crime by the
hardened criminal.[30]

Unfortunately, the story was as false as the notes that flowed from
Parkes's press. The engraver was not corrupted by the Cogniac Street
gang so much as hired by them on the basis of his burgeoning reputation as a counterfeiter. Sile Doty, a self-described "leader of a gang of
counterfeiters, horse thieves and burglars" in Vermont, recalled many

years later how he met "this very popular engraver" on the stagecoach to Boston in 1821. Doty devoted several pages to the famed forger, describing "this man . . . known only to men of our character" as a person "of refinement" and his family as "well-educated and stylish." Parkes's daughter, Julia, helped her father sign the notes, being "an accomplished penman [who] could imitate any handwriting or cut any flourishes with the pen she wanted." Parkes had been making counterfeits for some time, and Doty recalled the counterfeiter boasting that "I deal with men in high life; men of wealth and influence, living as far off as New Orleans, Charleston, Richmond, and Washington, many of them bankers and brokers." Though well connected, Parkes nonetheless understood the importance of seclusion. Parkes took Doty to a mountain high above a river and showed him his secret workshop, a cavern "with only a small aperture for a door, using a flat stone for that purpose." Doty recalled how Parkes, taking a "dark lantern, entered the place . . . Here was a rocky room . . . and here were his tools and implements."[31]

After arriving in Dunham, Parkes became an integral member of the gang, arguably the most accomplished engraver of the collective. His biographer spoke of him with unabashed admiration. "He had competitors in the engraving line, among the members of his own band, but his genius laughed them all to scorn, and by common acknowledgment, he at length bore away the palm." According to this same account, the newcomer enriched the fortunes of Paige, Adams, and the other members of the gang, because his superior imitations commanded high prices. Parkes spent much of the 1820s working with the Cogniac Street gang, though he spent two years in Charleston State Prison after an untimely conviction for forgery in Boston in April 1825. Two years later he returned to his workshop in Massachusetts, producing counterfeit plates from afar for his masters in Canada. The financial details of these arrangements have been lost, but the most likely scenario—and the one that eventually became the norm in the succeeding decades—was that the principals like Paige were acting as full-fledged capitalists, advancing funds to someone like Parkes, from whom they would take possession of the counterfeit plate, and thus extract the lion's share of the profit.[32]

Thanks in part to hired talent like Parkes, Cogniac Street prospered in the 1820s. After their botched attempts to crack down on the counterfeiters, the authorities in Montreal generally left the region alone, and local efforts to prosecute counterfeiting and related crimes generally proved ineffectual. In fact, the only real hindrance to the continued production of counterfeit notes in the region seem to have been the simmering tensions between the Cogniac Street collective and William Crane, who had founded his own gang on the other side of the border after his clash with Lalanne. The conflict erupted into violence in the summer of 1824, and the same correspondent who had reported Parkes's arrival trumpeted the news: "War! War! The Counterfeiting Gang of Berkshire . . . vs. Their Brethren in Iniquity, of Lower Canada." He reported that at "a general assembly of the Berkshire counterfeiting gang," the president, one "William Engraver" (the writer's nickname for William Crane) alluded to an existing "alliance" between his own gang and his colleagues in Canada. This agreement apparently stipulated that both gangs would share the market in counterfeit notes, but Crane accused Paige and his confederates of adopting "monopolizing principles," thus "wrenching from us . . . our share of the opportunities."[33]

With Crane playing the part of the upstart entrepreneur, and Paige the monopolist, the two gangs played out a drama that echoed the one brewing in the courts of the United States, where a growing number of judges ruled against exclusive franchises in favor of open competition. Crane, who could not sue, necessarily turned to other tools at his disposal. According to one account, Crane led his forces through the forests to Dunham in the middle of the night "armed with swords, pistols, and bludgeons." They attacked at dawn, and carried off "considerable booty," including a number of plates and $4,000 in notes; they also took several people prisoner, including Seneca Paige's father, who was working the presses when Crane and his associates arrived. As it turned out, Crane's victory proved fleeting, for shortly afterward, this same correspondent wrote another letter relating that Paige "has pitched battle with the Vermont rascals; has been successful in his turn, & it has resulted in their complete overthrow," along with the return of his plates, tools, and presumably, his father. An uneasy peace settled on Cogniac Street after this episode, and though Paige and his associates dominated the business, they tolerated continued competition from Crane, who engraved plates in Vermont for the Wing family, another counterfeiting clan that lived on Cogniac Street. The rest of the decade proved relatively uneventful, and dealers arrested in New York City frequently mentioned traveling to Cogniac Street to pick up new supplies of counterfeit notes on sale north of the border.[34]

As the states chartered more and more banks, the counterfeiting business boomed. Every new note issued by a bank represented an additional opportunity for the criminal capitalists who set up shop on the frontier. Each genuine note issued by a state-sanctioned bank surfaced in a more shadowy, less substantial form in the workshops run by these illicit entrepreneurs. Though people like Seneca Paige may not have been bankers in the strictest sense of the term, they came close to approximating their more reputable brethren in spirit, if not in practice. As one writer observed of the counterfeiters on Cogniac Street, "There is scarcely a dealer in all our country, who cannot produce abundant specimens of the ingenuity of this kind of *banking gentry.*" But the gentry were only the beginning. A host of lesser men on the make played a part in getting the notes out of the wilderness and into circulation.[35]

Imports, Exports, and Agents

In 1819, De Witt Clinton, the governor of New York, submitted his annual message to the legislature. He addressed various issues of concern to the state, lingering on one in particular: the problem of counterfeiting in Lower Canada, "principally carried on in a remote part of that country." For the edification of his listeners, Clinton gave a top-to-bottom view of the counterfeit economy, beginning with the "engravers of plates, makers of paper, and signers of notes," most of whom he observed "generally reside out of our jurisdiction." He then identified "messengers, who are constantly passing from various parts of the country to the seat of counterfeiting, to obtain spurious money and convey it to places of deposit," as the succeeding link in the chain. Next were "those who keep places of deposit, generally in the vicinity of large towns." These individuals, he explained, sell the notes to the fourth and final class of counterfeiters: the "utterers," or "passers," who put the money into circulation.[36]

This was a fairly accurate portrait of the counterfeit economy's many layers and players. While Cogniac Street was the fountainhead of the industry, the engravers who worked there relied heavily on an extensive network of mobile couriers and wholesalers as well as residential retailers who channeled counterfeits into the hands of the people who would undertake the more risky task of passing the notes on to unsuspecting shopkeepers, merchants, and grocers. In the early years of counterfeiting in the townships, this network was neither sophisticated nor extensive. Stephen Burroughs forged few commercial ties to the cities to the south; most of the notes he produced were sold directly to passers in

Vermont or to the many itinerant sellers of notes who hawked their wares throughout the New England countryside.

The experiences of William Stuart, a burglar and con man from Connecticut, epitomize the spirit of this early period. Writing many years later, Stuart recalled how as a teenager in 1807 he and a friend had been carousing in a tavern in Norwalk, Connecticut, when a man came in who had what "seemed to be a defect in one of his eyes; for he wore a green shade lying close over one eye ball." After watching Stuart attentively, the mysterious man beckoned the teens to follow him outside. The trio sat down in a field, where the man took off his eye patch. "The patch of silk over his eye was used to blind others—not himself," Stuart recalled. The man pulled out a roll of bank notes, "told us they were counterfeit, and offered to sell us some of them. Neither of us understood what counterfeit money was," he recalled with some embarrassment. The dealer explained, and as Stuart recalled, "we now saw how suddenly we could become rich . . . It was Burroughs' money, and to our eyes at least, as good as genuine." The dealer offered to sell them for "ten dollars a hundred, any quantity that we wished." Not having any cash, Stuart agreed to trade his horse, saddle, and bridle for counterfeit notes having a face value of three hundred dollars. In a symbolic moment, Stuart exchanged the barter economy for the market economy.[37]

Many of these early counterfeit salesmen or distributors had no fixed residence. They constituted a class of wayward capitalists who spent their days wandering the rivers, canals, turnpikes, and other commercial arteries of the new nation with "saddle bags richly laden," as one newspaper put it. Another described a dealer arrested with thousands of dollars' worth of counterfeit bills as "one of those counterfeiting gentry, whose traveling circuit extends from Canada to the Southern States." One dealer arrested around this time in New York City testified that he had "no particular place to live at," having spent the preceding months on the road between New England and New York; another apprehended a few years later related how he had spent the summer on the road, traveling to and from Ohio, Virginia, Washington, Baltimore, Philadelphia, Pittsburgh, Canada, and New York City. Some of these dealers combined their business with peddling, an obvious combination, given that itinerant peddlers and counterfeit salesmen both symbolized the democratization of capitalism and its commodities. Peddlers sold cheap goods; counterfeiters sold cheap money.[38]

The dealers who visited Cogniac Street and the other manufactories in Canada purchased notes under a variety of arrangements. In some cases, the purchaser would select from stock that the counterfeiters already had on hand, much of which Seneca Paige sold from behind the counter of a country store he had opened in Dunham. Paige apparently provided special containers for carrying the notes, such as the mahogany dressing case with hidden compartments found in the possession of a distributor arrested in New Haven.[39] Other customers purchased directly from one of the engravers, as did Daniel Bailey, a peddler who visited in 1814. Upon arriving in Dunham, he was "introduced to a man by the name of Adams" who supplied him with $2,000 worth of counterfeit notes on banks in New York. Bailey testified that he had agreed to "vend" these notes for Adams and "return to Canada and pay him a certain portion of the proceeds." Such arrangements were not at all unusual: even at the typical rate of ten genuine dollars for one hundred bogus, many visitors lacked the funds to buy goods outright, and the counterfeiters advanced credit in much the same way that country merchants did. They also accepted payments in jewelry, watches, stolen goods, and other commodities that circulated like money through the nation's shadow economy.[40]

Stolen horses became the most common currency among the counterfeiting fraternity. Like specie, but far more portable, horses simultaneously served as a source of capital, a means of exchange, and a means of transportation. Indeed, gangs of horse thieves doubled as distributors of counterfeit notes, using the horses to deliver shipments of worthless paper. Cogniac Street thus became not only the center of counterfeiting, but also a depot for people trafficking in stolen steeds, with visitors bringing purloined horses from the United States to Canada, or vice versa. In other cases the theft was a bit more subtle: visitors to Cogniac Street might buy horses with counterfeit money in one of the border states, then take refuge in Canada. Whatever the means of acquiring the horses, the same logic of border crossing applied, with distributors of counterfeit notes in the United States acquiring horses and distributing counterfeits as they crossed state lines, often extracting a double profit at the conclusion of their journey.[41]

While visitors to Cogniac Street often purchased whatever notes the gangs had in stock, some customers (typically a dealer) would bring the note they wished to have counterfeited and then wait while the engravers produced the plate and printed the notes. William Stuart, for example, wrote that after working with "Burroughs' bills," he eventually concluded that they "were not a good imitation" on account of the fact that "people began to examine their bank notes." Wanting something of a higher quality, he saddled his horse and "went to Canada, to a place called the Slab City, to the firm of Crane & Staples, superior copperplate engravers." Slab City was a code word for the village of Frelighsburgh in St. Armand, and the "firm" he visited was probably the counterfeiting partnership of William Crane. "They engraved notes of several different Banks *that were presented to them*," Stuart recalled. "In little more than a week they produced [for] me notes on Barker's Exchange Bank, some on New Jersey banks, and some genuine ones [one-dollar notes] on the Commercial Bank of Philadelphia." These banks, he explained, "had the most extensive circulation," making them easier to pass. Stuart, who was very pleased with Crane's work, paid him at the rate of ten dollars "real" money for every one hundred dollars counterfeit. "They received pay in watches, gold rings and old jewelry," recalled Stuart, "and the balance in cash."[42]

This practice of commissioning counterfeits became routine in the succeeding years. According to an undercover agent dispatched by the imperial authorities, a wholesaler named James Connor had informed him "that he had brought from New York a genuine five Dollar Bill of the Franklin Bank in the City of New York for the purpose of getting a Plate of it engraved." In an interesting illustration of the power of economic competition within the counterfeiting enclave, this same witness testified that Connor "had shewn [the genuine bill] to Adams who told him it could not be done." Disappointed, Connor "then shewed it to William Crane who informed him it might be done." As an inducement, he offered Crane $150 for the job, suggesting that Connor was a dealer of some means. After all, Connor had bragged to this same witness that he "had cleared fifteen hundred dollars over and above expenses" selling counterfeit money in New York City between July and September, but had decided to wait another month before returning because of a "Stagnation of Business," which the examiner understood to mean "the counterfeit Business." The market, in other words, was saturated, and Connor would wait until business picked up. Counterfeits, like every other commodity, obeyed the same laws of supply and demand.[43]

Anyone familiar with the market in bogus money knew that counterfeits were governed by the capitalist code. When the New York City police arrested Daniel Fowler, a well-known wholesaler, a local paper claimed that Fowler conducted his business "in as deliberate and systematic a style as any man of business ever conducted a cloth or other manufactory." Every year, the paper related, Fowler "went two or three times . . . to Dunham, in Canada, at which place is the counterfeit paper manufactory." There he placed orders and brought back large quantities of counterfeits in "hard little packages, about three inches thick." Like any good businessman, he then "exhibited his *samples*" to the dealers, "the excellence or defects of which were criticized in a grave, sober, business-like manner." Though tongue-in-cheek, the account hinted at a deeper truth: counterfeiting was not something practiced by lone individuals; rather, it involved an elaborate network of buyers and sellers whose activities spanned vast distances. Its cast of characters bore an eerie resemblance to the buyers and sellers of wheat, coal, cloth, or any other commodity traded at this time. And like those who trafficked in these goods, buyers of counterfeits looked for evidence that their bogus money would capture the confidence of the market. Wholesalers purchased counterfeit notes "at prices," one paper averred, "proportional to the neatness of the execution and the exactness of the imitation of the genuine notes." Those wholesale prices could range from as low as five or ten cents of "real money" per counterfeit dollar to as high as forty cents for a note that could command more confidence. The "exchange rate" depended as well on the size of the order, which could be as little as a few hundred dollars or as many as a million. If buying in bulk lowered prices, so did paying for counterfeits in genuine currency. As the *National Police Gazette* later observed, one hundred dollars in counterfeit money went for "ten dollars worth of valuable property, or for five dollars of bankable paper."[44]

In light of the complexity of the counterfeit economy, it should come as no surprise that wealthier distributors began to hire people to do the dirty work for them: so-called boodle carriers whose job it was to deliver the package of counterfeit notes (the boodle) to its destination. Louis Sampier, a laborer living near Dunham, recalled how John

Connor (a nephew of James) came to his house in December 1821 and "bargained with him to carry to the City of New York a bladder full of papers . . . and deliver it to his (Connor's) father old John Connor . . . and that Old John would then give him . . . forty Dollars in Silver money." Connor may have hired Sampier because he did not have the time to go to New York himself. Alternatively, he might have feared being caught with notes in his possession, much the way his son Timothy had been captured in Vermont the previous year. Law enforcement officials knew by sight the better-known distributors, and did not hesitate to seize and search them in the hopes of finding counterfeits in their possession. Employing a boodle carrier helped minimize the chance that a shipment would be seized. After delivering the goods, many of these hired hands then carried much-needed supplies to Cogniac Street on the return trip back to Canada, particularly bank note paper. For example, when New York City's high constable Jacob Hays arrested one such courier, he "found on him a Memorandum book containing his expenses to St. Albans which is called by them the Slabb City, sometimes Coniac St. so called by the Coniackers and also found in the same book samples of paper for the purpose of bank notes."[45]

If Cogniac Street was the cradle of the counterfeit economy, the wholesalers who marketed its wares constituted a vast, far-reaching web startling in its extent and complexity. In 1833, one of the gang gave a deposition listing approximately two hundred commercial contacts in places as far away as Boston, Indianapolis, and Wheeling, Virginia, as well as many more who lived within only a few weeks' travel. The proximity of many of these individuals to canal systems suggests that these waterways, aside from revolutionizing legitimate commerce, also transformed the distribution of counterfeit notes during the 1820s. Two such waterways proved especially important to the counterfeit trade. The

Champlain Canal, which connected Albany with Lake Champlain, gave distributors from New York City easy access to Cogniac Street. Dealers could now take a steamboat up the Hudson River, switch to a canal boat, and then sail to the northern end of Lake Champlain, a day's walk from Dunham. Likewise, the opening of the Erie Canal and its tributaries enabled Paige and his successors to reach all of New York, much of western Pennsylvania, and parts of Ohio and Indiana. Indeed, many of the individuals identified in the confession had direct ties to the canal system's economy: "Cisse Kerry, the owner and navigator of a packet boat on the Erie Canal . . . Captain Otis Allen, owner and navigator of a packet-boat on the western canal . . . [and] Z. W. Cowden, formerly a tavern keeper at Montezuma on said canal." This particular counterfeiter alluded to a number of others, noting simply that "I have known a great number of other persons engaged in this kind of traffic, perhaps not less in all than three hundred in the state of New York."[46]

While many counterfeit notes went to distributors living in rural areas, urban centers swiftly became the most important market for counterfeits from Cogniac Street. A large laboring population supplemented its meager earnings with bogus bills, and the growing size of cities made it easier to "pass" or "shove" counterfeits without detection. These men and women obtained their bogus money via an elaborate community of wholesalers and retailers related to one another by blood and marriage. A handful of clans typically dominated the business in each major city, and the selling and passing of counterfeit notes consequently remained an intimate business, dependent on complicated networks of relatives and friends who could be trusted to abide by their agreements. It was a world of face-to-face relationships, one that persisted and thrived within the larger urban milieu. There was, of course, a curious irony in this: an enterprise that exploited the growing anonymity of modern commercial society depended on old-fashioned communal ties, much the way many legitimate bankers built their enterprises on the foundation of familial contacts forged in close-knit communities.[47]

New York City swiftly became the most important export market for counterfeits, and what little evidence remains from the early nineteenth century suggests that the Connor family became the first to market Cogniac Street's wares. The patriarch of the clan, John Connor, moved his family from Albany to New York City around 1811. He had ties to Seneca Paige and other counterfeiters in Canada, and he soon gained a reputation, Jacob Hays reported, for being a "notorious passer or vendor of counterfeit money." Despite occasional harassment from the police, Connor grew wealthy working as a distributor for Cogniac Street. One witness testified that she did not believe "Conner does any thing" for a living, but nonetheless "appears to live very well," adding that the family had "every thing [in] plenty." This was a bit unfair. Connor, his son, John Junior, and his son's wife, Hannah, did have a legitimate line of work: they ran a tavern in the neighborhood of Mulberry Street. Each tended bar, serving their working-class patrons with drinks. But they also sold counterfeit notes, with Hannah Connor becoming especially infamous for handling bogus money. One retailer who purchased from them later testified that the family would "always keep a stock of counterfeit money on hand for sale."[48]

John Connor's brother, James, also worked in the business, shuttling back and forth between New York City and Cogniac Street at regular intervals. So, too, did James's son Timothy. Both brought genuine notes to Cogniac Street in order to have plates engraved, carried the counterfeits back to their parents for sale in the tavern, or sent the bogus bills in the hands of a boodle carrier. Sometimes James Connor recruited trusted friends of the family into the business. One suspect testified, for example, that after having known James Connor for some time, the latter "finally ... mentioned that he was concerned in dealing counterfeit money & that there was a great speculation to be made in it." This same suspect, "being poor," agreed to assist and accompanied Connor up to Cogniac Street, where they waited on Thomas Adams Lewis and William Crane to engrave, print, and prepare an order to be taken back to New York City.[49]

In time, many others besides the Connor family profited from the wholesale or retail market in counterfeit notes. Like the Connors, almost all of these entrepreneurs lived in the working-class neighborhoods east of Broadway and below Houston Street, and many sold their wares out of taverns and grog shops in or near the Bowery. Some of these individuals and their families had ties to John Connor and his family. A dealer named Guy Fuller, for example, married one of the daughters of James Connor, and set up a tavern with her brother. Similarly, a retailer named George Mariner apparently depended on John Connor for his supply of counterfeits, which he sold out of a grocery on Rutgers Street.[50] But others operating around the same time—Rufus Severance, Daniel Fowler, William Goldsby, and Selah Coles, to name a few—appear to have had limited dealings with the Connor family, and corresponded with Cogniac Street on their own terms. This increasingly became the case in 1820, when John Connor died and Jacob Hays secured enough evidence to convict other members of the family.[51]

In the 1820s, there arrived on the scene other dealers, some of whom had useful ties to other elements in the criminal underworld. Smith Davis, for example, who eventually acquired a reputation as the "King of the Koniackers," did time in prison for robbing a mail coach. After obtaining a pardon from President James Madison (a prison doctor helpfully testified that the future counterfeiter had "a complicated nervous debility that on some occasions seems to endanger his life"), Davis set up a tavern at the corner of Grand and Clinton Streets around 1825, just a few blocks from the wharves of the East River.[52] This "small, two story building," recalled the *National Police Gazette* a number of years later, "was devoted to the purposes of a porter-house," but doubled as "the resort of all the pickpockets and burglars about town." This same porter house became a key entrepôt for the wholesaling and retailing of counterfeit notes, which Davis brought back from Canada using a sophisticated relay of horses. Davis, whom the *National Police Gazette* described as a "dapper little man about five feet high, with a round, small head, and face, the prevailing expression of which was cunning," did not use force to secure his grip on the market; instead, duplicity and betrayal became his trademarks.[53]

Davis's occasional ally and frequent rival was Abraham Shepherd, the patriarch of an infamous family of counterfeiters. Shepherd, who worked as a wholesaler and dealer, had a talent for printing and engraving as well. Much of what is known about the clan comes from a chaplain at Sing Sing, who took down their history in 1845 after counting five members of the family in his care. This imperfect source, when combined with other scraps of evidence, provides some sense of the family's origins. It seems that Abraham Shepherd, a shoemaker from New Jersey, married Mary Earle, the daughter of a "respectable woman of some property" who lived in Belleville, a town on the Passaic River. They had four boys: Charles, William, Cornelius, and James. According to the chaplain, Abraham Shepherd initially had "the reputation of an honest though not very industrious man," but drifted into "idleness" and other vices far worse. He eventually moved to New York City, where he fraternized with "loose women and drunken men" and sold counterfeit money.[54]

There was some truth in this account. Shepherd had worked as a shoemaker, moving to New York City in 1822 or 1823. He plied his trade on Thompson Street, a respectable enough address, but the following year he moved to Orange Street, in the heart of the swampy region known as Five Points, a slum already infamous for its unpleasant sights and smells. He remained in and around Five Points for a number of years, just as it was becoming the focal point of criminal activity in the growing metropolis. Perhaps Shepherd drifted into crime on account of "idleness," but a more believable explanation lies with his original profession. Shoemaking underwent a devastating transformation in the 1820s, as competition from cheap factory-made shoes undercut and eventually destroyed the existing system of masters and apprentices, replacing it with an economy that relied on a growing division of labor among outworkers, many of them low-paid women and girls. Shepherd's own drift into crime coincides with the intensification of that process, for it was at some point in the mid-1820s that he quit making shoes and began dealing in bogus notes from Cogniac Street, eventually earning what one suspect called "the name of being a dealer in counterfeit money."[55]

Like John Connor, Shepherd put his children to work in the trade. James Shepherd, who related his life's story on his deathbed in Sing Sing, told the prison chaplain there that he first worked as a messenger for his father and his father's mistress. He recalled, for example, being "sent to the Washington Parade Ground with what appeared to be a basket of apples" but which actually concealed packets of counterfeit money. This may have been one of his father's favorite tactics: a witness in a case from 1832 testified that he had gone to the parade grounds and that "Shepherd's boy brought the money in the Bottom of a Basket which had Apples on top of it." As he got older, James Shepherd directed the distribution of larger shipments, and by his own estimation superintended the delivery of hundreds of thousands of dollars in counterfeit notes to Philadelphia, Baltimore, Pittsburgh, and other cities. "As I was only about seventeen years of age at this time," Shepherd recalled, "my father took all the profits of my hazardous labour; still, the infatuation was so great that I was led on without difficulty." James Shepherd eventually visited Cogniac Street and in his twenties assumed ever-greater responsibilities.[56]

Many of the families involved in the selling and shoving of notes intermarried, creating new criminal alliances. James Shepherd, for example, married Honora O'Brien, daughter of the patriarch of another clan of counterfeiters. Honora's father worked at selling and passing notes, as did her sister, Kate O'Brien, who became the wife of Oakley Beamer, who in turn had an alliance with Smith Davis. After her father's death, Honora's mother, Eliza O'Brien, cohabited with Rufus Severance, a counterfeiter who had gotten his start working with John Connor and Seneca Paige. And her brothers Michael and Peter O'Brien became the lieutenants of Jack Cantar, who in turn became "the heir," as the *National Police Gazette* later reported, "of the mantle which fell from the shoulders of Smith Davis, the veritable 'king of the koneyackers,' on his incarceration in the state prison, in 1838." This abbreviated family history, however convoluted, was by no means unusual. Almost every counterfeiter working in New York City had an equally complex web of kin ties to other players in the business of funneling counterfeits from Cogniac Street. This interconnectedness had its advantages: family members rarely "squealed" on one another. But like any extended family, conflicts inevitably erupted, sometimes leading to more serious breaches. In the late 1820s, for example, the different sellers and passers affiliated with Smith Davis clashed with several members of the Shepherd family, though no convictions resulted.[57]

Men tended to dominate these disputes, much as they controlled most of the buying and selling of counterfeit money. Women, by contrast, had a subordinate status within the counterfeiting community, even as they provided symbolic links of marriage between different families of forgers. There were, to be sure, a few exceptions: Hannah Connor, for example, sold counterfeits alongside her husband while tending bar at their tavern. But most women who sold counterfeit notes on the retail level did so only in the temporary absence of their husbands. Women tended to help in more subtle ways: secreting "boodles" among their own possessions, where officers would be less likely to look, or raising money to bail their husbands out of jail.[58] But these contributions counted for little when their husbands died or received a lengthy prison sentence. When these women were unable to assume control of their husband's business, many turned to other counterfeiters for support, and it was not uncommon for them to live with or marry another dealer, even if the previous husband was still alive. One account published in the papers related how the wife of a dealer in counterfeits already had "two husbands in the state prison: the first for dealing largely in counterfeit money, the other for grand larceny—and she is still young enough to adventure half a dozen times more yet, in the hymeneal lottery, if she dare."[59]

This kind of serial dependency was not, perhaps, the kind of life that many women would have chosen for themselves. But it was not uncommon: Abraham Shepherd's wife did much the same thing, living with a succession of small-time dealers in counterfeit money after her husband went to prison. It was a grim life, as she herself testified some years later. "Abraham Shepherd is my husband," she admitted, "but I have not seen him the last 7 or 8 years." As for her children, she noted that "they are scattered about, I don't know where they are except one living in the Jerseys." And when asked what she had been doing for work, she simply said, "Anything I can get to do." She claimed to work as a tailoress on occasion, but in Mary Shepherd's case, as with so many women in a similar position, "anything" included passing notes, for it was at this stage of the counterfeiting enterprise that she and others like her had an important role, however dangerous. By putting the notes in circulation, they oversaw the culminating act of criminal alchemy, one in which the imitations made on Cogniac Street would finally slip unnoticed into the wider world of commercial exchange, commanding confidence as if they were the real thing.[60]

In this final transaction and transmutation, a long and torturous journey came to an end. Hundreds if not thousands of miles away, on a dirt road in the back woods of the northern frontier, a community of criminal capitalists had founded a business that became the nerve center of a counterfeit economy that thrived alongside the growing number of banks and bankers below the border. The business they built depended on countless participants—buyers, distributors, jobbers, wholesalers, and retailers—who moved the goods from manufactory to market, eking out narrow margins of profit at every turn. In passing from hand to hand, these imitations affirmed a common faith in a shadow economy founded on the same principles embraced by capitalists who issued genuine bank notes: the sanctity of self-interest, the power of credit, the quest for profit, and the centrality of competition. Indeed, what the counterfeiters practiced was capitalism, stripped of its pretenses and dubious claims to morality, and reduced to its fundamental impulses and motives. How appropriate, then, that the illegitimate notes they manufactured swelled the streams of credit that underwrote more accepted and sanctioned avenues for accumulating wealth.

If counterfeiting and capitalism shared a fundamental set of values, there was another, related point of convergence. Both counterfeiters and bankers issued paper money, and the value of a counterfeit note, just like the value of a genuine note, depended on its power to instill faith and confidence. And of all the counterfeits in circulation, imitations of the notes of the Bank of the United States commanded the most confidence and the highest prices—and carried with them the prospect of the steepest penalties. The Bank of the United States supplied the nation with the closest thing it had to a uniform currency, and its fiscal probity and stability made it a tempting target for counterfeiters. During the 1820s, the denizens of Cogniac Street breached the bank's defenses on multiple occasions, precipitating diplomatic imbroglios and fiscal crises. In time, bankers of a more legitimate cast attacked the bank as well, ushering in the titanic political struggle known as the Bank War. This accidental alliance led to a strange yet revealing intermingling of the cultures of counterfeiting, capitalism, and democratic politics. Counterfeiters, more than one commentator concluded, enjoyed the confidence of allies at the highest levels of government.

THREE

The
Bank Wars

F ew visitors to Philadelphia in the late 1820s left the city without a glimpse of the Second Bank of the United States. Spare, massive, and fashioned of gleaming white marble, this temple of commerce launched a rage for classical architecture when completed in 1824. Like the Parthenon that inspired it, the bank towered over its surroundings, helping to cement the city's burgeoning reputation as the "Athens of America." The building drew encomiums from otherwise harsh judges; as one English architectural critic wrote a decade after its completion, "[The bank] excels in elegance and equals in utility, the edifice, not only of the Bank of England, but of any banking house in the world." Indeed, anyone who stood before this incarnation of antiquity, watching the steady stream of supplicants coming and going beneath its enormous eight-columned façade, invariably resorted to hyperbole.[1]

While the Second Bank of the United States cast a long shadow on Philadelphia's Chestnut Street, it loomed far larger over the nation's economic landscape. Like its predecessor, the First Bank of the United

FIGURE 7. After Andrew Jackson refused to recharter the Second Bank of the United States, Nicholas Biddle secured a charter from the State of Pennsylvania. In this final stage of its existence, the bank issued high-denomination notes bearing a portrait of Biddle's "marble palace." *Courtesy, National Numismatic Collection, Smithsonian Institution.*

States (also located in Philadelphia), it served as the country's de facto central bank. It owed its existence to a federal charter, and the national government deposited funds in its vaults for safekeeping, relying on the Second Bank's many branches to serve as fiscal agents for the collection of taxes. In the 1820s, under the leadership of the aristocratic Nicholas Biddle, it strived to stabilize an economic system prone to boom-and-bust cycles by presenting state bank notes for redemption, making it difficult for these banks to issue paper far in excess of their specie reserves. As a central clearinghouse, the Second Bank also regulated domestic and foreign exchange, and served as what a contemporary called the "balance wheel" of the banking system, using its substantial assets to intervene in the nation's economy.

For most citizens, these activities remained cloaked in mystery. Far more visible and obvious were the Second Bank's ubiquitous notes, the closest the nation had to a uniform paper currency. Unlike ordinary bank notes, these circulated at par throughout the country, though it was precisely this stability and solidity that led counterfeiters to prey on the bank. As any banker (or counterfeiter) knew, the greater the confidence in the note imitated, the more valuable the counterfeit; indeed, counterfeiters gave new meaning to the old adage that imitation is the sincerest form of flattery. Established banks with reputations for conservative management—Boston's Suffolk Bank, for example—attracted the ingenuity of counterfeiters. And of all such reputable institutions, the Second Bank of the United States stood above the rest. In attacking it, counterfeiters confronted an institution that could command resources no other financial organization could muster. Yet even these proved incapable of stemming the tide of fraudulent paper. In the late 1820s, counterfeiters manufactured imitations that eroded faith in the bank and prompted Biddle and his allies to launch an offensive against fraudulent financiers.

Despite such efforts, the Second Bank of the United States saw its standing plummet in the early 1830s, inaugurating a slow period of decline that culminated with its demise a few years later. Counterfeiters were not to blame, though what one editorialist would later call "licensed counterfeiters" shared responsibility for the bank's downfall. In the early 1830s, a rising generation of upstart bankers who resented the Second Bank's regulatory meddling became enmeshed in a titanic political struggle between Andrew Jackson and Nicholas Biddle. Forging an unlikely alliance with "hard money men," these aggressive entrepreneurs lent their support to Jackson's campaign against the Second Bank of the United States. They shared in the spoils of victory, either as proprietors of the so-called pet banks that eventually took control of the government's money, or as entrepreneurs who benefited from the consequent expansion of credit.

In the vituperative language that characterized this clash, individual counterfeiters—and the metaphor of counterfeiting—were employed in both real and rhetorical ways. All parties to the conflict accused one another of counterfeiting, either literally or figuratively. This was no accident. In the ongoing battle to define the proper boundaries between capitalist enterprise and criminal mischief, the figure of the forger proved useful in understanding these distinctions. By likening their opponents to counterfeiters, the bank's defenders claimed the moral high ground. Jackson and his allies took umbrage at these comparisons, but nonetheless managed to make counterfeits—and counterfeiters—central to their own political sloganeering. And more than once in the midst of this battle, flesh-and-blood counterfeiters themselves made an appearance, most often as undeserving recipients of presidential pardons. Indeed, the very prosecution of counterfeiters— or the willingness to forgive them—came to be seen as an overt political act, a symptom of the growing divide between those who advanced an expansive vision of federal economic power and those who fought to keep it in the hands of the state governments and state-chartered banks.

The "Bank War" resulted in the destruction of Biddle's beloved institution, but contrary to Jackson's hopes, did nothing to slow the proliferation of bank notes, either bogus or real. Nevertheless, the quest to purify the currency continued under other auspices: shortly after Jackson issued his famous veto, the conservative banking establishment of Boston banded together in an association to prosecute counterfeiters, much as they had already worked together to rein in banks that issued notes far in excess of their specie reserves. In the end, these efforts at private law enforcement fell afoul of the corruption and provincialism that plagued policing at this time. But it was the financial chaos unleashed by Jackson and his followers that would ultimately destroy their campaign to combat counterfeiting, depriving them of funds, if not a lack of purpose. Indeed, amid the panic and depression that consumed the country toward the end of the decade, it may have appeared more than a little foolish if not futile to crack down on counterfeits when so many legitimate banks had ceased to honor their promises to pay.

Banks of the United States

Alexander Hamilton created the central banking system that Jackson destroyed. His proposal for a "National Bank," first submitted to Congress in 1790, was part of larger program to create a dynamic, commercial nation of financiers and manufacturers. Hamilton modeled his institution on the Bank of England, but sought to make it more powerful. While it would conduct commercial business, it would also serve as a depository for federal taxes and administer the public finances. The bank's capital would come from two sources: a fifth from the government itself, and the balance from private investors. Hamilton proposed that a mere fraction of this capital be paid in specie, with the balance in securities of the federal government, thus insuring a market for the government's debt. This move required a leap of faith, but Hamilton understood better than most the alchemical power of finance. While his plan drew criticism from the ranks of Jefferson and his allies, the First Bank of the United States opened its doors in Philadelphia late in 1791; some eight additional branches opened in cities across the country over the succeeding decade and a half.[2]

The money issued by the First Bank supplied the next best thing to the uniform national currency envisioned by the framers of the Constitution. That document called for a metallic currency, granting Congress the prerogative to mint coins and forbidding the states from issuing "bills of credit." Unfortunately, like the colonies before it, the new nation possessed little gold and silver, and until the 1850s, the U.S. Mint produced but a fraction of the coin in circulation; the vast majority originated elsewhere, particularly in the former Spanish colonies. Hamilton's expansive interpretation of the Constitution's monetary clause, however, enabled the First Bank of the United States to issue notes that became a substitute common currency.[3] These notes faced little competition at first; only a handful of conservative state-chartered banks in each of the major seaboard cities coexisted alongside the First Bank of the United States, and each enjoyed a near monopoly in their respective regions. That soon changed, as entrepreneurs shut out of these institutions petitioned state legislatures for banks of their own. Banking consequently grew at an exponential rate during the first two decades of the nation's existence, with nearly a hundred state-chartered banks issuing notes by 1810.[4]

The First Bank of the United States exercised a growing measure of control over the number of bank notes these institutions issued, though this happened more by accident than design. Because the First Bank transacted the business of the largest agent in the economy, the federal government, state bank notes inevitably drifted into its coffers. With its many branches, the bank could send these notes back for redemption with an efficiency that other banks could not match. In the process, the First Bank effectively restrained the lending of the smaller banks, because a bank that put too many notes into circulation via its borrowers would quickly find itself incapable of making specie payments, and would see its reputation suffer. In time, these activities became a matter of conscious policy, though not without opposition from bankers who resented the regulation of their affairs by Hamilton's creation. These opponents inevitably questioned the bank's constitutionality, arguments that gained new relevancy as the deadline for renewing its charter neared.[5]

In defending against these attacks, proponents of the First Bank of the United States made a number of arguments. One of the more effective was that the prosecution of counterfeiters conferred a practical constitutionality on the bank. If unconstitutional, one senator inquired, "was it not an act of usurpation . . . to pass laws punishing individuals for the forgery of its paper?" Were not those who "enforce such unconstitutional measures, and under their surreptitious authority inflict death upon our citizens, worse than usurpers? Are they not murderers?" The harsh punishment of counterfeiters, he averred, established the First Bank's constitutionality far more effectively than any judicial decision. "Are we ready to inform the American People that this body . . . [has] sported with the lives and illegally shed the blood of our citizens?" This was a bit misleading: the federal government never put anyone to death for counterfeiting, thanks to a reformation of criminal law that gathered steam at the turn of the century. But in the end, constitutional arguments against the bank went nowhere, and its opponents adopted a simpler, if more evasive, tactic for settling the matter, blocking attempts to renew its charter until it expired at the close of 1811.[6]

During the following years there occurred an explosion of state-chartered banks and an erosion of the boundaries between genuine and counterfeit currency. Emancipated from the strictures of the national bank (and flush with federal deposits), state banks issued far too many notes. Inevitably, a spark—the British invasion of Washington—set off a financial panic, and the banks suspended specie payments. Suspension was not the same as failure, however, and the notes of the afflicted banks continued to circulate, though at a steep discount. Coins of copper and silver simultaneously disappeared into private hoards, and a growing number of merchants began issuing their own crude paper money in fractions of a dollar in order to make change for business transactions. As every man became a banker, advocates of a sound currency took issue with the "rags" that now passed for money. One satirist inquired why "the privilege of coining money, one of the highest attributes of sovereignty, [was] permitted thus to be exercised by bankrupts, and tavern-keepers, whose notes will either not pass at all, or pass under a depreciation?" In "civilized countries," the writer continued, counterfeiting was "severely punished." What was the difference between a man passing a "fictitious note" versus "a note that he knows will not command the value expressed on the face of it? The one indeed is a forgery, the other a rank imposition, but the offence of the individual, and the injury to society, is of the same nature." It was hardly a new observation, but it captured the dissolution of the boundaries between the real and the counterfeit accelerated by the national bank's demise.[7]

In the wake of the war, the passion for democratizing the right to make money waned, and a growing number of bankers, legislators, and even the president pushed for a new national bank. After a few false starts, in 1816 Madison signed a bill chartering the Second Bank of the United States, an institution that would act as the fiscal arm of the government, house the deposits of the U.S. Treasury, and conduct the day-to-day business of the nation. But this time its responsibility to restrain the note issues of the state-chartered banks was made explicit in the debates leading up to its creation. Henry Clay, formerly a vociferous opponent of a national bank, now urged his colleagues in Congress "to recover the control which it had lost, over the general currency." While Clay did not wish to attack the right of the state banks to issue their notes, he contended that the new federal bank would offer an "indirect remedy" insofar as "the local banks must follow the example which the National Bank would set them, of redeeming their notes by the payment of specie, or their notes will be discredited and put down." Legislator after legislator made similar arguments: the Second Bank of the United States would regulate the state banks, restore confidence in the currency, and supply a uniform, national medium of exchange. It would, in short, as Hezekiah Niles subsequently observed, "protect [people] against *legal* and illegal counterfeiters of money."[8]

Nonetheless, when the Second Bank of the United States opened its doors in Philadelphia in 1817, it demonstrated that a central bank could do as much harm as good. It managed to coax the state banks into resuming specie payments, but extended too much credit and kept insufficient specie in its own vaults. State-chartered banks again issued notes far in excess of their ability to redeem them; new bank charters soared, especially in newly settled regions in the west. By 1818, the monetary system again showed signs of strain, and Hezekiah Niles blasted banks whose notes were circulating at a steep discount. "The issuing of such notes," he observed with his usual gift for metaphor, "is *counterfeiting* in fact, if not in law." The only consolation, he averred, was that "these remarks do not apply to the bank of the United States, as yet." Niles's concern was appropriate: revelations of fraud and embezzlement prompted much of the leadership of the bank to resign in disgrace that same year. The growing controversy led to the appointment of Langdon Cheves as president the following year. He moved quickly to restore the Second Bank's reputation and its control over the larger economy, ordering the bank's branches to call in the debts of state banks, which in turn pressed their own debtors. A calamitous financial panic ensued, and while most of the conservative banks of New England weathered the storm, banks in other parts of the country suspended specie payments, and some perished in the ensuing depression, leading many people to adopt a lifelong suspicion of paper money. As prices plunged, farmers in newer states found themselves unable to make payments on land purchased from the federal government, and lost their mortgages. In the finger-pointing that ensued, many people singled out the Second Bank of the United States as the cause of their misfortune, setting the stage for Jackson's crusade against Nicholas Biddle a decade later.[9]

Biddle himself joined the bank's board of directors in 1819, and succeeded Cheves as president in 1823, inaugurating what one historian has termed the "golden age" of the Second Bank of the United States. Biddle, whose brilliance was undisputed, proved a quick study upon assuming the reins. A member of the Philadelphia ruling elite, he had little sympathy for the no-holds-barred, risk-taking bankers who had suffered during the currency contraction orchestrated by Cheves. The bank would not countenance those state banks that blurred the line between legitimate and illegitimate commerce; it would regulate, restrain, and restrict. As Biddle wrote in 1826, "The Bank of the United States was established for the purpose of restoring the currency. It went into operation amidst a great number of institutions whose movements it was necessary to control and often to restrict, and it has succeeded in keeping in check many institutions which might otherwise have been tempted into extravagant and ruinous excesses." Under his stewardship, the national economy grew at a steady though not always dramatic rate. The states once again began chartering banks, and although the numbers of these banks almost doubled in the first decade of Biddle's tenure, they remained under close supervision. Still, some commentators like Hezekiah Niles continued to attack shady banks and bankers. In a typical dispatch from 1825, he wrote, "What else are dishonest bank managers than *counterfeiters?*" He considered counterfeiters "sinless," in comparison to their more conniving, "calculating" brethren who sat behind the counters of broken banks.[10] But in actuality, common counterfeiters far outnumbered bad bankers, and imitation, not irresponsibility, became the bigger challenge for Biddle and the banking system he managed.

Biddle's Cogniac Problem

In 1825, the habitués of Philadelphia's grog shops, rum cellars, and back alleys likely noticed a stranger in close conversation with the leaders of the city's criminal underworld. The man was unusually tall, and had a sallow complexion that contrasted sharply with his jet black hair and what one person remembered as his "black hollow eyes." His intentions and operations remained obscure to most, save for a close circle of confidants—many of them strangers as well—who came and went at odd intervals in the city's more lawless quarters. As one of his coterie would later report, the mysterious man moved with caution, for it was "his natural character," and he went by numerous aliases: Stephen W. Porter, Ebenezer Foster, George Parmeter, and Abraham Gleason, to name but a few.[11]

His real name was Ebenezer Gleason, and he hailed not from Philadelphia, but from Cogniac Street, as did those with whom he frater-nized. The oldest son of a powerful elder in the counterfeiting commu-nity, the younger Gleason had crossed the border a year earlier to dodge several outstanding warrants for his arrest. He settled in Phila-delphia, taking refuge in the poorer districts along the waterfront. He worked as an agent for Cogniac Street at first, but soon assembled his own company of counterfeit engravers and penmen in the city. They could operate with relative impunity: like New York City, Philadelphia had little in the way of a police force to regulate an emergent criminal class. While remote locations such as Cogniac Street still offered the best sanctuary for counterfeiters, the growing anonymity of the seaport cities proved attractive as well, and most of the men and women he employed emigrated from Canada, though almost all operated on both sides of the border before settling in Philadelphia.[12] Their ranks in-cluded men like John W. Craig, a distributor who moved to Canada af-ter serving time in a Baltimore prison for passing counterfeits. Craig likely fled Cogniac Street after attracting too much attention in Can-ada (he narrowly avoided the gallows after stealing some horses), and like many counterfeiters, forged family ties to others in the gang: he married Martha Gleason, Ebenezer's younger sister, whom an associate described as "a deep, cunning & artful woman." Among the others in the gang were Benjamin Moses, an engraver, and his feckless brother, Reuben, also an engraver; both men had extensive criminal records in both Canada and the United States. A host of secondary figures or-bited the gang, the most notable of whom was Charles Mitchell, an aristocratic Virginian of many talents and few scruples whose ability to forge the signatures of bank presidents and cashiers made him a valued member of the counterfeiting fraternity.[13]

Gleason and his gang soon achieved considerable notoriety. In the spring of 1825, he supervised engravers working on imitations of several state bank notes, including a three-dollar bill of the Hartford Bank that Benjamin Moses crafted. Gleason and a confederate named Russell delivered a "boodle" of the counterfeits to New York City, and then proceeded to Massachusetts and New Hampshire, distributing additional notes to customers. An agent of the bank caught wind of their movements and pursued them to Dover, where he arrested the duo and locked them in a third-floor hotel room. Such constraints proved futile: Gleason and Russell immediately tied the bedclothes together, dangled out the window, and dropped the remaining twenty feet to the ground. Though the authorities recaptured Russell, Gleason vanished without a trace, reappearing in Philadelphia later that summer. He immediately returned to work with the Moses brothers and churned out counterfeits on a number of banks, distributing them to other cities via prominent wholesalers like New York City's Smith Davis. By fall of the same year, the flood of counterfeits coming from Gleason's Philadelphia workshop made waves in the financial community, and a cashier from the State Bank of Georgia (one of the banks that Benjamin Moses had targeted) wrote Philadelphia's mayor, warning him that the quality of a counterfeit twenty-dollar bill worried him. "I must confess its execution surpasses anything of the kind I have yet seen."[14]

In the wake of these successes, Gleason turned his attention to bigger and better things. When and why he chose to do so remain a mystery. But as he walked the Philadelphia waterfront, he could see the hulking mountain of marble that stood at the corner of Chestnut and Fourth Streets. Completed the previous year, the Second Bank of the United States was hard to miss. It offered a tempting target: its notes circulated throughout the country and enjoyed a reputation for stability and solidity unmatched by the state-chartered banks. That the federal government—and for that matter, the entire business community—treated them as the equivalent of specie only added to their desirability, as did the fact that they did not depreciate the farther they traveled from their point of issue. An undetected counterfeit of the Second Bank's notes traded on these qualities, and in the shadow economy where bogus bills were bought and sold, these imitations commanded a premium.

An equally important factor drew the Philadelphia counterfeiters to trade on the bank's credibility: it supplied an inordinate quantity of the country's currency. By the late 1820s, the Second Bank of the United States had issued notes in excess of $10 million, approximately a fifth to a quarter of all paper money in circulation (despite competition from more than three hundred state-chartered banks). By contrast, a single state bank might have one or two hundred thousand dollars' worth of notes in circulation. When Gleason's gang preyed on state banks, these numbers constrained them: the market could not withstand enormous emissions of bogus bills. The circulation of the Second Bank of the United States, by contrast, could tolerate a massive number of counterfeits before it had a noticeable effect. Better still, while state banks printed many small-denomination bills, a far greater proportion of the notes of the Second Bank consisted of higher denominations: twenties, fifties, and hundreds. Such notes offered far greater opportunities for profit, though they also attracted far greater scrutiny than did the small-denomination counterfeits on state banks.[15]

In theory, the Second Bank of the United States could marshal considerable resources to combat counterfeiting. It did have a federal charter, giving it the imprimatur of the general government. It also had branches throughout the nation, enabling it to collect and disseminate information about counterfeits in a timely fashion. But as criminals like Gleason realized, the appearance of national power was an illusion. Take the matter of punishment, for example. A counterfeiter who insulted the majesty of the Second Bank of the United States ran at most the risk of a short prison term. Consider, by contrast, the likely fate of his counterpart in England, where courts considered counterfeiting a treasonous offence—*lèse-majesté*—that merited the death penalty without benefit of clergy. The vast gulf that separated these punishments originated with the Constitution, which broke with common-law tradition by reducing treason to its essence: levying war on the United States. That radical shift, combined with a general retreat from capital punishment, left the new nation with little to distinguish the crime of counterfeiting the national bank's notes from other criminal acts—and with little ability to deter enterprising forgers.[16]

The federal judiciary was equally unimposing. More often than not, counterfeiters caught imitating the notes of the national bank ended up in state rather than federal courts, thanks to legislation that granted state courts concurrent jurisdiction. In fact, while the individual states swiftly passed laws in the early 1790s making it a crime to counterfeit notes of the national bank and coins of the national mint, Congress waited seven years and fourteen years, respectively, before it imposed federal penalties. This delegation of powers from the national government to the state governments was a tacit acknowledgment that the nation lacked the personnel necessary to enforce its laws. For the first few decades of the nineteenth century, the federal government could at best field one or two dozen federal marshals, and these often corrupt political appointees rarely initiated prosecutions against counterfeiters. Thus the federal government, which had rightful jurisdiction over the problem but not enough power to do much about it, ceded responsibility to the states.[17]

Yet counterfeiting, whatever the currency being imitated, transcended state lines, and was most easily combated on a national level. All too often, states saw their efforts to capture criminals stymied by the limits of their individual sovereignty, which explains why the New

Hampshire authorities gave up after Ebenezer Gleason fled the state in 1825. That states failed to share information on criminals with one another did not help matters; indeed, when state officials arrested a counterfeiter, they rarely knew whether their captive was wanted in another jurisdiction—a task made more complicated by the many aliases that criminals like Gleason used. If arrested, counterfeiters could post bail and flee long before news of their capture had spread to other interested parties. States did not maintain the kind of bureaucratic police archives necessary for tracking criminals whose careers spanned many years, and whose wanderings criss-crossed the entire country—and other countries as well. Even in the most ideal circumstances, when a counterfeiter was captured and positively identified, extradition was a messy affair, often falling prey to political and sectional rivalries. When it came to the prosecution of counterfeiters, the United States was less a single nation than a multiplicity of competing jurisdictions, with no common interest in solving the problem.[18]

Gleason's escapade also illustrated a related obstacle to enforcement: most states, cities, and towns did not have the number of officers necessary to combat any crime effectively, much less an enterprise as extensive and complex as counterfeiting. Until the 1840s, rural areas and smaller towns depended on justices of the peace, sheriffs, and a handful of other authorities. While these officers dutifully dealt with countless misdemeanors and nuisances—loitering, drunkenness, cursing, and the like—they proved far less adept at handling the arrest and prosecution of peripatetic counterfeiters. Even when they managed to arrest a boodle carrier or shover, they faced a practical problem: where to put them pending arraignment or trial. A hotel or tavern was not much of a holding pen, as Gleason proved, and even jails at this time were sorry affairs, meant for holding drunks and the occasional rioter, and supervised by keepers who were readily bribed. Only state prisons posed much of a challenge to counterfeiters, but they escaped from those, too, with great regularity. And if prison reports are any indication, confinement did not stop counterfeiters from plying their trade from within the walls of the penitentiaries.[19]

Nonetheless, imitating notes of the Second Bank of the United States presented a far more formidable challenge than copying bills of ordinary banks. The ubiquity of the bank's currency meant that everyone was familiar with its appearance, and anyone worried about a counterfeit could readily compare a questionable note to an authentic note. That most of the bank's notes came in higher denominations only increased the level of scrutiny a counterfeit might face. Gleason knew this. He knew as well that the engravers he usually employed could not produce counterfeits of this caliber. Benjamin and Reuben Moses had talent, but not enough for the job. Only one man could produce counterfeits of the requisite quality: Lyman Parkes, the engraver whom Seneca Paige had recruited in the early 1820s. "Every job of Parkes' was good for a successful issue of several thousands," the *National Police Gazette* claimed. "For this reason the notes engraved by Parkes were always at a premium among the subordinate koneyackers in different portions of the States who dealt with Smith Davis and the other members of the band, and they were readily disposed of [for] ten to fifteen per cent higher than could be obtained for any other."[20]

After Parkes was released in the spring of 1827 from a two-year prison term for forgery in Massachusetts, Gleason apparently recruited the famed engraver to manufacture a twenty-dollar and a hundred-dollar counterfeit on the Second Bank of the United States. While relatively few people knew of Parkes's involvement, rumors of the pending attack on the bank's credit somehow reached the Philadelphia police and the Second Bank. Perhaps a passer of counterfeits caught wind of the plot and passed along information to the police, though it is more

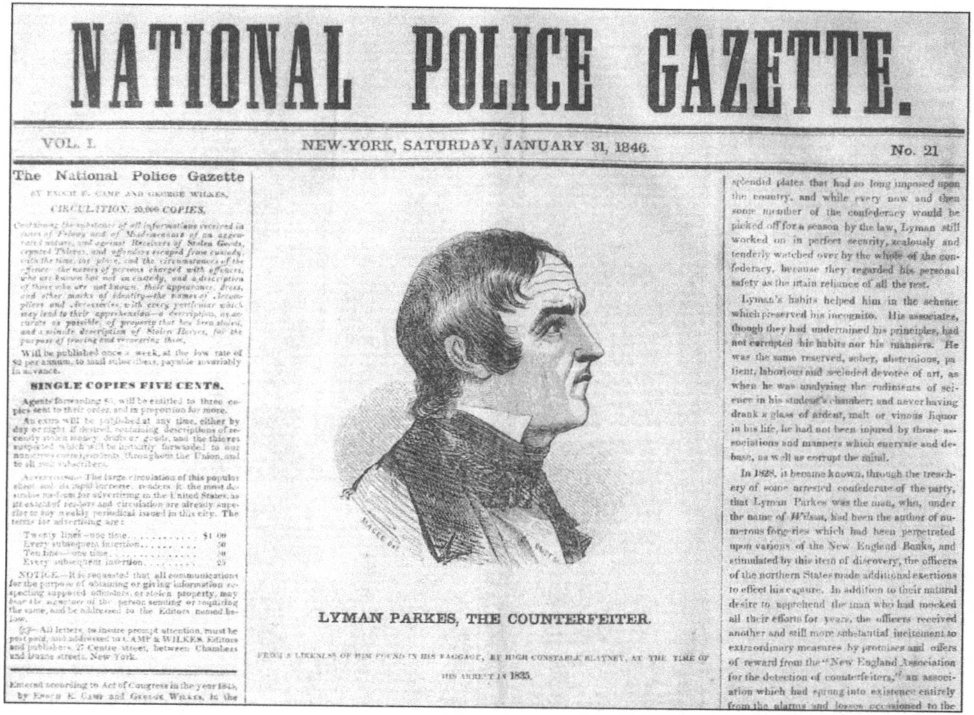

NATIONAL POLICE GAZETTE.

VOL. I. NEW-YORK, SATURDAY, JANUARY 31, 1846. No. 21

The National Police Gazette

BY ENOCH E. CAMP AND GEORGE WILKES.

CIRCULATION, 20,000 COPIES.

Containing the substance of all informations received in cases of Felony and of Misdemeanors of an aggravated nature, and against Receivers of Stolen Goods, reputed Thieves, and offenders escaped from custody, with the time, the place, and the circumstances of the offence; the names of persons charged with offences, who are known but not in custody, and a description of those who are not known, their appearance, dress, and other marks of identity—the names of Accomplices and Accessories, with every particular which may lead to their apprehension—a description, as accurate as possible, of property that has been stolen, and a minute description of Stolen Horses, for the purpose of tracing and recovering them.

Will be published once a week, at the low rate of $2 per annum, to mail subscribers, payable invariably in advance.

SINGLE COPIES FIVE CENTS.

Agents forwarding $5, will be entitled to three copies sent to their order, and in proportion for more.

An extra will be published at any time, either by day or night if desired, containing descriptions of recently stolen money, drafts or goods, and the thieves suspected, which will be instantly forwarded to our numerous correspondents throughout the Union, and to all mail subscribers.

ADVERTISING.—The large circulation of this popular sheet and its rapid increase, renders it the most desirable medium for advertising in the United States, as its extent of readers and circulation are already superior to any weekly periodical issued in this city. The terms for advertising are:

Twenty lines—one time	$1 00
Every subsequent insertion	50
Ten lines—one time	50
Every subsequent insertion	25

NOTICE.—It is requested that all communications for the purpose of obtaining or giving information respecting supposed offenders, or stolen property, may bear the signature of the person sending or requiring the same, and be addressed to the Editors named below.

☞ All letters, to insure prompt attention, must be post paid, and addressed to CAMP & WILKES, Editors and publishers, 27 Centre street, between Chambers and Duane streets, New York.

Entered according to Act of Congress in the year 1845, by Enoch E. Camp and George Wilkes, in the

LYMAN PARKES, THE COUNTERFEITER.

FROM A LIKENESS OF HIM FOUND IN HIS BAGGAGE, BY HIGH CONSTABLE BLATNEY, AT THE TIME OF HIS ARREST IN 1835.

splendid plates that had so long imposed upon the country, and while every now and then some member of the confederacy would be picked off for a season by the law, Lyman still worked on in perfect security, zealously and tenderly watched over by the whole of the confederacy, because they regarded his personal safety as the main reliance of all the rest.

Lyman's habits helped him in the scheme which preserved his incognito. His associates, though they had undermined his principles, had not corrupted his habits nor his manners. He was the same reserved, sober, abstemious, patient, laborious and secluded devotee of art, as when he was analyzing the rudiments of science in his student's chamber; and never having drank a glass of ardent, malt or vinous liquor in his life, he had not been injured by those associations and manners which enervate and debase, as well as corrupt the mind.

In 1828, it became known, through the treachery of some arrested confederate of the party, that Lyman Parkes was the man, who, under the name of *Wilson*, had been the author of numerous forgeries which had been perpetrated upon various of the New England Banks, and stimulated by this item of discovery, the officers of the northern States made additional exertions to effect his capture. In addition to their natural desire to apprehend the man who had mocked all their efforts for years, the officers received another and still more substantial incitement to extraordinary measures by promises and offers of reward from the "New England Association for the detection of counterfeiters," an association which had sprung into existence entirely from the alarms and losses occasioned to the

FIGURE 8. In the late 1840s, Lyman Parkes's reputation reached its zenith with the publication of a sympathetic biography in the pages of the *National Police Gazette. Courtesy, American Antiquarian Society.*

likely that Charles Mitchell tipped them off. He had reasons for doing so: convicted of passing a counterfeit note two years earlier, he hoped to betray Gleason in exchange for a pardon. In a letter written from his cell in 1827, he reminded the local authorities of his genteel origins (one missive begged his readers "not [to] class me with the common order of beings by whom I am unfortunately surrounded") and promised to betray his former associate's schemes, though he probably knew little about the details of the coming assault on the credit of the Second Bank of the United States.[21]

Whatever the source, it quickly became clear in the summer of 1827 that local counterfeiters sought to make more money than usual. As one local newspaper reported, early warnings indicated that a "stupendous fraud [was] about to be committed on the Bank of the United States, or some of its Branches . . . by forging their notes on a grand scale and distributing them throughout the Union." Not long afterward, counterfeits on the bank entered circulation throughout the country. They were "so admirably executed," one newspaper warned, "that it is with great difficulty that they can be distinguished from the genuine, even by the cashier, and other officers of the Bank." After surreptitiously pumping Gleason for information, Mitchell expressed his skepticism that an ordinary engraver like Benjamin Moses could have produced the counterfeits. "There are persons engaged in this affair (I mean relative to the United States money) of no ordinary case." Mitchell suggested that the engraver responsible "is a man of superior abilities . . . he is known to but few and those who did know him have kept it a profound secret." This was almost certainly Lyman Parkes.[22]

The prospect of a flood of superior counterfeits apparently prodded the officers of the Second Bank of the United States into action. Though records of the bank have not survived, what little evidence remains suggests that Biddle and his officers summoned all available resources to counter the threat, appointing a representative to work with local and federal law enforcement officials. What happened next remains a matter of some dispute. By one account, police arrested a small-time distributor, who led them to the gang. Other sources indicate that Biddle's agents tempted Reuben Moses with a "bribe" of $1,600 if he divulged the location of the counterfeiters. Moses apparently agreed, and on July 18, three officers led by High Constable McClean raided a house belonging to one of the gang, Barney Johnson. As they stormed through the front door, they captured John Craig on the stairs. Proceeding to the third floor, and throwing open a door, they found Johnson standing beside a table where Reuben Moses was forging Biddle's signature to some $30,000 worth of counterfeits. If Moses had intended to betray only selected members of the gang, his scheme swiftly unraveled, for the police pursued and captured Gleason, Benjamin Moses, and several accomplices. Additional leads enabled them to seize the counterfeiters' printing press, as well as a separate press in nearby Reading.[23]

The counterfeiters' grandiose ambitions soon came into sharper focus. Keys found in the garret of Johnson's house led police on a frantic search for a trunk thought to contain the remaining counterfeits. "Many a rogue [was] frightened by the questions and inquisitions then carried on by the officers and runners," reported one newspaper, "and a great number of vagrant and suspicious people were committed to prison, and held over for further hearing and examination." When the trunk eventually turned up, officers found $100,000 worth of counterfeits on the Second Bank of the United States, as well as counterfeits on state banks worth another $25,000. While this may have allayed Biddle's fears, the subsequent weeks brought news of more counterfeits on the bank: $200,000 found in the possession of a gang in New Orleans; $75,000 in the hands of two counterfeiters in far-flung

Matamoras, Mexico; and smaller amounts seized throughout the United States. By the end of the year, well over $300,000 in counterfeit bills had been removed from circulation, and Biddle took the unprecedented step of calling in all genuine twenty-dollar and hundred-dollar bills, replacing them with notes of "superior workmanship, with the latest improvement in the art of engraving."[24]

The courts meted out harsh punishments for the principals in the case. Ebenezer Gleason went first, tried on an outstanding indictment for counterfeiting state bank notes. For this crime alone he received a sentence of ten years' hard labor—harsh by any standard. Two months later, the jury in the federal court found Reuben Moses and John Craig guilty, and both earned similar sentences. The worst was yet to come, however. In the following spring and summer, Gleason and Benjamin Moses had their day in federal court. After the jury found both men guilty, the judge turned their sentencing into high drama, lecturing the counterfeiters on the enormity of their deeds. "Ebenezer Gleason and Benjamin Moses," he thundered, "you now appear before the Court to hear the sentence which is to dissolve your guilty . . . partnership, perhaps forever, in this world, since the duration of the punishment to which the offended laws of your country condemn you may exceed the ordinary length of man's life." He proceeded to heap scorn on the prisoners in a style better suited to a gallows sermon, weaving the story of their misdeeds into a grand morality tale. Speaking of their plot to "enrich" themselves by "the embarrassments of a great national institution," the judge gloated that neither man had realized that a "superintending Providence from whose all searching eyes the veil of light is no disguise" had espied their nefarious plans and foiled them. It was a grand performance, and he closed with a plea that the prisoners "devote the residue of [their] days to serious reflection and self examination, and [seek] to obtain genuine repentance." In sentencing both men to almost twenty years in prison, the judge gave the convicts plenty of opportunities for "reflection."[25]

The Second Bank of the United States had triumphed. Or had it? Lyman Parkes disappeared without a trace as soon as the police made their first arrests, and took with him the counterfeit plates, which Gleason desperately tried to obtain prior to his trial in the hopes of securing a plea bargain. Indeed, while the bank was to brag in its annual report of its success in preserving "the purity of the currency, and [saving] the community from the evils of its being counterfeited," Parkes would make a mockery of such boasts. Only two years after the raid, an agent of the Second Bank reported that Parkes, whom he described as "perhaps the most dexterous engraver ever in this country," had joined forces with Elijah Hurd, another graduate of Cogniac Street. In 1829, the two men and a host of accomplices turned up in Virginia with a printing press and counterfeit plates of the Second Bank of the United States, but Parkes and Hurd escaped prosecution, and continued to prey on the national bank.[26]

Perhaps Biddle took some solace from the fact that Parkes's former confederates toiled in their cells not far from his office on Chestnut Street. In 1829, three of the gang—Ebenezer Gleason, Benjamin Moses, and John Craig—were transferred to a single cell in the Norristown Prison, while Reuben Moses remained behind in Philadelphia. Whatever the reason for the move, Biddle regretted it. On the morning of November 22, 1830, when the Norristown sheriff visited the fortified cell where the three men lived, he found that a bar had been cut loose from the window, enabling the prisoners to wriggle through the opening and drop to the ground below, while an "ingeniously constructed rope ladder" allowed the escapees to surmount the outside wall. The sheriff likely received a far greater shock when, after realizing what had happened, he began to inspect the cell. Along with the prisoners' meager possessions, he came across a makeshift chalkboard upon which the counterfeiters had scrawled a pointed farewell: "You would not allow our friends to come and see us, so we are going to see them— good bye."[27]

The Mammoth Attacked

In 1827, as Charles Mitchell languished in his prison cell, he penned a letter to the local authorities, predicting that if the counterfeiters ever escaped, they would "proceed to some distant place, where they will again commence their labours and as [Gleason] says, *work to some purpose.*" Three years later, in the months following the prison break, news that the counterfeiters had fulfilled this curious prophecy began to reach the columned edifice on Chestnut Street. A confession, a whispered confidence, or perhaps another taunting letter: one way or another, Nicholas Biddle learned that the escapees had returned to their old haunts north of the border. In the summer of 1831, Biddle wrote Secretary of State Edward Livingston, requesting his assistance in arresting the counterfeiters. "If they were to be hanged, I would not apply to you—richly as they deserve the rope," Biddle wrote. He encouraged Livingston to secure their capture on the "frontier," suggesting that the men would "make excellent subjects of experiment 'in anima vile' according to any code you may prescribe . . . But, as the cookery books have it—Let us first catch the rogues."[28]

While attempts at extradition yielded nothing, more pressing matters took precedence in the early 1830s. Not long into Jackson's second term, a curious coalition of the Second Bank's enemies gathered behind the president's crusade to destroy what he called the "monster." During this conflict, counterfeits and counterfeiters became enmeshed in a war of words fought by those determined to destroy the bank and those

dedicated to saving it. Whatever the motives and whatever the rhetoric, much of the debate boiled down to a struggle over the right to
make money: who if anyone could issue bank notes, and how much
freedom did they have to do so? The final outcome of that contest—
the destruction of the Second Bank of the United States—would erode
the boundaries between legitimate and illegitimate banking, as well as
between capitalism and counterfeiting. In the absence of a "controlling
power," as Biddle once described his institution's regulatory mission,
the ease of making money—literally and figuratively—expanded with
the swelling ranks of bankers and counterfeiters.[29]

It was inevitable that the Second Bank of the United States would
attract Jackson's enmity: the president disliked banks and bank notes
generally, and he especially distrusted Biddle's institution, which he
considered a bastion of privilege and corruption. It did not help matters
that Jackson believed that the bank and its minions had worked behind
the scenes to destroy his chances at the presidency in 1828. Further, if
Jackson hated this "vast electioneering engine," so too did many of his
closest advisers in the so-called Kitchen Cabinet. But they had different motives for destroying the bank than Jackson did. They belonged
to the ranks of capitalists who resented the restraints that Biddle had
placed on the smaller state-chartered banks. Amos Kendall, for example, arguably the most powerful of Jackson's inner circle, despised government intervention in the economy. He believed fervently that Congress should "be content to let currency and private business alone,"
though he also believed—a little paradoxically—in banning the issue of
paper money. Roger Taney, another of Jackson's closest advisers, believed that the Second Bank of the United States was using its special
status to advance its own interests at the cost of the smaller, state-
chartered banks. Kendall, Taney, and others close to Jackson cultivated
political allies among state bankers who sought to break free of the

control of the national bank, and eventually, to lay their hands on the government deposits that sat in its coffers.[30]

Biddle viewed Jackson's allies with a mixture of disdain and alarm. Like himself, many were capitalists, but they belonged to a very different class. Biddle saw himself as a disinterested aristocrat, a philosopher-king of finance who made decisions with an eye to the public good, not private gain; he called his adversaries a band of "ruffians" and "gamblers" bent on hijacking his institution for their own private enrichment. In Biddle's opinion, they posed a more serious threat to his cherished bank than did the criminals who imitated its notes. As he once wrote at the height of the struggle, "this Kitchen Cabinet gang must be watched quite as much as their more respectable colleagues, the gangs of counterfeiters." Both "gangs" sought to make money, but the crime of counterfeiting paled next to the greed of Jackson's political advisers and their allies in the banking community.[31]

The opening salvos in the war on the Second Bank of the United States gave voice to the growing resentment these bankers felt toward Biddle's paternalistic ambition to encourage them, as the great banker once wrote, "into a scale of business commensurate with their real means." In the pages of administration mouthpieces like the *Globe*—motto: "The World Is Governed Too Much"—writers built the Second Bank of the United States into a monster, a hydra, a mammoth. In a typical dispatch, the paper's editor, Francis Blair, wrote that the bank "avows a design to destroy the State Banks, and admit of no paper currency but its own notes. By their own rights, by every principle of self-preservation, are the States and the State Banks called on, to rally around the President, and put an end to this grand monopoly." If Congress renewed its charter, Blair warned, the national bank would wage an "exterminating war" on the state-chartered banks, "*annihilat[ing] them every where* . . . until it shall reign without a rival in our monied world." In their rhetoric, the forces working against the Second Bank viewed the "monster" as conspiring to "crush local Banks" and destroy their right to make money.[32]

Biddle's private correspondence suggests that there was a bit of truth to these ravings. In a letter written to Daniel Webster, Biddle argued that the Second Bank of the United States operated to "prevent the abuse" practiced by state banks by "exercising the same function as to the state banks that the Genl. Govt. exercises towards the State Govts." A few lines later, he put it more bluntly: "The great object of the Bank is to control the State institutions." But control could take many forms. In a letter to a member of the governing board, Biddle observed that "the object in establishing the Bank was to purify the currency by the substitution of the notes of this Bank for the notes of State Banks." By the late 1820s, the country was well on its way toward consummating Biddle's vision of an exclusive, uniform currency. In time, the Second Bank of the United States might have become the sole bank of issue, much as the Bank of England became in nineteenth-century Britain and the Federal Reserve banks became in the twentieth-century United States. But this was a very different era, and the right to issue notes was a privilege that state banks would not yet yield. Biddle's vision of a singular, uniform federal currency was decades ahead of its time.[33]

Yet it would be a mistake to reduce the Bank War to a confrontation between a more conservative generation of capitalists and a rising generation of upstart entrepreneurs hungry for credit. Other opponents of the Second Bank included those who despised it on principle, viewing it as a dangerous concentration of power in the hands of an unelected elite; farmers who blamed it for foreclosures and bankruptcies that had occurred a little more than a decade earlier; and politicians and voters who distrusted all banks and all bank notes. Influenced by the writings of economist William Gouge, who decried the "evils" of paper money, the distrustful group pushed for the gradual abolition of all bank notes. Their putative leader, Senator Thomas Hart Benton of Missouri, was Jackson's chief congressional ally in the Bank War, and his nickname— "Old Bullion Benton"—fairly summarized his view of paper currency. "Gold and silver is the best currency for a republic," he characteristically claimed in a speech in 1831. How ironic, then, that Benton first discovered how counterfeit bills, wisely invested, could produce a fortune in political capital.[34]

In the fall of 1831, an Ohio country court tried a man for counterfeiting notes of the Second Bank of the United States. His attorney challenged the constitutionality of the notes, which were issued by the cashier and president of the local branch of the Second Bank rather than Biddle himself. Such "branch notes" had first appeared several years earlier, when Biddle's ambition to supply a uniform currency for the expanding economy was colliding with the impossible task of signing the growing number of notes issued by the bank. In order to circumvent the charter's requirement that he sign every note, Biddle ordered the individual branches to issue "drafts," notes by another name. In keeping with his desire to create a common currency—and "with a view to the prevention of counterfeiting," as he put it—Biddle made the branch drafts identical in appearance to notes issued in Philadelphia, save for the signatures. In the Ohio case, the defendant's attorney argued that, however identical to the currency signed by Biddle himself, the branch drafts were not the same "notes" described in local laws against counterfeiting. It followed that it was impossible to counterfeit something that had no legal standing. The court agreed, and set the counterfeiter free. One newspaper reporting the case concluded that the decision meant that all such notes were "*illegal,* and that the bank [was] *irresponsible for their payment.*"[35]

Benton called a meeting in St. Louis to laud the decision. The constitutionality of the Second Bank of the United States, he charged, "was exploded in Ohio on the trial of a counterfeiter." While he conceded that the decision had enabled a criminal to escape, he implied that the bank had itself sunk to the level of a counterfeiter by issuing an "illegal" currency. Congress, he claimed, refused to accede to Biddle's request to permit "subordinate officers" to sign the notes on the grounds that if the president and cashier "would attend to their business and avoid politics, [they] could sign as many bills as they could ever redeem in gold and silver." He conveniently ignored the fact that many legislators had turned down Biddle's request out of a fear that the bank's currency would supplant local bank notes. Benton also alleged that Biddle's request was refused because it would "facilitate counterfeiting" by introducing a multiplicity of signatures. "The poorest would suffer most because they would be most liable to take its notes and could not help themselves if the Bank['s] agents chanced to *cross*"—that is, cancel—"a good note instead of a counterfeit." This was a novel charge, but other politicians echoed it, claiming that the bank was extracting profit from unsophisticated country folk by claiming that genuine notes were counterfeits, then confiscating them without redemption in silver coin.[36]

This was not the last time that Benton would summon the specter of the national bank sinking to the level of a counterfeiter (or a counterfeiter rising to the level of the national bank), but another case decided the following month blunted his attack. A counterfeiter, caught with bogus branch bank drafts, advanced the same argument before the federal circuit court in Philadelphia to gain his freedom. This logic—that "the genuine paper [was] as worthless as its counterfeit"—may have worked in Ohio, but it did not pass muster in Biddle's backyard, and the judge ruled against the defendant. Not that this stopped the Jacksonians from echoing and elaborating the counterfeiters' legal logic. In the pages of the *Globe*, one article continued to assert that "to counterfeit [these notes] is *not* forgery, because they are *illegally* issued." Working the same vein, Benton introduced a resolution that branded the notes "illegal" and referred to them as an "illegitimate and bastard issue." Benton further argued that this spurious currency cloaked a far greater fraud. The Second Bank, he claimed, was teetering on the verge of bankruptcy, and was issuing "perennial streams of paper" in a giant pyramid scheme. "It is this currency," he bellowed, that enabled the bank to "flood the South and West . . . with paper for which it has not the means of redemption."[37]

In reality, the Second Bank of the United States was solid and solvent, and notwithstanding Benton's accusations, stood a very real chance of obtaining a renewal of its charter. As Benton railed against the bank, Biddle's request that it be rechartered another twenty years was already taking shape in legislative committees. Encouraged by his political allies, and convinced of the righteousness of his cause, Biddle moved forward with the campaign for renewal a full four years before the expiration of the charter, brushing aside Jackson's requests for modifications in the bank's governance. Biddle gambled that Jackson would not dare stake his candidacy—and more specifically, his electoral prospects in Pennsylvania—by attacking an institution that most of Congress supported. But Biddle was not so skilled at games of chance. By foolishly challenging Jackson, he triggered a titanic political struggle in which counterfeiters came to play a significant role.[38]

In the opening months of 1832, the rechartering bill moved through Congress. Benton continued his attacks, as did his allies, but Biddle marshaled his forces, and the bill eventually passed the Senate in early June, with the House following suit a month later. The bank enjoyed strong backing in Massachusetts, home of a banking community fa-

mous for its stability and conservatism; other states with similar traditions—Pennsylvania and Connecticut, for example—threw their support behind it as well. Despite Benton's campaign, a significant number
of legislators in the west voted for renewal, a reflection of their distaste
for shaky, state-chartered banks. Some of the bank's detractors also
hailed from western states, though many more came from the South.
New York City, home of the nation's largest and fastest-growing concentration of banks, mounted some of the strongest opposition of all,
seeking to wrest financial power from Biddle's native Philadelphia.
Biddle viewed the stakes of the struggle in this way, at one point char-
acterizing the contest as "a question between Chestnut Street and Wall
Street."[39]

Yet credit—if that's the word—for destroying the Second Bank belongs with Jackson. Though grounded in genuine constitutional concerns, his hatred for the bank assumed peculiar proportions, as an of-
ten-told anecdote about the president illustrates. While the nation's
capitol withered in the July heat, Martin Van Buren made a midnight
visit to Jackson, finding him sick in bed. Grasping Van Buren's hand,
Jackson quietly made a pronouncement: The bank . . . is trying to kill
me, but I will kill it!" This might be dismissed as an idle boast coming
from most men, but as anyone on the receiving end of the president's
dueling pistols could attest, Jackson carried through on his threats. Indeed, the veto message, unveiled a week after Van Buren's visit, unleashed a political maelstrom. In slash-and-burn rhetoric, Jackson assailed the bank as a monster bent on bending the nation to its will.
Along with employing the usual constitutional arguments, Jackson bat-
tered the bank for being autocratic, monopolistic, beholden to foreign
investors, and inimical to democratic institutions. His tirade left no
room for compromise, no room for maneuvering. Biddle called it a
"manifesto of anarchy," and compared it to "the fury of a chained panther biting the bars of his cage."[40]

Furious, yes, but effective: the message emboldened Jackson's allies, enabling them to frustrate an attempt to override the veto. It also prompted another of Jackson's supporters to approach the president directly on a related matter: the forlorn condition of former counterfeiter Reuben Moses. Within days of the veto message (which itself made much of the alleged unconstitutionality of the bank), Moses's attorney wrote to Andrew Jackson, informing him that the counterfeiter's conviction was "illegal," as was the bank's original charter. "I denied then & I always have denied the Constitutionality of that Act," he averred. He also disputed its power to prosecute counterfeiters in federal court, claiming that state courts alone possessed jurisdiction over such crimes. Several months later, a juror in the case added his voice to the chorus demanding that the counterfeiter be released, though he appealed less to Jackson's constitutional scruples than his visceral hatred of Biddle and the bank. Moses was an "honest industrious man" whom chance had thrown in the path of a gang counterfeiting the notes of that "mammoth of iniquity, the U.S. Bank." Captured after a "wily officer of the Bank" had lured the poor man into a scheme to entrap the rest of the gang, Moses was but another victim of "an Institution that now threatens the very existence of the liberties of our beloved Country!" This was laying it on a bit thick, but Moses himself upped the ante not long afterward, penning the first of two missives to the president in which he painted himself as a "truly penitent & suffering individual who will never cease imploring the throne of grace for your peace, happiness, and immortal welfare in return for the mercy you extend." Lest this be insufficiently obsequious, Moses subsequently reminded that president that "To err is human, but to forgive is divine."[41]

As 1832 came to a close, Jackson may have been feeling rather powerful: he swept to a resounding reelection that fall and launched his final assault on the bank. As this last stage of the Bank War unfolded, Jackson took the time to review the case of Reuben Moses. Jackson pardoned far more counterfeiters of the Bank of the United States than any other president preceding him (Thomas Jefferson, who detested the First Bank almost as much as Jackson hated the Second, was not far behind). Whether he exercised the pardoning power as a matter of political revenge is impossible to determine, though not implausible. It made sense: why punish someone for counterfeiting the notes of a bank that in his opinion had no constitutional authority to exist? Whatever the reason, Jackson penned a pardon for Moses on March 14, 1833. The counterfeiter had earlier promised to maintain a "strict adherence to the paths of rectitude and make atonement to his friends and society for the errors he . . . committed," but making it up to his friends seems to have required a trip northward—to Cogniac Street.[42]

The Final Assault

The demise of the Second Bank of the United States meant the end of any coordinated campaign against counterfeiting. That burden would pass to the state-chartered banks, few of which showed any inclination to make a common cause against the country's counterfeiters. There was one exception: the tight-knit conservative banking establishment of Boston, which on previous occasions had pooled resources to combat counterfeiting. A month after Jackson's election victory, representatives from Boston's banks gathered in the grand hall of the Suffolk Bank, the region's most powerful financial institution. The Suffolk's director, Benjamin Ropes Nichols, pushed his fellow bankers to mount a more aggressive campaign to address the growing threat, and in the succeeding decade, his organization, the awkwardly named New England Association against Counterfeiters, achieved many of its aims, delivering a crippling blow to Cogniac Street and capturing Lyman Parkes. Nonetheless, these victories would prove Pyrrhic.[43]

That the Suffolk Bank took the lead against counterfeiting was not surprising. With the exception of the First and Second Banks of the United States, the Suffolk was arguably the most stable—and stabilizing—financial institution of the era, imposing order on the region's banking system. Founded in 1818, it became the nexus of banking transactions throughout New England, thanks to a series of innovative policies instituted with the cooperation of other conservative banks in Boston. The most notable of these was its regulation of so-called foreign money, which referred not to the currencies of other countries, but to notes issued by "country banks" outside of Boston. From the perspective of the city banks allied with the Suffolk, the banks of rural New England *were* foreign: the financial condition of these institutions was difficult to ascertain, and their notes circulated at a discount. The eastward flow of money meant that the country banks' notes ended up at the counters of banks in Boston, burdening city banks with transaction costs and displacing more stable currencies from circulation.

The Suffolk eliminated the risk, uncertainty, and costs imposed by these multiple currencies. It began buying up the notes of country banks, sending them back to the issuing banks for redemption in specie—and it soon made country banks keep a permanent deposit of coin in the vaults of the Suffolk to cover these transactions. City banks assisted in this effort to centralize control, funneling all of their foreign money through the Suffolk, which would then send it back for redemption. It was a private solution to a public problem, and it made the region's banking system one of the most reliable in the nation by the time Nichols became director in 1826. Under his tenure, the Suffolk consolidated its power. It centralized and streamlined the redemption of bank notes; guaranteed that notes from any bank in New England would circulate at face value without a discount; forced country banks to maintain sufficient specie reserves; and curtailed the overissue of bank notes. All of these measures together reduced the level of uncertainty that came with having a system of multiple currencies, and lowered the number of bank defaults and suspensions throughout the northeastern states. Not everyone applauded these policies—more aggressive bankers and entrepreneurs derided the conservative banks behind the organization as the "Holy Alliance"—but no one had the clout to challenge them.[44]

The Suffolk's campaign against counterfeiting was an extension of Nichols's efforts to rein in "easy money" financiers, and it relied on the same close-knit community of conservative bankers. Within weeks of the first meeting, the association counted every bank in Boston as a member, along with the local branch of the Second Bank of the United States. Only one institution refused to join: the Commonwealth Bank, an interest of David Henshaw, the head of the Democratic Party in Massachusetts and one of Jackson's most important allies in the assault on the Second Bank of the United States. Unlike Nichols and his circle, Henshaw came from a poor farming family, and typified a rising class of aggressive entrepreneurs who had little use for the coercive communalism that an older generation of bankers advanced in the name of the public interest. Henshaw, like many men on the make who constituted a powerful segment of Jackson's political base, put his own interests first (most famously when, as federal collector of the port in Boston, he deposited the government's money in his bank to underwrite his own speculations). That Henshaw refused to join (and that everyone else did) suggests that the association drew its greatest support outside the Democratic Party: from the National Republicans, and eventually, the Whigs, most of whom supported the Second Bank of the United States.[45]

But Henshaw was in the minority in Boston, and the rest of the bankers closed ranks around the Suffolk. A standing committee consisting of Nichols, a representative from the Bank of the United States, and four other bank directors (most of whom had close ties to the Suffolk) drew up articles of association that required each member to subscribe to a fund that would underwrite investigations and prosecutions of counterfeiters as well as rewards, or bounties, to agents hired to make arrests. The banks of Boston also invited other banks in the region to join at a reduced fee. At its peak, the association managed to enroll a little over half the banks in New England. But while they managed to secure the support of most banks in Massachusetts, they had less luck farther away in states such as Vermont and Maine, which remained suspicious of the aims and intentions of the association.[46]

Nichols and his associates also made overtures to the banks of New York, but received little in return, save for vague assurances of cooperation. The aggressive capitalists of New York City had little in common with the genteel Bostonians and their ongoing campaign to preserve what Nichols once described as the "purity of our currency." The association attracted controversy in Massachusetts, too. The legislature refused to reimburse its expenses, and when it tried to expand its mandate to prosecute bank robbers as well, the state attorney general vetoed the idea, arguing that doing so would "prevent convictions, on account of the odium which might be excited in the communities against prosecutions conducted by large monied institutions."[47]

Nonetheless, in 1833 Nichols and the association forged ahead, arresting small-time counterfeiters and securing some convictions before turning to more important quarry. The capture of the occasional boodle carrier or retailer meant little if Cogniac Street remained in operation, and beginning in the spring of 1833, Nichols laid plans for a massive cross-border attack on the counterfeiters' headquarters. The members of the association did not look to the federal government, instead using their strong ties to elites in Lower Canada. The most powerful of these allies was Horatio Gates, president of the Montreal Bank. Born in the United States, Gates spent most of the early nineteenth century working in firms that brokered business between Canada and the United States, and he maintained extensive connections to families and businesses in both places. He persuaded all three banks in Canada to join the association and worked as an intermediary with law enforcement officials on his side of the border. The final strategy he and Nichols developed was simple: capture the counterfeiters and convict them in courts in Canada, thus obviating the need to extradite them.[48]

In the summer of 1833, the association's attorney assembled a diverse coalition of forces near Cogniac Street in preparation for the final assault. The Second Bank of the United States sent an emissary, as did several state banks. They joined several sheriffs, constables, and magistrates from both sides of the border (likely hired with the prospect of reward money), as well as law-abiding neighbors of the gang who helpfully identified the counterfeiters' houses. At daybreak on August 14, the entire force, thirty men, surrounded the house of Ebenezer Gleason. They found father and son asleep in the house, as well as Reuben Moses, Benjamin Moses, and another member of the gang. After securing the captives, the party ransacked the premises, finding bundles of counterfeit notes stashed in various hiding places, including the chimney and the manger in the stable—even some in the fireplace, where the counterfeiters had attempted to burn the evidence. A separate search of the cellar revealed a cache of thirteen counterfeit bank note plates secreted in a sheepskin. A search of the home of another local counterfeiter, Benjamin Wing, yielded more of the same: some counterfeit money, a press used to print bank notes (Wing implausibly claimed it was used for making combs), and a number of crucibles, molds, and chemicals used for producing counterfeit coin. Additional searches in outbuildings and the surrounding countryside turned up more equipment belonging to the company, including engraving tools, magnifying glasses, one coin press, and four copper-plate printing presses. Several counterfeiters put up token resistance, barricading themselves in their houses, but the officers used a homemade battering ram to knock down the doors. By day's end, local officials counted tens of thousands of dollars' worth of counterfeit notes on a dozen state banks, along with numerous imitations on the Second Bank of the United States.[49]

The local bailiff marched the prisoners under armed guard to Montreal, where they stood trial the following month. In an attempt to shave a few years off his prison term, Gleason gave a detailed confession. He spoke of returning to Canada in December 1830 (a month after his escape) and "soon afterwards" connecting himself with fellow fugitive Benjamin Moses, who engraved the counterfeit plates. Gleason offered details of his criminal operations, reporting that "my part of the business was to print the notes and fill them up," though it was clear that he also managed the operation, hiring craftsmen to produce counterfeit plates. Like many artisan entrepreneurs in the early nineteenth century, he consolidated control over the production process. He testified, for example, that he had previously "employed" Thomas Adams Lewis and his son, Nathaniel Adams, to engrave counterfeit plates, along with Benjamin and Reuben Moses. The exact terms of this profit-sharing agreement remain unclear, though Gleason seems to have had the better end of the bargain. None of these revelations gained him preferential treatment from the court. The teller of the Second Bank of the United States testified, as did officers from banks represented by the New England Association, but the most damning testimony came from the defendants' neighbors. One testified that Ebenezer Gleason once remarked that he "made false bills & [sold] them, & that there was no law against it . . . if they could find purchasers, they had a right to sell it." This pithy (if somewhat mis-leading) advocacy of laissez-faire was echoed by Gleason's brother, who likewise claimed he "had a right to make money, and would do so." It was an argument that would have resonated with bankers who resented the meddling of "large monied institutions" like the Second Bank of the United States and the Suffolk Bank.[50]

The jury found most of the prisoners guilty, but their sentences fell far short of expectations. Gleason's father received two and a half years in prison; the court sentenced each of the others to only two years. The raid crippled Cogniac Street, and dealt it a blow from which it never fully recovered. Yet the counterfeiting fraternity was far from finished. Indeed, several individuals evaded capture that summer morning. Some would be captured in the succeeding weeks (including William Crane, who came close to killing his captors with a sword concealed as a cane), but Lyman Parkes remained at large, as did Reuben Moses, whom the court released for lack of evidence. News that Moses was consorting once again with his former associates did not go unnoticed, and came at a delicate moment in the war between Jackson and Biddle, which took a new and dangerous direction at the time of the raid on Cogniac Street.[51]

After his reelection, Jackson moved to destroy the remaining power of Biddle and the Second Bank of the United States. He had his rea-sons for wanting "the monster" dead: Biddle had meddled in the elec-tion, funding newspaper attacks on Jackson and paying for pamphlets defending the bank from Jackson's attacks. That Biddle used the insti-tution's funds (some of which originated with the federal government) made Jackson's revenge all the more appropriate. Against the wishes of several advisers, the president requested that the government's funds, or deposits, be removed from Biddle's control and placed in a number of state banks whose reputation for skillful management qualified them for this duty. Most of the banks whom Jackson and his advisers contemplated as sufficiently virtuous to guard the government's funds just happened to have political ties to the president's inner circle, earning them the epithet of "pet banks." But that did not stop Jackson from moving forward, and a month after the raid on Cogniac Street, the government announced that it would begin shifting funds from the Second Bank of the United States to banks that Jackson and his allies in the "Kitchen Cabinet" had selected.[52]

The reaction was predictable, though it took a peculiar turn that same month. On the day the new policy was announced, Philadelphia's *National Gazette* published a scathing editorial that elaborated on a parallel Biddle had made several months earlier. "For the last four years," the article began, "the [Second Bank of the United States] has been engaged in defending the country from two distinct sets of enemies. One is the gang of counterfeiters, the other the junto of the Kitchen Cabinet." The counterfeiters—here the writer named Reuben Moses, Charles Mitchell, and others in the Philadelphia gang—"are about the equivalents of the most confidential members of the cabal." The article took the parallel to elaborate lengths, linking the bank's criminal prosecution of counterfeiters to its propaganda campaign against Jackson. It laid out the expenses the bank had incurred defending itself against counterfeiters on the one hand and politicians on the other. "The Kitchen Cabinet cost more than the counterfeiters," averred the anonymous writer, "because, having the whole patronage of the government at their disposal . . . they have the power to manufacture and circulate their counterfeits more readily than the humbler worthies of the copper-plate." The piece defended the bank's practice of underwriting newspaper articles and printed circulars, observing that "it has cost $10,000 dollars to put nearly all the counterfeiters into the Penitentiary. It has cost $38,462.51 to make every honest man justly

appreciate the Kitchen Cabinet and its works . . . Now, the Bank interferes in politics exactly as it interferes with counterfeits," it concluded.
"While the gang of counterfeiters continued their trade, they should be
hunted to their dens [and] while the Kitchen Cabinet persevere in their
warfare, they too ought to be watched, and answered, and exposed,
whether it cost much money or little money." This moral equivalence
was not an isolated bit of rhetoric: not long after the editorial appeared,
the bank's board of directors issued a declaration that the institution
had a "clear right to defend itself equally against those who circulate
false statements, and those who circulate false notes. Its sole object, in
either case, is self-defense."[53]

This broadside against Jackson and his inner circle did not go unanswered, arriving as it did in the midst of the most heated phase of the
Bank War. "This man compares the President and others . . . to counterfeiters and convicts!" screamed Francis Blair in the pages of the
Globe. "He might have found a better parallel at home. What boots it
to the people, whether they are plundered by counterfeiters or robbed
by the President and Directors of the Bank?" Accusing Biddle himself
of authoring the piece, Blair claimed that he could not "be expected to
tell the truth to the public, any more than one of his counterfeiters
could be expected to plead guilty at the bar of justice." But it was one
particular counterfeiter that drew most of Blair's attention: Reuben
Moses. The piece in the *National Gazette* had accused the administration of pardoning him out of political spite; Blair's *Globe*, by contrast,
defended Moses, alleging he had been "seduced and overreached by
the superior subtilty of the Bank's agent." Blair reprinted Moses's entire pardon application file in an attempt to reveal the degree to which
the counterfeiter's guilt paled next to the "still deeper guilt of the
TEMPTER." The transformation of a career criminal into a political
martyr sent the opposition papers into a lather, leading the *National*

Gazette to describe Moses and his associates as "old friends" of the administration. Perhaps, but when Moses was again arrested and convicted only a few months later for counterfeiting state bank notes, the *Globe* wisely abandoned its peculiar defense of the man it had once called a "poor wretch."[54]

As the battle over the fate of the Second Bank reached its climax, the Jacksonian newspapers made political capital of another facet of the controversy: the fact that Biddle had rewarded prosecutors for mounting successful cases against counterfeiters. This was not new: many banks, including members of the New England Association, paid rewards, or bounties, to judicial officials who managed to capture or secure a conviction; it was a standard feature of the private prosecutions so common in the early nineteenth century. But the *Globe* recast these compensations as bribes paid to attorneys "to induce them to traverse allotted Districts of the several States, in hotly contested elections, to utter deceptive harangues for the Bank, and philippics against the President." The Jacksonians demanded an account of all those paid "extra compensation" for their services in detecting and convicting counterfeiters, claiming that if the information was released it would reveal the "secret inspiration, which has animated so many orators on behalf of the Bank." Biddle refused, claiming that to do so would jeopardize its ability to conduct future prosecutions, but by this time, the bank had more pressing problems.[55]

In removing the government's funds, Jackson precipitated a final clash. "This worthy President thinks that because he has scalped Indians and imprisoned Judges, he is to have his way with the Bank," Biddle would write at the height of the conflict. "He is mistaken." In October of 1833, he curtailed the bank's lending, triggering a financial panic. As the money supply shrank, businesses went under, and the Jacksonians faced growing pressure to reinstate the deposits. The

Jacksonians spent much of the following year in disarray, and for a very brief period it seemed possible that Biddle might secure a new charter. But the opposition failed to rally around a single vision for what would have been the Third Bank of the United States, and by the spring of 1834, the movement to salvage the national bank was moribund, a victim of growing resentment toward Biddle's heavy-handed tactics. Biddle eventually relented, and the Second Bank of the United States began its final spiral into oblivion, replaced by a growing number of pet banks that controlled the federal government's assets. The mammoth was dying, and with it, any means of reining in the growing number of state banks, much less the counterfeiters who thrived in their midst.[56]

The End of an Era

As Jackson moved on from the battle with the Second Bank of the United States, counterfeiters added a final insult to its accumulated injuries. The principal perpetrator was Lyman Parkes, who remained at large after the raids of 1833. Desperate to track him down, Benjamin Nichols enlisted Willis Blayney, the high constable of Philadelphia, requesting that he bring Parkes to Boston to face trial. Blayney was an assiduous detective, though his reputation for honesty was far from unsullied. He spent much of his time chasing reward money for patrons outside of Philadelphia, and maintained extensive ties to the criminal underworld, leading one critic to claim that it was his "custom . . . to eat and drink, carouse and consort ex-officio with the thieves." Nichols nonetheless hired him, and Blayney swiftly tracked Parkes to Newark, New Jersey, where the counterfeiter had joined a gang that included Smith Davis, New York's largest dealer in counterfeit notes.[57]

Blayney was not the only one tracking Parkes; the New York City police wanted him captured, as did the Second Bank of the United

States. In a symptom of the regionalism that hobbled these efforts, none of these pursuers cooperated with one another. As the *National Police Gazette* later explained, all of them "wished only to accomplish their object within the boundaries of their own jurisdiction." In the end, the Second Bank won this particular battle. Biddle, who could expect little help from the federal government at this point, turned to Mayor Swift of Philadelphia, who persuaded his entrepreneurial high constable to secure Parkes's conviction closer to home. That meant luring Parkes to Philadelphia, which Blayney accomplished by bribing—or blackmailing—Smith Davis to set up shop in the city. Davis, who had a longstanding reputation of double-crossing his associates, abandoned the other members of the Newark gang and moved Parkes to Philadelphia, where the counterfeiter began engraving a forged ten-dollar note of the Second Bank of the United States.[58]

While the *National Police Gazette*'s account of what happened next was filled with melodrama, the key facts of the case presented there are corroborated by a number of independent sources. Davis and Parkes did move to Philadelphia in the fall of 1834, renting a house on the south side of the city. Parkes assumed the name James Wilson, and witnesses remembered him as a quiet, industrious man who hired local mechanics to help with a mysterious machine. Parkes told people he was working on a patent model, which gave him an excuse for concealing his activities from prying eyes. He even hired a full-time blacksmith to manufacture parts of a printing press as well as a geometric lathe and a transfer press, machinery used to create the counterfeit plate. Parkes labored the entire winter of 1834 and 1835 while Davis kept the police apprised of the progress. He finished the job the following April, when he and Davis printed a handful of notes. Parkes then visited a hat store to pass a note, but the police, tipped off by Davis in advance, arrested him on the spot. Blayney made a show of arresting

Davis as well, but then permitted him to escape, leaving Parkes to take the fall.[59]

News of the arrest quickly spread, as did tales of the astonishing fidelity of Parkes's imitation. After many years spent engraving the finest counterfeits in the country, this was Parkes's swan song: a masterpiece of mimicry that drew grudging admiration from the local press. "We have seen thousands of counterfeit bank notes," proclaimed *Bicknell's Reporter and Counterfeit Detector,* "and we unhesitatingly say that this is decidedly the best that ever came under our notice. Not only are the beauties of the genuine plate closely imitated, but the most trifling blemish has also been counterfeited with the most faithful exactness." Had the signatures of Biddle been equally well forged, the paper observed, "it would have been impossible for the keenest eye to distinguish the genuine from the forged." Brokers given the notes likewise acknowledged them to be "fully equal to the genuine notes in all respects." The curious flocked to the mayor's office to catch a glimpse of Parkes's work, along with the plates, presses, and dies from the counterfeiter's workshop. "The whole apparatus is the completest ever seen," wrote Blayney shortly after Parkes's arrest. "It is impossible for me to describe."[60]

The trial took place in the U.S. District Court in Philadelphia, and was as brief as it was conclusive. It did not help that the judge happened to be a longtime associate of Biddle's, while the prosecutor sat on the board of the Second Bank of the United States. Parkes's lawyer, Benjamin Rush, put up a desperate defense, trying to make an issue of the alliance between Smith Davis and the Philadelphia police. "I have a right to know what led to this arrest," Rush argued before the judge. "If I can show my client is made the victim in the cause and others, equally guilty, are not prosecuted, I may avail myself of it." The court dismissed Rush's complaints, though it did come out that Davis had disappeared

FIGURE 9. Like its genuine counterpart, the counterfeit engraved by Lyman Parkes featured the seal of the United States, a shield, and a bald eagle clutching arrows and an olive branch. Such symbols of economic nationalism would not again enter into such widespread circulation until the Civil War. *Courtesy of the National Archives, Mid Atlantic Region.*

under mysterious circumstances. The trial lasted but a few days, and the jury found Parkes guilty on eleven separate counts. The judge contemplated sentencing him to a fifteen-year prison term, but was persuaded not to do so by Blayney, who brokered a reduced term of five years. In return, Parkes, who was not only a master engraver but also a skilled chemist, divulged his secret "chemical arts for the erasure, alteration, and transfer of signatures on bank notes" before being sent to Eastern State Penitentiary, where he would spend the remainder of the decade in solitary confinement.[61]

The other characters in this infamous case escaped condemnation. In an expression of their appreciation, the directors of the Second Bank of the United States subscribed an award of $2,280 to be given to Mayor Swift of Philadelphia for his "extraordinary services in bringing this great counterfeiter to justice." Whether Swift's high constable shared in the proceeds is not known. But Blayney nonetheless attempted to claim the reward money that had originally been offered by the association, writing lengthy letters to Nichols boasting of his role in the case, and asking for the balance of the five-hundred-dollar bounty he had originally negotiated. Nichols declined, complaining that the counterfeiter had been convicted in Philadelphia, not Boston, as originally stipulated (worse, Blayney had negotiated the shorter sentence, disregarding Nichols's request that Parkes be sentenced to "imprisonment for life"). A predictable exchange ensued, with Blayney sending angry letters and promising legal action, but nothing came of his threats. He had no recourse: after using Boston's money to do Philadelphia's bidding, Blayney was left with little leverage.[62]

Smith Davis, by contrast, managed to turn the entire affair to his advantage. Not only did he escape prosecution for his complicity in Parkes's crimes, but he also was never punished for another, more brazen crime. While the city's newspapers breathed a collective sigh of relief that neither Davis nor Parkes had "circulated a single note," things turned out otherwise. According to the *National Police Gazette*, Davis had pocketed $10,000 in counterfeit ten-dollar notes before Parkes's arrest. "It was a shrewd double cross," recalled the *National Police Gazette*, "for the bank would never dream of the existence of such notes, and if it did, could not deny that they were the *genuine* [having been] virtually manufactured under the very direction of the president, and by the authority of the High Priest of the Police." With these illicit funds, "the King of the Koneyackers slipped to New-York . . . and with his ten thousand dollars, built a row of cheap row houses in one of the upper wards of [the] city." Smith Davis, who conducted counterfeiting in a most businesslike manner, now became a full-fledged capitalist, not so different from the many other speculators seeking to get rich in the frenzied property market that took off the year Parkes was convicted.[63]

The fever for real estate speculation was but one dimension of a massive economic boom intensified by the removal of the federal deposits. The Second Bank of the United States ceased to exercise significant control over the state banks, and flush with funds, they pumped credit into the economy in the form of bank notes. The number of banks exploded as well, nearly doubling in the five years following Jackson's reelection. The Second Bank of the United States became just another one of those state banks in 1836, with Pennsylvania giving it a state charter to replace its soon-to-expire federal charter. The stability of the nearly six hundred banks in operation by 1837 varied greatly. Some, such as those that fell under the regulatory regime of the Suffolk Bank, may not have been significantly overextended. Others, especially new banks founded in recently settled states such as Michigan, were more similar to "licensed counterfeiters." Many more fell somewhere in between, but all participated and benefited from the economic boom, fueled by land speculation underwritten by the rising tide of bank notes.[64]

None of this sat well with Jackson and other hard-money advocates.

The destruction of the Second Bank of the United States did not, contrary to their naive visions, usher in a broader reformation of the currency. Thomas Hart Benton felt especially betrayed. "I am one of those who promised gold, not paper," he cried from the floor of Congress. "I promised the currency of the constitution, not the currency of corporations. I did not join in putting down the Bank of the United States, to put up a wilderness of local banks." His bitter lament drew little but silence from his former allies. Benton may have envisioned the struggle as the opening campaign in a larger war against paper money, but many of the Jacksonians welcomed the torrent of speculation unleashed by the removal of the deposits. The growing schism between "Democrats in principle" and "Democrats in trade" inevitably sparked accusations of betrayal. Jackson's "hypocritical friends," claimed one Theophilus Fisk, a steadfast hard-money man, "opposed all banks in Congress, but chartered them in shoals in the States—running riot into wild, irresponsible, unregulated banking, yet keeping up the cry of 'specie currency' to gull the people."[65]

Jackson, who held fast to hard-money doctrines, countered the rising tide of paper money by issuing the infamous Specie Circular. The idea originated with Benton, who tried to coerce Congress into requiring specie payments for public lands. The proposal went nowhere, but Jackson issued an executive order in 1836 prohibiting the receipt of paper money for public lands effective August 15. The move widened the split within the Democratic party, leading many veterans of the Bank War to rail against Jackson and Benton's "Gold Humbug" and join the ranks of the opposition. Congress quickly passed a bill rescinding the order, only to have Jackson issue a pocket veto. The Specie Circular survived, as did Jackson's animosity toward paper money. In his farewell address delivered March 4, 1837, Jackson spoke of the evils inherent in a "paper system . . . founded on public confidence, having of itself no intrinsic value." Bank notes, Jackson lamented, encouraged a "wild spirit of speculation" that distracted citizens "from the sober pursuits of honest industry" by fostering a "desire to amass wealth without labor." Jackson also bemoaned the fact that "all [bank notes] are easily counterfeited in such a manner as to require peculiar skill and much experience to distinguish the counterfeit from the genuine note."[66]

The address, written with the help of his newly appointed chief justice, contrasted with an opinion Taney's court had issued less than a month earlier that legitimized the "paper system" Jackson now decried. In *Briscoe v. Bank of Kentucky*, the plaintiff challenged the right of individual states to charter banks that issued notes, claiming that doing so violated the "bills of credit" clause of the Constitution. Taney's predecessor, John Marshall, had already issued an opinion in a separate case indicating his willingness to construe the ban on bills of credit in a broad manner, and had Marshall and his fellow justices decided *Briscoe* a decade earlier, state bank notes might have been ruled unconstitutional. But the court of 1837 (all but one of whom were appointees of Jackson) affirmed the constitutionality of the Bank of Kentucky, and by extension, all state-chartered banks. It was a decision founded on dubious legal precedent, and was largely motivated by fears that a ban on the notes of state-owned and state-chartered banks could have disastrous economic consequences. Whatever the reasoning, legal or otherwise, the *Briscoe* decision threw responsibility for paper money—and implicitly, counterfeiting—back to the states.[67]

As these final, contradictory messages of Jackson's administration entered the historical record, a cataclysm was unfolding that would eventually condemn all bank notes, whatever their claim to authenticity, to a monetary no-man's land. While the exact sequence of events remains the subject of considerable dispute, Jackson's sudden shift in monetary policy, combined with a series of uncoordinated interregional bank transfers precipitated by another of Jackson's parting acts—the distribution of the federal surplus—brought matters to a crisis point, draining the specie reserves of banks in New York City. Growing demand for specie from abroad exacerbated the situation, until disaster struck just a few weeks after Martin Van Buren took office. As gold and silver flowed out of banking vaults and out of the country, pressure began to mount on the bank note bubble. On May 10, 1837, banks in New York City suspended specie payments on their notes, and other banks throughout the nation followed suit.[68]

Few escaped the crisis that now beset the nation's economy. In the panic and ensuing depression, over a quarter of the banks in operation failed, as did countless entrepreneurs and businesses. Confidence, that precious asset that Melville would write about two decades later, was in perilously short supply, and what little specie remained in circulation swiftly disappeared into private hoards, replaced by irredeemable bank notes circulating at a deep discount from their face value. As coins vanished, ordinary monetary transactions became next to impossible to complete, and individuals and businesses—oyster cellar owners, tavern keepers, dry goods dealers, import and export firms, to name a few—began printing their own money in fractions of a dollar. Every man became a banker, but operated without the slightest sanction from the state. Their notes, known as shinplasters (because their detractors equated them with worthless bandages) obliterated the already shaky distinctions between genuine bank notes and fraudulent currency—a fact satirists did not fail to notice. Three years after the *Globe* prophesied that "a sound currency is fast extending itself through the country, and taking the place of rag dollars and counterfeits," this particular "shinplaster" took aim at the hard-money men. The note, dated the day the banks suspended specie payments, offered a fitting substitute for the usual pledge to redeem a note in gold and silver coin: a promise to pay Thomas Hart Benton in "counterfeit caricatures."[69]

FIGURE 10. Like many satirical prints, this one depicts Jackson and Benton chasing the "gold humbug" of a specie currency over a cliff. While Van Buren appears to chart a different course, he did not deviate from his predecessor's hard-money policies. *Courtesy, American Antiquarian Society.*

The proliferation of shinplasters prompted plenty of jeremiads, but "the more scientific rogues in the chartered banks," as one newspaper called them, drew the heaviest rhetorical fire. "The laws against counterfeiting the currency have ever been intensely severe," wrote Theophilus Fisk, "and yet our Banking incorporations counterfeit the constitutional currency of the country, or substitute for real value their worthless irredeemable paper, and it is all very respectable . . . let a poor laboring man follow their pernicious example, and he is sent to the Penitentiary." Bankers, he averred, "can be viewed in no other light than as counterfeiters armed with public authority, by an act of incorporation." Worse, as Fisk was soon to discover, prospective bankers (or counterfeiters, depending on one's point of view) would soon find it far easier to obtain those acts of incorporation. In the midst of the panic, New York became one of the first states to pass a so-called free banking law, which abolished the older system of special legislative charters and instead permitted anyone who could raise a certain amount of capital to incorporate a note-issuing bank. The right to make money became democratized, and several states swiftly followed suit. Others did not: bankers in Massachusetts passed a resolution in 1837 condemning the practice, claiming that a "free trade in banking is neither more nor less than a free trade in swindling."[70]

This sentiment was understandable coming from one of the more conservative banking communities in the nation. They too fell victim to the economic collapse, as did the New England Association against Counterfeiting. After its victory in 1833, the organization went into a state of decline, and by 1838 the Suffolk Bank had halted its own contribution to the cause, citing "the indifference of members in paying their yearly assessments." As a state report subsequently concluded, the association "was dissolved because the members were unwilling to devote so much of their own money and personal efforts for an object which concerns the general wealth more than their own interests." This erosion of interest in the public welfare in the nation's most cohesive financial community was a testament to the destruction wrought by the panic and ensuing depression. The region's banks suspended specie payments with the rest of the nation, and more than a few eventually went under, though the failure rate remained far lower than other parts of the country. Still, the collapse of the association's campaign against counterfeiting—and the demise of the Second Bank of the United States—meant that a new generation of criminal capitalists could operate with impunity.[71]

The era of Nicholas Biddle and Lyman Parkes was at an end, and the counterfeit economy that evolved in the succeeding decades was no longer dominated by a single manufactory any more than Benton's growing "wilderness of local banks" was ruled by a single national bank. The fate of this pair of accomplished men—the great banker and the great counterfeiter—diverged in the decade following the Bank War. Biddle died in 1844, his reputation forever tarnished by his inept handling of the Bank War and his alleged mismanagement of the national bank's successor, the awkwardly named Bank of the United States of Pennsylvania, which went under in 1841. The fortunes of Lyman Parkes, by contrast, improved after he emerged a free man in the spring of 1839, thanks to a pardon by Martin Van Buren. The prison warden noted the event in his log book: "I . . . set [Parkes] at liberty . . . He has served 4 years + 3 mos. out of 5 years & goes out with promises to do better." Parkes did just that, moving with his daughter to a village in upstate New York, where he set up shop manufacturing wooden rolling pins, mop sticks, and bowls. He cut an unassuming figure, save on the rare occasion when he would succumb to vanity and show off the talents that had brought him such trouble. One local chronicler remembered how Parkes, "a remarkable penman," would in-scribe "the Lord's Prayer, with his name, date and age, in a circle the size of a six pence, perfectly legible, with only ordinary spectacles to assist his eyesight." But this was a parlor trick, not a profession. Parkes apparently abandoned his former vocation, content to live a life of obscurity.[72]

Not so the rising generation of counterfeiters in the lands to the west. In states like Ohio, Michigan, Illinois, and Missouri, counterfeiters flourished on the outer reaches of the nation, their reputations reaching mythical proportions. They thrived thanks to lax law enforcement and a growing tolerance for illicit money-making of all kinds. This was a region that needed money, and counterfeiters provided it. While a banker in the East might be compared to a counterfeiter, it was not uncommon for a counterfeiter in the West to be likened to a banker, thanks to the public service he provided by pumping much-needed money into a developing economy. And it was here, more than ever before, that the boundary between legitimate commerce and outright fraud disappeared in an ever-rising tide of bank notes.

FOUR

The
Western Bankers

T he Cuyahoga River follows a torturous path from its modest beginnings in the rolling landscape east of Cleveland, Ohio, twisting and turning and doubling back for close to a hundred miles before finally joining Lake Erie. The native peoples who visited here called it the "crooked river," a name that took on a new meaning in the early nineteenth century, when white settlers began trickling into the region. While most of the newcomers settled in tidy, law-abiding villages, a handful staked claims on the banks of the Cuyahoga in the 1820s and began counterfeiting on a vast scale. The river valley, with its countless gullies, ravines, caves, and other hiding places, offered significant advantages to prospective counterfeiters, much as the borderlands of Canada did for Stephen Burroughs and his successors at Cogniac Street.[1]

Isolation, however, was not the principal reason the valley became a haven for the counterfeiting fraternity. Rather, it was the opening in 1827 of the Ohio & Erie Canal, which ran in a straight line through the valley, fed by the serpentine river. By connecting Cleveland to the

Muskingham and Tuscarawas rivers in the southern half of the state, the canal made the valley a conduit for the movement of goods and people from the Great Lakes region to the Ohio River, the Mississippi, and eventually, New Orleans. Much of that commerce was legitimate, but plenty more was not. The canal attracted hordes of itinerant horse thieves, "blacklegs" (cheating gamblers), and dealers in counterfeit notes, or what one visitor described as a "large number of finely-dressed, ruffle-shirted, plug-hatted, kid-gloved, lavishly-bejewelled, and apparently wealthy sojourners." These men came to the Cuyahoga to buy counterfeit money, both bogus bills and coins, which they would put into circulation while traveling aboard the canal boats and steamboats that plied the inland waters of the Middle West and the South.[2]

The counterfeiters doing business with these visitors attracted the ire of law enforcement officials and self-appointed vigilantes, but not everyone in the region minded their antics. Several counterfeiters in the Cuyahoga enjoyed a mythical reputation, becoming local folk heroes whose exploits were part of the common culture. The leaders of these gangs were not run-of-the-mill criminals, but larger-than-life visionaries whose schemes extended throughout the newly settled regions of the country, all the way to the coast of California, and perhaps, on one famous occasion, as far away as ports overseas. Their reputation for generosity, their legendary charisma, and their extraordinary ability to escape punishment only contributed to their celebrity. Though much of what has been written and said about them has the aura of myth, there is more than a bit of truth to the stories that circulated up and down the length of the Ohio & Erie Canal, and eventually, throughout the United States.

In the succeeding decades, comparable criminal enclaves arose throughout the Middle West, from Michigan in the north to Indiana and Kentucky in the south, and down the Ohio River to the Mississippi River Valley. Many counterfeiters congregated along the borders of states and territories, seeking refuge in the cracks and crevices of the federal system and fleeing to even friendlier jurisdictions when necessary. Others took refuge in geographical borderlands like the Cuyahoga, which offered plenty of places for counterfeiters to hide and ply their trade without interference. Wherever the counterfeiters settled, they benefited from living in a region where the machinery of policing and social control was weaker than almost anywhere else in the country. Indeed, they often won election as sheriffs, justices of the peace, and other officers of the law, making it all the more difficult to prosecute them. But this tactic was hardly necessary: counterfeiters far outnumbered honest local, state, and federal law enforcement officials, most of whom rarely communicated with their counterparts in other parts of the country. By contrast, counterfeiters during the antebellum era fashioned an extensive, clandestine network of underground commerce that crossed state lines, giving rise to what one inside account described as a "secret band of brothers."[3]

Nonetheless, the success of the western counterfeiters cannot be attributed solely to the legendary lawlessness of frontier regions, or to the inchoate condition of institutions responsible for maintaining the social order. Though often a nuisance, counterfeiters performed a public service. As one citizen of Michigan observed several decades later, "counterfeiting and issuing worthless 'bank notes' . . . was not looked upon as a felony as it would be today. Of course it was taken for granted that it was a 'little crooked,' but the scarcity of real money, together with the necessity for a medium of exchange, made almost anything that looked like money answer the purpose." In a capital-poor region where money remained in short supply (and where specie and the genuine bills of more reputable banks disappeared into private hoards and flowed to eastern cities for redemption), counterfeiters catered to an insatiable demand for credit. These "directors" of secret "banks" and "mints" primed the local economy, easing the transition from barter to more sophisticated means of economic exchange.[4]

The counterfeiters were not alone in the assistance they lent to economic development. More than anywhere else in the country, the Middle West was a place where bankers came closest to becoming counterfeiters. Unlike the more stable monetary regimes of the eastern states, the region gave rise to banking excesses that approached counterfeiting in spirit, if not in practice. So-called wildcat banks, unincorporated banks, and fraudulent, nonexistent banks established by frontier financiers all blurred the boundaries between legitimate banking and outright fraud. Working against this backdrop, counterfeiters who preyed on more reputable banks could only rise in the public's estimation. Indeed, the wildcat banker came to be seen as a more disturbing figure than a conventional counterfeiter. The one issued "real" notes that depreciated to the point where people lost confidence in them; the other issued "fake" notes that could command confidence as long as their genuine counterparts did. Which was worse?

The Boston Bankers

In 1829, the village of Boston, Ohio, consisted of a cluster of white clapboard buildings that stood on the strip of land between the Cuyahoga River and the newly opened Ohio & Erie Canal. One hot summer day, dark storm clouds rolled into the valley, bringing rain and lightning. Accounts vary, but most agree that the proprietor of the modest general store that stood in the middle of the settlement ventured onto his porch as the storm approached. Perhaps he stood still, watching the gathering clouds, or was hurrying, trying to finish the day's tasks before the rain sent him inside. Whatever his movements, they were interrupted when a bolt of lightning came coursing down out of the sky, enveloping him in flame. The force of the blast ripped his black suit into tatters, threw his body off the porch and onto the ground, and as one eyewitness recalled, tore his boots off his feet, hurling them over the roof of a neighboring saw mill. As the thunder from the strike reverberated up and down the valley, the man's half-naked body lay sprawled on the ground, steaming from the blast as the smell of sulfur filled the air. Shouts likely went up throughout the village moments afterward, and as the storm continued to rage, the man's neighbors ran to the scene, carrying his limp body inside.[5]

The man's name was James Brown, and he was destined to become the most famous counterfeiter of the Cuyahoga. The blast left no trace on his body, but he lay unconscious for several days. Though he eventually recovered from his "lightning scrape," as one of his business associates described it that fall, the event was more than a freak accident; it marked the symbolic beginning of Brown's career in local lore. "It was said that he was wont to boast, in referring to this incident, that no live man could lay him upon his back as quick as the Almighty did," wrote a local historian who knew Brown well. The same writer observed that Brown's tattered suit was kept, reliquary-like, by family members as a "memento of the dread visitation." The baptism by fire, the boastful quip, and the sacred vestments: Brown enjoyed a larger-than-life reputation, which makes sifting fiction from reality a difficult endeavor. Nonetheless, there was plenty of truth to the legend, and even that which has been fabricated is revealing in its own right. His contemporaries assumed he could surmount any obstacle that fate threw his way.[6]

Brown's resilience may have had something to do with his remarkable charisma. Accounts of his physical appearance invariably reflect an awestruck admiration. A bystander at one of his many court appearances described "as noble a specimen of humanity as I ever gazed upon,

being over six feet high, with broad shoulders, ample chest, small waist, and elegant limbs . . . He is, indeed, in outward port and bearing, one of Nature's noblemen." Likewise, a resident of Akron recalled his "black, deep-set penetrating eyes," and remembered how his height and girth gave him "a personal presence that would attract attention in any company." Though a champion wrestler and a frequent participant in brawls along the canal, Brown was intelligent; in addition, "the mildness of his voice, and the geniality of his conversation, rendered him a most captivating companion." Others were equally glowing in their praise, and while it is tempting to dismiss these claims as frontier myth-making, the sheer number of contemporaries who described Brown in such terms suggests that there was some truth to these fulsome accounts. So, too, does a charcoal portrait of Brown and his wife completed sometime in the 1830s.[7]

FIGURES 11 (OPPOSITE) AND 12. Though Daniel Brown's career is well documented, Lucy Brown's role in the counterfeiting operations in Ohio remains a mystery. What little evidence survives suggests that she played a significant role behind the scenes. *Courtesy, Peninsula Library and Historical Society, Peninsula, Ohio.*

Brown's older brother, Daniel, was also a counterfeiter and a remarkable figure in his own right. Though no portrait survives, many accounts indicate that Daniel was the more capable and mature of the two brothers. Jonathan Green, a "reformed" gambler who knew both men, described Daniel Brown as the mastermind and the younger James as a lesser figure. "Nature, as well as education, had done much for Daniel Brown," wrote Green. "He was fitted for the gentleman, and possessed the elements of a good man, and a fine personal appearance. The love of money, which truly is the root of all evil, carried him astray." Green was less impressed with James, claiming he "was the reverse of [Daniel] in disposition." While James's reputation would change after Daniel's untimely death, surviving letters written by the two brothers suggest that Daniel was the more intelligent—or at least better educated—of the pair, even if James was the more colorful character. Other accounts tend to confirm this view, describing Daniel as sober, cautious, and possessed of "extremely pleasing manners," and James as more tempestuous.[8]

There was little in the brothers' early lives to foreshadow their future career as counterfeiters. Daniel was born in 1789 and James in 1800, both in upstate New York. Their father, a Revolutionary War veteran, moved the family to Boston around 1805, not long after the village was first surveyed. Daniel enlisted in the War of 1812, and in 1813 married the daughter of a merchant from the neighboring town of Hudson. His father gave him two hundred acres of the family farm, though he soon sold it and moved his family to Cincinnati, and eventually, two towns farther down the Ohio River: Lawrenceburg and Rising Sun, Indiana. Daniel built a three-story brick store in Rising Sun sometime after 1816, and local histories report that he worked as a steamboat captain on the Ohio, Mississippi, and Alabama rivers. James remained on the family farm in Boston, and in 1819 married Lucy Mather, the daughter of a respectable merchant in Cleveland; a son was born the following year, whom James named after his brother.[9]

It is likely that the two brothers began counterfeiting at around this time. Jonathan Green later identified a man named "Sturtivant" as "one of their principal engravers," which may be an indication that they worked with Roswell Sturdivant. A prosecutor in territorial Illinois described Sturdivant as a "man of talent and address [who] was possessed of much mechanical genius, was an expert artist, and was skilled in some of the sciences." Sturdivant belonged to a larger family of counterfeiters in the Middle West who operated along the Ohio River close to the intersection of the borders of Illinois, Indiana, and Kentucky.

Land records indicate that Sturdivant purchased property in Illinois overlooking the Ohio River some ten miles south of Cave-in-Rock, a natural cavern at water's edge where another member of the Sturdivant family had operated a generation earlier. According to a letter written in 1821 by an officer of the Second Bank of the United States, Roswell Sturdivant's house stood "on the top of a high Bluff—his workshop is upstairs—but it is supposed he has a cave in the vicinity in which his plates [and] paper . . . are usually deposited." The writer lamented that "the people residing in that vicinity were disposed to countenance and protect the establishment," though several vigilante raids in the 1820s forced Sturdivant to relocate to more hospitable terrain. This was an inconvenience, and nothing more: the political and physical geography of the Middle West offered many hiding places for counterfeiters.[10]

It is likely that Daniel Brown crossed paths with Sturdivant, the most skilled engraver of counterfeits operating in the Middle West at this time. There is some fragmentary evidence that Brown, whose work on steamboats would have taken him by Sturdivant's lair, served as a distributor for the counterfeiter, or procured materials for him. Whether this particular charge is true or not, it is almost incontrovertible that Brown was connected to the larger counterfeit economy by the early 1820s, though he maintained an air of respectability. One resident of Rising Sun recalled that Brown was a "very gentlemanly man in manners and appearance, and as his conduct here was always exemplary, the older citizens always spoke of him respectfully," despite the fact that "he was long suspected of counterfeiting." He may have had a hand in other criminal enterprises, too. The region was plagued with horse thieves in the 1810s and 1820s, many of whom worked hand-in-hand with counterfeiters. Daniel Brown was reported to have made trips over the mountains with droves of horses, some numbering close to a hundred mounts.[11]

While Daniel Brown had close ties to the criminal underworld that was then emerging along the western rivers, his brother worked with counterfeiters in the eastern states. James Brown was first accused of counterfeiting in 1822, when he and an associate were arrested in Hartford, Connecticut. Even at this early stage in his career, Brown displayed an audacity that distinguished him from the run-of-the-mill rogue. According to newspaper accounts of the case, Brown passed a bogus five-hundred-dollar bill on the Phoenix Bank in Boston, along with a hundred-dollar counterfeit on the Farmer's Bank of Richmond. The high denominations were unusual enough, but more remarkable was that Brown passed them on a note broker. This was extremely risky, though the counterfeits proved so well made that they passed muster with several bankers before being detected. The two men had $1,200 worth of counterfeit money on them when arrested as well as a good deal of genuine notes, which they used to post bail. Then they vanished, with one newspaper concluding that they most likely had fled to Canada.[12]

Several of the counterfeiters who eventually joined forces with James Brown had close ties to Canada. One of the first to arrive on the scene was Colonel William Ashley, whom Lucius Bierce, a prosecutor in Ohio, described as having "an exterior, and manners, that would adorn any society." Ashley hailed from Vermont, and according to Bierce, fled to "Slab City," one of the towns attached to Cogniac Street, and arrived in Boston, Ohio, in 1822. Colonel William G. Taylor, who like Ashley appropriated a military title, joined the "Boston Bankers" in 1824, if not earlier. Taylor, who was a merchant in Cleveland—and by at least one account a lawyer—was spotted in Cogniac Street not long afterward, and was rumored to have close ties to Canada. He went into business with James Brown, setting up a general store in Boston and splitting the proceeds. Other counterfeiters from Canada materialized around the same time, including the engraver William Crane, who surfaced in neighboring Portage County as early as 1830. More damning evidence of the growing ties between Cogniac Street and the Cuyahoga counterfeiters surfaced a few years later, when Ebenezer Gleason identified both James and Daniel Brown as visitors to the criminal enclave.[13]

The Brown brothers, Taylor, and Ashley probably established their counterfeiting company around this time. Lucius Bierce gave a lighthearted account of their activities, noting that "Boston was long celebrated for its Banking Institution." He listed the four men as "officers of the Bank," adding that "excepting the fact that they never had a charter from the State, authorizing them to swindle, a more honest set of men never congregated as 'a Board of Control.'" Though facetious, Bierce was driving at a deeper truth: banking on the Ohio frontier was a murky business. The state chartered dozens of banks in the 1810s that issued vast quantities of notes. Many more banks operated without state sanction, despite legislative efforts to curtail their operations. It was a heady time, one when the line between banking and counterfeiting blurred. As one newspaper editor remarked with tongue in cheek, "Since the business of making new banks has become so easy and so familiar, it is to be hoped that the dishonest practice of counterfeiting the notes of old banks will be entirely done away."[14]

The counterfeiters of Ohio need not have worried. When the Second Bank of the United States attempted to redeem the paper issued by banks in the western states, it precipitated a crisis. Panic spread throughout the economy in 1819, and the banking bubble collapsed in Ohio, Indiana, and other states of the Middle West, destroying not only institutions founded by respected capitalists, but also banks founded by "knaves and swindlers," as one contemporary characterized them. Over the following five years, most of the banks in operation on the eve of the panic closed their doors. The "bankers" in Boston, Ohio, by contrast, suffered no such fate. Their notes, while counterfeit, at least had the virtue of being imitations of banks in good standing. They were swindlers, yes, but their money remained a more reliable medium of exchange than the rags issued by their competitors elsewhere in the state. That may help explain why local residents so often tolerated these illicit contributions to the regional money supply.[15]

By 1826, the number of counterfeits flowing out of Boston and the surrounding Ohio townships reached a new high. The success of the counterfeiters' banking operations had coincided with the start of construction on the Ohio & Erie Canal the previous year, when the Cuyahoga became a bustling corridor of commerce. Among those doing business on the canal was George Farr, a drover who sold some hogs to a member of the gang. He was paid in counterfeit money, and as Charles Whittlesey of Cleveland would later recall, he "determined upon revenge." Farr insinuated himself into the confidence of the gang, and amassed evidence against them. Thanks to his efforts, local authorities issued warrants in 1826 for the arrest of James Brown, William Ashley, and several subordinates belonging to what local papers described as a "company of *unchartered bankers* or counterfeiters." Whittlesey claimed that the sheriff who made the arrest drew a pistol, but because "the weapon had in his hand somewhat of a tremulous motion, Brown replied with a smile that he had better put it back in its holster or it might go off and hurt somebody."[16]

Although this account may have been just the first of many embellishments on Brown's reputation, what happened after his arrest is well substantiated: Brown easily assembled the requisite $4,500 bail (an enormous sum at that time), then had his lawyers obtain deferrals on the case for the next six years. While the details of these maneuvers have disappeared, it is likely (if Brown's subsequent history is any indication) that the "bank officers" bribed witnesses and secured perjured testimony. They also made threats: according to Whittlesey, Farr was hustled out of Boston to escape assassination by Brown's confederates. There is no evidence, however, that the counterfeiters ever killed anyone. They had other tricks up their sleeves. Dan Brown, for example, forged an affidavit in which Farr "confessed" that he had perjured himself, and testified that his earlier accusations against Brown and Ashley were "totally incorrect and groundless" and inspired by "motives of revenge."[17]

Farr's genuine testimony, which survives in secondhand accounts, revealed considerable sophistication among the counterfeiters on the Cuyahoga. He reported that his induction into Brown's inner circle required an "oath of secrecy" that bound the candidate to murder any member who revealed the company's secrets. According to one source familiar with the case, Farr discovered that the leaders of the gang manufactured some counterfeits themselves, but more often "they were associated with the Eastern engraving offices who furnished the blank impressions both to the bank and the brotherhood. Their impressions were often genuine and the filling up"—meaning the signatures of the bank officers—"was spurious." While it is difficult to corroborate this claim, the quality of the notes passed by Brown in Boston lends some support to it. What does seem clear is that the actual engraving of the counterfeit plates generally took place elsewhere, even if Brown and his associates printed the notes in or around Boston.[18]

In the end, only one member of the gang went to the penitentiary; the rest escaped prosecution. Ashley posted bail and forfeited his bonds, reappearing after the indictment had been dismissed. This became a favored tactic of the "Boston Bankers," and while it left prosecutors with nothing to show, the local government benefited. As Whittlesey observed, "The sums paid by Ashley, Brown and his confederates into the treasuries of Summit, Portage, and Medina counties, amounts to fortunes." Forfeited bail was a kind of tax, but one the counterfeiters happily paid in exchange for being left alone. This strategy went hand-in-hand with their takeover of town governments, which were largely responsible for law enforcement in the region. Whittlesey claimed that the "bankers" controlled local elections and secured favorable judicial appointments from the state: "Magistrates were elected, and held offices, administering justice many years, who were attached to this fraternity and acted in carrying forward its objects." That left law-abiding residents of the Cuyahoga valley with few options in dealing with the residents of Boston, which one local citizen labeled a "modern Pandemonium."[19]

In addition to being the capital of counterfeiting in the Middle West, the town of Boston, Ohio, was rumored to control ten or more satellite operations in the surrounding countryside. Many of these, like the "mint" that was temporarily broken up in 1827 in Painesville, manufactured counterfeit coin. Among those apprehended was Colonel Ashley, hinting that the Boston Bankers controlled the operation. In typical fashion, Ashley and all but two of the fourteen people indicted escaped prosecution. Other manufactories sprang up closer to home in a number of adjoining townships, including one founded by three brothers in Richfield, a sparsely settled area filled with ravines and gullies. According to Bierce, they "were in favor of a hard currency," and set up a "mint" on a point of land still known today as "Money Shop Hill." The emphasis on minting bogus coin was logical: the dubious reputation of local bank notes left many people in the Middle West with a preference for coin, a bias that the counterfeiters of the Cuyahoga were happy to accommodate.[20]

Other counterfeiters contributed spurious coin, too. The most famous was William Latta, a shadowy land agent who had close ties to Cogniac Street. He settled in the eastern half of Bath Township, to the west of the Ohio & Erie Canal. Samuel Lane, the future mayor of Akron, and a contemporary of Latta, counted him a "lieutenant" of James Brown who was "singularly urbane and persuasive in his manners and conversation, always superbly dressed, with ruffle-shirt front, gold watch, elaborate fob-chain, seals, etc." Latta set up a tavern in Bath, from which he directed his counterfeiting operations in the "labyrinthine and heavily timbered hills and gullies of the eastern portion of the township." While the exact nature of his business dealings with Brown and the other counterfeiters in Boston remains unclear, the picture that emerges from court documents and local histories suggests a loose confederation of criminal gangs that worked in concert with one another, even if they suffered the occasional falling-out. Many of these partnerships had roots in often elaborate webs of family ties: William Latta, for example, married the widow of a member of the Sturdivant counterfeiting clan.[21]

The first section of the Ohio & Erie Canal opened in the summer of 1827, connecting Cleveland with Akron. Additional sections opened in the southern part of the state shortly thereafter, and the Cuyahoga Valley experienced a dramatic increase in the number of visitors. The opening of a water route that would eventually connect Ohio with the port of New Orleans coincided with the growing power of the Boston Bankers, who catered to the peripatetic venders and dealers of counterfeits who passed through the canal on their way to points south and west. Aside from the aborted crackdown in Painesville, no other attempt to root out Brown and his associates succeeded for the rest of the decade, and as one frustrated resident would report in 1828, the counterfeiters were "increasing in skill and experience as well as in numbers to an alarming extent." This was true, but within the next few years, the problem was no longer restricted to Ohio. The counterfeiters' sphere of influence grew in the 1830s to encompass the entire country.[22]

The Brotherhood

On May 30, 1830, Colonel William G. Taylor composed a brief letter to his longtime associate James Brown. "I have a little business with you before I leave," he wrote. "The sooner you arrive, the better—It will promote your Interest—and I shall expect you as soon as Thursday—don't fail." Though the two men had corresponded on previous occasions—discussing shipments of lumber, pork, and whiskey, as well as the finances of the store in Boston that they both owned—there was an unusual urgency to this final communiqué. Perhaps there was a legitimate business opportunity that Taylor wished to pursue with Brown. More likely, the letter marks the beginning of a conspiracy that led to the eventual disgrace of William Taylor, the death of Daniel Brown, and the rise of James Brown as the leading counterfeiter of the Middle West.[23]

In late January 1831, the police arrested in New Orleans James Brown, Daniel Brown, and several accomplices, charging them with passing counterfeit hundred-dollar notes on the Second Bank of the United States. Estimates of the amount of money seized varied; some reports in the local and national press put the total at $40,000, but others claimed that over $90,000 had been seized. The quality was remarkable: one account of the arrest described the notes as "well executed—almost the only difference being in the paper." Still, the arrests begged a larger question. What were the brothers doing in New Orleans with such a large sum of counterfeit currency? And where were they headed? These puzzles resist resolution because it was at this particular moment in James Brown's career that myth and reality became thoroughly intertwined.[24]

Samuel Lane, who left behind the most elaborate account of what happened, claimed that the Browns and Taylor had secured "some very excellent plates of the several issues of the United States bank notes, and were preparing to flood the country with the spurious paper." This was audacious enough, but Daniel Brown went further, devising a "mammoth scheme" that would "entirely eclipse any other financial project, either legitimate or illegitimate, that up to that time had ever been devised." According to Lane, Daniel Brown proposed that the trio outfit a ship in New Orleans, sail to China and India, and use the counterfeit money to purchase "a large cargo of teas, coffees, spices, silks, and other merchandise, to be disposed of in the various ports of Europe and America" (notes of the Bank of the United States occasionally circulated outside the United States). The entrepreneurs purchased a ship, hired a crew, including "artists, [and an] expert penman," but on the eve of their departure, James Brown and William Taylor went ashore to "paint the town red," drank too much, and passed some counterfeits. The police, who traced them to the ship later that evening, arrested the entire crew and seized the equipment.[25]

The reality was less dramatic. Lane had relied on secondhand accounts when he wrote the history of this episode. More reliable was the testimony given by Lucius Bierce, who was prosecutor for Summit County at the time. He claimed that the scheme never came close to fruition, though he did report that the "bankers," as he preferred to call them, "contemplated visiting Europe, and even China, and exchanging the United States Bank paper for the products of those countries." A newspaper account published a few years after the episode told a similarly subdued story. The scheme, this writer reported, "was to fit out a ship from New Orleans to Canton in China, sending out a large amount of counterfeit notes of the U.S. Bank, with which to purchase a cargo of teas, &c. [but] the gang had not money enough to fit out their ship without broaching their counterfeit funds [and] they were detected in time to frustrate their plan."[26]

The most reliable set of sources survive in the case files of the federal court in New Orleans, which contain intercepted letters, sworn statements, and correspondence between the principals dating back to the mid-1820s. The files indicate that James and Daniel Brown landed in the city jail (or "calaboose," as it was then known), whereas Taylor escaped arrest. The brothers, who could not muster the money to post bail (set at the extraordinary sum of $20,000 apiece), wrote to Taylor, who agreed to provide help, but only if the Browns signed over the deed to farmland in Ohio as security. The request sparked a schism among the former business partners, with James Brown accusing Taylor of extortion. When a federal grand jury issued indictments against the brothers in March, James Brown took revenge, turning state's evidence against Taylor. Brown testified that he and Taylor "had transactions in counterfeit money" in the past, and gave extensive details of their business dealings. Lucy Brown corroborated this account, as did Daniel Brown. The court issued a warrant for Taylor's arrest the same week that the brothers gave their testimony, and charged him with counterfeiting the notes of the Second Bank of the United States.[27]

Was any of this true? In his initial appearance before the court, Taylor claimed that he had first become acquainted with James Brown in 1826, but that "no intimacy [had] ever existed between them." He repeated this claim in a self-published pamphlet the following year, conceding that he had "some mercantile transactions" with Brown, but stating that these ended after Taylor sued Brown for failure to repay a debt. Taylor conceded that James and Daniel had requested his help in securing bail—this was hard to deny—but he maintained that he was the victim of an elaborate conspiracy concocted by the brothers. "They represented to the prosecuting attorney . . . that I was the great head of counterfeiters—that they were the comparatively innocent victims of my superior sagacity, and that if they could be permitted to turn *states' evidence*, testimony could be adduced that would convict me."[28]

However outlandish, there may be some truth to Taylor's claims. According to Jonathan Green, at the end of 1830 the gambler had crossed paths with Daniel and James Brown in Memphis and had joined the party, which included Lucy Brown as well. Green claimed that Daniel Brown had told him of his plans to establish a grocery in New Orleans, though it seems far more likely that the gambler knew their real intentions. Green claimed that Taylor had entered the picture only after the brothers' arrest and their failure to post bail, when the brothers decided that "some innocent person must be implicated and made a scapegoat." Taylor, with whom they "had been accomplices, no doubt, in many a deed of darkness," was selected to take the fall. Green claimed that Brown's lawyer had asked him to falsely accuse Taylor of giving him counterfeit money, and other witnesses in the case complained about similar attempts at subornation of perjury.[29]

Perhaps Taylor was innocent of what the Brown brothers accused him of doing, though other evidence from the case hints at a more complicated story. Taylor claimed he cut ties with James Brown in 1828, but the letter that Taylor wrote in May 1830 says otherwise. More damning are letters written by Daniel Brown from his prison cell. In one half-literate missive sent to a dealer of counterfeits who lived in New York City, Daniel Brown wrote that "I acted as an agent for Col. William G. Taylor & Whitlock" (one of Taylor's business partners), adding that "they are the men that has got me in this scrape + they have Robed me of a great deal + left me in prison," while in another letter he complained that "Taylor wants to Lay the Hole Blame of the Hole Concern on us when he is the Hole Ring Leader of the Hole Affair." Brown's letters reflect a measure of desperation, even paranoia, indicating that many of his former confederates in the counterfeiting fraternity had deserted him, possibly at Taylor's behest. "If you [know] anything, you [know] that Taylor is Guilty and the damnest Raskell in the world," he wrote one associate who later betrayed him. "All the

Gold that Taylor has will have no affect on you." Little wonder he would write "I am suspicious of everyone and [every] thing."[30]

It is difficult to know what part Taylor did play. Perhaps his only crime was his refusal to assist James and Daniel Brown in their hour of need. That seems unlikely, given Taylor's reputation as "a notorious counterfeiter where ever he is known particularly in the Canadas and state of New York," as one witness put it. Likewise, one of the witnesses summoned in Taylor's defense admitted upon cross-examination that Taylor was "probably concerned in the counterfeiting business." What then was Taylor's role? He may have been the capitalist in the scheme, paying to have plates made and the paper procured. Whatever his involvement, it is significant that the Second Bank of the United States, which played a behind-the-scenes role in the case against the counterfeiters, evidently encouraged prosecutors to focus their efforts on convicting Taylor, not Daniel or James Brown.[31]

Nevertheless, the brothers were not innocent. In a sworn statement delivered shortly before his death, Rufus Whitlock identified Daniel Brown as having purchased a five-dollar counterfeit plate on the Second Bank of the United States from a man named "Adams" in Lower Canada: most likely Nathaniel Adams, the son of engraver Thomas Adams Lewis. Whitlock also testified that Brown had commissioned counterfeit fifty- and five-hundred-dollar bills on the national bank, along with other plates, from none other than the famed engraver Lyman Parkes. Daniel Brown and one Susan Turner—most likely Brown's mistress—then took the plates to Boston, Ohio, where they struck off "a large amount" of the bills. Intercepted letters written by Daniel Brown in the fall of 1831 confirm as much. "I have heard that Parkes was in trubel," he wrote a wholesaler of counterfeits in New York City. "Please write me if it is the case, I hope in God it is fals."[32]

There was plenty of skulduggery over the winter of 1831–1832, as

Daniel and James Brown vied with William Taylor for control over the outcome of the case. According to Jonathan Green, who served as a messenger for Daniel Brown as he awaited trial, "two or three hundred witnesses for and against [the Browns] had been summoned, and several attorneys employed." This was an overstatement, but the court records and the surviving correspondence of Taylor and both Browns point to a campaign to corral friends who could testify on their behalf in court. Events took an unexpected turn on March 15, 1832, when someone broke into the courthouse and made off with the counterfeit plates, the notes, as well as the indictments issued in the case. The clerk of the court accused one of Taylor's witnesses of masterminding the robbery, a charge that Green corroborated under oath. Whoever was behind the plot, the plates turned up in Natchez the following month, just in time for Taylor's second trial (the first one, held in May, ended in his acquittal after the jury had deadlocked, unable to reach a verdict).[33]

The rest of the year was no less dramatic. Taylor stood trial throughout the summer, and prosecutors hammered away at his credibility, aided by James Brown, who was now free on reduced bail. Daniel Brown was not so lucky: he languished in prison, then died in August. The circumstances of his death are difficult to reconstruct. In his less-reliable second memoir, Jonathan Green speculated that Daniel Brown's personal physician administered a drug designed to mimic the effects of a respiratory illness, in the hopes of securing a release from prison on the grounds of ill health, but "a slow poison was mingled in his medicine." Maybe Brown was murdered, but there is little evidence to suggest this actually happened. More likely he died of consumption or any of the other illnesses that plagued prisons at this time. Whatever the case, Taylor stood trial for the last time in December. Once again the jury acquitted him.[34]

In his dramatic account of Taylor's trial, Jonathan Green painted a portrait of a vast criminal conspiracy unfolding behind the scenes, one orchestrated by a mystical and secretive fraternal order whose sphere of influence spanned the nation. This was an exaggeration, but Daniel Brown's letters to his associates, along with other sources from this period, document sophisticated criminal alliances. Counterfeiters operated over thousands of miles of territory and maintained ties with potential business partners scattered throughout the country. Even small-time criminals drew on these clandestine networks. Sile Doty, a minor counterfeiter, horse thief, and burglar who published a memoir late in life, recalled "adding many names to my lists of acquaintances" as he moved across the country, forging alliances and tapping loosely affiliated bands of counterfeiters, horse thieves, burglars, and other "branches of the profession," as he referred to the different occupations within the criminal economy. By the 1830s, counterfeiters like James Brown, Daniel Brown, and William Taylor could enlist associates throughout the country to turn their dreams into realities. "Often have I been told by the wife of one of them," wrote Green of the Browns, that "they could call to their assistance, if necessary, a thousand men." An overstatement, perhaps, but one that hinted at a deeper, disturbing truth: counterfeiters could muster considerable resources when defending themselves against prosecution—or when making life miserable for one another.[35]

The New Orleans debacle left Daniel Brown dead and William Taylor an exile, but James Brown emerged as the premier counterfeiter in the Middle West. He would become what Sile Doty, when he visited Brown in the mid-1830s, described as "one of the leading knaves" in Ohio. "I found him to be a resolute, active man, highly educated in the art of making bad money." This was true, but Brown had plenty of company by this time—not merely from other counterfeiters, but also from shady financiers who flourished in the fast and loose times of the late 1830s, founding bogus banks that printed money with little or nothing backing it. The line separating a counterfeiter from a banker would soon seem all but irrelevant. Confidence in the currency, always a vexed question, would become an even more abiding obsession for anyone handling money, not only in the Middle West, but in the nation at large.[36]

Free Banks, Anti-Banks, and Wildcats

James Brown returned home from New Orleans a minor celebrity, and the villagers of Boston, Ohio, rewarded him in 1834 by electing him the local justice of the peace. The appointment gave him a measure of control over legal affairs in the township, though he does not appear to have been entirely corrupt. His longtime adversary Samuel Lane conceded that Brown discharged his duties as a justice of the peace "with marked fidelity" even as he continued to control what Lane called, tongue-in-cheek, the "Cuyahoga Valley Syndicate for fabricating and expanding the currency." Lane was to become an important person in Brown's life, and while his account of the counterfeiter's career before this time contains a handful of inaccuracies, his descriptions from 1835 onward stand up to scrutiny. Lane arrived in Akron that year and came to know all the principals in the counterfeiting fraternity, as well as the other players in the drama that would unfold over the following decade and a half.[37]

As Brown consolidated his power, a handful of men based in Boston and the surrounding townships served as his lieutenants. These included individuals like Colonel William Ashley, who resurfaced at this time in Boston, as well as several tavern keepers in neighboring townships, including William Latta. Scores of other, lesser figures participated in vending, distributing, and passing counterfeit money throughout Portage County. Though Brown and his associates had manufactured plenty of counterfeit money in the region's gullies and caves in previous years, during the early 1830s this activity increased dramatically, in large part because of raids on Cogniac Street in 1833, which crippled a key manufactory in the counterfeit economy. Though much of the production of counterfeit notes would shift into the poorly policed cities of the East by the mid-nineteenth century, a number of rural enclaves scattered throughout the West played an increasingly important role in manufacturing from the 1830s onward, with Brown's operations becoming one of the most famous. As Samuel Lane later wrote, Brown acted as the "chief of the Bureau of Bogus Banking, in the West, if not of America."[38]

Lane's facetious equation of counterfeiting with banking was rooted in the decade's financial upheavals. In the wake of the destruction of the Second Bank of the United States, the number of state-chartered banks soared in the 1830s. Some 379 banks issued paper money in 1832, the year Andrew Jackson issued his famous veto. That number jumped to 439 the next year, 489 the year after, and 569 in 1836—and leaped still further to 661 in 1837 and 691 in 1838. The financial panic put more than a few out of business, but the number of banks in operation continued climbing, however modestly, reaching a peak of 711 in 1840 before beginning a decade-long slide. This rash of bank chartering—and the explosion in the amount of money in circulation—has been blamed on a number of factors. Certainly, the disappearance of the Bank of the United States lifted constraints on bank credit, especially in the West, where a mania for land speculation gave rise to many banks. Just as important, however, was the passage of so-called free banking laws in several states in the late 1830s that made it possible to establish banks without a special act of incorporation from the legislature.[39]

Whatever the reason for the explosion in the number of bankers, many of them had more in common with counterfeiters than with reputable financial institutions. Some of the worst banking abuses occurred in Ohio. Take, for example, the Stark County Orphans Institute, located just over the border from Portage County. While ostensibly a philanthropic organization, it illegally claimed the right to issue bank notes after obtaining a state charter in 1837. Another group of financiers—most likely counterfeiters—established the Orphan Institute's Bank, a competing, fictitious financial institution whose notes were meant to be confused with the "genuine" notes of the Orphans Institute. Neither bank redeemed its notes. Nor did other societies, libraries, and organizations that issued money without sanction from the state. More infamous still was the Kirtland Safety Society Bank, the brainchild of the Mormon leader Joseph Smith, who in 1831 founded a settlement for his band of persecuted followers in Kirtland, Ohio. Inspired by a revelation that his bank would "swallow up other banks," Smith dispatched a church elder to obtain bank note plates and notes in Philadelphia, while another went to the state legislature to obtain a charter. When the legislature rejected the request, Smith attempted to circumvent the law by establishing an "anti-bank-ing" society that would, paradoxically, issue bank notes. In keeping with this charade, Smith ordered that the existing notes be overstamped with the words "Kirtland Safety Society Anti-Bank-ing Company." The capital of the bank—or antibank, depending on one's point of view—rested on overvalued local real estate, which collapsed in worth during the panic of 1837, and the progenitors of the Kirtland swiftly sank to the level of counterfeiters in the public's estimation. In late 1837, Samuel Lane wrote in the local newspaper that "if a gentleman is engaged in passing counterfeit money, and comes across a man who has a lot of 'Kirtland Safety Society' [notes] on hand with which he is trying to gull the people, he has found a 'kindred spirit.'"[40]

While experiments like the Kirtland Bank attracted the greatest ire,

FIGURES 13 AND 14. A one-dollar note of the "Kirtland Safety Society Anti-Bank-ing Co." (top) with a detail of the upper right-hand corner of the same note (bottom). *Courtesy, Q. David Bowers.*

FIGURE 15. The Bank of Gallipolis was one of many banks founded under murky circumstances in the late 1830s. *Courtesy, Q. David Bowers.*

plenty of other banks in Ohio followed the same rags-to-riches-to-rags trajectory. In 1839, for example, a group of financiers claiming to be from Buffalo arrived in the town of Gallipolis and chartered a bank whose notes self-consciously invited confidence in the currency and the economic opportunities it would underwrite. Look at the messages of this money: strongboxes and cornucopias overflowing with coins, canals and rivers pulsing with commerce. These scenes radiated a boundless optimism in the commercial possibilities of the era. So too did the appearance of Hermes, the ancient god of commerce. Yet Hermes was also the patron deity of tricksters and thieves—an appropriate choice, given that the managers of the bank printed a million dollars' worth of notes above and beyond what their charter permitted, and then circulated it as far away as possible from the bank, never intending to redeem it. The Bank of Gallipolis collapsed two years later, as did the majority of banks founded in Ohio at this time, even if they did not stoop to outright fraud. Many simply found themselves unable to redeem their more modest emissions of notes, and after suspending specie payments, most of these banks failed.[41]

Banking in other states in the Middle West suffered from comparable rates of failure and fraud. Michigan, which James Brown counted as part of his territory, was the scene of some of the worst swindles, not only in the region, but in the entire country. It passed one of the nation's first free banking laws in 1837, permitting anyone to start a bank who deposited personal bonds and mortgages as collateral for the bills issued. Prior to the law's ratification, a mere fourteen banks did business in the state. Over the following three years, some sixty-seven banks obtained charters under the new terms, though several of them never opened their doors. The hard times of the late 1830s left few of these banks standing, and by 1842, only three remained (a handful of those that failed eventually reopened their doors under new management in the 1840s). The problem in Michigan was that the bonds meant to back the notes rested on overvalued real estate and promissory notes, not "real money" like gold or silver coin, and when the panic destroyed the underpinnings of the economic boom, the notes issued by these banks became nearly worthless.[42]

The collapse of the banking system throughout the Middle West led critics to dub the failures "wildcat banks." The etymology of the term is obscure. One explanation holds that they earned the name because many shaky banks opened their doors in obscure, out-of-the-way places where wildcats and other frontier fauna outnumbered people. Whatever the origin, wildcat banking became part of the vernacular around this time, and people used it to describe any bank that did not have anywhere near enough specie on hand to redeem its outstanding notes. As the economic depression intensified after 1837, "wildcat banking" entered the vernacular, as did tall tales of shady banks founded in swamps, forests, and other remote places in order to frustrate attempts to redeem their bills. While these practices were hardly the norm in the rest of the country, wildcat banking became part of the national language, a way of talking about banking, whether fraudulent or not. Indeed, even a reputable bank might be labeled a wildcat if it suspended specie payments or went into receivership. Confidence in the currency, which rested on an already fragile foundation, now disappeared in a financial maelstrom of unprecedented intensity.[43]

It was against this backdrop that counterfeiters like James Brown worked in the late 1830s, and as the reputation of reputable bankers plummeted, it was inevitable that counterfeiters would rise in the public's estimation. Indeed, many counterfeiters in Ohio and elsewhere began to emulate bankers in the way they did business. In the summer of 1837, local officials arrested Colonel Ashley in Boston, Ohio, and found some $10,000 worth of signed bills on the Mechanic's Bank of Toronto, along with many more blank bills on the same institution. The notes were not, technically, counterfeit. "There is no such bank in existence," wrote one newspaper of the arrest. "But it appears there had been such a bank petitioned for, and supposing the charter would be granted, plates had been procured." When the bank failed to obtain a charter, Ashley "either bought or stole the plates for the purpose of going into the Banking business himself." Ashley planned to take the charade even further by contacting the publisher of *Bicknell's Reporter and Counterfeit Detector* and requesting that the bank be listed in its pages as a genuine operation.[44]

This was but one of several banks that Brown launched around this time. In September 1837, bills of a new bank circulated: the Exporting, Mining, and Manufacturing Company's Bank of Illinois. As with the Bank of Gallipolis, the note depicted Hermes, apparently in his trickster guise: the bank was a figment of Brown's imagination. He likely obtained the plates under false pretenses from unsuspecting engravers, just as he did the following year, when he visited the engraving firm of Gurley & Burton in New York City, claiming to represent the newly chartered Farmers and Mechanics Bank of Wisconsin. No such bank existed, of course, but this did not stop the firm from complying with Brown's request. After engraving the plates and printing $180,000 worth of notes, the firm asked Brown whether he wanted to deposit the plates for safekeeping in the vaults of the nearby Union Bank. While the details of this conversation have been lost, Gurley and Burton apparently mentioned to Brown that one of their other clients, the Bank of Kentucky, had taken this precaution. Brown declined the offer, taking the plates with him when he left the city. He printed additional bills when he returned to Ohio, and put them into circulation. Brown had become a banker, comparable to other fraudulent financiers operating at this time.[45]

But it was a scheme uncovered the following year that best high-lighted the blurring of boundaries between banking and counterfeiting. In the wake of his visit to New York, Brown launched a more audacious scheme using the information the engravers had told him. In the first week of January 1838, the Union Bank in New York City received a letter from the Bank of Kentucky requesting that the Kentucky bank's plates be forwarded to Gurley & Burton, whom the writer had requested to print five hundred impressions of each denomination (with the exception of the $5, $50, and $100 notes). Brown was the one who had composed the letter; the Bank of Kentucky knew nothing of the request. Nonetheless, the officers at the Union Bank accepted the letter as genuine and forwarded it to Gurley & Burton, who dutifully printed $300,000 worth of the genuine—or were they counterfeit?—notes. The plot was disrupted at the last minute when the engravers became suspicious of the man whom Brown had appointed to pick up the notes. Brown's lawyers managed to frustrate attempts to prosecute their client, fending off the charges until 1850, when the city's district attorney dropped the charges.[46]

These various enterprises attracted the attention of the more law-abiding citizens of the Cuyahoga River Valley, who launched a concerted effort to root out Brown and his confederates. Samuel Lane led this campaign from his perch in Akron. In the fall of 1837, he founded the *Buzzard*, a small-sheet paper edited under Jedidiah Brownbread Jr., his nom de plume. Lane composed much of the paper in a dialect modeled after the writings of Seba Smith, who wrote under the pseudonym Major Jack Downing. Like Smith's literary persona, Lane feigned ignorance as an artless, half-literate Yankee. In his inaugural issue, Lane explained that the *Buzzard* would "remove all the filth an carin [carrion] an so forth from the Streets," by which he meant the "monstrous site of Blacklegs, Kounterfitters an vagabonds of evry deskription prowlin about this section." Lane complained that "most evry day ether a Kounterfitter, a pickpockit, a horse thief—all brothers—or a renegade of sum deskription is taken up an tried," but almost never convicted. He promised to enforce the law, even if it meant resorting to extralegal means: a handbill he printed the same week depicted two men hanging from nooses tied to a tree above the words "As Did VICKSBURG, so Let AKRON Exterminate the GAMBLERS, To The Tune of Hanging On a Limb," a not-so-subtle reference to the lynching of five gamblers by Mississippi vigilantes two years earlier.[47]

The offensive sparked swift retaliation by Brown and other members of his gang. Not long afterward, Lane narrowly escaped a "drubbing" by one of Brown's associates. By this time Lane and his allies, who included the local prosecutor, Lucius Bierce, and Ithiel Mills, a deputy U.S. marshall, had managed to amass enough evidence to have Brown arrested in connection with the Bank of Kentucky fraud, and in February 1838, the grand jury issued an indictment against Colonel Ashley for "making the notes of a Bank which never did exist," a reference to the previous year's escapades. In revenge, a gang mobbed the bespectacled editor on the streets of Akron. Friends rescued Lane, but shortly afterward, another "black leg" accosted him on the street and beat him. Lane took to carrying a pistol in Akron, and tensions escalated as the rowdier inhabitants of the rough-and-tumble canal town attempted to disrupt the prosecutions, which enjoyed the support of a growing number of middle-class citizens in Akron. Lane received numerous death threats, and someone—possibly Brown—promised a thousand dollars to anyone who would burn down Lane's editorial offices.[48]

Nonetheless, Lane and his allies continued their efforts, and by the end of February 1838, Ithiel Mills had arrested twenty-six counterfeiters and seized some $662,000 worth of counterfeit notes, along with three printing presses and numerous plates. Brown managed to fend off an indictment in connection with the Bank of Kentucky: the witnesses from New York City never showed up to testify against him, probably after receiving threats or bribes. But then Brown's luck ran out: magistrates in a neighboring county arrested his son. Daniel Brown Jr. was carrying counterfeit money and the private correspondence of what one newspaper called "a league of villains which have for sometime infested the West." These letters revealed that the gang, which had contacts as far away as Florida, owned boats that delivered counterfeits throughout the West. Its members operated with considerable sophistication, going so far as to convene an annual meeting in St. Louis. William Latta, who had fled Ohio after forfeiting bail several years before, surfaced in the letters as the head of the "principal bank of the company" in Indiana, indicating that the manufacture of some counterfeits had been moved to more hospitable locales. The grand jury declined to indict Brown, despite the evidence and despite Brown's bad behavior in jail, where he had managed to break free of his leg irons on three occasions.[49]

Though Daniel Brown Jr. escaped prosecution, Colonel Ashley was not so lucky: he stood trial and was found guilty of what Samuel Lane called *"tinkering with the currency,"* despite efforts to intercede by James Brown. The court sentenced Ashley to seven years in prison, which turned out to be a death sentence: Ashley had tuberculosis, and died days after his arrival. Brown suffered additional setbacks that spring after Bierce, Mills, and their counterparts in two neighboring counties captured eighteen more counterfeiters engaged in manufacturing coin. In typical fashion, Lane adopted an arch tone in describing the arrests. "Another Bogus Bank," he reported, "has been discovered and eighteen of the officers, directors, stockholders, &c. have been arrested." In a veiled allusion to the current crisis, Lane ventured that "not an institution in the United States . . . has greater facilities for redeeming their bills . . . But the removal of the *deposites* will undoubtedly [affect] the credit of the concern." As he did on many occasions, Lane characterized the counterfeiters as "a gang of *hard currency gentlemen*," or as "*experimenters on* [the] *currency*."[50]

This sort of rhetoric would have had political resonance for Lane's contemporary readers. After Andrew Jackson issued the Specie Circular in 1836 requiring that land purchased from the federal government be paid for in gold or silver, coins disappeared from circulation. As mentioned previously, panic swept the country the following year, and much of the coin vanished overseas in payment of outstanding balances; plenty more ended up in private hoards or in banks, which suspended specie payments at the same time to protect their dwindling stocks of gold and silver. Retail transactions became next to impossible, because merchants could no longer make change. In response, many ferry companies, municipalities, and even grocery store owners and tavern keepers issued "shinplasters"—paper money in fractions of a dollar. They did so without any permission from the state, and with no intention of redeeming their notes in specie. As the condition of the currency deteriorated still further, entrepreneurs began minting cheap copper coins to meet the demand for small change, many of which carried political messages. These "Hard Times Tokens," as they came to be known, mocked the Jacksonians' hard-currency "experiments," particularly the war on the Bank of the United States and the removal of the federal deposits. Thomas Hart Benton's obsession with gold and silver was satirized by these tokens, as was Martin Van Buren's proposal for an independent treasury that would conduct the government's business exclusively in specie. The messages of these coins—like the larger political rhetoric they echoed—surfaced in accounts of the counterfeiters arrested in Ohio.[51]

While self-appointed regulators of the currency like Samuel Lane

launched attacks on the counterfeiters, not everyone appreciated his honesty. James Brown and his associates supplied what many demanded: a circulating medium to ease the hard times. Lane said as much when he sarcastically described the counterfeiters as "philanthropic gentlemen" who were doing so much "to *soften* the *hard* times, and alleviate the distresses of his fellow beings, by making money plenty." Though Lane had contempt for the counterfeiters, as well as for their close cousins, the printers of shinplasters and issuers of copper tokens, these attempts at private money creation represented a common response to the need for a circulating medium. That need was powerful enough when times were good, but it took on new urgency in the late 1830s. As one local historian later wrote, "Some of the most influential citizens of the township were induced to engage in the unlawful business, and it is even stated that a certain aspect of respectability was conceded to this occupation." That may help explain why it proved so difficult for prosecutors to secure a conviction against the counterfeiters: some men who served on juries, even if they did not belong to Brown's gang, viewed him in a more generous light than did Lane and his fellow reformers.[52]

Brown could still marshal considerable resources to defend himself,

FIGURES 16 (OPPOSITE) AND 17. In their hard-hitting symbolism, "Hard Times" tokens sent a political message while relieving the currency shortage. *Reproduced from the originals held by the Department of Special Collections of the University Libraries of Notre Dame.*

even without the subtle support he enjoyed from the community. For example, in June 1838, another one of Brown's gang, Willard Stevens, was arrested for dealing in counterfeit money. He turned state's evidence, promising to testify against his patron in exchange for immunity. When the day of the trial arrived in September, however, Stevens failed to appear. Deprived of their star witness, prosecutors turned to some of Stevens's associates, but as Lane would later recall, "the memories of those who were to corroborate him had mysteriously failed." As for Stevens, rumors circulated that he had been murdered—although several years later he surfaced in Georgia, and eventually he returned to Ohio. Why he refused to testify was anyone's guess, though he may have been persuaded to leave in much the same way that Brown had persuaded another "turncoat," Jonathan DeCoursey. Arrested in the spring raid on the "hard money men," DeCoursey was a tavern keeper and one of Brown's trusted lieutenants. Brown's allies apparently took DeCoursey aside, gave him $600 in genuine money, a gold watch, a promise of indemnity for his bail, a promissory note for $200, and another $400 for his wife, and then told him to "absquatulate" to Texas. He left in the company of one of Brown's "trusted henchmen." All of these efforts were to no avail: he was captured and returned to court to testify against Brown.[53]

Brown's own trial came first in March 1839, and despite the strenuous efforts of his lawyers, the jury actually convicted him. This was a minor inconvenience: Lucy Brown's brother, the lawyer William Mather, rode a relay of horses to a sympathetic member of the Ohio Supreme Court, obtained a writ of error and a stay of the proceedings, and then rode back, overtaking the stage that was carrying Brown to the state prison. That summer, Brown's lawyers managed to overturn the conviction and secure a new trial. Brown dutifully appeared in court the following month, but the state's key witness, Jonathan DeCoursey, did not, having been "persuaded" yet again to leave the state by members of Brown's gang. The case limped along for another year, but when DeCoursey failed to appear, the prosecutor abandoned the case. William Latta, whom Ithiel Mills had captured in Indiana, stood trial in September, but Brown declined to answer questions under oath on the grounds that he would incriminate himself, and the case fell apart. Latta disappeared, returning to northern Indiana to continue counterfeiting.[54]

The collapse of the case put an end to the efforts of Lane and other reformers in the river valley. Lane, who married a local woman late in 1838, stopped publishing the *Buzzard* "owing to fears of personal violence to myself naturally indulged in by my young wife." He may have grown tired as well of waging war on Brown, who continued to enjoy the tacit support of many people in the area. Indeed, Brown hardly kept a low profile: he sold his farm and moved his family to Akron at this time, purchasing a house a few blocks from Lane's former editorial offices. An uneasy truce settled over Akron, even though Brown was

FIGURE 18. James Brown's house sits today within the boundaries of the Cuyahoga Valley National Park. Aside from the barely visible remnants of the canal, the view of the valley below is much the same as it was in the nineteenth century. *Photograph from the author's collection.*

implicated in counterfeiting schemes as far away as New York City. In 1842 or 1843, Brown moved his family back to the valley, purchasing a stately Greek Revival home that sat on a commanding bluff overlooking both the Cuyahoga River and Ohio & Erie Canal. The house was rumored to be "one of the most splendid in that part of the state, being superbly furnished with costly side boards, sofas, couches, divans, ottomans, mirrors, and other ornamental articles." Though Brown probably purchased the house, his son Daniel owned the title to it, along with three hundred acres of choice farmland in the valley below. Transferring the title protected the property from legal entanglements, because Daniel spent most of his time overseeing counterfeiting operations in various borderlands in Michigan, Indiana, and points even farther west. Like his namesake, Brown's oldest son would demonstrate a remarkable ability to turn everything he touched into gold, and in the coming years, his feats of financial legerdemain would earn him a reputation that stretched from coast to coast.[55]

Go West, Young Man

The village of Genoa, Illinois, occupies a choice area of prairie about sixty miles northwest of Chicago. The first settlers arrived in 1836 and 1837, drawn by the cheap land and the numerous groves of trees that dotted the township. Among the newcomers was a tall, pale man with dark, deep-set eyes, who as one local historian would later write, enjoyed a "reputation of being a man of wealth, and began to talk about building flouring mills, starting stores, and otherwise contributing to the growth and enlargement of the business of the place." The man purchased land from another settler, planted a row of maple trees in the village, got involved in local politics, and otherwise adopted an air of respectability. His name was Ebenezer Gleason, and like many other veterans of Cogniac Street who moved to the Middle West at this time, he also established a criminal outpost on the frontier of the expanding nation—an outpost that built on the clandestine commerce overseen by James Brown and his allies.[56]

The frontier beckoned to counterfeiters like Gleason for many reasons. By the late 1830s, Cogniac Street's importance was on the wane. Local authorities harassed the counterfeiters in the region, and a few years later, the ratification of the Webster-Ashburton Treaty, which included an extradition agreement, ushered in a new era of cooperation between the United States and Canada on criminal matters. By contrast, law enforcement in the newly settled territories of the Middle West was generally inchoate, and the town of Genoa, part of Dekalb County, was no exception. As one resident later wrote, "The lawless element always seeks the frontier, as they are generally freer from detection, and are brought to justice with greater difficulty than in older settlements." James Brown's former associate, William Taylor, gave a dramatic demonstration of this fact when he was captured near Genoa in 1838 after passing some counterfeit money. The county, which lacked a jail, kept him under close guard at the house of one of his accusers for several weeks, then transferred him at considerable expense to a jail in neighboring Will County. Taylor proceeded to escape from confinement, but the jailor still billed Dekalb County for his services. The expense of this single embarrassment drained Dekalb's coffers. "After this dear experience in the capture of criminals," wrote one resident, "it became the policy to overlook all crimes that were not too public and heinous, and when an offence had been committed that could not be overlooked, the County officers sometimes contrived that a hint should be given to the offender that he would probably be arrested, and that it would be expedient for him to leave . . . before that event should occur."[57]

Gleason benefited from this hands-off approach to law enforcement. On multiple occasions he escaped arrest, or managed to tamper with witnesses and avoid prosecution. Despite his reputation as a principal player in the counterfeit economy, Gleason's neighbors left him alone, and he acquired a store, a saw mill, and a farm. He also married a local woman, Lydia Strong, and otherwise played the part of a good citizen, all the while controlling much of the counterfeit economy in Illinois. Gleason's career came to an abrupt end in 1848. As one local historian would later write, "He escaped the punishment of his crime against the law to meet a more terrible fate." A traveling doctor who boarded with Gleason's family—and who developed a romantic attachment to Strong—allegedly fed the counterfeiter a bowl of porridge laced with poison; Gleason died "in convulsions and delirium." Suspicion fell on the doctor and Strong, but the evidence was inconclusive, and the pair escaped punishment. Strong married the doctor after the trial, but he, too, would soon die "under circumstances that led to the suspicion that he had been poisoned."[58]

After Gleason's death, associates from Cogniac Street took his place. William Crane moved to neighboring Lake County, Illinois, sometime in the 1840s, as did Gleason's nephew, Valentine Gleason, a young man in his twenties who served as Crane's apprentice at this time; John Craig visited the area, too. The business transactions of these men remain obscure, though they occasionally came into focus, most famously when counterfeits on an uncharted but otherwise reputable bank— the Wisconsin Marine and Fire Insurance Company—began surfacing in Illinois. The officers of the bank deputized a young cooper named Allan Pinkerton to root out the gang. In the course of his campaign, which launched his career as a private investigator, Pinkerton ingratiated himself with Craig, who bragged about doing "a good deal of *business*" with William Crane. Pinkerton managed to capture Craig, only to have the aging counterfeiter escape once again. While the subsequent movements of veteran counterfeiters like Craig and Crane are next to impossible to reconstruct, they likely established alliances with the many horse thieves, gamblers, and "land pirates" who operated in equally hospitable locales scattered throughout the Middle West. Many of these other newcomers had come from Ohio, and as one exposé claimed in the 1850s, "probably received their first lessons of instruction from the notorious Jim Brown."[59]

The counterfeiters who settled in the states of Michigan, Indiana, and Illinois, and eventually Iowa and Missouri, often congregated along geographical and political fault lines. For example, William Latta and another of Brown's associates settled in the township of Orange in Noble County, Indiana, just over the border from Lagrange County and a few hours' ride from the border with Michigan. Another cluster of counterfeiters put down roots on a small island in the middle of Beaver Lake, a vast tract of water and marshland in Indiana a half mile from the border with Illinois. The hideout, which earned the nickname "Bogus Island," could only be approached on one side, and there only via a crude road of submerged logs. Its denizens manufactured counterfeit coin and trafficked in stolen horses. As with Latta's neighbors in Noble County, the counterfeiters "had their sympathizers everywhere among the early settlers," as one local chronicler later wrote, and "the theory seemed to exist that so long as the evil was not directed against the home community, it was a venial crime." This scenario would happen again and again: small enclaves of counterfeiters set up shop in the interstices of the nation's newest territories, while surrounding communities turned a blind eye.[60]

This tolerance does not seem to have extended beyond the Middle West. Though counterfeiters thrived in Kentucky and Missouri, few counterfeiters operated in Arkansas, Mississippi, Louisiana, Alabama, or Georgia, even if distributors of bogus notes and coins peddled their wares in these newly settled states. The reluctance of counterfeiters to site themselves in the slave states probably had something to do with the history of vigilante violence directed at "land pirates," gamblers, and other outsiders in the 1830s. It may also reflect the far greater resources dedicated to maintaining social control in the region. Local militias, slave patrols, and a well-developed urban police force in cities like New Orleans made much of the slaveholding South an inhospitable place for counterfeiters. Add to that local authorities' considerable experience in tracking down fugitive slaves, and it was not surprising that most counterfeiters would head farther up the Mississippi River, where there was a greater acceptance of infringements on state authority.[61]

While many "mints" and "banks" operated with little interference from outsiders in the Middle West, there were a handful of exceptions. Counterfeiters associated with the Mormon settlement at Nauvoo, Illinois, for example, attracted condemnation from their neighbors in the 1840s. The Mormons, who had established an autonomous state-within-a-state at Nauvoo, probably tolerated counterfeiters living in their midst, and may well have had a hand in manufacturing bogus coin themselves. The attraction to counterfeiters of highly autonomous Nauvoo was understandable; moreover, the Mormons had been accused of counterfeiting in the past, as well as other experiments that bordered on counterfeiting, including the Kirtland Bank debacle. The U.S. District Court eventually indicted a number of church elders for counterfeiting coin, although the Mormons left for Utah before any arrests could be made.[62]

For the most part, though, coiners operated with impunity. That so many people tolerated their illicit activities was a testament to the shortage of currency throughout the Middle West. After the banking collapses of the late 1830s, most states in the region refused to charter banks, or chartered very few of them. Iowa, which had a single, corrupt territorial bank prior to its admission as a state in 1846, prohibited individuals and corporations from issuing "paper to circulate as money." Missouri, Indiana, and Illinois had similar prohibitions. Though each chartered a single "state bank" that put notes into circulation, demand for money inevitably outstripped the supply. Michigan, where most banks collapsed by the early 1840s, refused to charter another bank until 1849. Ohio kept a tight leash on new banks, and restricted their size and the quantity of notes they could circulate. The limits set on banking, combined with a regional imbalance of trade, which sent coins and notes flowing to the eastern states, left the Middle West struggling to conduct business. In light of the shortage, it was not surprising that coiners flourished. They performed a public service, and as one frustrated federal marshal in Ohio observed, "among them may be found men of property and good standing in their neighborhoods."[63]

James Brown and his family may or may not have fallen into that "good standing" category. Still, what little evidence exists suggests that he moved heavily into counterfeiting coin at this time, probably with the assistance of more reputable partners throughout the state. So, too, did his son, Daniel, whom Samuel Lane, with his usual gift for metaphor, described as "promoting the 'resumption of specie payments' by the production of bogus coin of such an excellent quality as to almost defy detection." Though Dan owned the family mansion overlooking the Cuyahoga River, and married a cousin who lived nearby, he spent most of his time in the Black Swamp, an impenetrable marshland that stretched across fifteen hundred square miles of northwestern Ohio and northeastern Indiana. It was an ideal place for manufacturing counterfeit coin: swarms of mosquitoes attacked anyone who ventured into its depths, and few travelers strayed off the single road, often flooded, that traversed the swamp. Brown apparently spent much of his time here or in the adjoining counties of Michigan and Indiana, though some of his operations may have been underwritten or directed by his father.[64]

Dan Brown showed a remarkable ability to outpace law enforcement officials. In 1842, counterfeit coin flooded southern Michigan, attracting the attention of George Bates, the federal prosecutor for the state. After some detective work, Bates intercepted a press used for cutting, stamping, and milling coin that was being shipped to "Dan West," an alias used by Brown. Bates and a federal marshal plotted to arrest Brown in Cleveland, but the press disappeared in transit, along with Brown. Bates eventually secured the conviction of several of the counterfeiter's lesser accomplices in southern Michigan, but Brown continued to evade capture. Finally, Bates traced the counterfeiter to St.

Louis. According to Samuel Lane, Bates arrived at the hotel where "Dan West" had put up for the night. Bates, who had never seen his quarry in person, made the mistake of inquiring at the front desk if the clerk would fetch West. The "clerk" was none other than Brown himself, and "coolly and politely saying to the newcomers that he would call Mr. West, Mr. Brown passed out through the kitchen, and a few minutes later was on board a Mississippi steamer." Lane, who wrote this account many years later, may have relied a little too heavily on secondhand reports of this particular episode. Still, whether true or not, tales of Brown's escape burnished the young counterfeiter's reputation as a trickster extraordinaire. Like his father, he proved remarkably capable of outwitting his pursuers.[65]

Nonetheless, everyone's luck runs out at some point. In 1846, one of James Brown's former confederates, John Bellows, confessed to obtaining counterfeit coin from Brown. Bellows, whom two federal judges described as a "young man of respectable connection" who had otherwise "retained an excellent character until he was seduced by Brown," proved to be the master counterfeiter's undoing. Using information obtained by Bellows, the deputy U.S. marshal Ithiel Mills searched Brown's house, finding parts of a copper plate press, batteries used for electroplating counterfeit coin, blank bank note paper, and letters linking Brown to counterfeiting schemes. A federal grand jury issued indictments, and Brown stood trial in Columbus that summer. According to Lane, Brown went to the trial with foreboding, telling confederates that while he could "worry out a county," he feared that the federal government "would prove too much for him." His premonition proved correct: the jury deliberated for only two hours before handing down a guilty verdict, and the judge sentenced him to ten years in prison. Brown's lawyers did their best to overturn the conviction, but to no avail. His confederates took their revenge on Bellows and his family, burning their barns to the ground, but this could not forestall the inevitable trip to the state penitentiary in Columbus.[66]

Brown arrived at the prison gates on August 10, and received a new name: No. 1654. He was forty-eight years old that summer, and as the warden interviewed the newcomer, he jotted down the rudiments of Brown's biography, lingering especially on the counterfeiter's appearance, describing him as "Well made" and possessing a "Gentlemanly appearance." The prison chaplain, who briefed Brown on the day of his arrival, likewise described him as "a man of splendid talents [who] would be capable of filling almost any office." Brown, the chaplain concluded, was no ordinary convict: "He has been a good neighbor, kind and benevolent to all around him—has lived in good style, and his family connections are generally possessed of respectability." Nevertheless, Brown's standing did not exempt him from exchanging his clothes for the striped garb that all inmates wore, a change of appearance that left Brown disconsolate. "I have never seen a man apparently so mortified at the idea of his imprisonment," the chaplain wrote. Still, when Samuel Lane visited Brown a few months later, he found the counterfeiter had been promoted to a "file leader" of a leading platoon of prisoners, marching them in lockstep to and from their duties. In time, the warden promoted him to run the prison hospital.[67]

As James Brown adjusted to his new life, Dan Brown remained a fugitive in the Black Swamp. After George Bates stepped down as a federal prosecutor, Dan Brown sent word he wished to retain his one-time adversary as his attorney in order to face the outstanding charges against him. Emissaries went back and forth between Brown and Bates, and after considerable negotiation, Bates met Brown in a dilapidated stagehouse on the outskirts of the swamp in 1847 or 1848. Bates's account, which he published several decades later, may well be embroidered, but its portrayal of the dapper counterfeiter was corroborated by other accounts. "Brown received me with the grace of a prince," wrote Bates. "He made a pitcher of punch and offered it to me, but I declined to drink until he first did so, to which he replied with elegant grace; 'Bates, gentlemen of our profession never drink. It won't do.'" Bates drank alone that day, sipping punch from a silver goblet served on a silver tray. Having amassed much of the evidence against Brown, Bates was well placed to give advice on whether he should risk a trial. After hearing the evidence, Brown declined, and the two men parted, but not before the counterfeiter treated his guest to a concert. Taking out an ivory flute, he played a popular bit of music, "The Last Rose of Summer," a performance that Bates conceded was done with "exquisite taste."[68]

The year 1849 began with stunning news: gold had been discovered in California, launching a mad rush for the west coast. Dan Brown was apparently in Missouri by this time, having abandoned his hideout in the Black Swamp. Surviving court records from St. Louis suggest that at this time he may have traded in "Dan West" for a new, more elegant alias: Timothy Lacey. He was under indictment for counterfeiting in Missouri when he heard the news of the gold discoveries, and that spring headed across the plains for California. He did not pan for gold when he arrived, as almost every other newcomer did, but settled on a ranch and sold provisions out of a store. Some of his former neighbors arrived in California around the same time, including Samuel Lane and Lucy Brown's brother, William Mather, who crossed paths with one another late in the summer of 1849. Mather told Lane that he had seen Dan Brown and that when he had inquired as to what Brown was doing in the gold fields, the counterfeiter had laughed and said "O, I've been speculating a little."[69]

This was an understatement. Not long after he arrived in California, Dan Brown recognized that the gold rush presented an unprecedented opportunity to make money in both a literal and figurative sense. The usual problems that plagued the nation's economy underwent a surreal reversal in California. There was a shortage of paper currency, but a surfeit of raw gold that circulated as currency. While "real" in a way that paper money never was, unprocessed gold was an inconvenient medium of exchange, especially for miners heading back home. Dan Brown recognized that what the miners wanted—indeed, what they needed—was paper money, and he swiftly commissioned counterfeit fifty and hundred dollar bills on the State Bank of Missouri, an institution with an unquestioned reputation.[70]

As Dan Brown's plot unfolded, his father's fortunes took a turn for the better. In June 1849, a cholera epidemic broke out within the penitentiary walls at Columbus, and James Brown, whom fate had put in charge of the prison hospital, found himself at the center of a catastrophe. Brown was well suited to the challenge. According to Samuel Lane, the counterfeiter remained "cool-headed and calm," and assumed control of the efforts to nurse the hundreds of inmates who fell ill. Many died; prison officials believed that many more had been spared because of Brown's intervention. After the epidemic burned itself out the following month, the warden and other administrators at the prison argued that Brown's heroism should be rewarded, and they successfully lobbied President Zachary Taylor for a pardon. Brown walked away from prison a free man not long afterward, on July 22, 1849, promising that he would never return to his former vocation.[71]

There may have been time for Brown to reform, but it was too late to save his son. In September 1849, Dan Brown and two accomplices began putting the notes into circulation. They found an enthusiastic reception among the miners, particularly those from Missouri. As Samuel Lane wrote, "What wonder [was] it then, that, when a gentlemanly appearing traveling broker appeared among the miners, with bright, new and crisp $50 and $100 bills on their favorite home bank," that the Missouri emigrants "should eagerly jump at them, even paying a small premium in gold dust at current rates?" Brown swiftly converted his entire stash—close to $100,000 worth of counterfeit notes—into gold dust, a feat of alchemy unmatched by any counterfeiter prior to that time. In passing so many high-denomination notes in so short a time, Brown was taking an extraordinary risk, especially given the miners' fondness for vigilante justice. He apparently factored that into his calculations when he commissioned the counterfeits, which were of very high quality. Unsuspecting note brokers took in tens of thousands of dollars of the counterfeits, as did the tellers of the Bank of the State of Missouri.[72]

On October 5, 1850, Brown and two accomplices left San Francisco aboard the steamer *New Orleans,* bound for Panama. No telegraph connected California with the rest of the country, and so long as the counterfeiters could keep ahead of the miners, who eventually discovered the fraud, they would be safe. The three men occupied a large state room, where they set up a gaming table, inviting their fellow passengers to play cards and gamble. But all was not well. One passenger would later testify that Brown alias Lacey was "tall, sickly, and very yellow." His uncle, who had described Brown to Lane as "in mighty poor health," believed that he had consumption, or tuberculosis. Lane would later speculate that he had scurvy, though this seems improbable. Whatever the ailment, Brown must have realized that something was amiss by the time the boat docked in Panama and he crossed the isthmus. There he and his partners boarded a steamer bound for New York City, paying their fare in counterfeit money.[73]

The trio arrived home the first week of November. The counterfeits had by this time been discovered, and the police arrested Brown's accomplices in New York City; Brown managed to escape back to Ohio with the help of friends. Discovery of the plot in California sparked outrage, prompting the formation of a vigilante committee that sent detectives in pursuit of Brown. They would not reach him in time: Brown spent his final weeks settling his legal affairs, distributing his wealth, and transferring the title of the farm to his brother, James Jr., who never entered the family business. Daniel Brown Jr. died on January 21, 1851, and his parents buried him in the front yard of the house, very close to the edge of the bluff that overlooked the river below. A delegation of Californians arrived not long afterward, demanding to know the whereabouts of Brown. Most gave up after learning he had died, but one detective remained skeptical and ordered Brown's casket disinterred. One look at "the cadaverous remains therein reposing" was enough to convince this final skeptic, and Brown was buried once more.[74]

The death of James and Lucy Brown's oldest son left the family devastated. James Brown, already described as a "moderate drinker" in prison records, became a full-blown alcoholic around this time. According to an affidavit that Lucy Brown would file the following year, James Brown had been a "habitual drunkard for the last three years or more." She testified that her husband had driven her from the house in the fall of 1850, and threatened to hurt her. By the following spring she gave up, filing for divorce. After the court sided with his wife, Brown left the house, moved to Cleveland, and continued his counterfeiting operations from the safety of the city. In 1857, a local resident wrote that "Jim Brown survives. He may be seen, a gray haired, broken down old man in the grog shops of Cleveland, where he is revered by the gamblers and small rogues of that city." Even in his inebriated state, Brown continued to oversee counterfeit operations throughout the Middle West, though he spent most of his time in cities.[75]

He was not alone. By the mid-nineteenth century, the business of counterfeiting was moving from frontier regions to other places where the rule of law was tenuous at best: the nation's burgeoning urban centers. In western cities like Cincinnati, St. Louis, Louisville, and Brown's Cleveland, an urban criminal subculture was emerging. There was safety in cities: venal police officers, corrupt courts, and overburdened prosecutors helped make counterfeiting profitable enterprises in these places. But it was in the eastern cities, New York City in particular, that counterfeiting reached its zenith. There, more than anywhere, conditions favored the counterfeiters. Not only was the legal system ill-equipped to stop counterfeiting, but also the city's ever-growing number of inhabitants, most of them strangers to one another, made it the ideal place for passing counterfeit currency. As counterfeiters in New York City prospered, so too did publishers of so-called counterfeit detectors like the one that Herman Melville described in the closing pages of *The Confidence Man*. Indeed, the contest between passers of counterfeits and detectors of counterfeits was to undermine still further the nation's confidence in the legitimacy of its currency.[76]

FIVE

Passing
and Detecting

On February 3, 1854, sometime between seven and eight o'clock in the evening, the door to James Montgomery's New York City dry goods store opened with a rush of cold air. As the lamp light flickered, a young woman walked into the store. In all likelihood she was respectably dressed, despite the shop's proximity to the notorious Five Points neighborhood a few blocks away, and after browsing for a few minutes, she selected items costing fifty-eight cents, handing a three-dollar note on the Union Bank to the store-keeper's wife, who waited behind the counter. She peered at the bill, then handed it to her husband for closer examination. As the customer waited, Montgomery laid the bill next to a pamphlet called a counter-feit detector. He leafed through its pages, turning to the catalog of known counterfeits on the Union Bank. Finding nothing suspicious, he accepted the bill. The customer took her change, bade farewell, and left the shop, disappearing into the night. Only a few minutes later, Montgomery learned from the clerk of an adjoining store that the note was in fact a counterfeit, and the woman a "passer," or "shover," of bogus money.[1]

In ordinary, mundane transactions like these, the counterfeit economy infiltrated the conventional economy. Though the stage on which these acts of buying and selling took place might vary—a dry goods shop in the city, a general store on the frontier, a saloon aboard a steamboat—the actors and props remained the same: the proprietor struggling to divine the authenticity of money, the shover masquerading as an honest customer, and the often useless counterfeit detector or bank note reporter occupying an honored place at the table of exchange. In this case, the passer, an illiterate Irish immigrant named Mary Condon, went to prison for the crime. But her case was an exception: passers of counterfeits almost always escaped detection and prosecution, and their imitations generally slipped undetected into the wider world. That they did with such frequency was less a testament to the quality of the counterfeits than a measure of the shovers' talent. Adopting the outward trappings of respectability—expensive garments, jewelry, refined manners, clean bodies, and clean clothes—shovers like Condon worked hard to cultivate trust in settings where appearances mattered. In other words, the success of these fraudulent transactions required a convincing performance of class identity: that the shover was too much of a lady—or too much of a gentleman—to knowingly pass a counterfeit note.

Yet few shovers could count themselves members of genteel society. The majority came from the ranks of the working class, and while a few of these artisans of exchange reveled in the risks of passing counterfeits, most plied their trade out of economic necessity. The reasons varied: some shovers could not find work, while others, particularly women, were widowed and without sufficient means of support. Whatever the cause of their poverty or misfortune, however, most shovers could trace their troubles to the larger capitalist transformations of the era, which depended on the exploitation of a growing number of poorly paid workers. It was in cities like New York that these laborers came together in the greatest numbers, scraping out an existence from wage work and casual labor, very much at the mercy of the boom and bust cycles that convulsed the nineteenth-century capitalist economy. And it was these same men and women who fed the demand for counterfeit notes, passing the bogus bills to make ends meet.

The sanitized vision of capitalism that bank notes portrayed could not conceal an equally disturbing truth: in a nation increasingly composed of strangers and filled with an ever-growing number of banks and bank notes, it was impossible to assess the value of a note from its appearance alone. People doing business had to rely on the "look" of the person presenting it—that is, clues to their class status derived from the way they moved, talked, and handled the money. But all these emblems could be counterfeited, and were no more fixed and certain than was the amount of gold and silver backing the bills. Such ambiguity proved intolerable for most people, and by the 1830s, enterprising publishers began hawking counterfeit detectors like the one that sat on the counter of James Montgomery's dry goods store. Printed every week or month, these publications provided detailed descriptions of all known counterfeits in circulation. They claimed to offer the only reliable line of defense against the growing tide of fraudulent currency, but as Montgomery's experience confirmed, they often failed to include the newest counterfeit bills.

Nor did the counterfeit detectors restore confidence to the currency. Indeed, the publishers of these guides had little incentive to help in this regard: demand for detectors thrived in an atmosphere of fear, uncertainty, and rumor, and the more bad bills in circulation, the better their business. Worse, many of the publications proved far more useful to counterfeiters than to their subscribers. Engravers of counterfeits used them to refine and perfect their issues, while shovers often exploited the false sense of security they provided in order to pass new varieties of phony notes. Disreputable financiers—"*legal* counterfeiters"—likewise turned the detectors to their own ends, bribing publishers to "puff" notes of illegitimate, ill-founded, or shaky banks. In the end, the proliferation of these pamphlets demonstrated just how far the protection of the currency—originally a prerogative of the federal government—had fallen, like the money supply itself, into the hands of private entrepreneurs. That the detectors offered little protection against the chaos of the currency did not go unnoticed. As one critic observed, the counterfeit detector "only announces the extent of the evil; it does not cure it . . . The fact is, nobody can tell the good from the bad." Confronted with crumbling categories, many shopkeepers, merchants, retailers, and other money handlers abandoned the quest for certainty, substituting in its place a corrupt pragmatism. Their informal credo—better a well-crafted imitation on a reputable bank than a genuine issue of a bad bank—further eroded the divide between the real and the counterfeit.[2]

The Underworld

The members of what one newspaper jokingly called the "society for passing *cogniac*" had multiple motivations for shoving counterfeits. More than a few belonged to the growing class of vagabonds and confidence men who mingled in marginal spaces of the nation's burgeoning cities. These wanderers did not conform to the demands of an increasingly commercial society: hard work, discipline, and temperance were not the virtues they admired. Individuals of this stamp, one suspect recalled, spent their days "sporting [and] playing cards, dice, & wheel of fortune." By their own admission, many of these rogues—men, mostly—chose their profession. Sile Doty, a thief and occasional passer of counterfeit notes, recalled how he dreaded being caught, for fear of spending time in prison "passing the time learning a trade, that might be useful to my fellow beings," a prospect he found "not at all pleasing and entirely out of my line of business." To Doty and others like him, shoving offered a way around the work ethic of a middle-class, commercial society, though they usually resorted to passing counterfeits when other ventures proved less lucrative. Shoving was a way to make ends meet, not earn a living.[3]

For others, particularly women, passing notes became a career unto itself. The most famous of these characters was Honora Shepherd neé O'Brien, whom we met earlier as the daughter-in-law of Abraham Shepherd, one of the country's largest dealers in counterfeit notes. Described by one chronicler as "the most talented, sagacious, scheming, and dangerous female counterfeiter in the country," Shepherd proved adept at extricating herself from difficult situations. If confronted by a storekeeper, she would turn on the charm, "smile him out of his resolve, and eventually he would bow her out of his store, satisfied that she was too much of a lady to willfully attempt to defraud him." One contemporary described her as a "winning woman" and made much of her "youthful beauty," particularly her "dark hair and eyes, and extremely arching eyebrows," and recalled that Shepherd had remarkable "powers of language, and well understands the effects of female tears upon judge and jury." Though eventually convicted on a counterfeiting charge in New York City in 1843, Shepherd's reputation grew after she escaped from her holding cell at the notorious "Tombs" by disguising herself in boys' clothing. She spent several weeks at large before the city's leading officers captured her once again, though "not without a struggle," as one newspaper reported. "She is a very powerful woman."[4]

The court sentenced Shepherd to eight years and three months in Mt. Pleasant Prison, better known as Sing Sing. She swiftly attracted the sympathy of several matrons at the penitentiary, including Eliza

FIGURE 19. Famed shover Honora Shepherd passed this note in 1848. Not a true counterfeit, it is a "raised note," having been altered from a one-dollar bill to a ten-dollar bill. *Courtesy, New York City Municipal Archives.*

Farnham, who later became active in feminist and abolitionist circles. Farnham and her assistant, Georgiana Bruce, thought they saw in Shepherd the "dawn of a reformation," and with the help of the Prison Association managed to secure her a conditional pardon. "They procured her release," reported the association, and "encouraged her . . . to avoid for ever the society in which her early life had been spent." Bruce took Shepherd to rural Illinois, where Shepherd found work as a dressmaker and domestic servant. She did well at first, and Bruce reported "there is no turning back." But for some reason, Shepherd drifted back to New York City and into her old habits. She was caught in 1848 passing a counterfeit at an apothecary's shop, and put on trial once more. Her former supporters published several editorials portraying her "relapse" as "melancholy evidence of the difficulty of carrying on the work of individual reform in the midst of existing social tendencies." She was, mourned one newspaper, a testament to "the force of early habits and impressions."[5]

This assessment may have been true, but many of the individuals who became full-time passers did so for reasons that cannot adequately be explained by the "idleness" of men like Sile Doty or the "habits" of women like Honora Shepherd. These explanations, as compelling as they might have been to moral reformers, obscured the fact that most people passed counterfeits because they needed the money to survive. In New York City, for example, the vast majority of shovers who were arrested lived in the region of Five Points, the Bowery, or one of the many working-class neighborhoods that lined the East River. The people who flooded into these enclaves lived at the epicenter of a momentous transformation in economic relations, experiencing firsthand the disintegration of an older system of master craftsmen, journeymen, and apprentices, and their replacement by petty entrepreneurs, wage laborers, and outworkers. Some gained by these changes, but most lost, and a growing number of men and women found themselves at the mercy of a labor market that yielded scant wages when times were good, and nothing at all when times were bad. That these workers made up the difference by passing counterfeits of the same bank notes used to underwrite this economic transformation was an irony that did not go unnoticed.[6]

Many of those arrested for passing counterfeits cited their economic misfortune when explaining their behavior. Henry Pemberton, a barkeep who had been out of work for several months, told the examining magistrate that he and his "wife & five children were in want of many things." Others picked up for passing offered similar personal histories, even if they did not admit wrongdoing. When asked about his occupation, one man testified that he had been out of work for eleven months, adding, "I have rec'd money from my father & have tryed to get into business." One newspaper article likewise described novice passers as "blundering, miserable wretches, out of employment, and coaxed into the older villains' dens, by other agents, already broken in, who get five dollars, in bad money, for every customer they bring; and finally, they are induced, through absolute distress, to take their notes and pass them." The paper added that one of these new recruits had been "tempted to the crime in hopes of procuring a little money to buy potatoes for his family, a wife and three children, who were in great want." With needs of this nature, it was difficult to resist temptation. Women had even greater incentives to traffic in counterfeits, especially if they had lost a husband or other means of support, but even single women might supplement their income by passing the occasional counterfeit.[7]

But where to buy counterfeits? It was not difficult: residents in working-class communities in the nation's cities knew which of their neighbors bought and sold counterfeit notes. Dealers may not have advertised their wares, but they hardly tried to conceal their reputation. Sooner or later, in hushed conversations behind closed doors and in gossip traded on street corners, news of who sold "coney" eventually got around. More specific information about new counterfeits also originated with the shovers, most of whom would periodically approach their dealers to learn of new shipments. For instance, a New York City shover named Philip Selover told the court how he had visited his dealer, and asked him "if any thing was in market." The man replied that "there was none but old stuff," but assured Selover "that there would be something new, and good the latter part of the week, which would be good for this market." The news would travel fast, and in the city's oyster cellars, bars, and brothels, word of the impending shipment would circulate. Distributors would send "secret information to the passers of counterfeit money," reported one newspaper, who would then "meet at a particular time and place to make purchases." Though the police might hear of these new issues through informers, they generally could do little beyond issuing vague warnings.[8]

Counterfeit money often arrived late, if it arrived at all. In New York City, one shover related how he and two itinerant dealers in counterfeit money named Horace and Hannibal Bonney (identical twins, no less) met with others in the trade at a tavern named, appropriately enough, "The Exchange." "The subject of counterfeit money was talked of, and the cause of the delay," he testified. In this case, someone had been taken into police custody. Indeed, arrests were a persistent problem: two decades earlier, a police informer in Philadelphia had reported that the "Trade" had sustained a "considerable shock [because] there had been several arrests lately . . ." Other problems could crop up. The shover Philip Selover testified that he had heard from an associate who had learned from "Abm. Shepherd's boy" that the workmen who had been "striking off the Newport twos got Drunk & injured the plate," and that "the plate has been sent up to Canada to get fixed." Delays like these only stoked the counterfeit market, as supplies dried up and demand rose. In this way, if not in a more fundamental fashion, counterfeits mimicked the pricing movements of commodities bought and sold in markets sanctioned by the state.[9]

Like their more legitimate counterparts, dealers in counterfeits had a range of tactics for increasing demand. Some drummed up interest in impending issues by sharing samples of the notes for sale. One witness in the case of a retailer testified that the suspect had "shewed him two five dollar Counterfeit Bank Notes" and told him "that he could get any quantity that he might want of such notes," offering to sell them at the rate of thirty dollars genuine for every one hundred dollars counterfeit. In another case, a passer named Willard Warner alleged that a small-time retailer had sent him a note with several high-quality counterfeits attached. If Warner was interested, the note promised, a "man will be Here—at 12 o'clk. So you can have what you want. He Left these to be seen as a Sample." The price was forty dollars genuine per hundred counterfeit—a bit high, but reasonable if the notes were as good as the retailer claimed. Dealers often let customers judge for themselves, showing sample counterfeits side by side with a genuine bill. One witness in a case against Smith Davis testified that Davis had shown her the counterfeits and then pulled out a "a good Three Dollar Bill of said Bank to convince her by comparison that the Bills were well executed." For someone contemplating a purchase, it helped to know that the props to be used in a performance would command confidence. A passer's livelihood—and freedom—were at stake.[10]

Thanks to variations in quality, prices for counterfeits varied from issue to issue. In general, manufacturers sold their notes to wholesalers at the rate of ten dollars genuine per one hundred dollars counterfeit, though some issues might command a higher (or lower) price in the market. By the time a "boodle" had passed through the hands of distributors like Abraham Shepherd, the price for retailers might be twenty or thirty per hundred. "The price," one newspaper reported, "varies from 25 to 30 cents per dollar, according to the *merit* of the bill." Prices went up as the notes moved through the underground economy, and the arrival of each boodle tended to bring out the entrepreneur in anyone who had capital on hand to purchase some bills. As a consequence, the retail business was extraordinarily fluid, full of individuals trying to extract miniscule margins of profit from buying and selling counterfeit notes. This inevitably led to competition, and it was not at all unusual for shovers to shop around when contemplating the purchase of a new batch of counterfeits. One shover testified that he met a dealer through a volunteer fire company who offered to sell him counterfeit money at twenty dollars per hundred, but then "fell down to $18 per hundred" when the prospective customer declined.[11]

Not everyone had enough cash on hand to buy into a new emission. Dealers therefore accepted alternative currencies: jewelry, clothing, and other valuables. More common was the practice of advancing counterfeits for a promise of future payment. Sile Doty, for instance, related in his memoirs how he met with a dealer from New York City who sold him money for "thirty cents on the dollar." Doty purchased $1,200 worth of counterfeit notes, "paying him nearly all down; for the remaining amount he was to wait three months." Many shovers who had no capital of their own turned to more marginal dealers, who would buy up small batches of counterfeit notes and "advance" them, a method that mimicked the commission system. One suspect testified, for instance, that a dealer had been "in the practice of furnishing [him] with counterfeit Bank Notes, to pass off for one half of the proceeds of such notes." This system of advancing notes and splitting the change was most popular among single women, few of whom could purchase counterfeit notes outright. In a typical case, Smith Davis approached two women living in Five Points, offering to advance some high-quality counterfeits that they would then pass "for his and their mutual benefit." Not all dealers proved so generous. Thomas Lynch, a witness in a shoving case, related that he had been approached by an acquaintance named Brown who "asked him if he wished to make money fast." Yes, he replied, and Brown then told him to take a five-dollar note and buy some oysters, promising that he would give him a miniscule fraction of the change. Lynch argued that "it was a slow way of making money," to which Brown retorted, "not if you pass plenty of them." The same logic of exploitation persisted all the way down the economic ladder, with people engaged in counterfeiting continually shifting the burden of risk to individuals less fortunate than themselves.[12]

Counterfeit notes, like any other commodity, did not travel in a straight line from producer to consumer, but followed a circuitous path through chains of sellers and resellers, each of whom extracted slivers of profit. This resemblance to more acceptable forms of commerce did not go unnoticed, and even attracted a kind of grudging admiration. One paper characterized counterfeiting as "a regular business," one in which "the dealers fall short of other professions only in not putting up sign boards," while another observed that the selling and shoving of counterfeit notes "had all the form and system of a regular business." It possessed a comparable level of specialization, obeyed the same laws of supply and demand, and relied on the same exploitative practices used by petty entrepreneurs to turn a profit. But however much it resembled the market in wheat or corn or shoes, the inner workings of the counterfeit economy were only dimly understood by most people. Not that they did not think or worry about counterfeits. Far from it: every time a bank note entered their hands, it was scrutinized, examined, and held up to judgment. So, too, was the person who presented it.[13]

Commanding Confidence

Successful shoving required that both the shover and the counterfeit note perform according to the expectations of middle-class commercial society, which meant coming across as "authentic" and worthy of confidence. Conventional wisdom of the day held that the most obvious indicator of a bank note's authenticity was the quality of the engraving. As one authority opined, "No counterfeiter, working with his hand, can possibly attain the beauty and accuracy of engraving by the perfect and costly machinery of professional engravers." According to this view, only second-rate artists, "runaway apprentices, and cast-off journeymen" counterfeited bank notes. Nothing was further from the truth: both crude genuine notes and elegant counterfeit bills passed from hand to hand. Still, such assumptions became commonplace, and the quality of the engraving could become more important than the authenticity of the note itself. This was true of the signature on the note as well. The same authority believed that counterfeit handwriting was "almost invariably clumsy and *unbusinesslike*." Counterfeiters, he believed, could parrot but never fully impersonate the signature of a genuine man of commerce. In an era when handwriting was an index of character, a poorly signed note signaled base intent—or so the theory went.[14]

Shovers recognized these prejudices, and demanded high-quality imitations. But artful engravings and fine penmanship were just the beginning; shovers knew that the identity of the note imitated was just as important to the success of a shoving expedition. Counterfeits on dubious banks inevitably attracted scrutiny, increasing the chances of detection. But counterfeits on banks with a good reputation could often pass even when the person receiving it suspected a counterfeit. From a storekeeper's perspective, counterfeits on reputable banks were easier to dispose of than genuine notes of disreputable banks. The ideal counterfeit, then, was a well-engraved note (probably a three-, five-, or ten-dollar bill) on a bank with a solid reputation, but not so familiar that victims could compare it with an authentic note. In New York City, shovers favored notes of well-established banks in New England, Pennsylvania, or even upstate New York. Only rarely did they attempt to pass imitations of local banks. In western states, shovers preferred counterfeits of eastern banks, which enjoyed more confidence than local banks.[15]

People trying to detect counterfeits looked at more than the name, quality of the engraving, and denomination of the note presented to them; they also scrutinized the note for evidence of a past—evidence of confidence granted and accepted in previous lives. Did it, in other words, show signs of wear and tear, of having passed inspection with others? A crisp, clean bill was suspicious: it had no history, no hint of having withstood the test of trust. Shovers turned these prejudices to their advantage. William Stuart would oil his counterfeits, fold them in blotting paper and then iron them in order to remove the "stiffness and rattling" of new notes. In a similar fashion, a passer recalled how he dipped his counterfeits in a solution of tobacco and soap and then patted them dry with ash, "until they had the limber, yellow appearance of old bills." Honora Shepherd soaked her notes in tobacco juice, while Peter O'Brien (Shepherd's brother) advised a passer to soak the notes in a basin of water with tobacco and then "put two or three pin holes in them to make it appear as if they had been thro the Bank." This was a clever strategy: banks shipped notes for redemption in bundles sewn together with needle and thread. A pin hole in a bank note implied that the bank itself had authenticated it.[16]

Bank employees were thought to possess special powers of counterfeit detection. The average teller, a popular guide to New York City's banks claimed, "acquires an instinctive faculty for the detection of spurious bills. To stand by and observe him counting, it might be supposed that he could hardly get a glimpse of each, so rapidly do they pass through his hands." And yet this same account related that the teller would periodically toss a note back to a depositor, "without perceptible pause in the swift handling," and bark out "Counterfeit!" Though impressive, this talent for detecting counterfeits was restricted to a handful of people who processed money for a living. This may explain why shovers rarely foisted their notes off on these more knowledgeable figures. Dealers might brag to their customers that a new issue could pass undetected at banks and brokers' offices, but no self-respecting shover would take such a risk. Instead, shovers targeted people with enough coins and small bills on hand to change the note, but not so well versed in money that they might recognize the counterfeit.[17]

This meant seeking out petty entrepreneurs: grocers, dry-goods dealers, shoe sellers, oyster bar owners, clothiers, milliners, tobacconists, druggists, butchers, bakers, and other middling entrepreneurs. New York City had the highest concentration of these retail establishments in the country, thanks to its growing importance as a commercial entrepôt. Further, these stores had plenty of the sorts of small items that shovers purchased in order to receive both the items and true money as change. For example, when Honora Shepherd returned to her old haunts and began shoving notes once more, she was arrested after passing a counterfeit ten on a grocer in payment for a ham and a bar of soap. Mundane purchases, to be sure, but Shepherd received, the grocer later testified, "eight Dollars and seventy five cents in change." Anyone passing counterfeit notes had to be careful, though, not to present too large a note relative to the size of the purchase. This would lead to a minute inspection of the bill, if not a close examination of the person presenting it.[18]

Shovers developed a range of ingenious tactics to avoid detection. One newspaper observed that shovers usually passed their notes "at dusk, or in the evenings," or as one merchant complained, "just about candle lighting." This was not a coincidence: counterfeits had a far better chance of passing inspection in the faint interior illumination cast by candles, whale oil, or gas. Other shovers targeted people outdoors at night, where the light was even poorer. For instance, an omnibus driver in New York City testified that he received a suspect note around midnight, "and it being dark, [he] could not fully distinguish the character of the bill, and could not leave his box to ascertain its character." Rather than refuse it, the driver "presumed the bill to be good," only to discover in the morning that it was worthless. Likewise, passers of counterfeit coin tended to operate after nightfall because the "leaden appearance" of such coins was "not so perceptible."[19]

Passers of counterfeit notes also avoided detection by working in pairs. One person would hold the counterfeit notes and wait outside retail establishments while the other went inside to make a purchase. As the *National Police Gazette* explained, the shover would take "about twenty-five or thirty cents in his pocket," along with a single counterfeit note, and then enter the store and purchase a small item. Upon "finding his change insufficient to the price," the shover would then "present the note and receive good money in change." Having done this, he would meet up with his accomplice, transfer the good money to him, and receive another spurious note in exchange. "These measures," explained the *National Police Gazette,* "were pursued to prevent danger, in case suspicion should fall upon the passer, and a search ensue." Still, the person passing the note assumed most of the risk, and the relationship between the partners was anything but equal. One shover testified that his accomplice said, "If you are asked anything about the money you must not say anything," and warned him that if he "blowed"—squealed—he "would kill him."[20]

In the 1840s, shovers began working in groups, in response to the increased speed with which merchants and retailers alerted one another about new counterfeits. These gangs, which often passed vast quantities of notes into circulation before anyone realized, operated under the auspices of dealers in counterfeit money. An acquaintance of the Bonney twins, for example, remembered how one of the brothers told some shovers that he wanted "to make arrangements where to meet and which way we shall go so as not to run afowl of each other." Bonney divided up the city streets between two groups, ordering them to begin passing notes at exactly six o'clock and reconvene at the corner of Grand and Crosby Streets at "half past eight." In similar instances, gangs of shovers from out of town would visit New York City, "put off" their notes in unison, and then flee back home across state lines. Members of Abraham Shepherd's family, many of whom lived in New Jersey, perfected this practice, making fast-paced forays across the river to New York City. By midcentury, coordinated operations began to span entire states, and eventually, the entire nation. These elaborate ruses probably aimed to frustrate the growing use of the telegraph, which could spread news of counterfeits almost instantaneously.[21]

Shopkeepers tried to protect themselves, questioning and inspecting the person presenting the note. It was not uncommon to interrogate unfamiliar patrons, asking them where they lived. This tactic had its roots in the late eighteenth and early nineteenth centuries, when most passers lived a more peripatetic existence. "Wicks and I put our horses together, and under cover of night drove beyond the reach of familiar faces," recalled Sile Doty in his memoirs. "Here I was, for the first time to try my hand at passing counterfeit money." In similar fashion, William Stuart recalled how "we rode about the country, bought watches, jockeyed horses, bought sheep, and other stock, paying for them chiefly in counterfeit money." It was risky to linger in any one place after shoving notes in rural areas: the fraud might be discovered and an arrest made. Many shovers operating in the countryside thus passed themselves off as peddlers, circuit riders, drovers—anything to explain their wandering ways. Canal boats and river steamers offered even better means of moving from place to place, and many shovers worked on these vessels, leaving counterfeits in their wake.[22]

Yet it was the nation's burgeoning cities that provided the best opportunities to pass counterfeits with minimal risk. This was especially the case in New York City, where the expanding metropolis began to fragment into smaller neighborhoods defined by class. Shovers could now visit parts of the city where storekeepers and retailers might not know them, much less trace them back to their homes. Indeed, the population growth of cities like New York—and the consequent level of anonymity—meant that people no longer recognized everyone they saw in the street. Nor could retailers identify everyone who came in to purchase an item. Many city dwellers, especially members of the middle class, necessarily turned to other methods of determining character, "reading" a stranger's appearance for signs of their social status, if not their criminal intent. People receiving money looked not only for counterfeit bank notes, but also for counterfeit persons. This strategy had some merit: an inexperienced passer might come across as nervous and unsure, leading to an arrest. But more often than not, these attempts to read character out of trivial details only resulted in people falling back on preconceived biases. An ill-mannered laborer who presented a note would get a closer inspection than someone who had all the markings of the middle class. But the counterfeiting community again turned these prejudices to their advantage. Female shovers became especially infamous for passing off counterfeits—by passing off themselves as "ladies."[23]

Women had many advantages over men when it came to passing counterfeits. As one newspaper complained in 1820, "Many genteel

well-dressed females are engaged, and such is their favorable and imposing appearance, that when they are sometimes arrested and brought
into courts of law, juries cannot be brought to believe them guilty, or to
convict them." Another paper put the matter more bluntly, noting that
"the females, generally, on trial, escape conviction. They are decked out
in genteel attire and are called 'Ladies' [and] the police magistrate is lib-
erally abused before the Jury for having given a fair and impartial account of the character and career of the . . . 'most amiable, industrious,
virtuous, and persecuted lady,' who, by this time has performed . . . by
working herself into tears." These sorts of trials, complained the paper,
inevitably ended in a verdict of "not guilty," and "the 'lady' triumphantly
leaves the court, probably in a carriage, to return the next day in an altered dress to her vocation of passing counterfeit notes in another part
of the city."[24]

Such editorials betrayed a growing concern over the counterfeiting
not only of money, but of the very markers of "respectable society." In
1818, for example, one passer in New York City testified that an acquaintance "goes out evenings dressed up like a Lady & passes the
money." Ironically, many of the notes passed by women of this sort underwrote the purchase of the accoutrements of a middle-class wardrobe
and persona: combs, bonnets, lace, dresses, shoes, slippers, and per-
fumes. In an era when fashion was swiftly becoming democratized, it
did not take much (especially if one was paying in counterfeit money)
to buy the outward appearance of a woman from a different class. That
ease—and the concern it raised among anyone bent on policing class
boundaries—may account for an urban legend that began circulating
in the 1840s. In one variation, a passer checked into a respectable hotel, explaining that she was a widow. She would then mingle with the
other ladies in the hotel and "fall in love with . . . articles of jewelry or
dress which some one of them own," insisting that they sell them to

her "at *any price*, partly to please her fancy, and partly as a memento of the agreeable acquaintance she has formed." Having gained their confidence, she would then suddenly tell her "friends" that she had to leave sooner than expected, and "consummate whatever bargains she may have arranged, and in the hurry of the moment palm off her counterfeit money in payment, receiving in exchange for her larger bills more than sufficient good money to pay all the expenses of her visit." An account of this incident lamented that "in this *pleasant* way one class of our female counterfeiters manage to live at our best hotels, dress richly, and crowd themselves into most excellent society." The passer, who counterfeited class and cash, represented a double threat to the emergent social order. That passers patronized the stores and shops owned by members of (or aspirants to) the middle class only heightened the transgressive nature of the imposture. So, too, did the fact that it was women rather than men who proved most adept at performing these acts of duplicity.[25]

Yet men also clambered over social barriers. The key was confidence. One account of a successful shover marveled at how he "walks into a store, boldly takes off his hat, nods familiarly about, and addresses the shopboys as if he had known them for a long time, thereby keeping their attention fixed upon himself, whilst they scarcely glance at the bill. He comes in at broad daylight . . . and knows well that a bold front wins half the battle." This was the method favored by Jack Cantar, a famous confidence man and counterfeiter who moved with ease through polite society by representing himself as the son of a wealthy merchant. Cantar, who eventually usurped Smith Davis's title as "King of the Koneyackers," was famous for his dignified airs and taste in clothing. Unlike many high-ranking counterfeiters, he also passed notes, changing clothes and facial hair to deflect attention. Several individuals on whom he passed counterfeits seemed to have paid more attention to the clothing he wore than the note he presented—a rather intriguing strategy. One witness testified, for example, that Cantar had worn "French Pantaloons [of] light colored Cassimere & black & white gaiter boots," adding after some reflection, "I particularly noticed the pantaloons fitting remarkably well." Of course, most of this clothing was purchased with—what else?—counterfeit money.[26]

Cantar was a perfect specimen of the confidence man, the well-dressed (perhaps too well-dressed) stranger whose outward signs of gentility, tact, and wealth lay claim to the trust of his victims. For another illustration of this persona, look at one of Daniel Huntington's genre paintings titled *The Doubtful Note* or *The Counterfeit Note*. Critics had differing interpretations of the work when it was unveiled in the 1850s, but they generally agreed on one thing: the genteel bespectacled man with the slender walking cane (itself a totem of respectability) was trying to pass a counterfeit note. The shover, equal parts gentleman and confidence man, looks out of the corner of his eyes, a faint smile playing on his lips. As for the well-dressed woman seated in front, she too may be in on the fraud: note that her glove has been dropped in a most unladylike fashion on the floor. In the subtle vocabulary of genre painting, as among the appearance-obsessed middle classes, such details mattered. Perhaps she is his accomplice, trying to distract the storekeeper. An opening gambit like this helped set the stage for the final act in this theater of exchange: passing the counterfeit note.[27]

Shovers did not always imitate members of polite society; merely passing as an authority on monetary affairs was good enough. One account related a variation on this strategy: a man would enter a store and begin examining goods, "approving some, and condemning others." His rather "gawky air, vulgar voice and manner, when contrasted with his substantial though plain apparel gave him the air of a country store keeper." After a few minutes, his accomplice would enter the store as

FIGURE 20. *The Counterfeit Note.* This engraving duplicated Daniel Huntington's painting of the same name, which has since disappeared. *Courtesy, Newberry Library, Chicago.*

well, purchase an item, and tender a counterfeit in payment. If the note was questioned, the man posing as a storekeeper would take it and "looking knowingly at it . . . pronounce it genuine," and then offer to change it at a discount, saying things like "I fancy myself something of a judge, for I pass a pretty many of such things through my hands in a year." This "independent" authentication usually had the desired effect, and the original sale went forward. Shovers developed endless variations on this scheme, giving their victims a fleeting sense that a decent, humble, "genuine" individual had validated the note.[28]

Some shovers would cultivate confidence by giving demonstrations of their honesty and good nature. The ploys of Ellen Russell, who worked in the 1840s, are representative of this approach. In one instance, she went into an oyster cellar in New York City and treated the store owner and several others to drinks. She paid with a suspicious-looking five-dollar bill on the Albany Exchange Bank, but as one newspaper explained, "to inquire into its genuineness, coming from so decent a source as the one who had treated all hands, would be preposterous, so the bill was taken and the change given." In a similar case, a man attending the annual fair held by the American Institute in Castle Garden approached the managers, "telling them he wished to present five separate awards of $100 each 'in premiums to the most worthy mechanical inventor.'" He began visiting the fair daily, "enjoying the most distinguished consideration of the managers," and using his newfound respectability to pass off dozens of counterfeits. Better still was the shover who approached people claiming to be "employed by a company of Frenchmen to seek out poor families who wanted relief." After this masquerade, he would pull out a counterfeit five-dollar note and ask his victim to break it into smaller bills "for the purpose of having change to give away."[29]

But shovers need not make a show of superiority, knowledge, or generosity: they could simply strive to appear so artless or preoccupied as to seem incapable of mounting a fraud. Working-class women, for example, would borrow babies and cart them around while passing notes; working-class men might feign drunkenness. Some enterprising shovers also used children to pass their notes, given most shopkeepers' reluctance to order their arrest. White shovers sometimes used a similar strategy by paying blacks to pass their notes. One suspect, a black man named Jack Benson, testified that a shover came up to him and said "Jack here are two notes get them changed for me and I will give you something when you bring me [the change]." Such tactics were not uncommon; one newspaper account of a shover identified "a poor modest-looking woman, or a black boy" as being "customary instruments" for passing counterfeit notes. But the police rarely arrested—much less convicted—blacks for passing counterfeit notes in New York City. This may reflect blacks' limited numbers in the city at this time. Or it may be a testament to the conventional view then that blacks were ill-informed in monetary affairs, and thus incapable of such frauds.[30]

Yet shovers, whatever their identity, did more than play to the prejudices of their victims; many targeted individuals unlikely to detect a counterfeit, or better yet, unable to file a complaint. Men, for example, would pay for sex with counterfeit notes. A prostitute living near Five Points testified that she met a man on the street who "was a stranger to her—but she went with him to a house of assignation in Crosby Street—where she staid with him about one hour." The man gave her a bank note, but as she explained to the magistrates, "she [was] no judge of paper money and did not know the Bill was Bad"; she only learned it was counterfeit when she tried to use it to pay for a pair of shoes. In a similar vein, when the police questioned a single woman about where she received a counterfeit note, she replied, "I got it from a gentleman. I don't know who." Her interrogators pressed ahead. "For what?" they asked, to which she answered: "for the use of my body." Prostitutes had little recourse in the event a client paid in counterfeit cash, though some passed the bills to other customers when making change. So, too, did other marginal entrepreneurs—such as swindlers, gamblers, and mock auctioneers—who received them in the course of business.[31]

Some shovers targeted those least equipped to authenticate the different notes in circulation. "The poor and the illiterate are the sufferers," wrote one prison reformer. "They can easily be imposed on, because they are inexperienced." Too many of them, he noted, ended up in prison because they unwittingly passed a counterfeit received from someone else. "I can't read," complained one accidental shover, adding he could recognize "a one and a two dollar but no other bill." Immigrants had particular trouble detecting counterfeits, and they represented an ever-growing proportion of those arrested. "I have only been in the country 18 months and begin to speak English within the last three months," one French man charged with passing counterfeits told the examining magistrate in New York City. "I know nothing about the Bank Bills of this country." A petitioner in New Jersey likewise claimed that he was "only twelve weeks in this country when taken . . . was it not impossible . . . to be a judge of a Counterfeit bill or bills in the above time?"[32]

Even those skilled at the art of detecting counterfeits found themselves stuck with bad notes. John Neal, an early nineteenth-century merchant, recalled that he and his fellow employees adopted the maxim that "if you buy the devil, the sooner you sell him, the better," and set aside any counterfeits taken in the course of business. Neal, who was "by far the most innocent-looking," passed along these bad notes to "the ignorant and the helpless." Several decades later, a newspaper echoed his logic, stating that "it is a favorite maxim with some to 'keep bad money in circulation,' for they say it makes no difference whether a bill is counterfeit or not, so long as it will pass around freely." This practice—rationalized by one person as "tucking off a bad bill that somebody had tucked on to him"—became an accepted way of doing business. After all, the storekeeper left holding a counterfeit had few choices. He could try to find the shover, but this was difficult. He could also destroy it, and take a loss, but for most struggling entrepreneurs, the push for profit drove them to pass it off on someone less knowledgeable, who would in turn pass it off on someone even more ignorant. As the note moved back down the economic ladder, each person receiving it had even greater incentives to pass it along. As one reformer wrote, "There are so many cases where a Counterfeit Bill comes . . . into the possession of a man, whose penury will not permit him to lose its value, and whose duty to his needy family is paramount to his virtue." Eventually someone would pass the note and be arrested or have it confiscated, and there the chain of imposture would end.[33]

The morality of these exchanges did not go unquestioned. One editorialist, observing that "the country is becoming flooded" with counterfeits, complained that many persons stuck with bad bills "insist that as they took them in good faith, so they must pass them. But is this any better than receiving stolen goods ignorantly, and then refusing to give them up to the owner when discovered?" An intriguing question, but most people left holding counterfeits tended not to see the parallel. One bank officer wrote, "There is a lamentably lax tone of moral sense in some men . . . who find themselves caught with a bad bill. Their reasoning seems to be, 'I took it for good—it must go for the same.'" A passer of a bad note articulated the ethics of an entire generation when in one instance he dismissed his victim's accusations with the following memorable bon mot: "If it was good enough for me it was good enough for [you]."[34]

These rationalizations came easily for many people. After all, even genuine bank notes circulated on specious grounds, for there was never enough "real" money (gold and silver) in the vaults of the corporations issuing bank notes (as almost everyone who dealt in bank notes found out sooner or later). Banks suspending specie payments, or going out of business without honoring their paper promises, gave rise to a kind of economic relativism. One financial paper posed the problem as follows: "Some people live by counterfeiting—others circulate their promises by means of sham banks. Which are best?" Many who grappled with the question ultimately arrived at a subjective, instrumental theory of value. In their eyes, the value of a note depended not on whether the bank that issued it could make good on its promise, but whether someone else would accept it as genuine. One editor complained, for example, that "I have known men take a bill pronounced counterfeit, saying, coolly, 'Somebody will take it.'"[35]

The selling and shoving of bogus notes eroded the often arbitrary distinctions between counterfeiting and capitalism. In the hands of the wholesalers and dealers, counterfeit money was treated like real money: it had a value, even if it suffered from a rather heavy discount. And with a compelling performance on the part of the shover, these bills could pass at face value, and thus cross the divide between the counterfeit and the real. Absent some final arbiter of authenticity, there was little to stop this kind of categorical collapse. The federal government, which had divested itself from any meaningful role in regulating the money supply, could not be counted on to banish the ambiguities inherent in a system of private money creation. There was, however, a final line of defense for those interested in maintaining distinctions between the solid and the sham: the "counterfeit detectors," which could unlock the secret codes of the currency and restore value to its rightful owners. Or so the enterprising publishers of these paper talismans claimed.

Cataloging Counterfeits

Like the bank notes they purported to describe, counterfeit detectors came in many guises. Over the course of the antebellum era, a host of entrepreneurs published at least seventy-two different titles. The ma-

jority of publishers had their offices in Boston, New York, or Philadelphia, though several cities in the West, particularly Cincinnati, had
their own detectors, too. While a few printers began issuing lists of
counterfeits in the early nineteenth century, the more profitable publishers—Robert T. Bicknell, Sylvester J. Sylvester, Archibald McIntyre,
John S. Dye, and most famous of all, John Thompson—began publication in the 1830s, when the number of bank notes in circulation exploded. These men had an encyclopedic knowledge of the nation's paper money, having extensive experience as note brokers and lottery-
ticket salesmen.[36]

The connection between lotteries and counterfeit detectors was one
of those strange symbioses peculiar to this transitional stage in the
nation's capitalist development. The lottery-ticket business functioned
as an important precursor to private banking, investment banking, and
stock brokerage activities. In a cash-poor country like the United States,
lotteries became a means of raising money for business development.
And because lottery-ticket salesmen operated over great distances, they
had to take whatever form of payment was proffered. The diversity of
currency that these men handled led many to open offices that dis-
counted the notes of distant banks. In the inaugural issue of his counterfeit detector, editor Robert Bicknell thus boasted that he had "for
many years been engaged in the Lottery and Exchange business in
Philadelphia" and was consequently "in the habit, daily, of discounting
every description of paper money," making him well-qualified for the
task of assembling a list of all the genuine and counterfeit bank notes in
circulation. Like several of his competitors, Bicknell continued to operate his lottery business on the side, and in this same first issue, he published "the scheme" of the Union Canal Lottery.[37]

"Scheme" was an appropriate description. By the 1830s, lotteries had
fallen into disfavor, viewed by many as fraudulent enterprises. S. J.

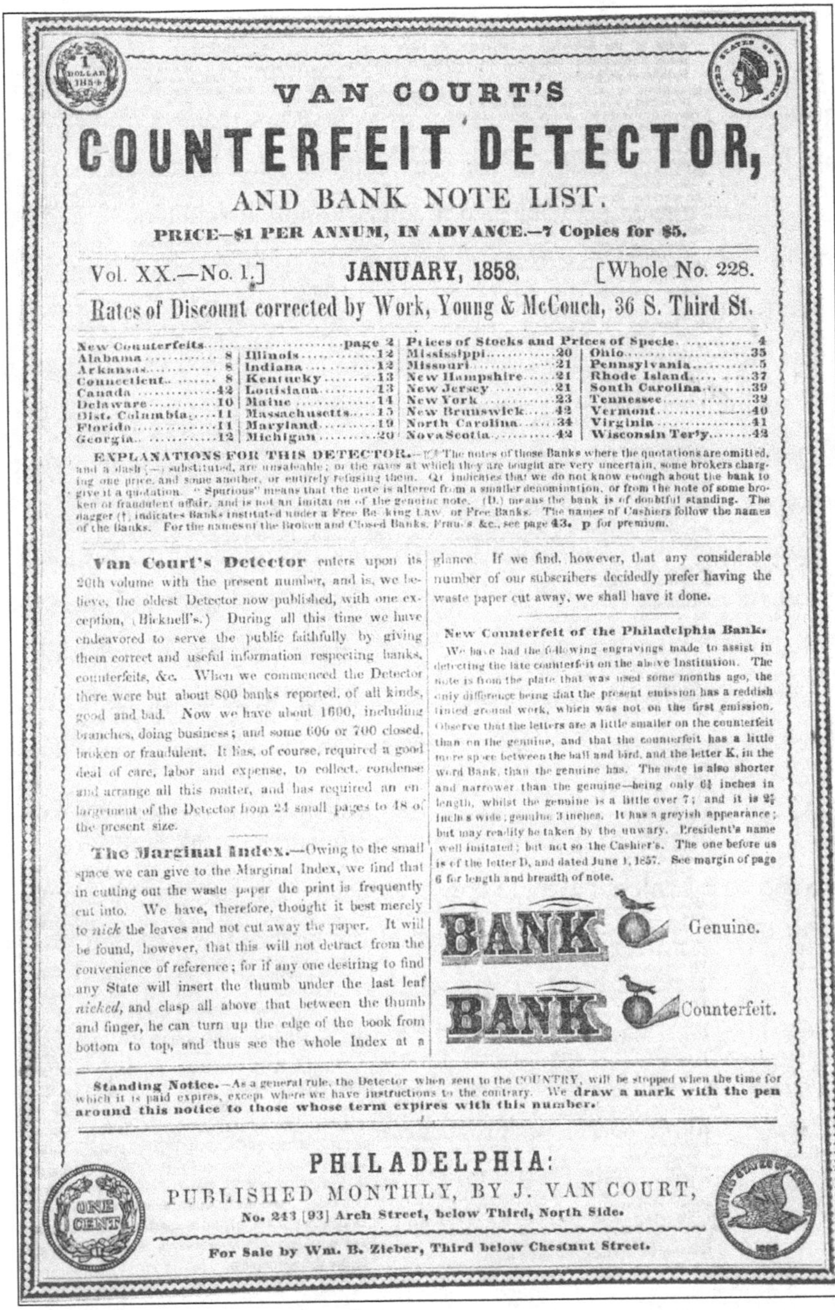

VAN COURT'S

COUNTERFEIT DETECTOR,

AND BANK NOTE LIST.

PRICE—$1 PER ANNUM, IN ADVANCE.—7 Copies for $5.

Vol. XX.—No. 1.] JANUARY, 1858. [Whole No. 228.

Rates of Discount corrected by Work, Young & McCouch, 36 S. Third St.

New Counterfeits .... page 2		Prices of Stocks and Prices of Specie 4	
Alabama 8	Illinois 12	Mississippi 20	Ohio 35
Arkansas 8	Indiana 12	Missouri 21	Pennsylvania 5
Connecticut 8	Kentucky 13	New Hampshire 21	Rhode Island 37
Canada 42	Louisiana 13	New Jersey 21	South Carolina 39
Delaware 10	Maine 14	New York 23	Tennessee 39
Dist. Columbia 11	Massachusetts 15	New Brunswick 42	Vermont 40
Florida 11	Maryland 19	North Carolina 34	Virginia 41
Georgia 12	Michigan 20	Nova Scotia 42	Wisconsin Ter'y 42

EXPLANATIONS FOR THIS DETECTOR.—☞ The notes of those Banks where the quotations are omitted, and a dash (—) substituted, are unsaleable; or the rates at which they are bought are very uncertain, some brokers charging one price, and some another, or entirely refusing them. Q. indicates that we do not know enough about the bank to give it a quotation. "Spurious" means that the note is altered from a smaller denomination, or from the note of some broken or fraudulent affair, and is not an imitation of the genuine note. (D.) means the bank is of doubtful standing. The dagger (†), indicates Banks instituted under a Free Banking Law, or Free Banks. The names of Cashiers follow the names of the Banks. For the names of the Broken and Closed Banks, Frauds &c., see page 43. p for premium.

Van Court's Detector enters upon its 20th volume with the present number, and is, we believe, the oldest Detector now published, with one exception, (Bicknell's.) During all this time we have endeavored to serve the public faithfully by giving them correct and useful information respecting banks, counterfeits, &c. When we commenced the Detector there were but about 800 banks reported, of all kinds, good and bad. Now we have about 1600, including branches, doing business; and some 600 or 700 closed, broken or fraudulent. It has, of course, required a good deal of care, labor and expense, to collect, condense and arrange all this matter, and has required an enlargement of the Detector from 24 small pages to 48 of the present size.

The Marginal Index.—Owing to the small space we can give to the Marginal Index, we find that in cutting out the waste paper the print is frequently cut into. We have, therefore, thought it best merely to *nick* the leaves and not cut away the paper. It will be found, however, that this will not detract from the convenience of reference; for if any one desiring to find any State will insert the thumb under the last leaf *nicked*, and clasp all above that between the thumb and finger, he can turn up the edge of the book from bottom to top, and thus see the whole Index at a glance. If we find, however, that any considerable number of our subscribers decidedly prefer having the waste paper cut away, we shall have it done.

New Counterfeit of the Philadelphia Bank.

We have had the following engravings made to assist in detecting the late counterfeit on the above Institution. The note is from the plate that was used some months ago, the only difference being that the present emission has a reddish tinted ground work, which was not on the first emission. Observe that the letters are a little smaller on the counterfeit than on the genuine, and that the counterfeit has a little more space between the ball and bird, and the letter K, in the word Bank, than the genuine has. The note is also shorter and narrower than the genuine—being only 6¾ inches in length, whilst the genuine is a little over 7; and it is 2¾ inches wide; genuine 3 inches. It has a greyish appearance; but may readily be taken by the unwary. President's name well imitated; but not so the Cashier's. The one before us is of the letter D, and dated June 1, 1857. See margin of page 6 for length and breadth of note.

BANK Genuine.

BANK Counterfeit.

Standing Notice.—As a general rule, the Detector when sent to the COUNTRY, will be stopped when the time for which it is paid expires, except where we have instructions to the contrary. We **draw a mark with the pen around this notice to those whose term expires with this number.**

PHILADELPHIA:

PUBLISHED MONTHLY, BY J. VAN COURT,

No. 243 [93] Arch Street, below Third, North Side.

For Sale by Wm. B. Zieber, Third below Chestnut Street.

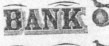

FIGURE 21. The information contained in a typical issue of a counterfeit detector swiftly lost its relevance, because new counterfeits appeared frequently on the market. *Courtesy, Library Company of Philadelphia.*

Sylvester, for example, was fined $150 for selling lottery tickets as late as 1840, and had to suffer through a lecture from the judge on the "enormity" of his misdeeds. But Sylvester was not alone: many detector publishers had dealings with the economy of chance and fortune, operating on the margins of the established financial community. They worked as intermediaries in the exchange economy, handling vast amounts of money, but they began their commercial careers with little cash of their own. Bicknell, for example, was described in his obituary as arriving in Philadelphia "a friendless orphan boy who by his own untiring exertions succeeded . . . in building up an extensive business," before dying young on account of his "unremitting devotion" to work.[38]

John Thompson had a similar biography, though he was a bit more fortunate in the lottery of life. Born on a Massachusetts farm, Thompson endured what he called "hard work and plenty of it" as a child. He eventually fled, becoming a dealer in lottery tickets for the firm of Yates and McIntyre, the same McIntyre who subsequently published a competing counterfeit detector, *McIntyre's Bank Note List.* In 1832, Thompson moved to New York City and opened a bank note brokerage. Because bank notes could only be redeemed in specie at the counter of the issuing bank, they depreciated the farther they traveled from home: a percentage point or two when times were good, much more when times were bad. Brokers like Thompson made their profit by purchasing notes of distant banks and then returning the paper to the bank for redemption in specie, with their profit coming out of the difference between the price paid by the broker and the price paid by the bank. The banks, which did not appreciate being forced to hand over their valuable specie reserves, resented brokers like Thompson, who did not hesitate to sue if notes went unredeemed.[39]

The failure to redeem bank notes, whether in times of panic or in the course of everyday business, inevitably prompted comparisons between bankers and counterfeiters. In many people's eyes, paper that could not be redeemed, for whatever reason, was as worthless as a counterfeit—or worse. At least a well-made counterfeit on a solid bank stood a chance of passing; a genuine bill of a defunct bank, by contrast, would find few takers. This blurring of categories helps explain why detectors—including the one Thompson launched in 1842—tracked not only counterfeits, but problem bank notes of all kinds, along with their perceived depreciation, rumored instability, and any other information that revealed the "confidence" that the marketplace had in various bills. Indeed, detectors documented an economy teeming with notes neither totally real nor completely counterfeit: genuine bills of banks that had suspended specie payments or had gone into receivership; notes of defunct banks that had been altered to imitate still-thriving concerns; genuine notes of solid banks that had been "raised" from a lower denomination to a higher one; notes that purported to be the issues of legitimate banks but looked nothing like the real thing; notes of banks that sounded genuine, but did not exist; and real notes of "wildcat" banks with little or nothing in the way of assets backing their promises to pay. Each of these species of notes occupied a place on the ever-changing continuum between the good and the bad, the real and the counterfeit, and all were described in elaborate, though not always accurate, detail in the pages of the detectors.

Thompson became the most successful of all the publishers of counterfeit detectors. He sold twice-weekly subscriptions for five dollars a year, and by 1855 was boasting a circulation of 100,000. He sold additional weekly and semimonthly subscriptions for three and two dollars, respectively, but even these more modest rates put *Thompson's Bank Note Reporter* out of the reach of the laboring classes; consequently, most subscribers hailed from commercial circles. Though many readers worked on Wall Street, far more lived in western states where the money supply was plagued by counterfeit and broken bank notes. *Thompson's*, which promised to restore some semblance of order to the blizzard of paper in circulation, became a standard fixture in any place of business. As one Wisconsin banker recalled, "The merchant in his store or the peddler on the prairies would as soon think of doing their business without scales, measure, or yardstick as without a 'Thompson's.'"[40]

Thompson's publications inventoried the nation's monetary system. Every bank in the United States was represented, along with the rate of discount on its notes (as offered at Thompson's many branch offices); a list of all the different denominations issued by the bank; and a compilation of all known counterfeits. His publications provided readers with a map to navigate the nation's economy. But as first-time readers soon learned, these pamphlets took practice to read. Aside from the front page, which usually contained two or three editorials and late-breaking news articles on recent counterfeits or bank failures, the bulk of the publication consisted of page after page of cryptic descriptions rendered in tiny type. Take, for example, the description of altered, counterfeit, and spurious notes circulating on the venerable Mechanics' Bank of New York City as of March 17, 1849:

> **Mechanics' Bank, 33 Wall St. . . . . . . (S.) par** [S. Knapp, Pres., Francis W. Edmonds, Cash.] Discount days—*Wednesday and Saturday.* 2s, let. A; A. B. Stevens, pres't, Jn. Clark, cash'r, dated April 2, 1840. The filling up and signing of a bill should never be relied on, as they can be altered at pleasure. 3's, altered from the 'Derby Bank' Derby, Conn., a broken institution. 5's, letter A., pay J. J. Astor, David Edmonds, Cash., Thos. D. Brown, Pres. Vig. a female & ship building. 5's altered from 1's, well executed. The word FIVE has been pasted across one end of the bill. 5's letter D. pay D. Bethune, dated May 4, 1828. 5's, let D. pay to P. Sharpe; others to A. Van Nest, July 1,

1828. 10's, good imitation of genuine, payable to P. Henry, R. Irving, and others. Filling up rather good—the signature of F. W. Edwards is not done with the ease and elegance of the original. Paper poor. 10's, altered from 2's. The word 'TEN' is printed much blacker than the rest of the note; well done. 20's, dated July 5, 1835, pay F. Hart, Fleming, pres. Baldwin, Cash.: others, let. C. pay to S. Jaudon. 20's, altered from 3's. Very well executed. 50's, let. C. pay J. J. Astor, May 13, 1835—easily detected by the signatures. Also, some pay F. Cooper, dated April 12, 1833, H. Baldwin, Cash.[41]

Translation: the bank is solid, insofar as the notes circulate at par. But the bills of the bank could be altered with ease, meaning that counterfeiters erased portions of the bill and reprinted them with different denominations and signatures. Other problems: spurious versions of the bank's three-dollar bills, printed from the plates of a broken bank; and several counterfeits (here clues to their detection were offered).

Yet without actual reproductions of the note in question, these telegraphic descriptions were vague at best and unintelligible at worst. Thompson once exhorted his readers to closely examine all one-dollar notes on the Cumberland Bank of New Jersey: "The bottom of the 'J' in JERSEY, turns to the 'E'—'PROMISE' is 1/8 of an inch from the left margin. In the genuine it almost touches it." In another issue, he told subscribers to scrutinize twenty-dollar bills on New York's Butchers' & Drovers' Bank: "20's, altered from 3's. In the true 20's, the words 'The Butchers' and Drovers' Bank are in capitals in semi-circles on the head of the bill, and the vignette representing cattle, is on the left hand margin; whereas, in 3's, all the words, 'Butchers' and Drovers' Bank,' are in a straight line in the center of the bill, and the vignette representing cattle, on the head." These distinctions, while not indecipherable, required more time than most people had in the rush of a retail transaction.

They also presumed a level of literacy that many laborers lacked, even if they had the money to purchase a detector.[42]

Other entrepreneurs exploited these shortcomings, issuing competing guides to the counterfeit economy called universal detectors. Publishers like Henry Foote and Wheeler Gillet marketed these booklets to tradesmen who could not afford a hefty annual subscription to *Thompson's* or one of the other reporters. Rather than force people to pore over esoteric listings of counterfeit notes, these pamphlets instead urged readers to look for certain fundamental signs: poor workmanship, design flaws, careless errors. Such telltale failings, Foote argued, arose because counterfeiters refused to purchase the machinery necessary to produce a genuine engraving. They would not invest so much money in an "illegitimate business"—indeed, engravers of counterfeit notes, he claimed, could not possibly be "first-class" artists and engravers. Genuine notes would look "natural" or "beautiful," while counterfeits would appear "stiff" or "scratchy." Gillet claimed that faces and features on genuine bills look "clear and natural," whereas counterfeiters "do as little as possible on faces, for the reason that the human countenance is one of the very hardest of all things to do well." Gillet therefore admonished his readers that "it is best to examine well the countenance of portraits whenever they are on a bill, and if you get the expression of the face well in your mind, it will be as impossible to deceive you with a false or counterfeit face, as it would be to deceive you with a counterfeit of one of your friends." That outward appearances inevitably betrayed a person's true, inner character was the conventional wisdom of the era, but it was no more accurate here than it was when a storekeeper tried to assess a suspected shover on appearance alone.[43]

Reliance on superficial appearances informed these authors' obsession with handwriting as well. "The round handwriting on the face of a good note . . . is invariably well done, and looks very perfect," claimed

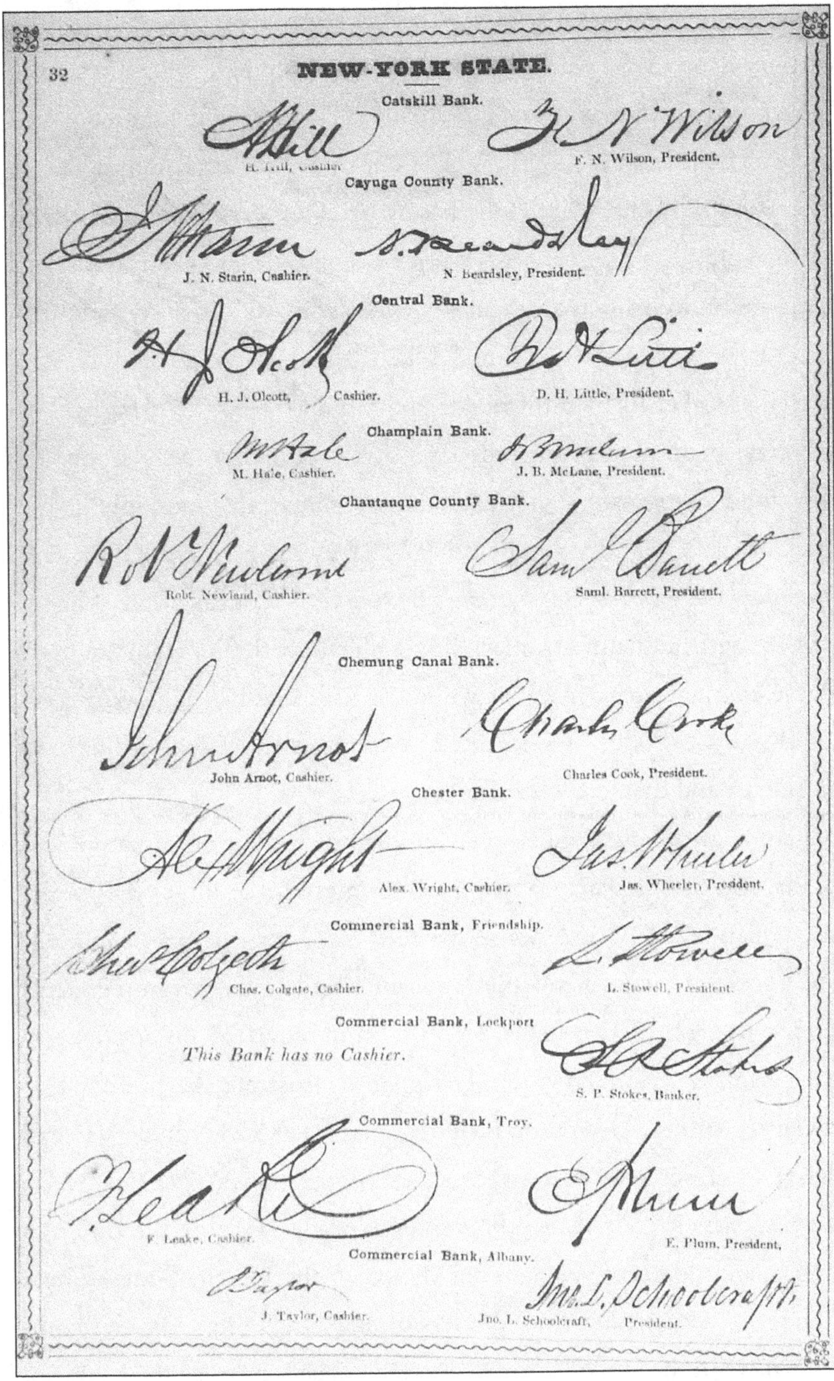
32

NEW-YORK STATE.

Catskill Bank.

H. Hill, Cashier — F. N. Wilson, President.

Cayuga County Bank.

J. N. Starin, Cashier. — N. Beardsley, President.

Central Bank.

H. J. Olcott, Cashier. — D. H. Little, President.

Champlain Bank.

M. Hale, Cashier. — J. B. McLane, President.

Chautauque County Bank.

Robt. Newland, Cashier. — Saml. Barrett, President.

Chemung Canal Bank.

John Arnot, Cashier. — Charles Cook, President.

Chester Bank.

Alex. Wright, Cashier. — Jas. Wheeler, President.

Commercial Bank, Friendship.

Chas. Colgate, Cashier. — L. Stowell, President.

Commercial Bank, Lockport

This Bank has no Cashier. — S. P. Stokes, Banker.

Commercial Bank, Troy.

F. Leake, Cashier. — E. Plum, President.

Commercial Bank, Albany.

J. Taylor, Cashier. — Jno. L. Schoolcraft, President.

FIGURE 22. John Thompson's guide to the signatures of the nation's financial elite was as useful to counterfeiters as it was to bankers trying to detect bogus notes. *Courtesy, American Antiquarian Society.*

Gillet. Foote went so far as to declare that bank clerks generally have "a very neat, rapid *business* hand," while counterfeiters' signatures were "*almost invariably clumsy and unbusinesslike.*" Such naive arguments reflected a belief that handwriting, like one's outward appearance, was an expression of individuality. One handwriting expert maintained that a person could "no more conceal" subtle peculiarities of his or her script "than he could his personal identity by drawing up his nose, squinting his eyes, or walking with a limp." Like the countenances on bills—the ones that Gillet likened to friends and familiars—handwriting was an inimitable extension of the self. That sort of thinking may account for why John Thompson published a book containing facsimile signatures of every president and cashier of every bank in the nation, *The Autographical Counterfeit Detector.* The romantic identification of handwriting with authenticity inevitably collided with the mimetic skills of the counterfeiters, many of whom had respectable handwriting, or could at least produce serviceable imitations of the signatures of bank presidents and cashiers who did.[44]

Like many of his competitors, Thompson put out other pamphlets, charts, and lists to clarify any lingering uncertainties about the money in circulation. His *Bank Note Descriptive List,* for example, contained additional information on the laws and regulations governing paper money in each of the states, along with abbreviated descriptions of every bank note in circulation. Designed to frustrate the proliferation of spurious notes, Thompson issued it once a year, giving it away free of charge to subscribers. Also free with a subscription was *The Coin Chart Manual,* which contained lithographic reproductions of the different foreign and domestic coins in circulation in the United States. These catalogs of coinage informed readers of new kinds of counterfeit coins (a problem in the antebellum era, though not so serious as the plague of counterfeit bank notes). They also provided a guide to the confusing array of hard currency in circulation. In 1849, for example, Thompson's

Coin Chart Manual listed no fewer than 850 different coins, of which only a handful came from the U.S. Mint. To be sure, few readers saw most of these coins. But well into the 1850s, foreign coins occupied a dominant role in the nation's hard currency supply, highlighting just how little control the national government had over monetary matters.[45]

Other guides, most notably John Dye's *Bank Mirror and Illustrated Counterfeit Delineator* and John Tyler Hodges's *American Bank Note Safeguard*, offered similar object lessons. Like the coin charts, these annual volumes relied on pictorials to convey their message, though they did so in a more schematic fashion. By 1860, the *American Bank Note Safeguard* ran to 378 pages, filled with crude facsimiles of the more than ten thousand different notes in circulation. Hodges sought to classify the country's currency, breaking it down to its constituent parts. He succeeded in this task, but his volumes also revealed just how much the currency—and perhaps the country as well—had splintered into thousands of disparate parts. Indeed, if there was any general conclusion to draw from an inspection of these countless guides, detectors, and manuals, it was that there was no such thing, symbolically speaking, as a national monetary system—or perhaps even a national economy—at this time. There were only innumerable far-flung fragments, each with its own territory, emblems of authority, rates of discount, and claims to confidence. The same, however, could be said of the detectors themselves, and how their self-interested assessments of the currency revealed the limits, if not the liabilities, of private solutions to what had become a public problem.[46]

Profiting from Anxiety

Indeed, the publishers of the counterfeit detectors entered this competitive business with an attention to private profit, not public virtue. As a consequence, while detectors promised to restore some measure of confidence to the currency, they often had the opposite effect, undermining readers' faith in the money supply as well as playing into the hands of the counterfeiters. Publishers, after all, had an incentive to play up news suggesting that the banking system was rife with fraud or teetering on the brink of collapse. The greater the anxiety they stirred up, the more subscribers they gained. "Counterfeit and altered notes are increasing at a terrible rate," trumpeted one, while another warned that "counterfeits continue to increase in almost every section of the country." The solution? Buy a detector. As Bicknell informed his readers, "While we regret this increase and perfection of knavery, we cannot but admit that we are advantaged by it [because] it is now almost indispensable for every store keeper to subscribe."[47]

Not everyone agreed with the publishers' point of view. One critic observed that "these descriptions, instead of enabling a person to detect a spurious or counterfeit note, simply call attention to the fact that there is a counterfeit, and leave the person as much in doubt as ever, unless you have a genuine note at hand to examine." Moreover, while detectors listed plenty of obvious imitations, an alarming number came with assessments like "so well done that good judges have taken them," or "the notes are exceedingly well executed, and calculated to deceive." After notifying readers of counterfeits like these, many detectors encouraged subscribers to reject entire categories of paper money as a way of minimizing risk. Thompson, for example, counseled his readers: "We would advise those who are not good judges of money to reject all notes described as *counterfeit* in the 'REPORTER,' agreeing in denomination and description with the genuine . . . unless they know them to be good." The ubiquitous warnings he and other publishers issued—"better refuse all [notes]" was a common refrain—led to the rejection of genuine notes along with counterfeits.[48]

Such admonitions did not endear the publishers to the banks they scrutinized. In one case, a bank in New York sued Thompson for libel after he reported that "there were 50's and 100's of notes of the bank said to be counterfeits" and that the officers of the bank "were in doubt as to which were good." The lawsuit claimed that the bank's customers had, since the publication of this warning, rejected its notes and "refused to have any dealing or business transactions" with it, causing "great damage" to the bank's finances. Other banks echoed these criticisms, including one whose directors complained to a Boston-based detector that they had "never seen any of the bad notes on their institution" described in its pages, adding that they "cannot believe that any exist." This was not far from the truth. As the publisher admitted, many counterfeits noted in its pages originated and circulated in western states, not in Boston—but it made no such distinction when reporting new counterfeits, leaving readers to assume the worst.[49]

Even more damaging to banks—and to confidence in the currency generally—was the detectors' self-appointed role as regulators of fraudulent banking. John Thompson, for instance, identified "the principles which called us into existence" as *War to all false systems of Banking,* whether practiced by individuals or authorized by State Legislatures. And in furtherance of these principles, we have been foremost in denouncing every species of shinplastering and unsafe systems of banking." Counterfeit detectors like *Thompson's* thus reported other kinds of problematic notes that, while genuine in principle, proved less so in practice. In one issue of his detector, Thompson listed some fifty banks in New York City, of which he deemed twelve "worthless," six "frauds," four "closed," and one, just plain "broke." He also had another classification: "D," for "doubtful." In the midst of the banking collapse of the early 1840s, Thompson branded plenty of banks this way. As he noted in 1842, "In answer to the oft repeated question, 'What bank will fail next?' we say look at the banks marked . . . (D.) in our list." Given that bankers and merchants looked to *Thompson's* as the arbiter of authenticity, these assessments often became self-fulfilling prophecies.[50]

More serious flaws in the system became apparent as the number of detectors proliferated. The publishers of these pamphlets, far from being impartial government auditors, had an active stake in the very business they claimed to regulate. Thompson, for example, helped found the America Bank of Trenton, New Jersey, and at any given time held substantial investments in the institutions he monitored, including a number of shaky western banks. This posed an obvious conflict of interest, as did some of the other activities he and other publishers pursued. In a typical example, Thompson loaned a "bogus concern" named the Tontine Insurance Company $200,000 so as to satisfy state regulators that the venture had the necessary capital to start issuing bank notes. Thompson apparently charged the fraudulent concern $2,500 for this "service," and as soon as the company obtained its charter, secretly withdrew his money, leaving it without capital "but with the [credit] of having one, thus enabling them to impose on the public." While his reputation suffered when the details of this transaction emerged, it hardly led to his ouster as the publisher of the nation's premier counterfeit detector.[51]

A larger problem, and one that afflicted the entire industry, was the obvious conflict of interest between counterfeit detecting and bank note brokering. These two branches of business tended to reinforce one another. One observer in New York City noted that because of Thompson's reputation as a publisher of a counterfeit detector, "when parties come here from the Country, they seek him out, & give him whatever Brokerage [business] they have to transact." This was all well and good, but brokers like Thompson made their money on the so-called discount rate, the few pennies on a dollar they subtracted for taking on the burden of returning the notes to the bank that issued them. The discount rate depended on several variables: the proximity of the bank, the perceived solidity of its finances, even the number of counterfeits in circulation. If a bank note broker turned publisher could undermine people's confidence in a particular bank's notes, he could then obtain them more cheaply, and thus achieve a higher rate of return when he presented the notes for redemption. And the easiest way of doing this was to cast aspersions on a bank in the pages of the counterfeit detector. Thompson himself was frequently accused of doing so. The president of the Erie Bank, for example, issued a disclaimer noting that "the anonymous article which appeared in *Thompson's Reporter* a few day's since, intended to discredit the Erie Bank, is without the least foundation, being only of the periodical efforts made to deceive the public at a distance from the bank, in order to purchase the paper at a discount."[52]

These allegations probably had some foundation; they almost certainly did in the case of other publishers, whom critics accused of numerous breaches of the public trust. One newspaper editor warned "the public to be careful how they put confidence in these 'Reporters' and 'Bank Detectors,' which inundate the community. These prints are more or less engaged in all the financial tricks of the age." The treachery of the detectors varied; some, for example, accepted bribes in order to "puff" a bank, meaning they falsely classified it as solid and testified that its notes passed at par. This same critic claimed that *Bicknell's Reporter* had announced the revival of the once-defunct River Raisin Bank of Michigan, only to have the corporation unmasked (or so the writer claimed) as "one of those impudent speculations which are got up in conjunction with such fraudulent prints as 'Bicknell's Reporter.'" A bit subtler was the accusation the *Bankers' Magazine* leveled at John Thompson. It noted that "until very recently" his detector had listed the Union Bank of New Jersey "on the eve of breaking; and the public have been continually warned to beware of their bills. For some reason unknown to us"—here the magazine appealed to the reader's imagination—"the *Reporter* has ceased blackballing the Union Bank, and expresses no doubt as of its soundness, although it is in fact no more sound that it was last January, when the *Reporter* represented it as on the eve of breaking." The writer stopped short of accusing Thompson of taking a bribe, but the implication was obvious.[53]

Allegations of equally outrageous behavior became commonplace toward the end of the antebellum era, occasionally spilling out in the financial press. The most common claim was that publishers solicited bribes or extorted low-interest loans from fragile (or fraudulent) banks, on the grounds that they needed to be indemnified in exchange for taking on the risk of accepting their notes. In 1857, for example, one bank claimed to have received a letter from a publisher warning that "unless you think it worth your while to guarantee me *amply*, against loss, I shall feel compelled to discredit your institution in my Reporter." In 1859, the *Bankers' Magazine* alleged that John Tyler Hodges confronted the directors of the Monongahela Valley Bank and "informed them that he wanted $3,000." The directors, a bit flummoxed, replied that "we are not aware the bank is indebted to you in $3,000," to which Hodges retorted, "I know all about your affairs, and can either run you up or run you down. If you have not the money, I'll take good negotiable paper." The officers of the bank apparently declined his "modest offer," at which point Hodges left "in virtuous indignation . . . remarking as he went, 'By G—d, I'll star you in my next issue!'" Sure enough, when the next issue appeared, the Monongahela Bank had the star affixed. The star in this case was the equivalent of Thompson's "D"—a mark of shame in the banking community.[54]

A truthful account? Perhaps, given that Hodges had a dubious reputation. A credit-reporting agency observed that although he was a "shrewd, sharp [business man]," he and his brother made much of their money in lottery tickets, pawnbroking, and other marginal speculations. Their business, one anonymous source claimed, "is [profitable] but not [considered] *reputable*." Even if Hodges did not attempt to extort money, plenty of other publishers apparently did: tales of "blackmailing bank notes lists" are too numerous to dismiss. In the 1850s, the *National Police Gazette* detailed the practice in several articles, claiming that banks supplied loans to publishers in order to secure a favorable rating in their detectors. Bank directors, it alleged, "submit to almost any exertion in the way of accommodations, and are liable to have among . . . small and great bank note publishers and bulletin brokers many thousands of dollars thus loaned out." The detectors typically accepted the loan in the form of notes of the suspect bank, then used their power to sell the public on the reliability of the notes, passing them onto customers in the course of pursuing their other vocation, bank-note brokering. According to the *National Police Gazette*, the most "merciless" of these publishers would, after passing off the notes, mark the bank as "doubtful" and "cause a sudden rush upon it for specie." This would lead the notes to depreciate, at which time the publisher would buy them "at twenty-five or fifty cents on the dollar from the swindled public." The publisher could then turn around and pay his debt to the now tottering bank in its own currency, which the bank could not refuse to accept at full face value. To do otherwise would be to admit that the bank's finances were as dubious as the blackmailing publisher had claimed.[55]

Publishers did not hesitate to accuse one another of this kind of chicanery, further eroding what little confidence people put in either the counterfeit detectors or the currency they claimed to protect. These running rhetorical battles often took place in tight markets, where competing detectors vied for the confidence of the local readership.

Detectors published in different parts of the country also took aim at one another in proxy battles over regional economic rivalries. For example, *Van Court's*, a detector published in Boston, complained of "gross and infamous libels . . . uttered by some of the New York prints against [banks in Massachusetts]," adding that "there is one of the N.Y. Counterfeit Detectors that we know of, that is prolific in getting up false rumors about banks, and leading the public astray; and yet that same Detector has a considerable circulation even in this city!" Another Boston-based detector, *Clapp, Fuller & Browne's Bank Note Reporter*, leveled similar accusations, claiming that "all other reporters that circulate in New England are owned in New York, though sometimes disguised in covers bearing the name of some Boston firm." This same anonymous writer went on to claim that these false detectors "are very often used for the purpose of giving credit to banks of doubtful character that are owned by New York parties . . . We would say, therefore, be patriotic, and support home institutions."[56]

The detectors' contradictory listings offered a vision of a monetary system run wild, a situation in which responsibility for the nation's currency (as well as its appraisal and assessment) had been ceded to countless competing parties. There was no single judge of the genuine who stood apart, symbolically or otherwise, from the economy; indeed, the counterfeit detectors themselves were not immune from the vicissitudes of the marketplace. At the height of the Panic of 1857, Thompson reported the latest bankruptcies to his readers, then added, "Your humble servant has also suspended [payments of debts], together with several other houses in Wall Street." By way of explanation, Thompson cited the present "want of confidence." His former competitors greeted the demise of this "regulator of the currency" with glee. In a typical dispatch, a publisher of a Cincinnati-based detector called him "the great

New York propagandist of 'wild-cat' money," accused him of taking bribes from bad banks, and ranked *Thompson's* as just one of many "bogus Counterfeit Detectors."[57]

These sorts of conflicts, similar to the ones that hobbled law enforcement efforts, reflected the profound divisions that fractured the antebellum marketplace. There was no single guardian of the public trust who could issue binding assessments of what was genuine and counterfeit, solid and sham, true and false; there was no central authority that stood above the fray of the national economy. Instead, a growing number of self-appointed judges emerged in the competitive economic environment of the antebellum era, exploiting this power vacuum to advance their own interests in the pages of their publications. Yet if the weaknesses of the system rendered many of these pamphlets next to useless, there was one class of capitalists who found them helpful indeed: the counterfeiters.

Accessories to Crime

In the summer of 1835, Nathan Barlow found himself in possession of a five-dollar note on the Whitehall Bank of New York. But there was a problem: he could not determine whether it was genuine or counterfeit. As he later recalled, the note "had been questioned by some but pronounced to be good & genuine" by others. Still uncertain, Barlow showed the note to his fellow passengers on a canal boat. One pronounced it bogus, but another, a peddler, asked to see the note, and "after comparing it with his bank bill detector," pronounced it genuine and even offered to change it "as proof of his confidence." Barlow, eager to dispose of the questionable note, gave it to the peddler in exchange for some other money. Secure in the knowledge the bill was genuine, the peddler went on to New York City, where he attempted to use the bank note to purchase some hymn books for his next peddling expedition—only to be arrested for passing a counterfeit.[58]

The incident encapsulated the problem with counterfeit detectors. By relying on these often inaccurate publications, readers opened themselves up to fraud. As one self-described "struggling dealer" wrote in the *New York Herald,* if people "had not these false guides they would be more circumspect in their examination of the money they take." He called for a ban on their publication, arguing that "there would be fewer attempts to entrap the unwary, who foolishly place too great reliance upon their honesty." An editorial in the *National Police Gazette* a few years later made much the same point, arguing that detectors often did as much harm as good, because "an ignorant person who looks in a counterfeit detector, and finds no exceptions . . . will receive the new counterfeit without hesitation; when, if he had no such thing as a detector to rely on, he would take the pains . . . to send out the offered note to a judge of money." Shovers of notes, this editorialist observed, could thus cheat "those who sleep with their eyes open."[59]

The principal problem was that detectors listed new counterfeits only after shovers had passed them in stores. As one critic noted, issues of bad notes "are generally 'rushed' in upon the community preconcertedly, from different points at once, and the greatest mischief is often done before [storekeepers] have time to get the description of the List." Indeed, gangs of shovers timed the release of counterfeits to coincide with the publication of the counterfeit detectors. As the *National Police Gazette* reported, "counterfeit bank bills are generally 'shoved' at night, immediately after the issue of the counterfeit detectors," at the very moment when readers put the most faith in them. In this way, shovers of notes made the counterfeit detector work for them rather than against them. One shover confided that as soon as his intended victim "turned to look at a 'detector,'" it was in "that instant he considered the note as cashed, and himself as safe."[60]

The dialectical relationship between shovers of counterfeits and counterfeit detectors eventually assumed a far greater level of complexity, with these publications becoming unwitting accessories to the very crimes they chronicled. A clue to this relationship can be found in descriptions of counterfeit notes, which reveal a surprising number of counterfeits with careless errors. One issue of *Thompson's* listed a counterfeit on the Farmers' Bank of Maryland in Annapolis: "genuine has a 'bee lit on a log'—counterfeit has no bee on the log." Similarly, a counterfeit on the State Bank of Ohio was described as "vignette—ploughman, etc. The ploughman has no whip (in genuine he has), only one of the forefeet of the dog are seen (in genuine both are)." Other detectors contain a staggering number of similar errors: hands with missing fingers, misspelled words, missing punctuation, and other bits and pieces absent from the counterfeit but present in the genuine.[61]

While some writers ascribed these errors to carelessness and ineptitude, there were more insidious reasons. An engraver named Waterman Ormsby, who published an exposé of counterfeiting in the early 1850s, offered the following explanation, citing examples from *Thompson's:* "The Forger will prepare his plate as perfectly as possible in every part but one, which is designedly left imperfect to attract notice. A horse, for instance, will be represented with but three legs. The Note will be immediately advertised in the Lists, as a dangerous counterfeit, with its imperfections specified." At that point, Ormsby explained, "the counterfeiter will now correct his plate, and forthwith print and circulate his Bills, with less chance of detection." When presented with the corrected counterfeit, readers of the detector would turn to the appropriate entry and find, much to their relief, that the bill in question did not have the telltale flaw and was therefore genuine. The *National Police*

Gazette echoed this assessment, noting that it was "a common thing for 'koniackers,' in getting up a new counterfeit . . . to make it differ slightly from the genuine notes. After this issue is circulated, and described in the detectors, the defect is remedied, and another issue is got out." In theory, the counterfeiters could do this ad infinitum, making minor modifications to their plates that would permit them to remain one step ahead. Detectors thus became a tool in the counterfeiters' arsenal, a means of safeguarding the passing of bogus bills. Detectors described the counterfeits, fostered new counterfeits, and described them yet again—in an ongoing contest between the counterfeiter and his adversaries. At times counterfeiters consciously pursued this strategy; in other cases, they did so in the normal course of producing imitations. As Ormsby explained, "If the counterfeiter has not the ingenuity to do this by design, he will soon find himself doing it by accident; for it is natural that the first thing he will think of after his fraudulent production has been noticed by the detector, will be to alter his plate, so that it will not correspond to the description given."[62]

Counterfeiters exploited other anticounterfeiting publications, too. Most popular among the counterfeiting fraternity was Thompson's *Autographical Counterfeit Detector,* with its facsimiles of bank presidents' and cashiers' signatures. The *National Police Gazette* predicted very early on that counterfeiters would turn these facsimiles to their advantage. Alluding to the *Gazette's* network of informers, the editors wrote that "certain organizations of counterfeiters . . . whose secrets we have obtained, have been looking forward to the appearance of the 'Autobiographical Counterfeit Detector' with the utmost interest." The reason was simple: the forthcoming volume promised to give counterfeiters access to the "signatures of every bank note in the United States." With this comprehensive catalog of "standard" signatures, the counterfeiter need only "consult the detector" and produce an imitation of the signature that could "set all apprehension at defiance." These predictions came true: counterfeiters in the 1850s frequently used the book to help duplicate the signatures on counterfeit notes. Perhaps because of these abuses, Thompson stopped publishing the volume after a few years.[63]

Shovers found other ways to turn the publications of Thompson and his competitors to their advantage. For example, rather than rely on genuine counterfeit detectors, some passers made their own *counterfeit* counterfeit detectors. *Bicknell's* reported that a shover had passed through the Ohio countryside, circulating a number of bogus bills. When someone "expressed doubts as to their genuineness," the shover produced a copy of *Bicknell's Reporter*—or so he claimed. "The newspaper was a *counterfeit*, as well as the pretended bank paper," wrote the editors in disgust. This became more common in later years, though there were variations on this technique. Most shovers did not go to the trouble of printing up an entirely new detector; rather, they obtained a few copies of the pamphlet, and as the *National Police Gazette* explained the technique, altered them. For example, "no counterfeit 50's on this bank" was made to read "no counterfeit 5's." One of the shovers would then take the bogus detector into a store, ask to see the detector, and "abstract it, and substitute a fraudulent one in its place." After the switch, an accomplice could go into the store and present the counterfeit in question. By the end of the 1850s, some shovers began adopting far more elaborate schemes to put their notes into circulation. In one instance, a shover named Knapp toured upstate New York, offering free classes on how to detect counterfeit bills and distributing free lists that detailed known counterfeits—only to have his assistants follow in his wake, passing notes that did not, needless to say, appear on these lists.[64]

In assessing the impostures, the *National Police Gazette* left readers with advice that presaged the words uttered by the characters in Melville's *Confidence Man:* "We caution shop-keepers and others . . . who are in the habit of taking paper money on the authority of their counterfeit detectors, not to place absolute confidence in them hereafter, and by no means in this age of counterfeits, to take a note which they do not know." This was wishful thinking: every week brought new banks, new notes, and new counterfeits—even new counterfeit detectors. Confidence in the money supply became difficult to establish and maintain. In the absence of reliable information, people necessarily adapted: they accepted money that might be counterfeit and passed it along to others. That otherwise law-abiding men and women became the accomplices of the armies of shovers who roamed the nation left some moralists uneasy. "If you find yourself in possession of a counterfeit note," wrote one, "throw it in the fire on the instant; otherwise you may be tempted to pass it [and] then it may pass into some man's hands as mean as yourself, with a new perpetration of iniquity, the loss to fall eventually on some poor, struggling widow." But most people did not consign the counterfeit to the flames. In a monetary system where the very distinctions between what was genuine and what was counterfeit were in constant flux, passing a dubious note to someone else was far easier to rationalize.[65]

Until the Civil War, then, a counterfeit could pass as genuine, and a genuine as counterfeit, depending on the misinformation, rumors, and false impressions that passed for knowledge in the marketplace. The nation-state, having ceded control of the money supply to private entrepreneurs, could do little to control the volatility that accompanied this abdication. Consequently, the value of a bank note was extraordinarily susceptible to the self-interested manipulations of bankers and counterfeiters. Counterfeit detectors promised to impose some order on shape-shifting bank notes, but the entrepreneurs who published them were as enmeshed in the system as the capitalists they claimed to regulate. Publishers did not monitor the money supply from a disinterested perch. Nor did they do so out of selfless motives. Their aim was to make money, and this they did, though not without lending considerable assistance to those who made money in a more literal fashion.

Other private industries also sprang up to curtail the worst excesses of the banks and counterfeiters. The most alluring of these promised to stop the problem where it began, with the complicated craft of engraving bank notes. Indeed, by the middle of the nineteenth century, the artistry and complexity of bank note design had reached its zenith in an attempt to defy counterfeiters. Unfortunately, like the counterfeit detectors, advances pioneered by this industry often played into the hands of criminal entrepreneurs, in no small part because the profit motive trumped all other considerations. Far from preventing fraud, the extraordinarily competitive business of bank note engraving gave rise to a new generation of counterfeits—and a new generation of counterfeiters—that further blurred the quaint distinctions between counterfeiting and capitalism.

Ghosts
in the Machine

One day in late July 1854, a jeweler named Buckley Benton threaded his way through the crowds that thronged New York City's financial district. At 111 Broadway, a block north of Wall Street, he stopped, walked up the stairs, and pushed open the doors. This was the home of the Mercantile Agency, a credit reporting firm that used a vast network of secret informants to assess the reputation of businessmen across the country. He came there in need of reassurance about a man named Waterman Ormsby, whose promissory note he held. Could the clerk provide some "intelligence" about Ormsby's character and credit? Was this individual truly worthy of Benton's confidence, the intangible asset that made commercial reputations and built fortunes?

The clerk summoned an assistant, who retrieved an enormous bound ledger that contained Ormsby's dossier. Benton probably knew a bit about his quarry already. An accomplished engraver and inventor, Ormsby had published in the previous year a widely read exposé of the banknote printing industry that had garnered considerable praise and attention in the press. In that book, and in numerous newspaper articles, he argued that the latest sophisticated engraving equipment, rather than preventing counterfeits, enabled far more dangerous imitations to pass undetected. Ormsby, who called for new safeguards to prevent counterfeiting, enjoyed the patronage of numerous banks, whose notes he engraved at his workshop only a few blocks away at 50 Wall Street. Yet when the clerk turned to Ormsby's entry, the lines in the ledger told a different story. "[Moral character] so infamous that we decline to [report] it and his [business character] ranks on a par with it . . . He has been tried for forgery & his chief [business] seems to be engraving for forgers." The clerk turned around and beckoned to another clerk, who peered at the entry and then summoned the owner of the Mercantile Agency, Benjamin Douglass. As a small crowd gathered at the counter, Douglass explained that he could not release the report, but advised Benton to steer clear of Ormsby, informing him that he "was a man of no responsibility; he was a bad man, and worked for counterfeiters, and was a counterfeiter."[1]

That the era's leading authority on bank note engraving and counterfeit prevention could stand accused of being a counterfeiter might seem, at first glance, a paradox. Or was it? Ormsby lived in an era when the vague border that separated capitalism and counterfeiting was far more nebulous, and like many craftsmen who struggled to survive in the brutally competitive business of engraving and printing bank notes, he spent time on both sides of that border, serving multiple masters. He and his competitors had plenty of opportunities to do so: the fast-growing cities where they plied their trade were home to not only many of the nation's banks, but also many of the country's counterfeiters. This new generation of urban criminal capitalists forged a symbiotic relationship with the printing and engraving industry, recruiting poorly paid craftsmen, out-of-work engravers, or in Ormsby's case, struggling entrepreneurs who needed to pay debts like the one that Buckley Benton held in his hand. In the process, counterfeiting became a collaborative effort that depended as much on legitimate artisans using a reputable firm's equipment as it did on career criminals operating out of clandestine workshops.

That collaboration was made possible by a revolution in the art of bank note engraving that played out over the course of Ormsby's career. Rather than craft each bank note plate as a single, unified composition, engraving firms began dividing notes into many different pieces: denominations, borders, and vignettes, or scenes. Each piece would be engraved on separate pieces of steel, otherwise known as dies, and then combined on a single plate in order to print the note. This creative division of labor shortened the time it took to engrave a bank note, and enabled engravers to reuse dies over and over, rather than begin new notes from scratch. Thanks to related advances, each die could also be copied and multiplied an infinite number of times. With the proliferation of these cheap, interchangeable, and reusable dies, copies inevitably found their way into the hands of counterfeiters. At the same time, the demand for skilled craftsmen declined, and many engravers found themselves at loose ends, easily tempted by offers to do piece work for counterfeiters, who might hire them to engrave the name of a bank, a denomination, or even a vignette.

In this curious fashion, the very features of industrialization that had fostered unprecedented economic growth—economies of scale, interchangeable parts, and the division of labor—also destabilized the financial system by providing an opening for the counterfeiter, who became the ghost in the machine of antebellum capitalism. That irony was not lost on Ormsby, who devoted much of his life to exposing the system's many liabilities, even as he engraved notes for members of the counterfeiting fraternity. A man of contradictions, he was one of the last craft engravers to fall victim to the corporate monopoly that took over the industry by midcentury, and his preferred antidote to counterfeiting called for a return to his profession's artisanal roots. At the same time, he was an accomplished inventor of the very same labor-saving machinery that had streamlined his profession and put skilled engravers like him out of work. Neither a committed capitalist nor a bona fide counterfeiter, he embodied the inconsistencies of the economic order behind the modernization of the bank note engraving industry. In the end, that transformation did more than produce ambiguous individuals like Ormsby; it also opened the door to bewildering new kinds of fraudulent bank notes that obliterated the already fragile divide between the real and the counterfeit.[2]

Ormsby's career also offers a glimpse into a series of transformations spawned by having capitalists, rather than the national government, control the manufacture of the country's paper currency. This was free-market capitalism at its most radical, and the inevitable consequence—rampant counterfeiting—belied claims that private economic interests inevitably contributed to the public good. Neither the banks nor the bank-note engraving firms had a stake in the larger consequences of their actions; neither had an interest or even an ability to make the sort of decisions necessary to frustrate counterfeiters. Rather, most bank note engravers and the bankers they served put profits—and their own economic survival—before the public interest. That meant producing notes as cheaply and efficiently as possible. But what was good for business was good for counterfeiting, too.

Machines and Money

"The present system of Note engraving is a system of counterfeiting in its very nature"—or so claimed Waterman Ormsby, who once described himself as an "agitator" on "the question of security against forgery." In an elaboration of this provocative thesis published in 1862, Ormsby observed that bank note engravers in his own time could trace their techniques back to the first person who had successfully counterfeited paper money. Recalling the case for his readers, he pointed out that this famous British forger, a man named Vaughan, did not counterfeit the note himself. Rather, Vaughan had cut a Bank of England note into twenty separate pieces—"as many parts as its pictorial arrangement would admit." Next, Vaughan divided the labor of engraving these fragments among some twenty legitimate engravers, each of whom produced a discrete scroll, number, word, or vignette, all without realizing the larger plan. Vaughan then collected the plates and printed the note in twenty separate steps. "This process of engraving the first counterfeit Note," Ormsby informed his readers, "is now employed in manufacturing our genuine paper currency . . . The first counterfeiter's system, has, in fact, been legalized among us; and those who advocate it and practise it are, in a sense, legalized Vaughans, in many cases as unable to engrave anything themselves as was their notorious predecessor."[3]

This claim was not far from the truth. Beginning in the early nineteenth century, a remarkable series of innovations and inventions had revolutionized the art of bank note engraving. Ormsby credited—or blamed—many of the changes on Jacob Perkins, a Massachusetts inventor who had set out to manufacture bank notes that would be both cheaper and more difficult to counterfeit. Perkins did so by abandoning the older system of relying on skilled craftsmen to engrave each bank note plate according to individual specifications. Instead, he divided the plate into dozens of pieces, or dies, and commissioned master craftsmen to engrave each one with discrete but highly intricate designs, figures, and letters. When complete, Perkins reassembled the

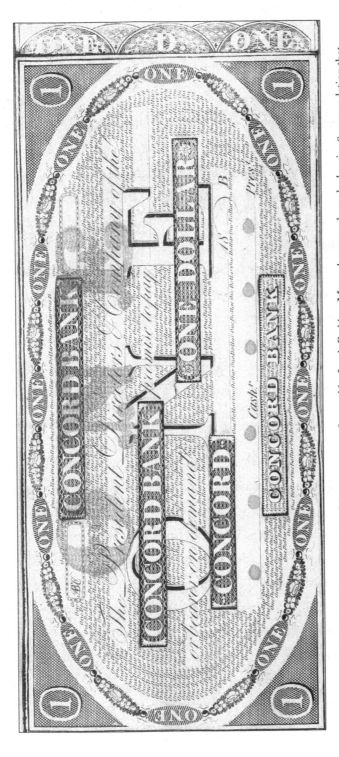

FIGURE 23. Thanks to the complexity of the notes manufactured by Jacob Perkins, Massachusetts adopted a law in 1809 mandating that all banks in the state use his plates. The system persisted until the early 1830s, when the counterfeiters on Cogniac Street managed to imitate the notes, leading the legislature to rescind the regulation. Nonetheless, some banks continued to use the notes designed by Perkins until the Civil War. *Courtesy, Q. David Bowers.*

dies in a strong frame to make a complete "stereotype plate." In theory, this concentration of artistic labor within a single design would deter counterfeiters. This was believable, at least at first: bank notes printed using the stereotype plate looked far more complicated than ordinary bills. Better yet, because the plate consisted of interchangeable parts, Perkins could serve multiple customers with the same plate. As he explained in 1806, his plate "should serve to print bills of any denomination, and for any bank, simply by removing the dies, which contain the name of the bank, town and denomination, and substituting others prepared for the purpose."[4]

In order to cater to many banks from a common set of engravings, Perkins could not rely on copper dies and plates, which wore out after several thousand impressions: he needed something that could endure countless printings. Steel was an obvious choice, but it was far too hard to engrave. Perkins solved this problem while inventing his stereotype plate sometime around 1804, discovering a method of "hardening and softening steel at pleasure." His innovation, which relied on heating and cooling the steel under special conditions, enabled engravers to soften a blank die, engrave it, and then harden it once again. The finished die could now withstand hundreds of thousands of impressions without wearing out, and a single set of steel dies could thus supply notes for hundreds of banks, all at a fraction of the usual cost.[5]

At the same time, Perkins devised a means of making copies of these engraved dies in almost unlimited numbers. The "siderographic process" worked as follows: a single element of a bank note—the denomination, the name of the bank, decorative borders, a portrait or scene—would be engraved on a die and then treated with heat to harden it. The workman would then place the die in one of Perkins's inventions—the transfer press—and roll a blank cylinder of soft steel over the die under extreme pressure. The cylinder would thereby pick up a

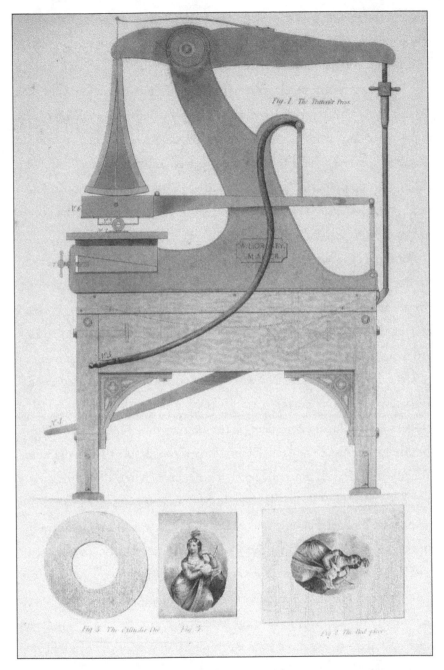

FIGURE 24. In the siderographic process, the original engraving (bottom right) was placed in the press and a "cylinder die" of softened steel (bottom left) was rolled over it under extreme pressure, picking up the impression in relief (bottom center). From Waterman Ormsby, *A Description of the Present System of Bank Note Engraving* (1852). *Courtesy, American Antiquarian Society.*

copy of the image in relief—what Perkins called "a perfect fac-simile of the original." Then the workman would harden this cylinder, place it once again in the transfer press, and transfer the image back onto a blank surface of soft steel, which could itself be hardened and used to print notes. This represented a remarkable revolution: henceforth, any element of any bank note need only be engraved once. An infinite number of copies could then be reproduced and transferred using the siderographic process. Perkins claimed with some justification that he now possessed "the power of re-producing and multiplying the works of the greatest artists."[6]

Perkins began working with expert engravers to push this system to higher levels of sophistication. He eventually moved to Philadelphia, where he entered into a partnership with three such artisans: Gideon Fairman, John Draper, and George Murray. Perkins continued to improve upon his machinery, while his partners handled the engraving of new dies. Perhaps dissatisfied with the aesthetic limitations of the stereotype plate, the engravers in Philadelphia developed a more flexible process for producing complete plates. Rather than bolt individual dies together, they used the transfer press to move designs from cylinders directly to a single common plate of soft steel. After all the elements had been transferred, the plate could be hardened and used to print a note. This had certain advantages. As Perkins explained, "Various engravings combined to form the figure of a note, can be *transposed at will,* so as *entirely to change its general appearance,* and by this means, the same original engravings may be used to form a great variety of notes, sufficiently distinct to produce the effect of entire novelty." Engravers were no longer constrained by the utilitarian design of the original stereotype plate.[7]

Though Perkins eventually moved onto other enterprises, his former partners began to market the system that became known as the "American system of bank note engraving." A close cousin of the much-lauded "American system of production," the new process contributed to a dramatic improvement in the quality of bank note engraving. As Perkins himself explained, *"each original engraving* may be accurately preserved and perpetuated *ad infinitum,"* making it feasible for firms like Fairman, Draper, and Murray to invest the time and money in extraordinarily detailed engravings—and then use and reuse those same elements in successive bank note designs. With a modest supply of quality dies, an engraving company could now produce an almost infinite variety of paper money to meet the growing needs of the state-chartered banks. During the 1820s and 1830s, Perkins's inventions and innovations spread throughout the country, becoming further refined by the next generation of bank note engravers, including Waterman Ormsby.[8]

Like other engravers of the era, Ormsby pursued some formal training (at the National Academy of Design in New York City) and learned the rest of his craft on the job. In the early 1830s he engraved illustrations and book plates for several firms, and then worked as a contract engraver for a bank note company in Boston. In 1835 he moved to New York City, which was swiftly becoming the unofficial capital of the engraving industry, thanks to the growing number of banks and financial service companies that made the city their home. Shortly afterward, he founded his own engraving company, supplying vignettes to some of the larger bank-note engraving firms, and eventually making the plates himself. Like many in the trade, he did more than make money: he also engraved postage stamps, checks, certificates, product labels, portraits, even scenes on the cylinders of Samuel Colt's mass-produced pocket revolvers. Ormsby was also an inventor of some repute, devising, among other things, a device for chopping wood. But he dedicated most of his mechanical talents to bank note engraving and developed some fourteen different machines for this purpose, including an improved version of the transfer press invented by Perkins; a ruling machine that engraved intricate background designs found on many bank notes; and a "grammagraph" that copied medals and medallions onto bank note dies in order to give the illusion of a bas-relief.[9]

All these accomplishments made Ormsby an authority in the field, and in 1852 he published his magnum opus, *A Description of the Present System of Bank Note Engraving, Showing Its Tendency to Facilitate Counterfeiting.* The quarto volume was profusely illustrated and garnered considerable publicity in the financial press, including an excerpt and review at the head of the *Banker's Magazine.* Noting that "the crime of counterfeiting is one that has increased alarmingly of late years in this country," the editors described Ormsby's book as "an elaborate work upon a highly important subject," one that "deserves the especial consideration of bank officers." Other commercial publications, like *Van Court's Counterfeit Detector,* encouraged their readers to purchase copies. "Those who have never had a 'peep behind the scenes,'" promised *Van Court's,* will be "astonished" to learn "that counterfeits can be so perfectly executed."[10]

Ormsby's exposé of the "American System" of bank note engraving had a simple thesis. The problem, he explained, "consists in the use of labor-saving machinery and dies, and in the piecemeal or patch-work system of Engraving necessarily resulting from their use." The division of labor pioneered by Perkins, combined with his techniques of copying individual dies, meant that counterfeiters no longer had to start from scratch when imitating a note. "Every Bank Bill in this country is composed of many separate and distinct parts; and as the original plates are engraved in parts, so the counterfeiting of them can be effected in parts also." Counterfeiters, in other words, could obtain copies of existing dies, eliminating much of the work of forging a note. And as Ormsby explained, because "the same dies are used many times on the same note, and also on many notes," a single die could be used to counterfeit many different bank notes.[11]

Ormsby's argument turned conventional wisdom on its head. As Ormsby observed in one of the many newspaper editorials he wrote in the 1850s: "It is the character of the work engraved upon a bank note which gives to the note a credit and circulation among the people—more than the signatures of a President and Cashier, which are appended to it." But "if a bank note plate is engraved and printed without skill . . . the community may be expected to look upon the notes with distrust; although the most dazzling autograph of a millionaire adorn the note." This equation of craftsmanship with authenticity was terribly misguided. "New and exquisitely engraved vignettes," he noted in his book, may be of "surpassing elegance. But let it be borne in mind that if a die be made, it must be made with the intention of using it many times. The privilege of using it for the FIRST time, may be granted, for an extravagant price, to the Bank; and a SUBSEQUENT impression may actually fall into the hands of the Counterfeiter, at a less price." That made it very difficult for anyone, even engravers, to detect counterfeits. "How can it be otherwise," Ormsby asked, "if genuine Bank Note dies are employed in making the counterfeit plates?"[12]

But where would counterfeiters obtain genuine dies? The most obvious sources were the banks themselves, which numbered close to a thousand by the time Ormsby was writing. Many of these institutions did not last, but went into receivership and bankruptcy during one of the many financial crises of the antebellum era. In most states, especially prior to the 1850s, the banks kept in their own vaults copies of the plates and dies used to print their notes. These assets would, when the bank failed, be auctioned off to the highest bidder. Ormsby highlighted this problem in an article in the *New York Times*, noting that when banks take back their plates "from the custody of the engraver, they take their place among the fixtures and personal effects of the institution; and when this expires they are sold, with the confusion of desks, stoves and spitboxes, for the benefit of heirs and assigns." Elsewhere, Ormsby urged those who used bank note plates "to protect them from abuse, and guard them with all the care and solicitude of Vestals. They should never be treated as merchandise—sold to satisfy clamorous creditors or starving stockholders." This became a serious problem from the late 1830s onward, when numerous banks failed and had their assets liquidated. Counterfeiters could thus feed on the castoffs of capitalism, collecting abandoned dies and plates in order to produce imitations of other, still-thriving banks. The plates and dies used to print notes of wildcat banks often ended up in counterfeiters' hands as well. All these materials could be copied *ad infinitum* once they had entered the underground economy.[13]

Failed engraving firms also became a source of dies for counterfeiters. Prior to the 1850s, hundreds of bank note engravers like Ormsby catered to the growing number of institutions issuing notes. These same engravers entered into a shifting series of alliances with one another, forming partnerships for a few years before consolidating, breaking apart, being absorbed, or going bankrupt. Many of these firms, Ormsby reported, auctioned off their inventory of master engravings. "Their stocks of beautiful dies have been sold at incredible sacrifices," he wrote in his exposé. "The original vignettes, denominations, etc., which are seen on scores of Bank Bills, now in circulation, have been scattered over the country, enabling any one who purchases them, to make duplicate Bank plates, so perfectly, that it would be difficult to detect the fraud." Ormsby listed half a dozen such bankruptcies, including firms that had employed artists such as Asher B. Durand and John Casilear. These failures, he lamented, had "flooded the market with the very choicest materials for Bank Note frauds." Contemporary accounts corroborate this claim: many defunct firms' dies ended up in counterfeiters' hands.[14]

But counterfeiters could also turn to still-thriving bank note firms to obtain dies and plates. Some counterfeiters, for example, posed as bank officers in order to obtain these materials. Several cases in the 1840s became especially infamous. In one, a well-dressed man named Captain Pollock called on the engraving firm of Rawdon, Wright, & Hatch in Cincinnati, and had plates engraved "upon the credit of forged letters, representing him to be an agent of a Banking Company, about to establish a bank at Wetumpka, Alabama." As was customary, Pollock dictated the design of the note, selecting from the firm's extensive collection of dies. After the firm engraved the plate on the "Planters' Bank of Wetumpka, Alabama," Pollock paid for it and took it to St. Louis. What the firm did not realize—or more likely did not bother to question—was that the design Pollock selected was identical to (and even used the same engravings as) the plate for the Planters' Bank of Nashville, Tennessee. Pollock and his associates simply hammered out the words "Wetumpka, Alabama" and inserted "Nashville, Tennessee" using a transfer press and another die. "Thus prepared," wrote one account of the incident, "a large amount of counterfeit Tennessee bills were put in circulation, and so genuine was their appearance that the Bank did not detect the imposition until a considerable sum was taken in at the counter."[15]

Over time, counterfeiters refined these schemes, and more than a few took the strategy to its logical conclusion, impersonating officers of an actual bank. In a typical case from 1850, a counterfeiter approached an engraving firm on Wall Street, passing himself off as the representative of the Wisconsin Marine and Fire Insurance Company and requesting that the firm engrave a "facsimile" of that bank's bills and print $10,000 worth of notes. Far more audacious was a venture of James Brown of Ohio. As mentioned earlier, in the late 1830s he and several accomplices forged a letter that purported to come from the cashier of the Bank of Kentucky. It arrived in the Wall Street office of Gurley & Burton, the engraving firm that printed the Bank of Kentucky's notes. The letter requested them to print $375,000 worth of notes from the plates in their possession. The engravers complied, and came close to handing over the cash to one of Brown's accomplices, who showed up in disguise at the engravers' office in order to pick up the proceeds. The scheme came apart at the last minute—"the transaction was blown," one witness testified—and Brown never took possession of the unauthorized notes. "The ingenuity of the attempt made is remarkable," one newspaper reported. "The plates were real—the impressions real." In cases like these, the dividing line between real and counterfeit disappeared altogether.[16]

Counterfeiters had plenty of other means of commissioning counterfeit plates. Rather than arouse suspicion by going to an established bank-note engraving firm, they patronized less reputable engravers of business cards and advertisements. Many of these artisans owned copies of bank note dies that they used to produce so-called advertising notes, slips of paper that resembled bank notes but were in fact used to hawk products and services. Many such bills, Ormsby explained, used the same vignettes found on bank notes, and if a counterfeiter obtained a plate for an advertising note, he could change the lettering and use it for more nefarious purposes. Evidence of criminal activity from this time tends to confirm Ormsby's theory. In 1840, for example, a man named J. T. Master approached a New York City engraver named Joshua Lowe. As the engraver later testified, the counterfeiter "examined several specimen sheets of die impressions [and] stated that he wished a plate made which was to be used for the purpose of making show bills to vend an Indian medicine." The counterfeiter selected a number of engravings of denominations and vignettes of the kind found on genuine bank notes. In this case, Master eventually aroused suspicion because he had told Lowe that he "did not wish [him] to do the lettering" for the note, a rather curious request. But in other instances, counterfeiters successfully adopted this pretense to obtain dies and plates.[17]

Ormsby's writings show him to be remarkably well versed in these various forms of imposture and fraud. That may have had something to do with his occasional dealings with the counterfeiting community. Indeed, Ormsby came close to being convicted for counterfeiting early in his career. According to court papers, he was approached in 1838 by a Philadelphia counterfeiter named Charles E. Ely, who asked Ormsby to engrave portions of plates for the Farmers' Bank of Orwell, Vermont. Ely was arrested by the police, and apparently implicated Ormsby. When examined by the authorities, Ormsby confessed that he had "never been authorized nor has he received any order from any of the officers for a plate of the Farmers' Bank of Orwell to engrave, stamp or transfer any plate or part or parts of [a] Plate or plates for the said Bank," though he claimed that "he was not aware" that the engravings he supplied would "be used or made a part of any Bill or Note for the said Bank."[18]

Perhaps. But two letters confiscated from Ormsby point toward another interpretation. These missives, written from Ely to Ormsby late in the fall of 1838, suggest that Ormsby's subsequent exposé of the connection between legitimate bank note engravers and counterfeiters was rooted in personal experience. According to the court records, Ely hired Ormsby to transfer vignettes onto a plate and then forward it to Philadelphia. Ely promised Ormsby that if he "made such a plate, I will letter it in that manner as a set off to the stamping, and own it between us." Ely assured Ormsby that the finished plate would be well worth their time. "Stamp the plate and send it on," he wrote, and "I will make your eyes slick out like a lobster's when you see it." He promised that the resulting counterfeits could be "passed in every Bank and Broker's office in the city." He also tried to answer Ormsby's concerns about some unpaid bills: "You talk about the expense of printing," Ely wrote, alluding to an earlier letter. "Bah! If you like it better, I will forward you five Hundred sheets of the new plate when done and charge it on account." Ely, in other words, was offering to pay Ormsby for his services in counterfeit notes.[19]

Ormsby managed to escape an embarrassing trial in this instance—as did Ely, who posted bail and fled. But Ormsby may have continued to work for counterfeiters on occasion, even if he avoided prosecution. According to the records of the Mercantile Agency, Ormsby cared "nothing for the motives or purposes of what he engraves. Has no credit whatever; & the only wonder is that any one should have to inquire about him in the way of business." The allegation came to Ormsby's attention after Buckley Benton's visit to the Mercantile Agency in 1854, prompting the engraver to sue the credit reporting company for slander. In subsequent litigation, the Mercantile Agency alleged that Ormsby had engraved a number of counterfeit plates on several banks, though it offered no evidence to corroborate these charges. It also alleged that he had engraved copper plates with discrete words or numbers: "ten dollars," "State of New York," "fifty dollars," "10," "Merchants' Bank," "Bank of North America," and other curious commissions, though he was hardly the only engraver to supply such items to customers. Indeed, the firms had thousands of these bits and pieces of bank note plates in stock, and would make copies with few or no questions asked. According to the *New York Times*, the credit agency likewise testified that Ormsby "was in the habit of engraving for any casual applicant for plates without inquiring into his character or the object for which the plates were to be used, and that in this way he engraved counterfeit plates on a number of banks in this and other States."[20]

In the end, Ormsby lost his suit, on the grounds that the agency's assessment was delivered in private, not public, and did not show evidence of malice or bad faith. Ormsby appealed the ruling, only to lose on the appellate level a decade later. But as to the more pressing question—was he a career counterfeiter?—the courts remained silent. Possibly, though credit-reporting agencies often depended on hearsay and other circumstantial evidence, and indeed, Ormsby attributed the rumors to his competitors—a defense that was, in retrospect, not entirely without foundation. But posing the question this way misses a larger point: a number of developments at this time conspired to bring legitimate engravers into contact with the counterfeit economy, blurring the line between what was lawful and what was criminal. Ormsby was hardly alone in the way he responded to the radical transformation of his chosen profession. Bank note engraving underwent the same process of industrialization and consolidation that other crafts did in the nineteenth century. Competition between engravers grew especially fierce, and the older system of masters and apprentices broke down, replaced by wage workers and entrepreneurs whom Ormsby derided as "capitalists." A growing number of freelance engravers began working for counterfeiters as a way of supplementing their income, though much of this illicit work was done with a "no questions asked" attitude to avoid charges of outright complicity. Like their clients, the engravers needed the money.

The Engraving Demimonde

The symbiotic relationship between counterfeiters and engravers had its origins in the 1830s, when distant production centers like Cogniac

Street lost their hold on the market. Deprived of their usual sources of bogus notes, urban dealers and wholesalers in the eastern half of the country began to commission counterfeits closer to home. New York City, which by this time was well on its way to being the center of bank note engraving, was a natural place to look for unemployed bank note engravers and printers willing to prostitute their skills for new masters. It, along with Philadelphia, was home to close to three-quarters of the nation's printing and engraving firms, and soon became the source of most counterfeits in the United States, with imitations flowing into New England, New York, Pennsylvania, New Jersey, Maryland, and western states such as Ohio, Indiana, Illinois, Wisconsin, and Michigan. In Missouri, the city of St. Louis harbored far fewer firms, but nonetheless became an important regional production center, supplying notes throughout the Mississippi River Valley, and to a lesser extent, the Missouri and Ohio river systems. (The South, by contrast, was home to only a handful of engraving firms, and produced almost no counterfeits.) By midcentury, counterfeiting was well on its way to becoming an urban industry, much like the printing and engraving business that it depended on for paper, plates, dies, and corrupt craftsmen.[21]

There was little these cities could do to halt collaboration among criminals and engravers. Though New York City established a preventative police force in 1844, and several cities followed suit in the 1850s, officers did not enjoy a reputation for professionalism. Certainly, a handful of more honest policemen led prosecutions of counterfeiters during these years, particularly in New England, where a revived Association for the Suppression of Counterfeiting monitored arrests and prosecutions. But the vast majority of policemen throughout the rest of the country seem to have approached their job with an eye toward profiting from their daily responsibilities. Some stood accused of taking

bribes in exchange for freeing suspected counterfeiters, while others refused to pursue alleged counterfeiters unless banks paid them to do so. And
more than a few fell under suspicion of collaborating with counterfeiters. For example, Horace and Hannibal Bonney, the infamous identical
twins who dominated New York City's counterfeiting operations through
much of the 1840s and 1850s, initially worked as officers on the First
Ward Police before branching out into more lucrative lines of business.[22]

Even when the police did do their job, they arrested very few engravers or other principals in the counterfeit economy, netting small-time
shovers and petty retailers instead. In the event the authorities captured
a key player in the counterfeit economy, they rarely secured a conviction. One problem was the so-called straw bail system, in which suspects would post bail with the assistance of confederates who would
pose as "reputable" men and pledge the necessary funds. The prisoner
would be released and promptly vanish; the person bailing them often
disappeared as well. In other cases, the surety (the person who assumed
responsibility for the suspect) would obtain the necessary funds from
the fugitive, pay the court, and the case would be dismissed. From the
standpoint of city governments, resolutions like these were welcome:
they provided a reliable source of funds. Many more suspects managed
to secure their freedom by "turning up" counterfeit plates, dies, or
money, or by serving as "stool pigeons" for the police. Such concessions
do not seem to have diminished the size and scope of the counterfeit
economy, and in fact may have cloaked bribes that counterfeiters paid
to police and prosecutors in order to resume their vocation. On those
rare occasions when juries and judges sent someone to prison, most inmates did not serve out their full sentences, thanks to state governors'
extensive use and abuse of their pardoning powers.[23]

These pardons were supported by many voters, who thought it
preposterous that fraudulent bankers walked free while counterfeiters

went to prison. For example, one newspaper that favored a specie currency applauded the release of several notorious counterfeiters, writing, "This was right. These men had been counterfeiting *spurious money,* the rags of the Banks, and there was no reason why the *counterfeiters* of the spurious money should be subjected to a severe punishment while the *manufacturers* of it are suffered to go at large." The rage that many felt toward banks and bank notes might, absent any ban on paper money generally, find expression in the decisions of judges, juries, and even prosecutors toward those who made, sold, and passed counterfeit bills. In a country where, as one newspaper sputtered, passers of notes risked ending up in the penitentiary, "while the banker, who swindles the public out of thousands, lives respected in the community," criminal laws went unenforced, and prison sentences went unserved.[24]

In the case of counterfeit engravers who walked the delicate line between legal and illegal enterprise, prosecution was particularly difficult. These artisans could always claim that they did not realize that a commission was destined for a counterfeiter's press, or could refuse to ask the obvious questions. For example, when Waterman Ormsby was confronted in 1848 about his "don't ask, don't tell" policy toward patrons of his engraving business, he supposedly replied that "it was *not* his place or duty to inquire into the object of his employers, or the uses to which they intended to apply his work after it had passed out of his hands" and that he would continue to work for "any person who would employ and pay him, without regard to their characters or purposes." Whether or not Ormsby actually said these words is impossible to determine, but the philosophy they articulated was one held by any number of struggling engravers and firms operating in the 1840s and 1850s, most of whom put their economic survival ahead of the public interest. They lived in an economy that commoditized their labor, and inevitably acceded to its demands, selling their skills to the highest bidder.[25]

The practice of freelance counterfeit engraving became rather common during the hard times of the late 1830s, when the self-described "capitalists" of the counterfeit economy began hiring out-of-work machinists, engravers, and other skilled workers to fashion counterfeit plates. Late in 1837, for example, the arrest of several engravers revealed that Abraham Shepherd, Smith Davis, and other powerful dealers had hired workmen to fashion counterfeit plates on multiple banks. One witness testified that a machinist named John Packer who "puts or transfers the Die work on the plates . . . had done the machine work for four or five plates . . . for Abraham Shepherd." Packer himself denied this, claiming that "I know Shepherd, he has hinted to me that he wanted me to do work for him but I never have done any for him, unless through other persons." This may have been true: Shepherd managed to hire Packer by sending an emissary who asked him to engrave several plates at the rate of ten dollars apiece. Packer apparently agreed to do the job, setting up a secret workshop outside of his daytime establishment. "I suspected the plate was for counterfeiting Bank Notes," he told his examiner by way of explanation, "[and] I did not want my family to know anything about it."[26]

This was hardly an isolated instance. A few years later, a man named Isaac Baker set off for New York City to find an engraver who would supply counterfeit plates. After poking around the city's printing workshops, he found an engraver named Lee on Courtlandt Street who supplied a partial plate for fifty dollars; another engraver in the same neighborhood added a border to the plate, along with the words "promise to pay" and "or bearer on demand," as well as the denomination figures and the words "County Bank of Plattsburg." Additional engravers lent their labor to the effort, supplying dies and pieces for the project, as well as for other plates, including one on the Clinton County Bank and the Seneca County Bank. Baker testified that although a handful of engravers he approached had refused to help him, they did not report him to the police.[27]

Counterfeiters commissioning plates often did so in a piecemeal fashion so as to avoid implicating either themselves or the engravers they hired. There was no law against ordering words engraved on a copper plate, even if the choice of words was suspicious. In 1839, an engraver was hired to manufacture the words "America," "People's," "Winthrop," "The Concorde Bank," and the "Commercial Bank," all pieces of full-fledged counterfeit plates taking shape under the watchful eyes of a single counterfeiter, using much the same system that Ormsby described. This strategy could push up against legal limits, as it did in this same case. The man employing the engraver eventually commissioned him to engrave a copy of a note on the Greenwich Bank of New York, but quickly thought better of it, requesting that he leave out the name of the bank. As the counterfeiter explained, "If the Police found the plate on him they could not harm him [as] he had read the Statute and found that neither [the engraver] or himself could be harmed"—because the plate was not, strictly speaking, a counterfeit of the original, even if a transfer press could readily turn it into one with very little effort.[28]

These collaborations did not cease once the hard times had passed, but instead became even more common, and often occurred with a more explicit understanding of the ultimate purpose of the engravings. In 1851, Joseph Rosencrans, a counterfeiter from upstate New York, visited the shop of Alexander Dangerfield and had a business card engraved. When Rosencrans picked it up, he asked Dangerfield if he could engrave bank notes, too. The engraver said he could, to which Rosencrans replied: "[You] would be surprised to find how quick men go rich in this country if they only got in the right channel." Dangerfield replied that he, too, would like to be rich, at which point

Rosencrans took out a bank note and asked if he could imitate it. "I told him I could," testified Dangerfield. "This was the first thing that excited my suspicions against him and put me on my guard." Perhaps, though, the engraver went on to do work for Rosencrans, selling him dies and plates with no questions asked. In cases such as these, the counterfeiter typically would take possession of the plates and print them at a separate workshop.[29]

In other cases, the criminal entrepreneurs who provided the financial backing for new counterfeits went straight to the source, infiltrating engraving firms and bribing low-level apprentices and journeymen to print notes using genuine plates. As early as 1839, an alumnus of Cogniac Street named Russell Moore paid a workman at a firm in New York City to surreptitiously borrow the plates of the Bank of Seneca County and strike off a number of notes. In an attempt to prevent these "genuine counterfeits," New York passed a law in 1843 requiring that banks deposit their plates with the state's comptroller of the currency. Other states passed similar laws in the 1850s, but many banks ignored them. As one newspaper explained, "For the convenience of the Banks these plates are frequently, and perhaps generally, left in the hands of the engraver"—despite laws to the contrary. Other cases made headlines in the 1850s, prompting additional calls for reform of what one what newspaper described as "the loose laws on the subject of bank note plates," but these did not lead states to expand their oversight. Absent federal intervention, state regulations governing the disposition of bank note plates remained as much a patchwork as the engravings that constituted those plates.[30]

Over time, it became easier to hire corrupt employees on the "inside" because even the lowliest workman could deliver counterfeit plates and dies. Indeed, many of the workmen who transferred and copied dies for counterfeiters lacked advanced engraving skills. This was a logical outgrowth of the growing mechanization of the profession, a trend that Ormsby lamented, even as he contributed toward it by refining the inventions of Perkins and others. As mentioned earlier, Ormsby's innovations—a refined transfer press, ruling machines, geometric lathes, and several other devices—helped move the work of engraving out of human hands. Ironically, Ormsby may have invented these devices because he lacked the human resources of the larger firms: he worked by himself, with the help of only his son and an occasional assistant. Whatever the reason, his innovations, and those of other inventors of the day, meant that the twin crafts of counterfeiting and bank note engraving became far easier to learn than they had been in the opening decades of the nineteenth century. "The Forger," observed Ormsby, "need only possess a degree of low cunning and hypocrisy, without a particle of artistic talent."[31]

No person better represented this trend than William Brockway, a counterfeiter who worked in a print shop in New Haven in the late 1840s. Ormsby, who devoted a whole chapter of his exposé to Brockway, described how the counterfeiter produced one of the most successful forgeries of the era without an iota of "artistic talent." According to Ormsby (and other accounts published at the time), counterfeits on the New Haven Bank surfaced in 1848. Unlike most imitations, which typically had slight imperfections in the arrangement of the vignettes or the denominations, these new frauds could not be distinguished from the original except for the handwritten serial numbers, which did not match the banking records. Over the course of the next year, other counterfeits exhibiting the same astonishing verisimilitude plagued additional banks in New Haven. The only thing that connected these different imitations was the fact that all had been printed in the shop where Brockway worked. But the shop only printed notes; it neither engraved bank note plates nor owned dies. Instead, banks brought the plates to the shop and supervised while workers like Brockway printed the notes.

Brockway had devised a method of copying the plate without resorting to a transfer press or any of the other contrivances used by engravers. As authorities later learned, Brockway had been taking classes at Yale with the famed chemist Benjamin Silliman. It seems that the learned professor had lectured his students on new discoveries in electrotyping, and Brockway had realized the implications. It was astonishingly easy: first, dip a bank note plate in a solution of sulphate of copper. Then set up a galvanic battery and run an electric current through the solution. This would cause a deposit of copper to form on the bank note plate. After a layer of sufficient thickness had coalesced, the counterfeiter could remove the plate and peel the copper crust. This negative mold could then be placed back in the solution and the current applied once again. After another layer formed, producing an exact facsimile of the original plate, it too could be peeled off, treated, thickened, and used to print bank notes identical to those produced by the genuine plate.

But how to obtain the plate without arousing suspicion? Brockway realized he did not need the plate; a simple metallic impression would do. When it came time to print notes from the plates entrusted by the watchful bank officers, he made a show of testing the pressure of the press before commencing work, and managed to slip a piece of copper foil beneath the plate, secure an impression, and stow it in his apron. He then subjected it to the electrotyping process, producing perfect copies of the original. Brockway was eventually caught (though he became infamous again in the 1860s). But electrotyping became standard practice among counterfeiters who, Ormsby claimed, could now multiply plates "more perfectly . . . than can the original Bank Note Engraver by means of his Transfer Press." Better yet, it could be done at a fraction of the cost: transfer presses sold for five hundred dollars or more, but a pair of galvanic batteries and the chemicals used for electrotyping could be obtained for as little as five dollars.[32]

Brockway was not the only one to exploit these technologies for the purpose of counterfeiting. Others, including the dapper Jack Cantar, also began exploiting electrotyping and other technological contrivances. In one of several cases in which Cantar had a role, a steam engineer named Alfred Scott testified that Cantar had researched patent reports and experimented with galvanic batteries, and speculated on the possibility of using the daguerreotype process in order to counterfeit bank notes. Scott recalled that Cantar had described himself on two occasions as "nothing more nor less than a Scientific Counterfeiter." Indeed, Cantar and his many associates distinguished themselves in the application of technological advances to the "science" of counterfeiting.[33] Yet if several of the techniques they pioneered eased the manufacture of counterfeits, their real contribution lay elsewhere. In time, the growing sophistication of forgers like Cantar gave rise to a new generation of fraudulent notes that further obliterated the already fragile divide between the real and the counterfeit.

Broken Banks and Phantom Notes

As counterfeiters became more sophisticated, so did their products. They no longer restricted themselves to simple imitations, but began to manufacture other varieties of bogus bank notes. Classifying and defining these other frauds can be maddeningly difficult, especially because many writers in the nineteenth century frequently called any kind of problematic note a counterfeit. That said, these other subspecies of counterfeit notes can be broken down into three general categories: raised notes, altered notes, and spurious notes. These varieties of bogus notes became common as banks and bank note engravers went out of business in the increasingly volatile economic climate of the 1830s. They also became easier to pass—and more popular among retailers and shovers—as the currency itself became more confusing and chaotic.

Raised notes—genuine bank bills that had their denominations changed from a lower to a higher number—had been around the longest. Though earlier generations of counterfeiters had occasionally resorted to inflating the value of a note in this fashion, the practice became progressively easier as the "patchwork system" of engraving became widespread, and copies of denomination dies fell into the wrong hands. Forgers like Cantar would procure these dies, collect genuine small-denomination notes (usually ones and twos of reputable banks), and then apply solvents to erase the existing denomination. After the note dried, the counterfeiter would stamp the higher denomination die in the blank space. Such notes became easier to pass in later years, as it became more and more difficult to remember the appearance of the growing number of notes in circulation. Moreover, because each raised note was a sui generis piece of handiwork, and surfaced in relatively small quantities, few of the detectors bothered to keep track of them. John Thompson, for example, asserted that "these are frauds we do not pretend to keep the run of, as no genuine Bill is exempt from its practice."[34]

Though Cogniac Street occasionally manufactured raised notes, such frauds did not become especially common until the late 1830s, when a new generation of counterfeiters began producing them in urban centers. This made sense: the production of raised notes required little equipment aside from some chemicals and a handful of dies, making it easy to conceal their production. Moreover, the necessary raw materials—low-denomination bank notes—could easily be obtained in banking centers like New York City. In one such case, for example, a witness testified that a counterfeiter named Standish "shewed me a [vial] of liquid which he said would take out the ink from Bills." Eager to help, the witness accompanied Standish to Wall Street and visited several money brokers' offices, changing larger bills for one-dollar notes of the Manchester Bank. Standish then treated the notes with acid, transforming them into five-dollar notes. In time, this became a thriving cottage industry in the urban underworld, with countless criminal entrepreneurs engaged in acts of petty inflation.[35]

Using similar methods, counterfeiters also made "altered notes" using the bills of defunct, or "broken banks." Typically, the counterfeiter would erase the name and location of the bank and replace these elements with the title of a solvent institution. As an alternative, the counterfeiter might remove the location only. As Ormsby explained in his book, "Thus 'the Farmers' Bank, Mich.' . . . is made to read 'The Farmers' Bank, Mass.' . . . by substituting for I C H the letters A S S!" Such selective deletions became a common practice: one witness in an alteration case in New York City testified that a note had been "altered from a Bill of the North River Banking Co. which is said to be a worthless concern . . . The said Bill was altered," he explained, "by striking out the letters 'ing' after the word 'Bank' and also by defacing the letters 'Co,'" transforming it into the North River Bank. Even more cosmetic alterations could transform previously worthless notes. One counterfeit detector, for instance, warned that bills of a defunct bank in Romeo, Michigan, had been reincarnated as the genuine issues of the Bank of Rome, New York, simply by extracting the letter "o."[36]

Most alterations required more work, with counterfeiters erasing and replacing multiple elements of the note. Few counterfeiters left behind a description of these feats of erasure, but one such case from 1845 gives some indication of their working methods. According to testimony gathered in January of that year, the police burst in on Michael O'Brien (brother of Honora Shepherd) and Peter Van Pelt while they were altering notes of different denominations. When the officers searched the room, they found notes of the dead and disreputable Lapeer County Bank of Michigan undergoing a remarkable metamorphosis into the far more respectable and thriving Fairhaven Bank of Massachusetts. O'Brien and Van Pelt apparently began with the one-dollar notes of the sort at the very top of the photograph. They would then extract the words of the bank, the county, and the words "Safety Fund," as shown by the specimen in the middle. Typically, counterfeiters accomplished this feat by cutting holes in a glass plate that corresponded with the sections to be erased, pasting the bill to the glass, and then dripping acid on the exposed parts of the note. After the note had dried, O'Brien and Van Pelt would stamp the blank areas with separate dies bearing the words "The Fairhaven Bank," "Fairhaven," and "Massachusetts." Though the resulting bank note did not resemble the authentic issues of the Fairhaven Bank, it had the general appearance of a genuine note.[37]

This practice of resurrecting and reincarnating broken bank notes was fueled by changes in the banking system itself. In the decade that spanned Jackson's war against the Second Bank of the United States, the number of note-issuing banks grew dramatically from 321 in 1830, to 531 in 1835, to 711 in 1840. Many of these corporations, especially those in the western states, issued notes far in excess of their capital, and eventually went bankrupt. As a consequence, by 1842 their numbers had declined to 654; hundreds of others disappeared throughout the 1840s and 1850s. But these figures only begin to hint at the explosion—and eventual implosion—of the paper money economy. In this same period, the total face value of bank notes in circulation went from $61 million in 1830 to $104 million in 1835 to $149 million in 1837, before plummeting back down to $59 million in 1843.[38]

Many of the banks active in the 1830s died in this financial cata-

FIGURE 25. A bank note of the dead and defunct Lapeer County Bank (top) stripped of its identity (middle) and resurrected as the issue of the reputable Fairhaven Bank (bottom). *Courtesy, New York City Municipal Archives.*

clysm, but their notes survived. Brokers often purchased these for pennies each, hoping to lay claim to the remaining assets of the defunct corporation. These notes usually ended up in the offices of brokers in New York City, where speculators bought and sold them for a tiny fraction of their face value. But counterfeiters also purchased these paper corpses with an eye toward resurrecting them as corporations in good standing. One New York City broker, for example, testified that Otis Allen, a well-known counterfeiter, had asked him if "he had any broken Bank Bills to sell." The broker showed him several bundles of notes, including some on the Citizens' Bank of Augusta, Maine. Allen bought most of the broker's stock, taking special interest in the Augusta notes. A short time afterward, Allen "casually mentioned that 'there would be a neat thing out in a few days,'" which turned out to be two-dollar notes on the Citizens' Bank of Worcester printed from the dead notes of the Citizens' Bank of Augusta. The notes of defunct banks thus lived on in another guise, however fraudulent.[39]

Note brokers became central players in this subspecialty of the counterfeit economy. In one well-publicized case, the New York City police arrested two note brokers named Thomas and Seldon Brainard, who had been supplying Horace Bonney and his (other) brother Erastus with tens of thousands of broken bank bills. The officers who arrested the counterfeiters found them engaged in "altering and re-creating the notes of broken or defunct banks, so as to pass for the issues of monetary institutions of Boston and elsewhere." As the police prepared to take the prisoners back to the station, "a Wall street broker" walked through the door (one of the Brainards) "who at the sight of the officers . . . thrust a large package of something in the fire." The officers pulled it out and found thousands of dollars in notes from banks that had perished in the financial disasters of the 1840s. When they searched the broker's office, they found an additional $30,000 in notes of lifeless banks, awaiting resurrection through feats of chemical leger-demain.[40]

During the 1850s, the business of reanimating broken bank notes be-came a thriving business. Langdon Moore, a burglar and occasional counterfeiter, recalled how he had gotten into the business in the late 1850s. "I visited a number of brokers, purchasing several thousand dol-lars in broken bank bills on the Metropolitan Bank of Washington, D.C. These bills I altered to a bank with the same title in New York City." Pleased with his success, Moore purchased a small press, "made the acquaintance of an engraver, who furnished me with engraved State and location plates," and then set to work "altering notes from failed banks, first extracting the title, State, location, and signatures." After substituting the names of new banks, and "taking especial care in se-lecting inks that would compare with the rest of the notes," Moore forged "the names of the officers of the solvent banks in their place." The counterfeiter further recalled that "this was a new industry, and as the notes were so much better than a regular counterfeit, I could not keep up with the local demand, to say nothing about the country trade." By all accounts, he was only one of many engaged in the busi-ness, which became an integral part of the counterfeit economy by the 1840s and 1850s. By 1862, a bank note reporter observed that "counter-feits, or fac-simile notes, are comparatively rare . . . Very few of this description are in circulation." By contrast, the reporter estimated that some "nine-tenths of the bad bills in circulation [are] altered, raised, or spurious."[41]

This final class of illegitimate bills—so-called spurious notes—was the most sophisticated kind of fraudulent currency to appear in the mid-nineteenth century. Such bills, explained Ormsby in 1852, "are not imitations of any genuine Bills in particular, but [are] made to bear a general resemblance to all Bank Notes, and [purport] to be the issue of some solvent bank." The appearance of the spurious note did not matter. For example, an engraver charged with forgery testified that the counterfeiter who hired him "left [it] to my discression, to put on the plates what I pleased." In a case such as this, the counterfeiter would take possession of the plate, then add the name of a plausible-sounding bank: a "Farmers' Bank of . . ." or a "Mechanics' Bank of . . ." or a "City Bank of . . . ." Scores of real banks already had these common prefixes. In 1858, one newspaper counted sixty "Farmers'" banks, forty "Merchants'" banks, and twenty-five "Commercial" banks. When a counterfeiter "incorporated" another such institution, he was trading off the comfort, if not trust, that these conventional names generated in people handling paper money.[42]

Though counterfeiters often commissioned spurious notes, it was more common for them to print them from the plates of defunct banks. "Genuine plates of exploded banking concerns, with the best workmanship, have got into the hands of counterfeiters, by purchase," complained one newspaper in 1855. "The names of the banks have been altered readily, so as to be similar to that of well-established banks." Few states had regulations governing the disposition of a dead bank's plates on the assumption that they would be of little use to counterfeiters. This was wrongheaded, and in New England, the second incarnation of the Association for the Suppression of Counterfeiting managed to have legislation passed in Massachusetts requiring that these plates be destroyed. But this was an exception, and the plates of many defunct banks enjoyed a curious afterlife, reincarnated as nonexistent banks.[43]

Such frauds worked because most people rarely looked beyond superficial signs of authenticity. It was sufficient for a note to appear well engraved and vaguely familiar. Take, for example, a two-dollar note of the Globe Bank of New York, which was engraved as well as any other genuine note from the era. But there was no such institution

as the Globe Bank of New York. Nor, for that matter, was there any
such bank as the Danbury Bank or the Lockport Bank, other spurious
notes printed from this same plate. As the counterfeit detector magnate John Thompson testified in a trial of one of the counterfeiters
concerned in passing these notes, the bill was "fraudulent & worthless,
as there is no Bank of that title or name, nor any Banking Company
doing business under that title or name." He added that while "there
was a Bank called the Lockport Bank, about ten years ago . . . it was
closed & there is now no such Bank in existence." This also became a
common strategy of the new generation of counterfeiters: produce a
note that evoked memories of a once-extant bank.[44]

There was some poetic justice in all of this. The casualties of capitalism's relentless competition arose from the dead and moved with
new purpose. Cast-off plates and dies, lifeless paper promises of broken banks, out-of-work engravers, reputations of now-defunct corporations: all came to life, animated by the necromantic powers of the
counterfeiter. Once resurrected and reincarnated, they mingled with
their genuine counterparts, further eroding confidence in the currency.
The growing number of these fraudulent bills gave rise to a serious
symbolic crisis, as engravings of bank names, denominations, and other
emblems of value slipped their material moorings and began appearing on an ever-multiplying variety of fraudulent notes. As a consequence, the question of how to prevent these new species of counterfeit
notes became an abiding obsession of the financial community by midcentury. Waterman Ormsby had his opinions on how to best prevent
the fraud. So, too, did his many detractors.

The Search for a Solution

During the 1840s and 1850s, engraving partnerships grew ever larger,
absorbing competitors, pooling collections of dies, and making greater

use of the "labor-saving machinery" that Ormsby derided. As one of the few bank note engravers who continued to operate his own firm at this time—the New York Bank Note Company—Ormsby witnessed and experienced this process of consolidation firsthand. He would later recall that "as the original founders of engraving companies passed away, men of capital occupied their places, until at last the latter alone remain, in power supreme, and Bank Officers are brought face to face with the Engraver no more." As a consequence, "when business is dull, the hired Engraver is turned away, and still the capitalist lives in affluence on the profits constantly accruing from the use of the artist's previous labor, in the shape of accumulated dies." Marx never identified the bank note industry as a signal example of the revolution in production so characteristic of his age. But Ormsby did, and in rhetorical offensives like these, he fought to maintain the artisan-engraver's control over his own labor—to maintain ownership of the "means of production." That his labor was going toward the manufacture of bank notes—the sacred totems of capitalism that had already underwritten a similar revolution in labor relations in other parts of the economy— made his campaign all the more quixotic.[45]

Ormsby nevertheless spent most of the 1850s and 1860s advancing a new method of engraving that he believed would restructure his profession along more equitable lines. It would also, he promised, put an end to counterfeiting. Ormsby's solution was to "dispense entirely, and for ever, with the use of dies, machinery, and other mechanical contrivances, by means of which the business of Bank Note Engraving is rendered so profitable to those engaged in it." In effect, he tried to turn back the clock to a time before Perkins's inventions (as well as his own improvements) and restore the artisan craftsman to his rightful place. The "Unit System," as Ormsby's solution became known, called for an end to the discrete symbols, signs, and vignettes that made up most bank notes. Instead, he urged banks to commission plates engraved as a

FIGURE 26. Engravings like these embodied Ormsby's philosophy: "A bank note should be one thing, one design, one picture, with the necessary lettering interwoven, one—inseparable—and unalterable." *Courtesy, Q. David Bowers.*

single, highly detailed, interwoven scene that blended the lettering, denomination, and all other parts of the note into a unified whole. The artisan, in other words, would retain control over his creation, rather than having it appropriated by the hated "capitalists" who bought and sold the products of his labor.[46]

The few notes that Ormsby produced using this system became masterpieces of the engraving art, studied, collected, and treasured by numismatists. The one-dollar bill of the Carroll County Bank, New Hampshire, was the first that he engraved under the dictates of the unit system. Though Ormsby evidently used existing dies for a handful of elements, the central vignette is intricately woven into the denomination and the name of the bank, a feat of artistry that took weeks if not months to accomplish, and cost the engraver almost five hundred dollars. But the time devoted did yield a dividend. A decade after Ormsby finished the job, the cashier of the Carroll County Bank testified that no counterfeiter had altered or imitated Ormsby's plate. This was probably true: someone trying to alter the note using acids would have destroyed the vignette in the process. Moreover, the intricacy and size of the engraving tended to discourage counterfeiters from spending time fashioning an imitation plate. There were far simpler bank notes that could be counterfeited using existing dies.[47]

Ormsby obviously had complicated motives for advancing this system. His solution, which dispensed with the use of dies and other contrivances that enabled the division of labor between workmen, was an expression of economic anxiety as much as anything else. Those anxieties only intensified in the 1850s, as mergers and acquisitions reduced the number of bank note engraving establishments to only a few, each of which employed scores of employees and contract workers to do the most specialized tasks. Ormsby nonetheless continued to cling to the older model of a family proprietorship, working with his son and occasionally hiring an assistant or two. His solution—the unit system of engraving—would have required everyone else to reverse course and follow his lead. Indeed, he once wrote that if everyone adopted his system, "instead of only seven gigantic monopolies, there would be *seven hundred*." Ormsby naively envisioned a world in which "every bank would choose its own engraver [and] the design of every bill should be a large, original picture, engraved by the hand of the artist on the plate itself." To those who might object that "there are not engravers enough to do the work," Ormsby had a revealing retort: "Well, if all engravers are *sought after*, and fully employed, there would be NONE to do the counterfeiting." This was an acknowledgment, perhaps, of the assistance he and many others had lent to the counterfeiting community, as well as a seething indictment of his profession's industrialization.[48]

Only the Carroll County Bank commissioned Ormsby to engrave notes under this system, though many other banks hired him to produce bills using more conventional methods. Most made this choice because they did not want to spend the extra money required by the unit method. "When a bank is about to order a set of plates," wrote Ormsby in an editorial in the *New York Times*, "it generally . . . regards, first, what it considers to be economy—a saving of expense . . . 'Of course' they want the best work. But, of course, they want to declare a dividend on their first six-months' business, and so . . . they can't pay much for their plates and printing." New banks generally chose from an existing stock of dies rather than go to the trouble of having new vignettes engraved. Many bank note companies cut prices further by producing "general plates" for their more cost-conscious customers. A financial newspaper, explaining the practice, noted that one engraving company has "prepared several sets of general plates, leaving apertures for the name of the bank, the town and the State" in order "to accommodate banks who do not wish to incur the expense of a set of special plates." One counterfeit plate could thus do the job of many, the paper observed: "It will be the easiest thing imaginable to use the same plate for all the banks using the plates, and thus counterfeits may be almost indefinitely multiplied."[49]

The financial press assailed these arrangements, complaining, as one newspaper did, about this "miserable spirit of false economy." Striking a similar tone, another financial journal complained that "banks have been multiplying on all sides, with small capitals, necessarily restricting themselves to economise in procuring plates." But banks proved deaf to such criticisms because they had little to gain from making their notes impervious to counterfeiting. Though banks lost some money by mistakenly redeeming counterfeit notes, tellers caught most of the bad bills. The burden of bad notes fell instead on those least able to afford it: the working class, the illiterate, and others who lacked a strong familiarity with the different bank notes in circulation.[50]

Still, inventors and bank note engravers besides Ormsby attempted to develop techniques for frustrating counterfeit, altered, and spurious notes. The firm of Danforth Wright & Co., for example, printed one-dollar bills bearing a single circle; two-dollar bills had two circles; three had three; and so on. A similar safeguard used an image of coins. A discrepancy between the number of circles or coins and the denomination of the note indicated a raised note. Yet an article assessing this technique dismissed it, noting that "it is difficult . . . for the masses to recollect these devices." Indeed, few people kept track of these inconsistent and uncoordinated anticounterfeiting measures, which also included special kinds of paper, watermarks, and what was called "uniformity" in design. Proponents of this last solution often invoked the example of the Bank of England, which had few problems with counterfeiters by the mid-nineteenth century. As one would-be reformer observed, the fact that their notes were "the principal circulating medium throughout the country . . . so familiarizes every one with Bank of England notes, that the most casual observer could readily detect a spurious imitation if exhibited." This same inventor proposed that "instead of the [three hundred and thirty one] Banks in the State of New-York issuing different forms or devices of notes as they now do, there be but one *form* of note for all." An excellent idea, but most banks in New York and elsewhere refused to abdicate control over the design of their notes. This was the price of private money creation.[51]

Some banks and banking associations turned to special inks as a substitute for these more radical reforms of the banking system. The New England Association for the Suppression of Counterfeiting took a special interest in this issue, thanks to the growing problem of altered notes. In 1853, the association opened a competition promising five hundred dollars to any inventor who could create indelible ink. As an added safeguard, it invited readers to test specimens submitted to the association, promising one hundred dollars to anyone who managed to alter them successfully. A year (and many altered notes) later, the association was forced to conclude that "nothing has yet been offered which the Committee can recommend as a perfect protection against alterations." The committee members who had overseen the inquiry could only recommend that banks print different denominations on different-sized pieces of paper—which would, in theory, make it more difficult to pass an altered note.[52]

Meanwhile, several new kinds of bogus bills made using calotype photography had surfaced, creating a small panic among the membership of the association and in the larger banking community. These new notes triggered an ontological crisis, obliterating the fragile divide between real and fake. "One such note, or copy, has been taken and presented to the Cashier of a Bank in State Street," reported the association in 1855. "Expressing some surprise at the appearance of the Note, [the cashier] unhesitatingly declared it to be a true bill, beyond all doubt, because the signature was genuine—was his own signature; of *that* he was sure!" Alarmed, the association could only recommend to its members that banks frustrate these new counterfeits by printing notes in black and red ink, an idea it subsequently abandoned after counterfeiters managed to tint their photographic notes.[53]

The association continued to pursue its quest for tamper-proof bank notes, but not without becoming enmeshed in a bizarre controversy over the feasibility of special ink and paper developed by Christopher Seropyan, an inventor residing in New York City. His patented invention consisted of "oil-colored paper" printed with a translucent indigo ink that was "equally or more fugitive than the color of the paper itself." In addition to preventing photographic counterfeits, Seropyan claimed that his notes could not be altered. Intrigued, the association put his invention to the test, but found it wanting. One member reported that Seropyan's invention had "proved to be quite vulnerable." In fact, the notes were especially dangerous because they "circulated as unalterable, and would, therefore, probably not be so closely scrutinized, upon that point, as ordinary Bank Notes." Another member concurred, warning that "the public is thus thrown off its guard upon this point" if the notes issued came with an "assurance from highly respectable authorities that they CANNOT BE ALTERED."[54]

Most every method of detecting counterfeits attracted this criticism sooner or later. It made sense: any defense that could be breached would play into the hands of the counterfeiters, who could exploit the false sense of security such assurances induced. It was the same problem many readers had with the detectors, and the association consequently began to view the possibility of a technological fix with serious skepticism. Seropyan and his allies, of course, did not see it this way, and they launched a public relations campaign that culminated in a flurry of accusations published in the financial papers. Much of the dispute was rooted in regional rivalries, with banks in New York lining up behind Seropyan and banks in Boston supporting the association. The New York banks, already suspicious of their counterparts in New England, dismissed their concerns as somehow politically motivated. In the end it did not matter: whatever its merits, few banks adopted the indelible ink. Nor was any particular safeguard adopted en masse, and by the end of the decade, the problem of altered, spurious, and counterfeit notes had only worsened.[55]

Ormsby followed these developments, perhaps delighting in evidence that a simple technological panacea was beyond reach. But by the late 1850s, he had more pressing concerns. Aside from his ongoing lawsuit against the Mercantile Agency, Ormsby was struggling financially, thanks to yet more changes in his industry. In the wake of the Panic of 1857, almost all of the surviving partnerships had combined into a sprawling entity: the American Bank Note Company. It was the first bank note corporation (all the others had been partnerships) and amalgamated no fewer than seven separate firms—"all the firms now engaged in the business of Bank-Note Engraving and Printing in the United States," one announcement proclaimed. This was not entirely accurate: Ormsby's New York Bank Note Company remained on the sidelines, barely clinging to life. His competitors, he claimed, had orchestrated his downfall, spreading rumors of his alliances with known counterfeiters. In a bitter screed published in 1862, he could only lament that "the entire control of the Note Engraving business . . . has passed from the artist into the hands of mere capitalists."[56]

This accusation was accurate, but not in the conventional meaning of the word "capitalist." The new monopoly was unlike any corporation before it, completely dominating the industry and centralizing its production, distribution, marketing, and sales divisions into a single building in New York City. "Its business is thoroughly systematized in its operations, and is divided into separate departments," noted one journalist who visited company headquarters. "Each department [is] under the charge of a competent superintendent, and all under the direction of a general manager, who is held accountable by a Board of Trustees." The new monopoly also adopted a "systematic division of labor" and other tools of scientific management. The bank-note engraving business thus became the first business in the nation to achieve the vertical and horizontal integration characteristic of the modern industrial age. This was a paradox: the very industry that had manufactured the paper symbols of an anarchic system of capitalism now became the harbinger of an entirely new economic order, one populated by corporate combines, industrial behemoths, and monopolies. Indeed, so dominant did the American Bank Note Company become that, as this writer observed, it "begins to hold the same relation to the paper currency of the country, that the United States Mint holds to the specie currency."[57]

The consolidation did not, however, put an end to counterfeiting. In 1862, with the Civil War entering its second bloody and inconclusive year, the *New York Times* offered a gloomy assessment of not only the war but also the currency that was supposed to pay for it. In a lead article that repeated many of Ormsby's arguments (and indeed, may have been written by the failed engraver), the paper warned its readers that counterfeit notes had become so ubiquitous that they threatened to undermine what little faith people still had in the money supply. Citing the "six thousand varieties of counterfeit money" in circulation, in addition to the many other kinds of bogus bills passing from hand to hand, the *Times* lamented what it described as a "spectacle . . . degrading to our National character, as well as an overwhelming condemnation of the system of Banking and Bank-note Engraving." Counterfeiting, the article concluded, was "undermining our morality as a Nation." It was, the headline proclaimed, a "National Evil Demanding a National Remedy." The editorialist's plea was impassioned as well as prescient: the Union was under siege, and out of the exigencies of war came an answer to the long-standing question of how to protect and maintain confidence in the currency. All the parties to the problem—engravers like Ormsby, his former competitors, the publishers of counterfeit detectors, banks and bankers, even the counterfeiters—found themselves drawn into the war. All would play a role. None, however, could have anticipated how very different their world would be once the firing stopped.[58]

SEVEN

Banking
on the Nation

L ate in the summer of 1861, as the Union and the Confederacy prepared for a long, punishing war, a novel form of paper money made its appearance: the greenback. The most common denomination was the five-dollar bill, which offered an object lesson in economic and political nationalism. The federal legislation sanctioning the issue—"ACT OF JULY 17, 1861"—crowned a portrait of Alexander Hamilton, advocate of a robust federal presence in the economy. The oversized assurance that dominated the center of the bill—"THE UNITED STATES PROMISE TO PAY TO THE BEARER FIVE DOLLARS ON DEMAND"—was one that would have resonated with Hamilton, a firm believer in the unifying power of the national debt. So, too, would the symbolism of Thomas Crawford's statue *Freedom Triumphant in War and Peace*, which occupied the left side of the bill. As a piece of propaganda, the money conveyed a message of national unity aimed not only at the Northern financiers who would underwrite the war, but also at the Southern states whose secession had triggered the conflict.

FIGURE 27. Though originally designed amid the deteriorating political situation of the 1850s, Liberty served here as a symbol of national unity: a brooch marked "U.S." held her robes in place, the shield in her left hand contained the national seal, and the national motto—E Pluribus Unum—encircled the base. *Courtesy, Federal Reserve Bank of Atlanta Monetary Museum.*

These notes did more than convey patriotic sentiment; they simultaneously underwrote the military campaign to preserve the Union. The federal government, faced with a financial crisis after the outbreak of war, turned to this new, national currency to pay its bills. But what began as a struggle over the financing of war swiftly acquired a deeper significance in both the North and the South. Whereas the South remained wedded to an older model of monetary policy in order to finance its bid for secession, a growing number of reformers in the North came to see the fate of the currency as interdependent with the fate of the nation. In articulating this vision, they fashioned not only a new system of currency, but also a new United States, one that made confidence in the nation synonymous with confidence in the nation's money—and vice versa. Their program, enacted in a series of halting and tentative steps, gradually spelled an end to the private monetary system and the counterfeit economy it had fostered. In place of the inchoate and confusing system of state bank notes, national leaders created a uniform currency, of equal value and acceptable everywhere, that rested on the public credit of the country rather than private assets of countless corporations.

As symbolic expressions of the authority of the federal government, these new bills had a sanctity that the old notes lacked. But like most symbols of authority, they meant nothing if the government could not safeguard them from imitation. This threat did not take long to materialize: shortly after the first greenbacks appeared, counterfeiters set to work producing their own versions of the new money, with often spectacular success. Indeed, the potential profit involved in counterfeiting a national currency far outstripped the more modest issues of the previous decades, and the ranks of the counterfeiters swelled during the war. But their enterprise, once tolerated and even celebrated, provoked a very different response now that the survival of the nation was at stake. What was once a nuisance or even an alternative source of currency was now a crime against the state, a treasonous assault on the nation's finances, and one that demanded a swift and ruthless response by the federal government.

The federal campaign against counterfeiting took shape in the shadow of Crawford's statue, which by the end of 1863 graced not only the greenbacks, but also the dome of the nation's capitol in Washington. The towering bronze figure faced east, overlooking a ramshackle cluster of dilapidated brick buildings a block away that was anything but a symbol of freedom. Known as the Old Capitol Prison, this makeshift penitentiary housed thousands of deserters, bounty jumpers, blockade runners, spies, rebel soldiers, and as the Civil War dragged on into the summer of 1864, counterfeiters. They arrived in small groups that year in the company of a short, powerful man dressed in a black coat, his eyes shaded by a broad-brimmed black hat. This was Colonel William P. Wood, the warden of the Old Capitol Prison and the founder of the U.S. Secret Service. From his base in the heart of the federal city, Wood launched the government's campaign against counterfeiters of the new national currency. What began as an informal, uncoordinated effort soon gained momentum, and after gaining official sanction for his operations, Wood started building what would become the first national police force in the country's history. From its humble beginnings in the precincts of the Old Capitol Prison, the Secret Service waged a ruthless campaign to suppress and dismantle the counterfeit economy that had thrived for close to a century. In the coming years, Wood and his successors fashioned a powerful bureaucracy that safeguarded the government's monopoly over the money supply, insuring the symbolic and material union between the country and the currency first forged during the Civil War.

Legal Tender

In the decades leading up to the Civil War, the federal government adopted a policy of benign neglect on monetary matters. After Andrew Jackson vetoed the rechartering of the Second Bank of the United States, the Hamiltonian vision of a strong central government linked to the interests of the capitalist class became ever more irrelevant. This trend intensified in the 1840s, with the establishment of the Independent Treasury, which conducted all of the government's business in gold and silver coin. As William Gouge, a longtime opponent of paper money, would observe in 1854, "Having separated itself entirely from paper money banks, the United States government [was] no longer responsible for the evils they produced." The spread of a sprawling system of state chartered banks was one consequence of this disengagement. The proliferation of bogus bank bills was another.[1]

The combination of a weak federal government and a multifarious money supply proved a liability in the opening months of the crisis between North and South. Salmon P. Chase, Lincoln's secretary of the treasury, had the misfortune to inherit this system. Though blessed with experience as a governor and senator from Ohio, Chase had almost no knowledge of business or finance (though he had, by most accounts, a fairly generous estimation of his own abilities). Upon assuming office, he found a sizable deficit bequeathed by the outgoing Buchanan administration as well as a sharp decline in tax revenues. Worse, the Independent Treasury Act of 1846 required that what little funds the government possessed be locked up in gold and silver and that all expenditures be paid for in the same. This, then, was the unpleasant situation of the federal government on the eve of a war that would ultimately cost more than two billion dollars.[2]

Chase, like most everyone else who came to play a role in the financial revolution of the Civil War, moved toward solutions to these problems with a mixture of confidence, blindness, and trepidation. Certain that a quick victory was at hand, he and others initially saw little need to overturn the monetary system already in place. But as the South held on longer than expected and the aims of the war grew more ambitious, Chase and his allies sought to do more than cleanse the nation of slavery; they also moved to assert federal control over the money supply. In the process, the war on slavery and states' rights became curiously intertwined with a constitutional and legislative war on the system of banking and counterfeiting that had served and plagued the country for decades. But that joint agenda was slow to coalesce. In the opening months of the conflict, the more pressing problem was how the North would finance the war.

In the summer of 1861, Chase managed to convince Congress to pass legislation authorizing him to borrow up to $250 million by issuing bonds payable in twenty years, along with two different kinds of treasury notes. The first was a short-term note that matured in three years and yielded interest payments of 7.3 percent. The second did not yield interest but was in theory repayable in specie when presented at the subtreasuries. Called "demand notes," these latter issues were meant to circulate, and marked a faltering first step toward a uniform national currency. There was some precedent for this step: the U.S. treasury had issued small quantities of federal notes in the past as a stopgap measure during wartime or periods of financial panic. But these earlier forms of federal currency rarely circulated as a medium of exchange, and generally came in high denominations. By contrast, the demand notes consisted of fives, tens, and twenties. In a symbolic gesture, the five-dollar notes depicted Alexander Hamilton, the first secretary of the treasury and an early proponent of a national currency. Still, in a sign that Chase did not comprehend the magnitude of the undertaking, Treasury Department officials signed every note, as was the custom with currency issued by state-chartered banks. As the burden of signing several million notes became apparent, the department substituted engraved signatures in place of handwritten ones.[3]

Had the North won a few decisive battles during that first summer, the impetus for a national currency would have ended with the initial issue of demand notes. But Bull Run and a series of Confederate victories crushed hopes that the war would soon be over. Chase therefore turned to the financial community of New York City in the hopes of selling the bonds approved by Congress. In August 1861, he met with the city's bankers to secure the purchase of $150 million in government securities. In a misguided bid to maintain the hard-money doctrine symbolized by the Independent Treasury, Chase insisted that the participating banks pay for the bonds in specie. As a consequence of this requirement, specie began to flow from the banks into the government's coffers and out again into the hands of people presenting the recently issued demand notes. Neither the government nor the banks managed to accumulate specie, which rapidly disappeared into private hoards or into the safes of speculators. By December, the banks had suspended specie payments on both their notes and their obligations to the government.[4]

Chase's insistence on specie payments had led to an unfortunate impasse, one that demanded an even more revolutionary solution that would ultimately expand the federal government's control of the currency at the expense of the state-chartered banks. His initial mistakes aside, Chase was well suited to orchestrate that revolution, even if he had misgivings about the constitutionality of some of the more radical provisions that passed into law. As governor of Ohio in the 1850s, he had already intimated that a uniform national currency was far preferable to the hodgepodge of currencies then in place, a view shared by many westerners. And in a letter to a newspaper editor in October 1861, Chase proclaimed, "I never have entertained a doubt that it was the duty of the general government to furnish a national currency. Its neglect of this duty has cost the people as much as this war will cost them. It must now be performed, not merely as a duty but as a matter of necessary policy."[5]

The same message, further elaborated, furnished the centerpiece of his report to Congress in December 1861. He used the occasion to revisit the infamous *Briscoe* decision of 1837, which had declared state bank notes constitutional. The result, he observed, had been a bank note circulation governed by the "laws of thirty-four States and the character of some sixteen hundred private corporations." Such variety did not lend itself to stability. "Under such a system, or rather lack of system," Chase observed, "great fluctuations, and heavy losses in discount and exchanges, are inevitable." Even worse, the inevitable failures of less solvent institutions meant that "considerable portions of the circulation become suddenly worthless in the hands of the people." The solution, Chase averred, was an expanded issue of demand notes combined with a "moderate tax, gradually augmented, on bank notes," which would, over time, yield a uniform currency issued and controlled by the federal government. This alone would not solve the pressing financial needs of the nation, and so Chase suggested that the government sanction the creation of national banks that would, as a requirement of incorporation, purchase federal bonds as a security for the notes they issued. Such banks, while underwriting the war effort, would also issue notes "bearing a common impression," or what would become another kind of uniform national currency.[6]

All of Chase's proposals eventually became law, but not in the order he envisioned. Dismantling the existing banking system, whether by taxing its notes or creating competing institutions chartered by Congress, was not feasible at this point; resistance from the banking community was too strong. Nor would such moves meet the government's desperate need for money to pay its creditors. When the House Committee on Ways and Means took up Chase's report, they addressed the need for money first—and for good reason. The demand notes already issued had begun to depreciate, thanks to the scarcity of specie; doubts now began to circulate about the government's ability to redeem its promises. Moreover, the legislation passed thus far had not made the demand notes legal tender; that distinction was held by gold and silver coin alone. As with the depreciated bills of state-chartered banks, creditors could refuse the demand notes when presented in payment of debts, making them an unreliable medium for the banks and the government to pay their bills.

The solution to this conundrum was relatively straightforward: make the existing notes legal tender while simultaneously issuing new notes. This fiat currency—which like the earlier demand notes came to be called "greenbacks"—was approved only after considerable debate. To its detractors, the move was eerily reminiscent of the moment when the Continental Congress resorted to the printing press to underwrite the Revolution, with disastrous results. "The whole argument used in favor of the issue of these legal tender notes," proclaimed Representative Owen Lovejoy, "is based upon precisely the same foundation as the old theological dogma, *crede ut edes, et edes*—believe that you eat the real flesh of Christ in the wafer, and you do eat it. Believe that this piece of paper is a five dollar gold piece, and it is a five dollar gold piece." Dismissing such "legislative legerdemain" as nothing more than "a delusion and a fallacy," Lovejoy warned that "there is no precipice, there is no chasm, there is no possible, yawning bottomless gulf before this nation, so terrible, so appalling, so ruinous, as this same bill that is before us." Abandoning the specie basis of the currency, Lovejoy warned, would mark the beginning of the end of the nation itself.[7]

Representative Samuel Hooper thought otherwise. A Boston merchant of conservative credentials, Hooper had devoted much of his career to the cause of banking reform, writing extensively on the problems of the nation's increasingly inchoate currency. In a series of pamphlets published in the 1850s, he had warned of the "great system of counterfeiting" that the state-chartered banks had fostered and he campaigned to force banks to hold greater reserves of specie to back the notes they issued. Hooper was not the sort of politician who could be counted on to support legislation that eschewed the widely held belief that specie alone was the basis of a sound currency. But that made his conversion to the legal tender cause all the more effective. As he explained in a pragmatic plea to the House on February 6, 1862, "Every intelligent man knows that coined money is not the currency of the country." The real issue, he noted, was "whether the Government shall depend on the irredeemable and depreciated notes of suspended banks, and use them as the medium in which to pay its debts to contractors and soldiers and others, or whether it shall make use of a paper issue of its own." That paper issue, Hooper suggested, should consist of legal tender notes that could be converted on demand into the twenty-year bonds authorized the previous year. They would not, however, be redeemable in specie any time in the foreseeable future. His earlier views notwithstanding, Hooper was adamant about making the issues legal tender. "To strike out the legal tender clause from this bill would make it useless," he warned, adding that "many of the banks now refuse to receive and pay out the demand notes." Simply issuing more would mean a further depreciation in their value.[8]

In the end, the arguments of Hooper and his allies won the day, despite the misgivings of Chase himself, who thought making the greenbacks legal tender a dangerous, if inevitable, step. Having passed the House, the bill proceeded to the Senate, where it fell into the protective custody of allies like Senator John Sherman of Ohio, who had replaced Chase when he departed for the Treasury Department. The younger brother of William Tecumseh, Sherman shared Hooper's growing conviction that the existing circulation of state bank notes must be replaced with a uniform national currency. And as Sherman's like-minded colleague, Senator James Doolittle of Wisconsin, observed, making greenbacks legal tender was a first step in that direction. "This government," he argued, "must assert its constitutional authority over the currency in some practicable way, and it seems to me that the mode proposed in this bill is the simplest and most direct." That Sherman and Doolittle hailed from the West was no accident: the region's troubled monetary history led them to embrace the new, national currency.[9]

The final legislation, signed into law by Lincoln on February 25, conferred legal tender status on the emission of some $100 million in greenbacks, as well as the $50 million worth of demand notes already issued. Public response to the issues was favorable, at least in the Northern press. In a typical dispatch, the *New York Herald* spoke of the "general joy and satisfaction" that greeted the greenbacks, citing them as "proof that the people are, and have been, long dissatisfied with the irresponsible bank money with which they have been flooded. Hence they hail with joy a currency standing on the good faith of the nation— a currency as secure as the nation itself." A few months later, the *Herald* observed that the greenback was a proxy for the "patriotism of the people, who, under no circumstances, will depreciate them; for that would be only destroying their own public credit, and the loss would have to fall ultimately upon themselves."[10]

That message was reinforced by the appearance of the greenbacks, which became miniature emissaries of the federal government, providing evidence in everyday life that the fate of the nation was now entwined with the banalities of economic exchange—and vice versa. The

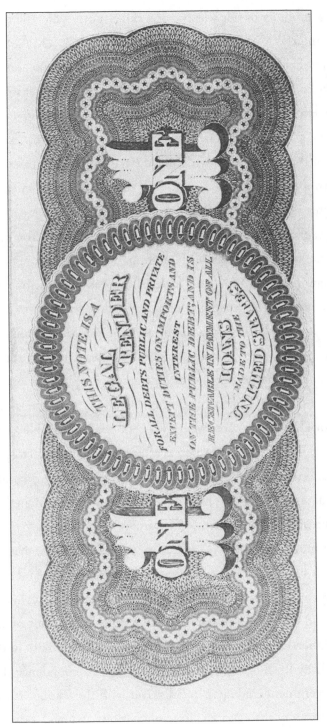

FIGURES 28 AND 29. A confident Salmon P. Chase stared from the front of the one-dollar notes, which earned the nickname "greenbacks" on account of the dye used to print the back of the bill. Unlike the first emission of greenbacks, which reassured readers that they would be redeemed in five years, subsequent issues—including this one—made no such promise. *Courtesy, Federal Reserve Bank of Atlanta Monetary Museum.*

most obvious reminder of this was the one-dollar note, which bore the visage of Salmon P. Chase on the left side of the bill. This feature marked a remarkable departure from existing practice and a momentous, if symbolic, expansion of federal sovereignty. In the past, citizens might never encounter a representative of national authority (aside from their local postmaster); now, Chase's countenance and the federal stewardship of the economy he symbolized circulated widely throughout the North—and as discussed later, even the South. In an interesting twist, notes of higher denominations made historical reference to the growing expansion of federal power by portraying the patron saint of economic nationalists, Alexander Hamilton, on three of the remaining denominations: twos, fives, and fifties. Lincoln's portrait, by contrast, was relegated to the ten-dollar bills alone, though this may have had more to do with Chase's low opinion of the president than anything else. Every note proclaimed its status as "legal tender, for all debts public and private except duties on imports and interest on the public debt" and on the initial emission promised that it was "exchangeable for U.S. six per cent twenty years' bonds, redeemable at the pleasure of the United States of America after five years." This last part raised more questions than it answered, but for the moment, the notes averted a fiscal crisis. They also marked a paradigm shift, unifying the interests of the nation with a common currency.[11]

This was a momentous step. The illusory promise of specie-backed paper had been superseded by something that rested on a far more abstract and transcendent notion: the credit of the nation. This was not a credit that could be reduced to piles of coin sitting in the vault of any given bank; rather, this was a credit that rested on a nascent faith in the nation itself. Initially, this meant nothing more than a confidence that the federal government could pay its bills. But with the war effort cast as a struggle to unify the country, these obligations assumed a deeper

significance. For many people in the North and the South, the greenbacks came to represent the United States in a way that the money of
the antebellum era never did. The greenbacks were issued by the nation, for the nation, in order to pay for the preservation of the nation.
Backed by nothing more than the future credit of the nation (and the
vague promise of some interest), their value was dependent on the outcome of the struggle that had prompted their issue in the first place. A
pyramid scheme, perhaps, but a rather successful one. The South em-
barked on an equally audacious plan. But whereas the North's program
yielded a source of funds and a revitalized sovereignty, the South's fiscal
experiment collapsed under the weight of its own contradictions.

Counterfeit Confederates

When the Confederate Congress met to draft its constitution in 1861,
it used the original from 1789 as its model. Nonetheless, it made a
few significant clarifications, changes that crippled its efforts to raise
money for the war. It eliminated, for example, the clause that forbade
individual states from issuing bills of credit. At the same time, it prohibited the Confederate states from making such notes legal tender,
reserving that status for gold and silver coin alone. According to the
Jeffersonian and Jacksonian traditions of constitutional interpretation
popular in the South, with their veneration for the Tenth Amendment,
this meant that both the states and the central government could issue
notes. Yet neither could make them legal tender: the central government because it had not explicitly been given the power to do so; the
states because they had been denied that privilege. The result was a
flood of paper from all quarters.[12]

Some measure of the problem can be gained from comparing the
source of the two regions' funds. The North, on the one hand, tapped a

relatively wide range of revenue sources to underwrite its war effort. Some 21 percent of the total came from taxes, with another 62 percent coming from the sale of interest-bearing bonds. The greenbacks accounted for only 13 percent of the total raised—a not insignificant amount, but hardly an unhealthy reliance. The South, on the other hand, was forced by a range of circumstances (some imposed on it and some of its own making) to resort to the printing press to fund its attempt at secession. It had no apparatus for collecting taxes, and what little was collected was paid in paper money that the states themselves had issued. Worse, gold and silver were in very short supply; indeed, at the outset of the war, the entire Confederacy had less specie on hand than the banks in New York City, despite having seized the assets of the mint in New Orleans. Banks consequently suspended specie payments in the South long before they did in the North.[13]

All of these problems exacerbated the central contradiction at the heart of the Confederate enterprise: in order to win the war, it needed to create a strong central government. But that need inevitably collided with the impulse, intensified by decades of wrangling over slavery, to protect the sovereignty of the individual states. Consequently, when the newly appointed secretary of the treasury, Christopher Memminger, convinced the Confederate Congress to levy a property tax to fund the war, the legislation ran afoul of the states. Suspicious of centralized authority, they denied that the Confederate Constitution permitted the "general government" to force the states to collect taxes on its behalf. The various taxes that the Confederacy attempted to impose on its recalcitrant members were denounced in no uncertain terms as "tyrannical," "unconstitutional," and "anti-republican." Prior to October 1864, less than 5 percent of the Confederate government's total revenue over the course of the war came from taxation.[14]

Memminger had other options at his disposal, but these proved equally problematic. Sales of government securities, while promising at first, were hampered by rising prices, which made bond yields unattractive on anything but patriotic grounds. Indeed, much of the price inflation stemmed from the other strategy adopted by the Confederate Congress in August of 1861: the production of treasury notes similar to the demand notes and greenbacks issued by the North. The first emission was approved in March 1861, and consisted of $1 million in mostly high-denomination ($500 and $1,000) notes bearing 3.65 percent interest. Every subsequent emission, however, consisted of non-interest-bearing notes representing the obligations of the Confederate government. By the end of the war, the Confederacy had put more than $1.5 billion of these into circulation. Despite sporadic attempts to declare these notes legal tender, they remained otherwise, meaning that they could be refused in business transactions without any penalty. With their purchasing power undercut, the "graybacks," as they came to be called, lacked the very authority of the government whose finances they were meant to sustain.[15]

Worse, the Confederate treasury soon found that the very simple act of printing this dubious currency proved extraordinarily difficult. This was a direct consequence of that truism of Civil War history: the North's industrial superiority. Most bank note engravers and printers resided in the North, and prior to the war, most state-chartered banks in the South commissioned Northern bank note engravers to manufacture their notes. In fact, before the formal declaration of war, the Confederacy hired the National Bank Note Company of New York to print its initial series of interest-bearing notes. After U.S. authorities seized the plates, Memminger commissioned Solomon Schmidt, director of the New Orleans branch of the American Bank Note Company, to produce some $20 million in treasury notes. Schmidt, one of Memminger's deputies later explained, was "illy provided with men and tools to execute a large order." That fall, the Confederate treasury seized Schmidt's plates and presses and moved them to Columbia, South Carolina, where the government centralized its printing and engraving operations.[16]

Lacking skilled steel-plate bank note engravers, the Confederacy sent emissaries overseas to recruit the necessary talent. In the meantime, the government was forced to turn to a number of different lithographers working in the South. These included Hoyer and Ludwig, a partnership between a German lithographer and a goldsmith-watchmaker, whose crude efforts Memminger described as "peculiar"; the firm of Keatinge and Ball, founded by a former employee of the American Bank Note Company whom the Confederacy had lured away; and Colonel Blanton Duncan, an entrepreneur with no experience in printing or engraving. These and several other firms and partnerships with equally negligible qualifications became the sole source of the Confederacy's money supply during the course of the war. (An eleventh-hour attempt to hire a British engraving firm ended when the plates were captured by the Union blockade.)[17]

Shortages plagued the production of notes throughout the war. Most troubling was the perennial lack of skilled engravers. The arrival of foreign craftsmen alleviated the problem, but only for a short time. As the New York Herald reported later in the war, "The rebel authorities imported a number of Englishmen for the purpose of manufacturing rebel notes." Faithful at first, the workers soon "tired of the slow manner of their own enrichment [and] set up an establishment of their own," where they produced several hundred thousand dollars' worth of notes for their personal use. Attempts to recruit engravers from the ranks of Union prisoners proved even more fruitless. One soldier taken prisoner at Bull Run recalled how a fellow captive, a "superior engraver" who had been "formerly employed" by the Union Bank Note Engraving

Company in New York, "received frequent personal applications from Richmond bankers to furnish bank note engravings, or plates." The nameless engraver was alleged to have turned them down, and escaped from prison shortly thereafter.[18]

Several design flaws made Confederate money especially susceptible to counterfeiting. The few firms that produced notes using steel plates often reused existing vignettes and dies confiscated at the outset of the war rather than engrave new designs. Moreover, the same vignettes surfaced over and over on different notes and bonds, making the labor of counterfeiting one note applicable to other notes as well. Worse, the majority of the notes produced for the Confederacy relied on lithographic engraving, which produced fuzzy, indistinct prints that could be imitated with less effort than those printed from steel plates. To complicate matters, the peculiar conditions of currency production in Columbia—an ever-changing number of firms and partnerships involved in engraving and printing—yielded countless variations of each denomination and issue, making it more difficult to keep track of genuine issues, much less counterfeits. Additional variations resulted from the many different kinds of bank note paper used in production, most of which was smuggled from the North in small shipments. Compounding this bizarre situation was the insistence of the many different engravers and printers that they sign their notes. The coup de grâce was the government's insistence on counter-signing each note by hand, which required the employment of some 262 different clerks. Though Memminger warned that this system only made it more difficult to keep track of the different issues, and hence made them easier to counterfeit, his concerns went unheeded.[19]

The first known counterfeits went into circulation late in 1861. Few of these originated with counterfeiters, who seem to have considered the Confederate notes unworthy of imitation. Rather, they came from

legitimate printers and engravers in the North who sought to undermine the Southern currency while turning a profit. The most famous of
these printers was Samuel Upham, the owner of a newspaper stand in
Philadelphia who also sold stationery (including patriotic envelopes
mocking Jefferson Davis) and patent medicines with colorful names
like "Upham's Pimple Banisher." As he would recall in a letter written
to a historian many years later, Upham got his start in March 1862,
when he noticed a great demand for a local newspaper. Curious, he
soon learned that the day's issue contained a facsimile of a five-dollar
Confederate note, "the first that had been seen this side of the rebel
lines." Being an enterprising sort, Upham immediately called on the
editor and purchased an electrotype plate of the note, and had them
printed up on French letter paper. "They sold like 'hot cakes,'" he rec-
ollected, and Upham decided to add counterfeiting to his repertoire.
Drawing on skilled engravers in the Philadelphia area, he commissioned facsimiles of Confederate tens, hundreds, and other notes. In
order to distinguish himself from his competitors, and avoid being labeled a counterfeiter, Upham printed the following on the outer border
of his notes: "Fac-simile Confederate Notes Sold, Wholesale and Retail. By S. C. Upham, 403 Chestnut Street, Phila." Purchasers, however, could easily trim off the margin and then use them in lieu of the
genuine notes.[20]

Upham, who by his own estimate sold some $15 million worth of
Confederate notes on both the wholesale and retail markets, relied on
an elaborate advertising campaign to promote his product. Testimo-
nials taken from newspapers appeared in circulars and broadsides, at-
testing, for example, that "his lithographed notes are worth just as
much as those issued by Jeff Davis" and "are as valuable . . . as the originals." In fact, Upham's facsimiles and the other imitations that flooded
the market approached and in some cases exceeded the crude engrav-

ings produced by the firms under contract with the Confederacy. Many soldiers carrying Upham's notes into the Confederacy found, as one correspondent did, that Upham's notes were "invariably preferred by the unsophisticated rebels to their own productions." This was not an isolated incident. As the Confederate currency began to depreciate, the quality of both the engraving and the paper became a more credible measure of value than the bills' false promises of redemption.[21]

While there is little evidence that the Union actively encouraged the purchase and dissemination of counterfeits as a means of undermining the Southern currency, the Confederates increasingly came to see these notes as evidence of Union plots and conspiracies. Southern newspapers carried accounts of Union prisoners found with "bogus Confederate bills of small denominations, which they attempted to palm upon boys on the streets for bread, confectionary, &c" in an orchestrated attempt to "injure the Confederate currency." Likewise, a diarist in New Orleans wrote of how the Union soldiers "go to the battles with their pockets stuffed with counterfeit Confederate money which they intend to pass off if they succeed in getting into the country," an allegation corroborated in a number of accounts, including a print of soldiers purchasing counterfeit notes. News of these incidents caused considerable consternation in the offices of the Confederate treasury. As early as November 1861, Memminger received letters warning him that unnamed individuals "encouraged by the authorities" were "preparing in New York and Philadelphia a larger issue of counterfeit Treasury notes of the Confederate States . . . with a view to destroy the genuine notes as a currency." Memminger wrote Alexander Stephens in August of 1862, complaining of the growing number of counterfeits, and arguing that "the fact that they are publicly advertised for sale at the North proves the connivance at least, and probably the complicity, of the Government"—a view shared, it seems, by Jefferson Davis.[22]

FIGURE 30. Detail from Adalbert John Volck's engraving *Counterfeit Confederate Notes Publicly Offered for Sale in the "City of Brotherly Love."* Courtesy, Collection of The New-York Historical Society.

In all probability, the federal government took little interest in counterfeiters of Confederate notes. There is evidence that the Treasury Department, curious as to Upham's activities, paid him a visit shortly after he began advertising his notes. According to one newspaper account, Upham "said he was engaged in crippling the rebel treasury, and thought it was very strange he should be molested." When asked to elaborate, Upham allegedly said, "You see . . . these are better than the original article; the originals are worthless; they are unauthorized by law; so I am not counterfeiting." In the end, the case was referred to Secretary of State William Seward and then passed on to the War Department, which apparently permitted Upham to resume his sales, which he continued until August of the following year. By that time, he had plenty of competition in the facsimile business, the most prominent being Winthrop Hilton, a lithographer, counterfeiter, and pornographer in New York City. According to Upham's account, Hilton "copied several of my fac-simile notes" and began selling them to "bogus . . . cotton brokers and other scalawags, who passed through the Confederate lines and purchased cotton from the Rebel planters." There is plenty of anecdotal evidence to support Upham's claim, and the Southern papers gave accounts of "sharpers" purchasing items at blockade auctions using counterfeit money. Furthermore, Hilton advertised his notes as early as October 1862 in *Harper's*, where he promised "perfect fac-similes of confederate treasury notes" at a somewhat higher price than Upham's products (also advertised in *Harper's*). By some accounts, this was a testament to Hilton's superior product.[23]

Hilton was eventually arrested in January 1864 on suspicion of being a supplier of genuine Confederate currency to the South, and the authorities found at his workshop no less than $6 million in bonds and $1 million in treasury notes, along with the lithographic stones for printing a variety of denominations. He languished in jail for months, and the local newspapers congratulated the federal government on having robbed the Confederate government of its money supply. But what made the case preposterous in retrospect was the fact that the bills were indeed counterfeit, as attested by Memminger in a letter he wrote to an associate who had read of the arrest. Assuring his correspondent, who had worries that the stories were true, Memminger counseled him to leave "the Yankee police under their present impressions, as I have very little doubt that it is some establishment for the issue of counterfeits that they have ferreted out." Though Hilton's case eventually ended up on Lincoln's desk, he does not seem to have been prosecuted for supplying the Confederacy. Nor, for that matter, was he punished for counterfeiting its notes.[24]

This kind of categorical confusion between the genuine and the counterfeit was mirrored by the Confederate treasury's own policies. As expenditures mounted and revenue declined, it became necessary to pay debts with additional issues of treasury notes. With each issue, the notes depreciated further, driving up prices in an inflationary spiral and prompting the production of still more notes. This vicious cycle reached a point where the treasury began to have difficulty keeping up with the demand for paper, a condition exacerbated by paper shortages. In what can only be described as either a perverse financial experiment or a tacit acknowledgment that the Confederate government was having trouble meeting the demand for money, Memminger suggested in 1862 that the South should begin honoring counterfeit currency as genuine. After all, Memminger wrote Alexander Stephens, many of the "notes were so well counterfeited that they will be freely received in business transactions." Legislation passed shortly afterward sanctioned this notion under certain circumstances, and banks began counting counterfeit graybacks as part of their legitimate assets, inflating the currency still further. With the distinctions between the counterfeit and the genuine obliterated, the Confederate treasury effectively abdicated whatever remaining sovereignty over the currency it possessed. It had, by implication, become just another counterfeiter, and judging from the quality of its notes, a pretty lousy one at that.[25]

As the graybacks became ever more worthless, citizens of the Confederacy began to discount their own currency in exchange for greenbacks. So began a process by which the South was absorbed once again into the nation—not through brute military force or territorial conquest, but via the green slips of paper that denoted a reinvigorated Union. Intimations of this trend surfaced fairly early on in the conflict. "Rebel officers have been here and offer $5 to $15 Confederate for $1 in greenbacks," a Northern soldier taken prisoner in 1861 confided to his diary. "They have a curious faith in success." The following November, a clerk in the Confederate War Department made an equally portentous observation. Noting that farmers were refusing the graybacks, "the only money we have in circulation," he speculated that "five millions of 'greenbacks' . . . might be more effectual in expelling the Confederate Government and restoring that of the United States than all of Meade's army." By 1863, that possibility seemed much closer at hand, with the Confederate Congress investigating rumors that "brokers and others in the city of Richmond are publicly offering the currency of the United States, known as 'greenbacks,' for sale or exchange for Confederate money, at a ruinous discount on the latter."[26]

Certainly, many Confederates made clear their preference for the South's new currency, with its pictures of slaves, regional heroes, agrarian scenes, allegorical figures, and Confederate leaders. As one former Northerner taken prisoner in 1863 recounted in a newspaper, "A Virginia white boy came into the camp to sell tobacco, for which he charged one dollar a plug. Col. Tilden and one of his captains wanted two plugs, and offered two dollar greenbacks for them." This Virginian, the prisoner reported, "didn't take that kind of money, and wanted Confederate paper." By contrast, he noted, "Negroes who sell bread and fruit to the prisoners are too shrewd to take anything other than Union money." A year later, many white Southerners began following the lead of slaves and ex-slaves. On the front lines, one Southern officer reported that "Confederate currency . . . has ceased to have even a nominal value," and warned that "unless the most stringent measures are adopted we shall soon have Federal currency . . . to the entire exclusion of Confederate paper." By 1864, the situation had become so serious that the Confederate Congress passed a law prohibiting its citizens—free or otherwise—from "dealing in the paper currency of the enemy." But by then it was too late.[27]

The National Banks

Despite the popularity of the greenbacks and the growing enthusiasm for nation-building in the North, there remained the circulation of state bank notes, which for many seemed an incongruous reminder of states' rights. But when the U.S. Congress passed a revenue bill in July of 1862 that imposed the first ever federal taxes on property and income, the prospect of taxing state bank notes, as had been proposed a year earlier, became a realistic prospect. Later that year, Lincoln pushed the debate even further, calling for the organization of a system of national banks that would circulate notes uniform in appearance and secured by U.S. bonds—the same bonds that had been approved as a means of borrowing money to pay for the war. Such bank notes, Lincoln promised, would "protect labor against the evil of a vicious currency and facilitate commerce by cheap and safe exchanges." Several days later, Chase followed up with his own plea for an end to the system of state-chartered banks, calling instead for the "establishment of one sound, uniform circulation of equal value throughout the country

upon the foundation of national credit combined with private capital."
The same Hamiltonian argument was put forward shortly thereafter in
even starker terms by Robert J. Walker, a lawyer, politician, journalist,
and recent convert to the nationalist cause. Using the pages of his *Continental Monthly* as a forum, Walker called on the federal government
to resume "the great sovereign function of regulating the currency and
giving to it uniformity and nationality." In no uncertain terms, he cast
the Confederacy as the inevitable progeny of "state supremacy, state al-
legiance, and state secession," and complained that "now the government is paralyzed financially . . . by a question as to state banks."
Critics of Chase's plan, Walker asserted, spoke "the very language of
rebellion—the echo of South Carolina treason."[28]

It is unlikely the banking community of New York City saw it that
way, but then again, almost all of them jealously guarded their right to
issue notes, and viewed the plan to nationalize the banking system with
understandable trepidation. One exception was John Thompson, an
entrepreneur and publisher of the most ubiquitous of all the counterfeit
detectors. Back in June 1861, Thompson had written to Chase and Lincoln, proposing the adoption of a bond-backed "system of Government
currency" that would be "free from discount, free from failures, conve-
nient for remittances by mail and much more desirable to carry when
traveling or marching than gold." Echoing the argument that a national paper currency gave citizens a stake in the outcome of the war,
Thompson claimed that "every well wisher of our country's cause will
feel that holding these notes if for only a day is contributing a mite in
time of need." But Thompson was very much an exception, if an important one. At the beginning of 1863, he could do little to move legislation along, save for publishing editorials promoting Chase's plan. The
real heavy lifting fell instead to allies in Congress, notably Representative Samuel Hooper and Senator John Sherman.[29]

Sherman's line of attack began with legislation he introduced on January 5, 1863, only a few days after Lincoln issued the Emancipation Proclamation. The proposed bill called for a tax on state bank notes aimed at phasing them out of existence. Two days later, Hooper introduced unrelated legislation in the House that spelled out the administration's recommendations for a system of federally chartered national banks. The day after, Sherman began a rhetorical offensive against the state banks that attacked them on both constitutional and practical grounds. Citing an impressive list of precedents, authorities, and arguments, Sherman distilled his case down to a few simple propositions: "Congress has the power to regulate commerce; Congress has the power to borrow money, which involves the power to emit bills of credit; Congress has the power to regulate the value of coin. These powers," he argued, "are exclusive . . . No State has the power to interfere with this exclusive power in Congress to regulate the national currency [or] provide a substitute for the national coin." Sherman avoided any explicit discussion of the *Briscoe* decision, but hammered away at it indirectly, citing evidence of something that could sway his listeners: original intent. "It was the intention of the framers of the Constitution," he proclaimed, "to destroy absolutely all paper money, except that issued by the United States."[30]

Sherman made a more pragmatic plea for the adoption of a national currency by raising the specter of counterfeit notes. "The losses to the people by counterfeiting never can be avoided when you have such a multitude of banks," he warned. "You cannot prevent the people from suffering largely from counterfeiting when you have sixteen hundred different banks, issuing each of them several different kinds of bills, under the laws of twenty-eight different States." The resulting confusion meant that anyone handling the currency rarely bothered to memorize the appearance of any given note. "When a stranger presents a bank bill for circulation, the person about to receive it looks rather at the man who presents it to see whether his face is honest, than at the bill to detect whether it is counterfeit or not." The creation of a uniform national currency, he argued, would eliminate the problem. "When the notes are few in kind, only three or four of them, all issued by the United States, all of a uniform character," Sherman predicted, "they cannot be counterfeited because their face will become so familiar that every man will know a genuine note; he will detect it in a moment as the countenance of a familiar friend."[31]

Here was an answer to the dilemma that Herman Melville had outlined only a few years before in the *Confidence Man*. In a nation increasingly composed of strangers and filled with a growing number of banks and bank notes, it was impossible to assess the value of a note from its appearance alone. People doing business had to rely on other securities: the demeanor of the person presenting the note, for example. But this, too, could be counterfeited, as Melville himself warned, and was no more fixed and certain than the amount of gold and silver standing behind the note. Sherman offered a solution: the nation would become, by virtue of its infiltration into every facet of commercial life, a "familiar friend" or familiar face, much the way that Salmon Chase's visage reassured citizens handling the greenbacks already in circulation.

During that January, the prospect of a radical reform of the country's currency began to gather momentum, and Sherman's allies published articles in the press echoing his arguments. On January 26, Sherman introduced a version of the national bank bill that was largely the same as the one proposed by Hooper several weeks earlier. At the same time, he wrote a series of articles in the *New York Times* that repeated many of the practical arguments already put forth, while clarifying the patriotic justifications for eradicating the existing currency and replacing it with something both uniform and national. Doing so, he claimed in one such article, would confer an added, Hamiltonian benefit: "Government and the people . . . would for the first time become inseparably united and consolidated. The people would have acquired a new and direct interest in the support of the Government, because their currency would depend for safety on the maintenance of that Government." To opponents of the plan, particularly the note-issuing banks, Sherman had an effective, if inflammatory reply, contending that their claims were nothing more than an assertion of "the accursed heresy of State Sovereignty, laying at the foundation of the slaveholders' rebellion."[32]

On February 10, Sherman again spoke at length on the bill, elaborating with ever more force and urgency both the evils of the existing system and the necessity of reforming it. The problem of counterfeiting was again addressed, with Sherman asking, "How is it possible for any honest man to detect the genuine from the counterfeit, when he has to select from seven thousand different kinds of bank bills?" By contrast, Sherman promised that under his proposed system there "will be but six or seven kinds of notes. They would become familiar to us, so that every man would be a counterfeit detector in himself, and would not be compelled to look through a long list to ascertain whether a bill was genuine or not. This very fact would give a credit and currency to bank circulation which it has not now." He urged nothing less than the creation of a system of national banks. "The policy of this country," he argued, "ought to be to make everything national as far as possible; to nationalize our country so that we love our country."[33]

His pleas had the desired effect, and the Senate passed the bill two days later. Though many thought it would die in the House, the taint of states' rights became too much of a liability to the bill's opponents, and after a few key defections to Sherman's camp, the legislation passed and was signed into law on February 25, 1863. In its final form, the bill was a compromise between federal and state sovereignties. Rather than create a single, national bank, it empowered the federal government to grant charters for a new system of national banks. Any group of five or more individuals with sufficient capital could now apply for a charter. Though the bill led to a few new banks, its aim was to encourage established note-issuing banks to relinquish their state charters in exchange for federal charters. These new "national banks" could then issue notes, the amount of which depended on the government bonds these institutions had purchased as security to back their issues.[34]

At the same time, the design, engraving, and printing of the new notes was taken out of the hands of the banks and vested with the federal comptroller of the currency. Because there was not yet a Bureau of Engraving and Printing, the treasury turned to private parties to do the work. Toward that end, Secretary Chase put out a call to "artists, engravers, and others" to submit designs for notes in denominations of $5, $10, $20, $50, $100, $500, and $1,000 (an amendment passed in 1864 permitted the issue of notes in denominations of $1, $2, and $3). The circular was printed and reprinted; John Thompson, for example, published it in his *Bank Note and Commercial Reporter* in April 1863. Chase made it clear in the competition's announcement that "the designs must be national in their character; and none will be considered that have been used, in whole or in part, upon any currency, bond, certificate, or other representative of value." In a further restriction, he prescribed that completed bills be of the "uniform size" of seven inches by three inches. Engravers also had to leave room for two blocks of text. The first would contain a message declaring the notes legal tender; the second was to contain the text of sections 57 and 58 of the National Currency Act, which spelled out in no uncertain terms the maximum punishments for counterfeiting the notes: fifteen years' hard labor and a fine of $1,000. Chase concluded his call with a notice that "special attention will be given to security against counterfeiting."[35]

The winning designs came from three bank-note engraving corporations. The first was the American Bank Note Company, which had

FIGURES 31 AND 32. Waterman Ormsby engraved the scenes that appeared on all the five-dollar bills of the new national banks: Christopher Columbus in sight of land on the left, and an allegorical image of the meeting of Europe and America on the right. The design of this new national currency permitted banks to personalize the bills by leaving space for their name and location. *Courtesy, National Numismatic Collection, Smithsonian Institution.*

been spawned by the massive merger and consolidation movement of the late 1850s. The other two were short-lived competitors: the National Bank Note Company, formed in 1859 by engravers who had refused to join the American Bank Note Company; and the Continental Bank Note Company, an organization formed in coordination with suspect engraver Waterman Ormsby. The American and the National, both of which had already won contracts for printing the greenbacks, received the bulk of the work for the new notes, but Ormsby's Continental was responsible for the balance (despite Chase's misgivings about hiring someone of Ormsby's reputation). The designs, per Chase's request, depicted people and events central to the nation's history and myth: Columbus sighting land; Sir Walter Raleigh in England, exhibiting corn and tobacco from America; the baptism of Pocahontas; the departure and landing of the Pilgrims; Benjamin Franklin capturing electricity with his kite; the Battle of Lexington; the signing of the Declaration of Independence; Washington crossing the Delaware; Washington resigning his commission; and others. The remainder of the vignettes consisted of stock allegorical figures, including the ubiquitous Liberty.[36]

It was an eclectic set of designs, but all sought to create, through the medium of the currency, a common history that transcended not only the histories of the individual states, but also the formal chronological boundaries of the nation itself. That most of the vignettes predated the ratification of the Constitution testified to the need to establish a shared history between North and South that avoided the controversies over slavery during the antebellum era. The rarest note—the $1,000 bill—did make reference to the Mexican-American War, an event that ultimately fueled tensions between North and South. But taken as a whole, the notes represent an imperfect attempt to paper over sectional divisions and set the stage for a reunion. The most common of all the notes—the one-dollar bill—showed two young women shaking hands before an altar, a not-so-subtle allusion to hopes of unification. (The South, by contrast, printed notes at this time bearing an allegory of the South slaying the Union.)[37]

At first, the national bank notes remained a curiosity, dwarfed by the sheer number of greenbacks already in circulation. This was largely Chase's fault, for he initially insisted that any bank applying for a federal charter give up its name in exchange for a number. Few banks took him up on the offer, though a handful of individuals applied for charters in order to set up entirely new banks. The first to do so was John Thompson, who with his two sons founded the First National Bank of New York. It was not a popular institution in New York City, and Thompson's competitors led the opposition to create a uniform national currency. "I had up-hill work at the start," Thompson later recalled, for the other state banks had refused to let him into the Clearing House, which facilitated the settlement of accounts between banks in the city. In an attempt to help, Chase enlisted Thompson to sell government securities. As payments for these (drawn on other New York City banks) flowed into Thompson's vaults, he presented them at the banks that held the accounts, demanding specie payments. Eventually, the other city banks relented, and Thompson was admitted to the Clearing House.[38]

Thompson aside, most banks were reluctant to abandon their names and reincorporate under federal charters. By the end of 1863, a mere sixty-six national banks had begun operation, compared to more than 1,500 state banks still in business. Chase, realizing his error, rescinded his request that banks give up their names, and by March 1864, some 469 national banks had incorporated. The treasury, seeking to draw the remaining state banks into the fold, suggested to Congress that it "prohibit the further issue of bank notes not authorized by itself and compel, by taxation . . . the withdrawal of those which have been already issued." Senator Sherman, taking up a familiar cause, introduced legislation that imposed a prohibitive tax of 10 percent on state bank notes. Lincoln signed the measure into law the day before his second inauguration. Over the course of the next year, the remaining state chartered banks fell into line, adopting federal charters and issuing the new uniform currency. A few hundred banks retained their charters, but stopped issuing notes.[39]

The shift from a decentralized system of banks and bank notes to a uniform money supply did more than tie together the country and the currency; it also solved, at least in part, the problem that Melville had identified. Confidence in the currency, which had formerly depended on a host of often contradictory variables—the perceived soundness of a bank, the character of a customer, the appearance of a note—now rested on something far more abstract, yet paradoxically more solid: trust in the nation. It was a profound transformation, one that helped usher in a new economic order in which the state assumed stewardship of the economy for both the public and private interest. It also meant that counterfeiting, once tolerated or even applauded, now posed a direct challenge to federal sovereignty. As the Civil War came to a close, the national government began to grapple with this threat, creating a police apparatus that transcended state lines: the Secret Service. This bureaucracy, the first of its kind, finished the job initiated by the currency reforms of the 1860s, cementing the authority of the new nation-state.

Policing the Economy

For all its celebrated efficiency and professionalism, the Secret Service emerged under murky, even suspicious circumstances. It did not originate with an act of Congress, but grew out of schemes concocted by a motley collection of individuals, people whom historian David Johnson has described, in a memorable turn of phrase, as "bureaucratic entrepreneurs." The most important and famous of these self-promoters was William Patrick Wood, a man one contemporary remembered as "short, ugly, and slovenly in his dress; in manner affecting stupidity and humility, but at bottom the craftiest of men." It was precisely this combination of contradictory qualities that enabled Wood to triumph where other more conventional figures might have failed. Indeed, though he had rather mixed success in suppressing counterfeiting, he left behind a more important legacy: a bureaucratic fiefdom that became the foundation for all future efforts to protect the currency. This organization, like many bureaucracies, outlived its creator, far exceeding its original limited—and perhaps questionable—mandate.[40]

Wood's path to power was a curious one. A veteran of the Mexican-American War, he was a skilled machinist and patent model maker who supplemented his income by working as a freewheeling detective and bodyguard. In the 1850s, Wood made the acquaintance of the lawyer Edwin Stanton, assisting him during the legal battle over the patent rights to McCormick's reaper. Stanton eventually became Lincoln's secretary of war, and installed his protégé as superintendent of the Old Capitol Prison. The former corporal, paid at the rate of a regular cavalry colonel, took to calling himself Colonel Wood. His prison soon filled with inmates: runaway slaves, prisoners of war, hostages, deserters, spies, people accused of defrauding the government, blockade runners, as well as individuals Wood simply described as "suspicious characters" and "tough citizens generally." As the war entered its second year, Wood processed and questioned thousands of captured Confederates, extracting valuable military intelligence that he passed on to Stanton. By his own admission, he read all the incoming and outgoing mail, and once bragged to Belle Boyd, the alleged Confederate spy, that "there warn't any thing going on in the prison that [I] didn't know of." Much of his information apparently came from merciless interrogations of prisoners. According to one source, "Wood used to counterfeit testimony convicting the prisoner, and read it to him." He often denied prisoners the right to lawyers, bail, and many of the other privileges typically granted to suspects. Stanton either overlooked—or more likely, sanctioned—these violations of civil liberties.[41]

During 1862 and 1863, Wood expanded his powers, taking advantage of his friendship with Stanton to indulge in a series of adventures behind enemy lines. On one occasion he posed as a Confederate soldier and visited a prison in North Carolina containing captured Union soldiers. To the inmates he handed out thousands of dollars in graybacks, most likely counterfeit. He then proceeded to Richmond, ostensibly to help broker an exchange of prisoners between the two sides. In a typical case of Wood's willingness to take matters into his own hands, he opened negotiations with the Confederate government over the fate of other prisoners, something he expressly lacked authorization to do. Exasperated, one Union officer telegraphed officials in Washington and complained that "Mr. Wood is doing the most absurd things in Richmond." Wood eventually returned empty-handed, and the commissioner in charge of prisoner exchanges wrote him a blistering letter: "You assumed power and formally signed your name to an agreement . . . which would virtually have paralyzed [the United States government's] power to act upon rebels under the Law of treason."[42]

This, then, was the man who launched the federal government's decades-long campaign against the counterfeit economy. He was not an obvious choice to lead a federal bureaucracy; he certainly lacked the propriety that became so valued a trait in civil servants in later years. But the very qualities that led him into such trouble—both before and during his tenure as head of the Secret Service—also enabled him to carve out a permanent bureaucratic empire where others might have failed. There was a paradox here: one of the most successful law enforcement campaigns in the nation's history began with an individual whose operations often bordered on lawlessness. Indeed, Wood managed to establish his anticounterfeiting police force without any resolution from Congress granting him the authority to do so. The rise of the Secret Service, in other words, was not inevitable. It was very much the creation of Wood, who recognized an opportunity and constructed the necessary infrastructure, circumventing obstacles with guile and pure persistence.[43]

Wood accomplished this feat in stages, beginning in 1864, when he joined forces with another Stanton protégé, a detective named Lafayette Curry Baker. Like Wood, Baker was a military adventurer who viewed the federal government's wartime expansion as a splendid opportunity for carving out a bureaucratic domain of his own. Baker, with Stanton's blessing, had set up a covert national police force called the "secret service." This outfit, financed with cotton seized from blockade runners, investigated frauds against the government, gathered intelligence on the Confederacy, and eventually, prosecuted counterfeiters. In the summer of 1864, for instance, Wood accompanied Baker on a well-publicized raid on counterfeiters operating in St. Louis, Indianapolis, and Nauvoo, Illinois. They swept in and arrested ten individuals, seizing plates, dies, presses, ink, and paper. In an intriguing development, the detectives did not imprison the counterfeiters in the local penitentiary to await their trials, but instead took them in chains to Washington and deposited them at Wood's Old Capitol Prison. Baker led other raids shortly thereafter, capturing members of gangs operating out of New York City and New Jersey who had been counterfeiting the new currency.[44]

FIGURE 33. After the end of the Civil War, the Old Capitol Prison hosted
the executions of the Lincoln conspirators and, shown here, of warden
Henry Wirz, who mistreated Union soldiers held in Andersonville Prison.
Courtesy, Library of Congress, Prints & Photographs Division, Civil War Photographs, LC-B8184-3287.

In the succeeding months, Wood took control of the federal campaign against counterfeiting. This was not a response to a legislative mandate. When Congress passed the Legal Tender Act, it did not allocate money to protect the new currency from counterfeiters; nor, for that matter, did it fashion the legal machinery necessary for combating the problem. Rather, as Wood recalled, Lincoln, Stanton, and the new secretary of the treasury, William Fessenden, appointed him to "give the counterfeiters a shaking up, which I proceeded to do under an order from the War Department." Baker did not participate in these efforts, possibly because he fell out favor with Stanton after being caught tapping the military's telegraph line. Wood went alone, and as he later recalled, "independent of all civil process, I proceeded to Ohio, Indiana, and other States west of the Alleghenies, making arrests and . . . bringing many persons to Washington and providing them with special quarters in the Old Capitol prison."[45]

At the same time, Wood forged an alliance with Edward Jordan, solicitor of the treasury. The man who appointed Jordan, Secretary Salmon P. Chase, had given his chief attorney carte blanche to prosecute counterfeiters. Drawing on that authority, and Wood's own experience chasing counterfeiters, Jordan hired Wood late in 1864 and appointed him an "Acting Agent" charged with "detecting frauds of Government Securities." Wood spent the first half of 1865 strengthening his mandate, arresting counterfeiters, and hiring "operatives" to assist in his campaign. He continued to arrest counterfeiters throughout the United States, and in each case brought them back to the nation's capital to await trial. He simultaneously maintained his position as keeper of the Old Capitol Prison, using information gathered from new inmates to further his campaign against the counterfeiters.[46]

As the war came to a close, Wood moved to consolidate his power. According to one unsubstantiated report, on April 14 the newly appointed secretary of the treasury, Hugh McCulloch, asked Lincoln's permission to establish a permanent national police force aimed at suppressing counterfeiting. Lincoln gave his assent, only to be shot dead that evening. This story, with its tragic anticipation of the agency's later mission (the Secret Service did not begin protecting the president until century's end) is probably apocryphal. More likely, McCulloch and Jordan acted independently in the political chaos that followed Lincoln's assassination. Whatever the impetus, Wood resigned his position at the Old Capitol Prison on June 1. Shortly after, on July 4, McCulloch appointed Wood "Chief of the detective force to act under the directions of the Solicitor of the Treasury, in detecting and bringing to punish-

FIGURE 34. One prisoner said of Wood: "His is a peculiar eye—keen and gray; at times cold and perfectly expressionless, at others full of shrewdness and keenness." *Courtesy, U.S. Secret Service.*

ment persons engaged in counterfeiting." Wood was sworn in the next day. A photograph taken after he assumed control of the new agency shows a face that counterfeiters would come to know well.[47]

In 1865, Wood and his operatives began to catalog and classify the country's counterfeiters. This took detective work on a larger scale than had been attempted in the nation's history, and during these first few years, Wood's small but growing circle of operatives—some twenty to thirty individuals—logged hundreds of thousands of miles in travel, interviewed thousands of suspects, and arrested and convicted hundreds of counterfeiters. As federal officials, Wood and his operatives moved throughout all corners of the country. Each judicial district had its own operative, though Wood assigned multiple operatives to key cities. Each operative, Wood included, sent detailed reports back to Washington, which a growing cadre of clerks transcribed and filed away into enormous bound volumes. From the beginning, Wood maintained detailed dossiers on different counterfeiters complete with miniature biographies, criminal associations, distinguishing physical features, past convictions, current status and location, and alleged violations. A composite portrait of the counterfeit economy began to emerge.[48]

Much of what Wood and his agents discovered was a relatively recent development. Though counterfeiters operated on a national scale prior to the 1860s, the system of locally issued monies limited the reach of their operations, even if it made counterfeiting relatively easy. The new uniform paper currency, by contrast, could circulate anywhere. Consequently, like their predecessors who had preyed on the notes of the earlier Bank of the United States, counterfeiters of greenbacks and national bank notes had a strong incentive to invest the necessary time and money to fashion high-quality imitations. As one report on the counterfeiting of federal currency concluded, "It will pay counterfeiters to take special pains in the preparation of a bill that can be circulated everywhere from New York to New Orleans, and which will not be subjected to the scrutiny attending the issue of counterfeits upon local banks." The new federal currency helped nationalize the capitalist economy, but it did the same for the counterfeit economy as well.[49]

As Wood and his agents began investigating the criminal operations behind these new imitations, they quickly realized that by the 1860s New York City had consolidated its position as the center of counterfeiting in the United States; Philadelphia was a distant second. In New York, counterfeiters clustered in the area north of the Bowery, much as they had during the antebellum era. The most important counterfeiters conducted meetings, sealed business deals, and took orders in a handful of saloons along East Houston Street. Jerry Cousden, a notorious printer and dealer, could be found at 16 East Houston Street at "The Exchange," a saloon run by another longtime dealer and burglar named Langdon Moore (alias Charley Adams)—whom Wood later described as a "well-bred, ingenious, intelligent man." William "Blacksmith Tom" Gurney, another dealer, often loitered on the premises, or spent his days at 50 East Houston, the address of a restaurant and criminal haunt called "The Arbor." Jim Colbert, probably the biggest dealer of all, kept "The Gem," a "drinking house of low character," on the corner of Crosby and Houston. It served as a clearinghouse for the buying and selling of counterfeit notes, and operatives found cards advertising it in the possession of counterfeiters as far away as James Brown of Ohio. A similar set of meeting places could be found in Philadelphia, where that city's principal counterfeiters—Bill Cregar, William Tarr, Ransom Abrams, Minnie Price, Phineas "Fin" Dizard, and others—met to place orders, distribute notes, and settle accounts.[50]

These meeting places functioned as a façade for far more extensive operations spread throughout the city and the surrounding towns. As one exposé published around this time explained, "counterfeiting . . . is a complicated business, and like every business is divided into its several branches." The author of this treatise further noted that counterfeiters of federal currency required "skillful hands, expensive presses, and other equally expensive working material." It is, he explained, "a business that cannot be commenced without considerable capital." As a consequence, "a man of considerable means . . . is generally at the head of it, who furnishes the necessary capital, and therefore takes the larger part of the profits." It was an intriguing parallel: just as conventional capitalism came under the sway of a dwindling number of plutocrats at this time, so too did the counterfeit economy. By the 1860s, a small circle of these capitalists were controlling the trade in bogus notes, employing a vast army of low-paid workers.[51]

New York City and Philadelphia had a number of these magnates, and many began their careers, à la Horatio Alger, on the lower rungs of the counterfeit economy. Joshua Miner (or Minor) started life as a small-time shover and trader, before landing in prison out West in the 1850s. After his release, he drifted to New York, became a paving contractor, and built a fortune, mostly from the manufacture of counterfeit money. He had many partners, but his favorite seems to have been Valentine "Frank" Gleason, an engraver who had become a capitalist as well. Gleason had a distinguished lineage: he was the nephew of Cogniac Street's Ebenezer Gleason. According to one source interviewed by a Secret Service operative, Gleason had "learned the trade of Old Crane who died out west sometimes since"—a reference to William Crane, the engraver who had clashed with the Cogniac Street gang back in the 1820s. After a long apprenticeship in the counterfeiting fraternity, Gleason became a wealthy man, and had taken to wearing what one operative described as "a large diamond cross and a long chain."[52]

But the most important and infamous of all the capitalists was William "Long Bill" Brockway, who had been arrested and imprisoned for using the electrotyping process to produce perfect facsimiles over a decade earlier. He emerged from prison in the 1850s and changed his name to William Spencer, moved to Philadelphia with his wife, and like William Wood, arrogated a military title for himself. Colonel Spencer née Brockway dabbled in real estate, made legitimate investments, and began to move in Philadelphia's high society. Probably the most secretive of all the magnates, he remained a shadowy figure during the early years of the Secret Service. There is no evidence that he fraternized with other counterfeiters, save for a handful of trusted intermediaries through whom he exercised his influence and made his investments. A towering figure—Allan Pinkerton called him "the most successful counterfeiter known to modern times"—Brockway eventually became the public face of the counterfeiting fraternity.[53]

Capitalists like Miner, Gleason, and Brockway employed various master engravers (many of them skilled immigrants) in New York City and elsewhere. But few such men became wealthy from plying their trade. As one guide to the criminal classes noted, engravers arrested by the police "present no indication of unusual prosperity, and they say they have barely made a living. They make the plate or plates and the dealers make the money." This observation, confirmed by agents of the Secret Service, echoed the observation that Waterman Ormsby had made a decade earlier: engravers generally worked for counterfeiters out of economic need. And so it was appropriate that in the course of his investigations Wood discovered that Ormsby had been engraving plates for Miner and Gleason, along with at least one other criminal capitalist. Wood, determining that Ormsby had only engraved counterfeits on state-chartered banks, not the new federal notes, never pushed a prosecution. And to Ormsby's credit, the little evidence that remains suggests that he had stopped producing counterfeits as soon as he started the Continental Bank Note Company, which produced substantial quantities of (genuine) federal currency.[54]

Wood and his agents discovered a complicated set of wholesaling relationships as well. Many of these individuals, particularly those doing business on Houston Street, would contribute part of the capital necessary for producing a counterfeit plate. For example, one operative reported that Jim Colbert was trying to "sell out . . . his interest in the manufacture of counterfeit U.S. monies." By advancing the capital and obtaining what was called an "interest," counterfeiters like Colbert were entitled to a certain percentage of the bogus notes. They then sold these to a number of trusted dealers, whom Colbert called "customers." In turn, these dealers sold the notes to other dealers, who in turn sold them to shovers. As Wood and his agents soon discovered, most of these dealers plied their trade outside New York City, distributing counterfeit notes throughout the United States. One individual, for example, was described as purchasing counterfeits, then traveling "around the country with them for sale." Many of these dealers had elaborate networks that spanned the nation. In some cases, dealers used "boodle carriers" to deliver the goods; more often they depended on other means of distributing their wares. As one writer noted, "The mails and expresses are made the medium for exportation from this city." In response, Wood's operatives began monitoring the mail, arresting dealers as they dropped off or picked up bundles of counterfeit notes.[55]

Over the first few years of the Secret Service's existence, Wood and his operatives used these scraps of information to map the contours of the national counterfeit economy. Though New York City and Philadelphia dominated the business, several additional key entrepôts were identified as being dominated by members of the counterfeiting elite. In St. Louis, Frederick Biebusch, a German immigrant who had run a criminal empire as early as the late 1840s, served as a middleman and financier of multiple counterfeiting gangs operating in Missouri, Indiana, and other states along the Mississippi River. Operatives described him as "an old offender in the bogus currency business," and "open for the transaction of any species of rascality whereby he can make money illegitimately." Wood soon discovered that Biebusch maintained close ties with a number of associates: an engraver and dealer named Peter McCartney, better known as the "King of the Koniackers"; a skilled engraver named Ben Boyd, who produced a number of stunning counterfeits of greenbacks and national bank notes; Nelson Driggs, a "capitalist and outside manager" who financed many counterfeit plates;

and John Frisby and Louis Sleight, who lived in Nauvoo, Illinois, and controlled that state's counterfeiting business. If these men dominated the Mississippi River Valley, James Brown of Akron remained the key player in Ohio, western New York, and Michigan. One operative described him "a celebrated counterfeiter," and "the largest dealer in counterfeit . . . Government Securities in the North West."[56]

In 1865, Wood launched an aggressive campaign against counterfeiters on multiple fronts. James Brown was one of the first arrested, and Wood extracted a confession from him that led to the prosecution of scores of associates throughout the country. Brown never stood trial; he fell to his death off a canal boat on his way home from a court hearing the following year. "His career, from dawn to manhood, has been one of 'counterfeit presentment,'" wrote the *Cleveland Herald* in a lengthy obituary of a man whose life, "if written, would put fiction to the blush." "He has put more bogus coin into circulation than would a freight ship," wrote the paper, "and his inflation of the paper currency exceeded the wildest schemes of wild cat bankers." Lest these exploits seem too romantic, the paper ended on a somber note: "Jim Brown, the counterfeiter, is dead. Let his deeds be buried in the same dishonored grave."[57]

Other counterfeiters suffered less cruel but equally decisive fates. Wood secured the conviction of New York's Jerry Cousden in 1866, which sparked additional prosecutions. Several of Philadelphia's capitalists were captured and convicted the same year, including Minnie Price, Ransom Abrams, and Bill Cregar. In addition, Wood and his operatives dealt several blows to the counterfeit economy of the western states, managing to orchestrate the arrest of the Johnson clan in Indiana and Fred Biebusch in St. Louis. During the 1860s, the Secret Service also put away hundreds of less important figures, mostly petty dealers, shovers, and boodle carriers. At the same time, Wood and his agents confiscated engraving machines, plates, dies, paper, and considerable quantities of expensive equipment, bringing these materials back to Secret Service headquarters in Washington.[58]

Much of Wood's success depended on finding ways to circumvent local law enforcement officials, many of whom colluded with counterfeiters. Wood later recalled, for example, that he had to work hard to ensure that counterfeiters had "no opportunity to dicker with local detectives, and prove alibis and good character under the management of able counsel." He had good reason to be suspicious. As one of his operatives reported in 1865, "I have already demonstrated the truth of your suspicions that many of the officers whose duty it is to suppress counterfeiting . . . are themselves in concert with the principals." Other agents reported similar findings, especially in urban areas. One counterfeiter in Philadelphia, for example, bragged that "he was in with one of the best detectives in the city." In New York City, an operative likewise reported that no fewer than five detectives had been "posting Jim Colbert . . . of the movements of all other officers when they know." Other operatives encountered more subtle resistance to federal authority, with state and municipal authorities undermining their efforts at various turns.[59]

Wood pioneered several rather questionable methods to steer clear of these obstacles. As he later recalled, "I was permitted to use my own methods to effect the desired results." Wood did not go to the trouble of obtaining warrants or follow any of the usual rules governing search and arrest procedures. Nor, he later recalled, did he "solicit assistance from State and local authority." Instead, he and his agents relied heavily on the common-law custom known as "citizen's arrest," which enabled people outside official positions to apprehend criminals caught in an illegal act. Wood and his men would thus shadow suspects and arrange to buy counterfeit notes from them while other members of the force

watched the transaction. Once the money had changed hands, the "citizens"—Wood's men—would sweep in and collar the suspect on the
basis of having witnessed a crime. By exploiting this convention, Wood
arrogated policing powers not expressly granted to him by Congress
(though he did manage to obtain an appropriation of $100,000 per year
beginning in 1866). Only later did the Secret Service gain statutory authority for its right to pursue and arrest counterfeiters.[60]

Wood and his agents came to rely on other equally dubious methods.
Most infamous was the practice of hiring shovers and small-time dealers to entrap the more important wholesalers and engravers. This was
a dramatic shift in policy: though municipal police departments had
relied on informers, or "stool pigeons," they rarely put them on the
payroll. But Wood made a practice of it, deputizing counterfeiters as
"Assistant Operatives." In 1866, the *New York Times* reported that one
George Hyer, an accused murderer, forger, and former counterfeiter,
had been arrested for selling counterfeit money, and in the course of
the trial it came out that Hyer's sale of bogus bills had been approved
by Wood himself. The following year the *Times* professed that "the
dealings of the Government with *counterfeiters* have long been a mystery to the common mind," citing William Brockway, who had been
arrested for counterfeiting and a few days later "turned up *in the employ
of the Government.*" The *Times* claimed that Wood had hired him, and
that when Brockway finally came to trial, the head of the Secret Service attended the proceedings, acting "as volunteer counsel, suggesting
points for his defense and doing all in his power to secure his acquittal
against the regular Government officers [seeking] to convict him!" The
article went on to detail other instances of the practice, and concluded
with a not-so-rhetorical question: "Can the Government punish [coun-
terfeiters] in no other way than by taking them into partnership?"[61]

It was an excellent question, and one that shadowed Wood throughout the 1860s. Even by the standards of the day, his methods were unorthodox, and they did not always yield the desired results. Many of the counterfeiters hired by Wood betrayed the government. Some passed along information to their former associates, while others used government agents to punish competitors, much as counterfeiters had exploited local law enforcement agents in the antebellum era. At the same time, the growing paranoia of many counterfeiters testified to the success of Wood's efforts. After operating with impunity for decades, counterfeiters found that their chosen profession had grown far more perilous. One counterfeiter, for example, told an undercover operative, "It won't do to tell ones best friends now days his business," while another admonished an undercover agent to "look out . . . for we have traitors in the camp." Still another complained that Wood's campaign required "both friend and foe to be watched."[62]

Nonetheless, the campaign against counterfeiting suffered setbacks by the late 1860s. In some cases, the Secret Service obtained a conviction, only to have President Andrew Johnson grant a pardon. Part of the problem lay with worsening relations between Johnson and Wood's patron, Edwin Stanton, in the wake of Lincoln's assassination. Johnson attempted to evict Stanton and replace him with an appointee of his own choosing. In response, Stanton's allies in the Republican Congress passed the Tenure of Office Act to keep Stanton ensconced. Frustrated, Johnson attempted to circumvent this restriction by suspending Stanton, resulting in a bizarre standoff that lasted for several months. Johnson simultaneously fought back on a number of other levels against the Republicans. In what seems to have been an attack on Stanton, McCulloch, and other Republicans who favored federal control over the currency, Johnson began pardoning scores of counterfeiters arrested and convicted through the efforts of the Secret Service. The Republican Congress, perhaps angered by this erosion of the Secret Service's prerogatives, passed a resolution in November 1867 demanding that Johnson release details on all pardons he had granted to people accused of making, possessing, or passing counterfeit money.[63]

Though Johnson may have had personal reasons for undermining the Secret Service's authority, the documents he released to Congress suggest other motivations. Johnson claimed that Wood continued to violate prisoners' civil liberties after the end of the Civil War, arresting and detaining suspected counterfeiters without benefit of counsel. Wood later admitted as much. According to one recollection, he arrested William Brockway and his wife in New York City and dragged them to a hotel room in Newark, New Jersey, keeping them prisoner there for five days. During that period, he relentlessly interrogated the counterfeiter until he agreed to cooperate. Wood saw nothing amiss in all this: as he later recalled with glee, "Our interviews were spicy." Inevitably, working methods like these began to hamper the effectiveness of Wood's campaign and attract denunciations in the press. By the late 1860s Wood could point to few recent successes and spent most of his time fending off charges of improper behavior. As one Secret Service employee later recalled, "The term 'Secret Service' conveys to uninformed minds, an irresponsible body of men, with an almost [unlimited] supply of money, adopting unscrupulous means to accomplish infamous ends." It was not a reputation that inspired confidence in the Secret Service, much less the currency it was supposed to protect.[64]

As criticism of the Secret Service mounted in the late 1860s, Wood issued a detailed list of rules and regulations that reflected a growing attention to professionalism. He instructed operatives to maintain a "strict conformity to the civil law," and forbade them from exploiting a number of once-common practices. These included using their status as government employees to obtain credit or borrow money; receiving gifts, payments, or gratuities from anyone outside the government;

and delivering counterfeit materials to unauthorized individuals. Other rules aimed to improve the agency's bureaucratic record keeping. All operatives, for example, now had to submit more detailed reports, and had to obtain receipts—and written explanations—for all expenses. In addition, operatives had to maintain itemized accounts of all counterfeit notes coming into their hands. As mundane as these various reforms seem, they testified to a dramatic shift. Increasingly, operatives were required to subordinate their personal interests to objectives of the federal bureaucracy. They thus became instruments of a higher power, the face of a resurgent national government. In a curious turn of events, confidence in the money supply—and by extension, a capitalist system dedicated to the pursuit of profit and individual self-interest—had come to depend on government bureaucrats.[65]

Most of that transformation did not take place under Wood's reign, however. By 1868, Wood's days were numbered, thanks to Johnson's having survived impeachment proceedings. This made Stanton's continued claim to a cabinet position untenable, and the secretary of war soon resigned. His patron gone, Wood's power diminished. He ceased to have any control once Grant assumed the presidency in 1869 and appointed his own officials at the treasury, including Edward C. Banfield to the solicitor's position. Banfield, described by one journalist as someone who "when tested gives the true ring of the genuine coin," promptly demanded that Wood resign. Banfield had reason to do so: Wood by this time had been indicted for having falsely imprisoned a suspect. In his letter written in response to Banfield's request, Wood noted that "flattering myself that I am sufficient Philosopher to reason that when an official desires a change of their subordinates, there is no alternative but to comply with their wishes, hence I tender you my resignation." He also published a less temperate letter addressed to George Boutwell, the new secretary of the treasury, alleging unfair treatment, but to no effect. Wood returned to civilian life, becoming a private detective and, eventually, a newspaper columnist.[66]

Still, it is difficult to underestimate Wood's signal accomplishment: the establishment of a bureaucratic beachhead at the heart of the federal government. His personal ambition became the unlikely medium through which the federal government exercised its newfound sovereignty over the currency, and he forged the rudiments of what would become a powerful and permanent extension of the nation-state's authority. That expansion was already evident in the closing years of Wood's tenure, as growing numbers of citizens wrote the headquarters in Washington complaining about counterfeiters, identifying suspects, and supplying leads to investigators. These missives heralded an important shift in the relationship between ordinary people and the federal government. Rather than report bogus notes to local law enforcement authorities or the publishers of counterfeit detectors, they looked to Washington to solve the problem. Only the federal government had the power to pursue counterfeiters operating on a national scale.[67]

And only the federal government had the right to issue money. The same year that William Wood stepped down from his post at the Secret Service, the Supreme Court heard a challenge to the constitutionality of the tax on the notes of state-chartered banks. As luck would have it, Salmon P. Chase, who had resigned as secretary of the treasury in 1864, was chief justice, and in *Veazie Bank v. Fenno*, he affirmed his own policies, ruling the tax constitutional. In the closing lines of the decision, Chase asserted that Congress, having "undertaken to provide a currency for the whole country . . . may, constitutionally, secure the benefit of it to the people by appropriate legislation." Congress had already taken steps toward that end, he observed, by passing laws "against the imposition of counterfeit and base coin on the community." Similarly, he argued, "Congress may restrain . . . the circulation as money of any notes not issued under its own authority. Without this power, indeed, its attempts to secure a sound and uniform currency for the country must be futile."[68]

The language was striking. The right to make money was now the federal government's alone. A decade earlier, such an assertion—that the nation could rightly rein in "notes not issued under its own authority"—would have been greeted with derision and unyielding opposition. But the outbreak of the war had set in motion forces that had unified the nation and coalesced support for the notes that had helped preserve it. Indeed, by the time Chase heard the case, the question at hand had already been decided—not in courts of law, but in the hands of the nation's citizens, whose day-to-day handling of the greenback and its close cousin, the national bank note, testified to a sea change in economic practice. In their casual exchange of these paper totems of nationalism, people were unconsciously expressing a newfound faith in the power of the government to control and regulate the currency. Chase's opinion was merely stating the obvious: the era of the state bank note—either real, counterfeit, or somewhere between—had come to a close.

EPILOGUE

Confidence
in the Country

I n his *History of Banking in the United States* published in
1896, the political economist William Graham Sumner recalled for his readers the state of the money supply before
the Civil War, dwelling in particular on the problem of counterfeit
money. "It is difficult," he observed, "for the modern student to realize
that there were hundreds of banks whose notes circulated in any given
community. The 'bank notes' were bits of paper recognizable as a species by shape, color, size, and engraved work. Any piece of paper which
had these appearances came with the prestige of money." He then con-
jured a scene remarkably similar to the one that Melville related in the
closing pages of *The Confidence Man*. Prior to the Civil War, Sumner
told his readers, a person receiving a bank note would inevitably turn to
a counterfeit detector and "scrutinize the worn and dirty scrap for two
or three minutes, regarding it as more probably 'good' if it was worn
and dirty than if it was clean, because those features were proof of long
and successful circulation." From the vantage point of his own era,
Sumner could only marvel that "free, self-governing, and at times, ob-

streperous people" tolerated this currency for as long as they did. As he noted with some disbelief, "They treated the system with toleration and respect."[1]

Sumner's incredulous tone highlighted the sea change that had taken place during the previous half century. Though devoted to the proposition that government could do little to address problems of social and economic inequality, Sumner and other boosters of free market capitalism had no interest in returning to an era when, in the oft-quoted words of one historian of banking, it was "somewhat harder to become a banker than a brick-layer, but not much." Indeed, Sumner spoke of the rise of a national banking system with reverence. "Its first great feature," he wrote, "was that it was national and federal . . . a thing which in the days of misery under the local bank system people had sighed for again and again as an unattainable hope." He then went on to extol the national banking system's many virtues: its uniformity, stability, and the fact that it operated under what he termed "federal control." Confidence in the currency had been restored. The nation had intervened in the workings of the economy, assuming control of the money supply so as to eliminate the uncertainties and inconveniences associated with a system of private currency creation.[2]

The relationship between the country and the currency thus underwent a profound shift in the decades following the Civil War. Confidence in the currency had formerly been associated with highly subjective, ever-changing criteria: the appearance of the note, the demeanor of the person presenting it, the corresponding information in a counterfeit detector. But by the time Sumner was writing, it had become entwined with faith in the nation itself, thanks to the abolition of the monetary system controlled by state-chartered banks and its replacement with a uniform currency of greenbacks and national bank notes adorned with nationalist symbols. This raised a curious paradox:

the most vocal defenders of nationalizing the currency were also, like Sumner, proponents of laissez-faire economics. For these reformers, the nation had an important, but singular, role to play in the economy. It would provide the currency; entrepreneurs, speculators, and other practitioners of capitalism would provide the rest. Whether this was a "tremendous gain" as Sumner claimed or a more mixed blessing depended on one's point of view. But there was no denying that the nation-state exercised unprecedented authority over the money supply by the end of the nineteenth century.[3]

This outcome was by no means inevitable. In the decades following the Civil War, political leaders and economic nationalists who anticipated Sumner's worldview labored mightily to consolidate federal control over the currency. The most distinguished and powerful of these reformers was John Sherman, who had shepherded the nationalization of the money supply during the Civil War. As early as 1871 Sherman used the specter of the older system of banks and bank notes in political speeches, recalling for his listeners the "incongruous hotch-potch of State banks, founded upon the laws of thirty-seven States, without security, without uniform value, of local circulation, and endangered by a swarm of counterfeits." The adoption of a national banking system, he reminded his listeners, had replaced this system with something far more worthy of confidence. As Sherman's political ally and friend Jay Cooke had observed not long before, "It is impossible to alter National Bank notes from a lower denomination to a higher, and there is not now one dangerous counterfeit where under the old system there were a hundred." More to the point, Cooke noted, it was "impossible for a National Bank note to become worthless, or even to depreciate in value, so long as the Government shall exist and continue to fulfill its pledges."[4]

Yet one pledge remained unfulfilled: the federal government's original promise to make the greenbacks fully convertible into gold. Doing so would provide a dramatic demonstration of the nation's ability to meet its obligations, and make greenbacks distinct from the irredeemable notes, comparable to counterfeits, that state-chartered banks had issued before the Civil War. As an editorialist argued in the *New York Times* in 1874, "There is no absolute safety for the business of the country until the last vestige of a legal-tender currency is wiped out and the Government retires completely from the business of manufacturing paper into the 'counterfeit presentment' of money." In 1875 Sherman helped steer through Congress the Resumption Act, which held that the United States would begin paying out gold in exchange for greenbacks on January 1, 1879. Appointed secretary of the treasury by President Hayes after the contested election of 1876, Sherman assumed responsibility for delivering on the legislation's promise. As he did so, he kept new political forces at bay, most notably the "greenbackers," a populist movement of laborers and farmers who favored an elastic and inflationary money supply. In a carefully orchestrated public event, Sherman moved to assure the public that the government could redeem its outstanding notes. He ordered gold stockpiled at government subtreasuries and made sure that on January 2, 1879, the government opened its doors to the public, ready to make good on its promise. But as one chronicler of the event has written, the day proved "anticlimactic." In New York City, few people showed up that day to demand coin for greenbacks. Instead, far more gold was exchanged for greenbacks than greenbacks exchanged for gold. Confidence in the nation-state was now as good as gold—or better.[5]

It was on Sherman's watch as well that the government moved to consolidate its control over the currency in a more subtle way, nationalizing the means of production—in other words, the means of making money. Starting in 1869, the government began to annex bits and pieces of the production process away from the privately owned bank-note engraving companies. In 1874 the companies began lobbying Congress to regain these lucrative contracts, arguing that it, not the government, would better safeguard the currency from counterfeiters. Sherman disagreed, eventually overruling the recommendations of a congressional committee that sided with the bank-note engraving firms. In 1877 Sherman gave the Bureau of Engraving and Printing total control over all aspects of the country's currency production. Though the maneuver prompted vociferous opposition from the American Bank Note Company and its allies, Sherman's move was hardly unexpected. This was the man, after all, who a few years earlier had proclaimed that "if anything should be national, it should be bank notes." Thanks to his efforts, the government now had a complete monopoly over the making of money on both a symbolic and a material level. The only thing that remained was to safeguard the money supply from counterfeiters.[6]

The formidable challenge of protection fell to William Wood's successors at the Secret Service, who turned the agency into a far more faceless and professional bureaucracy that symbolized the power of the nation rather than the power of a single individual. Hiram Whitley, the capable administrator who replaced Wood, introduced a number of reforms aimed at securing the confidence of the public. Whitley fired most of the counterfeiters whom Wood had hired, along with many of the more corrupt operatives on the force, replacing them with middle-class men, a number of whom had worked in business or the professions prior to joining the force. He also standardized procedures for arresting suspects, seizing evidence, receiving reimbursement for expenses, and circulating correspondence. In addition, Whitley issued badges to operatives, giving them the imprimatur of federal authority. Finally, he worked to secure a steady appropriation from Congress—approximately $125,000—throughout the first half of the 1870s.[7]

The reforms he instituted yielded immediate results: Whitley and his operatives captured a number of counterfeiters who had previously escaped prosecution. William Gurney, the famed wholesaler, was taken in 1870, while Frederick Biebusch, who had managed to secure a pardon after his previous conviction, was captured and sentenced to a long term in prison that same year. Other counterfeiters fell into the hands of the Secret Service over the next two years, most notably Joshua Miner in 1873. Miner eventually bribed his way to an acquittal, but Whitley ruined the counterfeiter's chances of regaining a share of the market. Though several other counterfeiters remained at large, Whitley's agents pursued them relentlessly, instituting what Whitley would later describe as "a reign of terror." By this time, the Secret Service had begun acquiring a reputation for omniscience. As one journalist noted when he visited its offices in 1873, "The ramifications of the Secret-Service Division of the Treasury Department extend . . . all over the country . . . There is a branch office of the division in every city of importance, as a commercial or monetary centre, in the United States, and each of these branches is under the immediate supervision of a chief operative." Though he conceded that the Secret Service was "a *terra incognita* to most people," he assured his readers that however invisible it might seem, it enjoyed a subtle omnipotence. It is, he noted, "a gigantic machine, having its ramifications everywhere."[8]

Whitley's successor, Elmer Washburn, presided over the Secret Service from 1874 to 1876, and largely completed its overhaul. An engineer by training and a bureaucrat by nature, he instituted a web of regulations that required operatives to fill out paperwork at almost every stage of an investigation, thus holding his employees to an even higher level of accountability. More generally, he issued edicts exhorting them to maintain their integrity—informing operatives, for example, that "employees will be judged by the character they sustain, by the results they accomplish, and by the manner in which they accomplish them."

He also obtained statutory recognition of the Secret Service from Congress, insuring the agency's continued, if not permanent, existence. He proved equally adept at prosecuting counterfeiters. During his brief service, Washburn oversaw the arrest and conviction of numerous fugitives, including Nelson Driggs, the "magnate of money making," and Driggs's business partner, John Peter McCartney.[9]

Most devastating to the counterfeiting industry, perhaps, was Washburn's arrest and conviction of the engraver Ben Boyd in 1876. So valuable was Boyd that a handful of accomplices developed a scheme to secure his release. Several counterfeiters—described by one chronicler as a "gang of desperadoes and ghouls"—plotted to steal Abraham Lincoln's body and hold it hostage in exchange for the release of Boyd. The counterfeiters, who had an apparent fondness for ambiguous symbolic gestures, planned to steal the corpse on the centennial of American independence: July 4, 1876. The plan eventually went awry, but was revived that fall, and almost succeeded: two men broke into the crypt, lifted the lid of the sarcophagus, and were in the process of lifting the coffin when Secret Service agents, who had gotten wind of the plot, broke up the proceedings. Abraham Lincoln's body remained in its crypt; Ben Boyd remained in his cell. The incident exemplified the Secret Service's growing mandate to protect the reliquaries and prerogatives of the nation. After all, Lincoln's body was as sacred as the currency that displayed his visage, and in foiling the plot, the Secret Service delivered a double blow on behalf of the nation's authority.[10]

As the Secret Service captured and convicted the remaining counterfeiters during the 1870s and succeeding decades, the money supply took on an ever more sacrosanct quality. Indeed, the Secret Service began prosecuting anyone who trifled with the symbolic value of the currency. They began by arresting people who produced so-called flash notes, imitations of paper money that businesses used as advertisements. The agency undertook a similar campaign against manufacturers of toy money used in children's games, with R. H. Macy of department-store fame forced to surrender some 160 boxes of play money to the Secret Service. As Andrew Drummond, head of the Secret Service in the late nineteenth century, solemnly explained, "The Securities and Coins of all countries should be held sacred, that people, especially manufacturers, should not seek to transform them into curiosities." The Secret Service consequently prosecuted painters of trompe l'oeil images of paper money, an artistic genre that came into vogue in the 1870s. William Michael Harnett, a painter based in New York City, began producing a number of these compelling imitations of federal currency. They could never pass as money; their mimetic quality had an aesthetic, not a practical value. But the federal government did not see it this way, and as Harnett later recalled, a pair of Secret Service agents raided his studio. As one interrogated Harnett, the other poked his cane in the corners of the room, demanding to know whether Harnett had any more of "those counterfeits," meaning his paintings. Harnett attempted to explain that what he was doing was not counterfeiting per se, but as he subsequently learned, "Harmless though it was, it was clearly against the law, and I was let go with a warning not to paint any more life-like representations of the national currency." Harnett abandoned his project, as did most artists when confronted with this warning. The money supply had become a sacred and inviolable symbol that was not to be manipulated by banks, counterfeiters, or even artists.[11]

In policing artists like Harnett, the defenders of the new monetary system sought to eradicate any lingering ambiguity between the genuine and the counterfeit. The confusing classifications that readers might have found in an old counterfeit detector—genuine, solid, spurious, altered, broken, wildcat, depreciated, doubtful, and of course, counterfeit—vanished, replaced by inviolable black-and-white distinc-

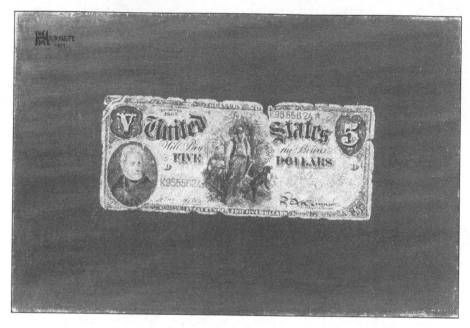

FIGURE 35. William Michael Harnett's trompe l'oeil painting *Still Life: Five Dollar Bill* (1877) earned him an appearance in court and persecution by the Secret Service. *Courtesy, Philadelphia Museum of Art: The Alex Simpson, Jr., Collection, 1943 (1943-74-5).*

tions enforced in everyday exchanges and courts of law. In the process, counterfeiters ceased to be the ghost in the capitalist machine; counterfeiting as a metaphor for the larger capitalist enterprise ceased to resonate. That counterfeiters no longer had such a purchase on the popular imagination was a testament to the fact that the dual meanings of "making money"—circulating currency and accumulating wealth—were increasingly drifting apart. Indeed, if there was a profit to be made, it was not in the circulation of bank notes, but in the purchase of stock shares on margin, the trading of commodities in futures markets, and other mysterious operations. To the uninitiated, these mechanisms for making money seemed no less alchemical than the dubious bank notes of an earlier era; to those who understood the power of confidence, such instruments offered new and increasingly esoteric opportunities for making money. If anything, the machinations of speculators like Jay Gould, Jim Fisk, and other infamous figures took the capitalist confidence game in new and startling directions in the decades after the Civil War, putting to shame the more modest feats of an earlier generation of bankers and counterfeiters.[12]

From the late 1870s onward, complicated debates over the composition of the currency became the focus of tremendous political struggle. While some parties to these debates believed that the federal government should provide an elastic supply of irredeemable greenbacks and plentiful silver coin, others countered with proposals to link national bank notes to the gold standard. Yet whatever the monetary vision, few people questioned the idea that the federal government would, whether directly or indirectly, furnish the paper money and coin in circulation. The idea of returning to a time when states chartered banks that issued notes in a dizzying number of denominations and designs—a time when, as secretary of the treasury Charles Foster recalled in 1892, "only an expert could distinguish counterfeits from genuine notes"—was unthinkable to most participants in these debates. Though a handful of politicians proposed lifting the prohibitive tax on state bank notes the same year Foster made his speech, the idea never gained serious consideration.[13]

If anything, there was a movement toward greater government control over the currency. Proponents of a new, powerful central bank gained credibility after the panics of 1893 and 1907, which highlighted the need for a lender of last resort. In 1908, after the U.S. Treasury had been forced to deposit government funds into banks in New York City, Congress passed the Aldrich-Vreeland Act, which permitted the national banks to issue notes not backed by government bonds, an emergency measure that threatened to sever the ties between the national currency and the national government. At the same time, Congress called for the establishment of a National Monetary Commission,

FEDERAL RESERVE NOTE
10
THE UNITED STATES OF AMERICA
WILL PAY TO THE BEARER ON DEMAND
AUTHORIZED BY FEDERAL RESERVE ACT OF DECEMBER 23, 1913
11-K
C
K527303A
11-K
SERIES OF 1914
11-K
JACKSON
Washington, D.C.
C2
John Burke
Treasurer of the United States.
TEN DOLLARS
W G McAdoo
Secretary of the Treasury.
FEDERAL RESERVE NOTE

FIGURES 36 AND 37. The back of the ten-dollar Federal Reserve note attempted to reconcile the nation's agrarian past with its industrial future, while the front was an exercise in historical amnesia: Andrew Jackson, slayer of the Second Bank of the United States, was here resurrected to lend credence to a new, more powerful central bank. *Courtesy, National Numismatic Collection, Smithsonian Institution.*

which would research the idea of establishing a central bank in the United States. As one proponent of the legislation said before its passage, "What the country needs is not a makeshift legislative deformity . . . but a careful revision and a wise reformation of the entire banking and currency system."[14]

That reformation was not long in coming. The National Monetary Commission's reports laid the foundation for the creation of the central bank, as did congressional hearings on the dangers of the "money trust," the nickname for the handful of Wall Street banks that controlled a disproportionate share of the nation's wealth. On December 23, 1913, the Owen-Glass Act established the Federal Reserve, which would supervise and intervene in the nation's monetary affairs. A six-member Federal Reserve Board oversaw the system, which consisted of a dozen regional Federal Reserve banks. The capital for these government banks came from a levy on the assets of the national banks, along with any state banks that joined the system. Aside from serving as a lender of last resort and regulating the nation's money supply, the Federal Reserve issued its own money (the individual Federal Reserve banks also issued their own short-lived notes, similar to the national bank notes). These new notes circulated alongside the national bank notes, but soon became the exclusive paper currency of the United States.[15]

As the twentieth century began, the counterfeiting profession was in its final, slow decline. Counterfeiting was on its way to becoming one of the "lost arts," the New York Times reported in 1908. "The counterfeiters of the present—what few there are—are what race-track men would call 'pikers,'" the paper observed. "Their income is less than a hack driver's." The fate of the counterfeiting fraternity seemed to be linked to the growing respect accorded the Secret Service. As the same paper observed in awe a few years earlier, readers "have perhaps been moved to admiration of the silent, unsleeping detective branch of the Government, which never appears in the public eye except in the act of pouncing on a victim and which never forgets a crime or a criminal." That image of bureaucratic omnipotence was rooted in results. According to one government survey conducted in 1911, counterfeits constituted a mere thousandth of 1 percent of the total paper currency in circulation, a dramatic decrease from the nineteenth century.[16]

Though counterfeiting underwent a brief revival during the hard times of the 1930s, the Great Depression also spurred legislation that completed the nationalization of the money supply begun during the Civil War. The Gold Reserve Act of 1934 effectively removed gold as the direct foundation of the money supply, making most of the federal currency "redeemable in lawful money," as opposed to precious metals. Toward that end, the law mandated that private citizens could no longer own gold bullion, and the federal government bought up all domestic gold supplies, which would henceforth be used to underwrite the buying and selling of the various foreign currencies used to stabilize the dollar. While gold would continue to have an indirect role in the money supply for several more decades, this legislation made confidence in the currency synonymous with confidence in the government. Separate legislation passed at the same time abolished the system of national banks. The right to make money was now firmly in the hands of the federal government alone, and paper currency was backed by nothing more—and nothing less—than the public's confidence in the nation-state.[17]

This state of affairs would have seemed deeply alien to the bankers and counterfeiters who plied their trade in the first half of the nineteenth century. They lived in an era of unsettling change, a time when even the simplest economic exchanges required people to place their trust in strangers—the unknown customer standing at the store counter with a strange bank note in hand, or the founder of the bank whose signature appeared on that note, but whose bank vault holdings remained a secret. Yet it was also an era of boundless opportunities for a certain colorful class of self-made men to make money from—and for—the country's chaotic economy. Whether they did so in clandestine workshops in the backwoods of the frontier or in the chambers of a marble-columned bank in the nation's burgeoning cities, they shared a common impulse to conjure wealth out of thin air. They were modern-day alchemists, and they succeeded on a grand scale, even if the bank notes they made seemed neither entirely real nor completely counterfeit.

It was a curious time, but it could not last. The cataclysm of the Civil War, and the search for national unity it fostered, compelled the federal government to secure the right to make money as an exclusive privilege of the nation-state. Something was lost in that transition: a sense of the limitless possibilities for freewheeling entrepreneurs to make money and orchestrate new means of exchange. But much was gained. The federal government's conclusive victory over counterfeiters, combined with the nationalization of the currency, has paid significant dividends. Beginning in the twentieth century, people handling paper money ceased to inspect and question its authenticity. Money became almost invisible, the subject of a quick glance, but little more. What had been a country of counterfeits became a genuine nation, enjoying complete control over the money that circulated within its borders. And so it remains today. The little slips of green paper pass from hand to hand, emblems of our faith, trust, and perhaps most important of all, our confidence in both our country and its currency.

ABBREVIATIONS

ACG	*Appendix to the Congressional Globe*
ANA	American Numismatic Association, Colorado Springs, Colorado
ANQ	Archives Nationales du Québec, Montreal
BL-HBS	Baker Library, Harvard Business School
BMSR	*Bankers' Magazine and Statistical Register*
BRCD	*Bicknell's Reporter, Counterfeit Detector, and Prices Current*
CFBD	*Clapp, Fuller & Browne's Bank Note Reporter, and Counterfeit Detecter*
CG	*Congressional Globe*
DIC-USSS	Description and Information of Criminals, U.S. Secret Service (RG 87)
HPE	*History of Political Economy*
JEH	*Journal of Economic History*
JMCB	*Journal of Money, Credit, and Banking*
JPE	*Journal of Political Economy*
JWP-HSP	Joseph Watson Papers, Historical Society of Pennsylvania, Philadelphia
LoC	Library of Congress, Washington, D.C.
MHS	Massachusetts Historical Society, Boston
MiHS	Missisquoi Historical Society, Stanbridge East, Quebec
MSA	Massachusetts State Archives, Boston
NAC	National Archives of Canada, Ottawa

NARA	National Archives and Records Administration, College Park, Maryland
NPG	*National Police Gazette*
NWR	*Niles' Weekly Register*
NYC	*New-York Columbian*
NYCIP	New York City Indictment Papers, Municipal Archives of New York
NYDT	*New York Daily Tribune*
NYEP	*New York Evening Post*
NYH	*New York Herald*
NYT	*New York Times*
OHS	Ohio Historical Society, Columbus
OSA	Ohio State Archives, Columbus
PADA	*Poulson's American Daily Advertiser*
PCCR	Portage County Court Records, Ravenna, Ohio
RR-USSS	Register of Reports, U.S. Secret Service (RG 87)
TBNR	*Thompson's Bank Note Reporter*
VCCD	*Van Court's Counterfeit Detector*
VSA	Vermont State Archives, Montpelier
WCCD	*Willis & Co.'s Bank Note List and Counterfeit Detector*
WFP	*Washington Free Press*
WRHS	Western Reserve Historical Society, Cleveland, Ohio
WSG	*Washington Sunday Gazette*
WWS-SSA	*William Wood Scrapbooks, Secret Service Archives, Washington, D.C.*

NOTES

Prologue

1. This final figure is derived from an examination of *Hodges' American Bank Note Safe-Guard,* an annual that listed all bills in circulation. The number of different notes was likely higher, given that *Hodges'* did not list scrip, fractional currencies, and other marginal paper. Richard H. Timberlake Jr., "The Significance of Unaccounted Currencies," *JEH* 41 (1981): 853–866. On unchartered note-issuing banks, see Richard Sylla, "Forgotten Men of Money: Private Bankers in Early U.S. History," *JEH* 36 (1976): 173–188. On the number of banks in operation, see Warren E. Weber, "Early State Banks in the United States: How Many Were There and When Did They Exist?" working paper 634 (2005), Research Department, Federal Reserve Bank of Minneapolis.

2. Bray Hammond, *Banks and Politics in America: From the Revolution to the Civil War* (Princeton, N.J.: Princeton University Press, 1957), 89–450; James Willard Hurst, *A Legal History of Money in the United States, 1774–1970* (Lincoln: University of Nebraska Press, 1973). A similar narrative unfolded in the realm of public works. See John Lauritz Larson, *Internal Improvement: National Public Works and the Promise of Popular Government in the Early United States* (Chapel Hill: University of North Carolina Press, 2001).

3. Herman Melville, *The Confidence-Man: His Masquerade* (1857; New York: W. W. Norton, 1971), 5.

4. Ibid., 213–214.

5. *NYT,* 30 July 1862, 1.

6. *NWR,* 4 July 1818, 315; *NYT,* 30 July 1862, 1–2; *Proceedings of the American Geographical and Statistical Society* 1 (1863), 43–58. Counterfeiting in the nineteenth century has not received scholarly attention, save for David R. Johnson's pathbreaking *Illegal Tender: Counterfeiting and the Secret Service in Nineteenth-Century America* (Washington, D.C.: Smithsonian Institution Press, 1995), 1–64. On detectors, see Chapter 5.

7. *NYT,* 30 July 1862, 1; James A. Haxby, *Standard Catalog of United States Obsolete Bank Notes, 1782–1866,* vol. 1 (Iola, Wis.: Krause, 1988), x–xi; Q. David Bowers, *Obsolete Paper Money Issued by Banks in the United States, 1782–1866* (Atlanta: Whitman, 2006), 157–176, 227–261.

8. *NWR,* 14 March 1818, 36, emphasis in original; *New-Yorker,* 5 August 1837, 315.

9. *United States Magazine and Democratic Review* 5 (1839): 225, emphasis in original.

10. Allan Pinkerton, *Thirty Years a Detective* (New York: G. W. Carleton, 1884), 518; Neal, *Wandering Recollections*, 124.

11. Melville, *Confidence-Man*, 111. On the tale of the goose and the golden eggs, see Elizabeth Knowles, ed., *The Oxford Dictionary of Phrase and Fable* (New York: Oxford University Press, 2000), 326, 424. On capitalism and confidence, see Jean-Christophe Agnew, *Worlds Apart: The Market and the Theater in Anglo-American Thought, 1550–1750* (Cambridge, Eng.: Cambridge University Press, 1986); David M. Henkin, *City Reading: Written Words and Public Spaces in Antebellum New York* (New York: Columbia University Press, 1998), 137–165.

12. Joseph J. Klein, "The Development of Mercantile Instruments of Credit in the United States," *Journal of Accountancy* 12 (1911): 321–345, 422–449, 526–537, 594–607; Fritz Redlich, "Bank Money in the United States during the First Half of the Nineteenth Century," *Southern Economic Journal* 10 (1944): 212–221; Fritz Redlich, "Early American Checks and an Example of Their Use," *Business History Review* 41 (1967): 285–302; James P. Baughman, "Early American Checks: Forms and Functions," *Business History Review* 41 (1967): 421–435. On the role of reputation in the culture of credit, see Craig Muldrew, *The Economy of Obligation: The Culture of Credit and Social Relations in Early Modern England* (New York: St. Martin's, 1998).

13. On changing perceptions of money, credit, and bank notes, see Janet Riesman, "Republican Revisions: Political Economy in New York after the Panic of 1819," in William Pencak and Conrad Edick Wright, eds., *New York and the Rise of American Capitalism: Economic Development and the Social and Political History of an American State, 1780–1870* (New York: New-York Historical Society, 1989), 1–44. On the disembodiment of economic and social life and its attendant crises, see Karen Halttunen, *Confidence Men and Painted Women: A Study of Middle-Class Culture in America, 1830–1870* (New Haven: Yale University Press, 1982); Jackson Lears, *Fables of Abundance: A Cultural History of Advertising in America* (New York: Basic Books, 1994), 54–74; and Henkin, *City Reading*. On demographic changes, see Peter D. McClelland and Richard J. Zeckhauser, *Demographic Dimensions of the New Republic: American Interregional Migration, Vital Statistics and Manumissions, 1800–1860* (Cambridge, Eng.: Cambridge University Press, 1982). None of this is to suggest that this process was new or unique to the United States. See, e.g., Agnew, *Worlds Apart*.

14. *NPG*, 4 August 1849, 2.

15. Contrary to popular myth, the American economy was never a laissez-faire enterprise. Nonetheless, banks and other note-issuing corporations operated with a remarkable degree of freedom, in part because mechanisms for enforcing laws governing their activities did not yet fully exist. Thus while the regulation of activities (economic or otherwise) within communities may well have been firmly established, as William Novak and others have argued, I would contend that the intended and actual regulation of banks and banking was far more limited, especially outside of New England. See William J. Novak, *The People's Welfare: Law and Regulation in Nineteenth-Century America* (Chapel Hill: University of North Carolina Press, 1996). On the growth of the state in the early republic, see Rich-

ard R. John, "Governmental Institutions as Agents of Change: Rethinking American Political Development in the Early Republic, 1787–1835," *Studies in American Political Development* 11 (1997): 347–380; Ronald P. Formisano, "State Development in the Early Republic: Substance and Structure, 1780–1840," in *Contesting Democracy: Substance and Structure in American Political History, 1775–2000*, ed. Byron E. Shafer and Anthony J. Badger (Lawrence: University Press of Kansas, 2001), 7–35.

16. Currency, whether real or counterfeit, has escaped the close attention of most historians chronicling the transition to capitalism in the United States, despite the fact that bank notes made the so-called market revolution possible. For an introduction to the vast literature on the transition to capitalism, begin with one of the more recent salvos in the field: Joyce Oldham Appleby, "The Vexed Story of Capitalism Told by American Historians," *Journal of the Early Republic* 21 (2001): 1–18.

17. *NWR*, 4 July 1818, 316; *Working Man's Advocate*, 1 June 1833, 4. On the antithesis of the Protestant ethic, see Jackson Lears, *Something for Nothing: Luck in America* (New York: Viking, 2003). On *The Confidence Man* as the embodiment of the American character, see Walter A. McDougall, *Freedom Just around the Corner: A New American History, 1585–1828* (New York: Perennial, 2004). On Weber, see Max Weber, *The Protestant Ethic and the Spirit of Capitalism*, trans. Talcott Parsons (1904; New York: Routledge, 1992).

18. For related accounts that address the connections between capitalism and gambling, see Ann Fabian, *Card Sharps, Dream Books, and Bucket Shops: Gambling in Nineteenth-Century America* (Ithaca, N.Y.: Cornell University Press, 1990); and Lears, *Something for Nothing.*

1. Bordering on Alchemy

1. This reimagining of Burroughs's capture is based on visits to the former Burroughs farmstead as well as the *Green Mountain Patriot*, 27 May 1806, 3; *Balance and Columbian Repository*, 17 June 1806, 5; Silas McKeen, *A History of Bradford, Vermont* (Montpelier, Vt.: J. D. Clark & Son, 1875), 188–191.

2. McKeen, *History of Bradford, Vermont*, 190.

3. Ibid., 191. On Burroughs's bad aim, see *Farmers' Cabinet*, 13 October 1807, 3.

4. Stephen Burroughs, *A View of Practical Justice* (Trois-Rivières, Quebec: G. Stobbs, 1836), 7, emphasis in original; *Green Mountain Patriot*, 27 May 1806, 3; *Connecticut Gazette*, 28 May 1806, 3; *Northern Post*, 31 July 1806, 2. On the origins and appeal of outlaws, see Graham Seal, *The Outlaw Legend: A Cultural Tradition in Britain, America, and Australia* (Cambridge, Eng.: Cambridge University Press, 1996); Richard E. Meyer, "The Outlaw: A Distinctive American Folktype," *Journal of the Folklore Institute* 17 (1980): 94–124.

5. *Montreal Gazette*, 24 November 1806, 2; *Providence Gazette*, 3 January 1807, 2; see also the letter transcribed in *La Patrie*, 27 January 1934, 42, in "Burroughs, Stephen," Alumni File, Rauner Special Collections, Dartmouth College Library, Hanover, New Hampshire.

6. On Burroughs and the breakdown of authority, see Jay Fliegelman, *Prodigals*

and Pilgrims: The American Revolution against Patriarchal Authority, 1750–1800
(New York: Cambridge University Press, 1982), 245–246; Robert A. Gross, "The
Confidence Man and the Preacher: The Cultural Politics of Shays' Rebellion,"
in Gross, ed., *In Debt to Shays: The Bicentennial of an Agrarian Rebellion* (Charlottesville: University Press of Virginia, 1993), 297–320.

7. On the larger Elizabethan underworld, see Frank Aydelotte, *Elizabethan Rogues
and Vagabonds* (Oxford, Eng.: Clarendon Press, 1913). On colonial con men,
see Steven C. Bullock, "A Mumper among the Gentle: Tom Bell, Colonial
Confidence Man," *William and Mary Quarterly* 55 (1998): 231–258.

8. Curtis P. Nettels, *The Money Supply of the American Colonies before 1720* (Madi-
son: University of Wisconsin Press, 1934); Leslie V. Brock, *The Currency of the
American Colonies, 1700–1764: A Study in Colonial Finance and Imperial Relations*
(New York: Arno Press, 1975), 1–16. For alternative explanations of the specie
shortage, see John Kenneth Galbraith, *Money: Whence It Came, Where It Went*
(Boston: Houghton Mifflin, 1975), 47; Roger W. Weiss, "The Issue of Paper
Money in the American Colonies, 1720–1774," *JEH* 30 (1970): 770–784.

9. Nettels, *Money Supply;* Galbraith, *Money,* 47–50; Richard Doty, *America's Money,
America's Story* (Iola, Wis.: Krause, 1998), 21–29. On book credit, see David
Terence Flynn, "Credit and the Economy of Colonial New England," Ph.D.
diss, Indiana University, 2001.

10. Joseph B. Felt, *Historical Account of Massachusetts Currency* (1839; New York: Burt
Franklin, 1968); Doty, *America's Money,* 29–32; Act of 10 December 1690, quoted
in Nettels, *Money Supply,* 254.

11. On Locke, see Joyce Oldham Appleby, *Economic Thought and Ideology in Seventeenth-Century England* (Princeton, N.J.: Princeton University Press, 1978), 199–
241; and Constantine George Caffentzis, *Clipped Coins, Abused Words and Civil
Government: John Locke's Philosophy of Money* (New York: Autonomedia, 1989).

12. Samuel Hartlib, *An Essay upon Master W. Potters Designe: Concerning a Bank
of Lands to be Erected throughout this Common-Wealth* (London: Richard
Wodenothe, 1653), 28, quoted in Carl Wennerlind, "Credit-Money as the Philosopher's Stone: Alchemy and the Coinage Problem in Seventeenth-Century
England," *HPE* 35, suppl. (2003): 248. On Hartlib, alchemy, and paper money,
see John L. Brooke, *The Refiner's Fire: The Making of Mormon Cosmology, 1644–
1844* (Cambridge, Eng.: Cambridge University Press, 1996), 105–108;
Wennerlind, "Credit-Money," 234–261; Henry Robinson, *Certain Proposals in
Order to the People's Freedom and Accommodation* (London: M. Simmons, 1652),
19, quoted in Wennerlind, "Credit-Money," 252.

13. Andrew M. Davis, ed., *Colonial Currency Reprints, 1682–1751* (New York: A. M.
Kelly, 1964), vol. 1: 241, 249–250, quoted in Brooke, *Refiner's Fire,* 107, emphasis in
original; Hans Christoph Binswanger, *Money and Magic: A Critique of the Modern Economy in the Light of Goethe's Faust* (Chicago: University of Chicago Press,
1985); Antoin E. Murphy, *John Law: Economic Theorist and Policy-Maker* (New
York: Oxford University Press, 1997); Wennerlind, "Credit-Money."

14. Davis, *Colonial Currency Reprints,* vol. 2: 209, quoted in Brooke, *Refiner's Fire,*
107, emphasis in original.

15. Henry Smith, ed., *The Writings of Benjamin Franklin*, vol. 2 (New York: Haskell House, 1970), 127–155, emphasis in original; Theodore Thayer, "The Land Bank System in the American Colonies," *JEH* 13 (1953): 145–159.

16. Brock, *Currency of the American Colonies*, 17–129.

17. Ibid., 130–243; Bray Hammond, *Banks and Politics in America: From the Revolution to the Civil War* (Princeton, N.J.: Princeton University Press, 1957), 24–25; Jack P. Greene and Richard M. Jellison, "The Currency Act of 1764 in Imperial-Colonial Relations, 1764–1776," *William and Mary Quarterly* 18 (1961): 485–518; Joseph Albert Ernst, *Money and Politics in America, 1755–1775: A Study of the Currency Act of 1764 and the Political Economy of Revolution* (Chapel Hill: University of North Carolina Press, 1973).

18. John Styles, "Our Traitorous Money Makers: The Yorkshire Coiners and the Law, 1760–83," in John Brewer and John Styles, eds., *An Ungovernable People: The English and Their Law in the Seventeenth and Eighteenth Centuries* (New Brunswick, N.J.: Rutgers University Press, 1980), 172–249. The principal work on the colonies is Kenneth Scott, *Counterfeiting in Colonial America* (1957; Philadelphia: University of Pennsylvania Press, 2000), 70–92, 132–133.

19. Carl Wennerlind, "The Death Penalty as Monetary Policy: The Practice and Punishment of Monetary Crime," *HPE* 36 (2004): 131–161; Leon Radzinowicz, *A History of English Criminal Law and Its Administration from 1750*, vol. 1 (London: Stevens and Sons, 1948), 644–648; Peter Linebaugh, *The London Hanged: Crime and Civil Society in the Eighteenth Century* (New York: Penguin, 1991), 55–57.

20. Scott, *Counterfeiting in Colonial America*.

21. Stephen Burroughs, *Memoirs of Stephen Burroughs . . .* (1811; Boston: Northeastern University Press, 1988), 3–43; *Knickerbocker* 51 (1858): 129–131.

22. On the democratization that accompanied the spread of evangelical religion, capitalism, and revolution, see Richard Bushman, *From Puritan to Yankee: Character and Social Order in Connecticut, 1690–1765* (New York: W. W. Norton, 1967); Robert H. Wiebe, *The Opening of American Society from the Adoption of the Constitution to the Eve of Disunion* (New York: Knopf, 1984); Fliegelman, *Prodigals and Pilgrims;* and Gordon Wood, *The Radicalism of the American Revolution* (New York: Vintage, 1991), 95–225.

23. Excommunication of Stephen Burroughs, 26 March 1785, in Frothingham Papers, 1683–1865, Historical Society of Pennsylvania, Philadelphia; Burroughs, *Memoirs*, 71. Burroughs preached in the spring of 1785. See the discussions of his exploits in *Norwich Packet*, 8 September 1785, 3; and *Essex Journal*, 14 September 1785, 3.

24. Burroughs, *Memoirs*, 60–63. On Lysander, see Arthur Hugh Clough, ed., *Plutarch: Lives of Noble Grecians and Romans*, trans. John Dryden (New York: Modern Library, 1992), 584–606.

25. Burroughs, *Memoirs*, 83.

26. Ibid., 83; Brooke, *Refiner's Fire*, 108–128. On Wheeler, see *Boston Post Boy*, 10 October 1763, 3; *Boston Evening Post*, 7 February 1774, 3; *Salem Gazette*, 11 October 1785, 3; and Scott, *Counterfeiting in Colonial America*, 157, 222–236.

27. *Massachusetts Spy*, 20 October 1785, 3; Castle Island Commitment Register, 1785–

1798, p. 1, Massachusetts State Prison Records, MSA; Burroughs, *Memoirs*, 80, 96–97; Gross, "Confidence Man," 315. On his stint in prison, see *Massachusetts Gazette*, 1 May 1786, 2; Linda Kealey, "Punishment at Hard Labor: Stephen Burroughs and the Castle Island Prison, 1785–1798," *New England Quarterly* 57 (1984): 249–254. On Burroughs's relationship to Shays' Rebellion, see Gross, "Confidence Man," 297–320.

28. Burroughs, *Memoirs*, 84. On the tense economic situation in Massachusetts, see Leonard L. Richards, *Shays's Rebellion: The American Revolution's Final Battle* (Philadelphia: University of Pennsylvania Press, 2002).

29. Hammond, *Banks and Politics*, 89–113; *Records of the Federal Convention of 1787*, vol. 2, ed. Max Farrand (New Haven: Yale University Press, 1937), 308–310; Janet A. Riesman, "Money, Credit, and Federalist Political Economy," in Richard Beeman, Stephen Botein, and Edward Carter II, eds., *Beyond Confederation: Origins of the Constitution and American National Identity* (Chapel Hill: University of North Carolina Press, 1987), 128–161.

30. Charles C. Tansill and H. H. B. Meyer, eds., *Formation of the Union*, 69th Cong., 1st sess., House Document 398 (Washington, D.C.: Government Printing Office, 1927), 475, 556–557, quoted in Hammond, *Banks and Politics*, 92–93. On the Revolutionary and post-Revolutionary experience, see Scott, *Counterfeiting in Colonial America*, 253–263; William G. Anderson, *The Price of Liberty: The Public Debt of the American Revolution* (Charlottesville: University of Virginia Press, 1983); and Mary M. Schweitzer, "State-Issued Currency and the Ratification of the U.S. Constitution," *JEH* 49 (1989): 311–322.

31. Hammond, *Banks and Politics*, 103–118; David Jack Cowen, *The Origins and Economic Impact of the First Bank of the United States, 1791–1797* (New York: Garland, 2000).

32. Hammond, *Banks and Politics*, 146; Fritz Redlich, *The Molding of American Banking*, vol. 1 (1947; New York: Johnson Reprint Corporation, 1968), 5–23; Robert Wright, *Origins of Commercial Banking in America, 1750–1800* (Lanham, Md.: Rowman & Littlefield, 2001).

33. Hammond, *Banks and Politics*, 146–147; Q. David Bowers, *Obsolete Paper Money Issued by Banks in the United States, 1782–1866* (Atlanta: Whitman, 2006), 62–65. On the spread of banking and entrepreneurial activity, see Wiebe, *Opening of American Society*, 150–154; Wood, *Radicalism of the American Revolution*, 316–318.

34. On Burroughs's entanglements in Worcester, see *American Mercury*, 6 June 1791, 3; *Worcester Magazine*, 23 June 1791, 4; and Burroughs, *Memoirs*, 208–218, 343–345. On Burroughs and Long Island, see Aurelia Grether Scott, "The Strange Case of an Early Long Island Schoolmaster," *Journal of Long Island History* 7 (1967): 10–23.

35. Burroughs, *Memoirs*, 343–348; Barbara Ann Chernow, *Robert Morris, Land Speculator, 1790–1801* (New York: Arno Press, 1978), 170–198.

36. Minutes and Reports of Land Committee, vol. 14, June–December 1802, pp. 5222, 5245, Lower Canada Land Papers, RG1, L3, NAC; Lists and Returns of Petitions Presented to the Lt. Gov., vol. 2, 1797–1802, p. 535, RG 1, L3, NAC; Burroughs, *Memoirs*, 223, 367.

37. Solon Robinson, *The Green-Mountain Girls* (New York: Derby & Jackson, 1856), 399; Charles P. DeVolpi and P. H. Scowen, *The Eastern Townships: A Pictorial Record* (Montreal: Dev-Sco Publications, 1962), 3–7; Jean-Pierre Kesteman, Peter Southam, and Diane Saint-Pierre, *Histoire des Cantons de l'Est* (Sainte-Foy, Quebec: Les Presses de l'Université Laval, 1998).

38. DeVolpi and Scowen, *Eastern Townships*, 5–6; Audrey Martin McCaw, "United Empire Loyalists in the Eastern Townships," in *Missisquoi Loyalist Legacies* (Dunham, Quebec: Missisquoi Historical Society, 1976), 29–35; Mrs. C. M. Day, *Pioneers of the Eastern Townships* (Montreal: John Lovell, 1863), 117.

39. Charles Stewart, *A Short View of the Present State of the Eastern Townships in the Province of Lower Canada* (London: J. Hatchard, 1817), 12–13; Joseph Bouchette, *The British Dominions in North America*, vol. 1 (1831; New York: AMS Press, 1968), 308, 400; André Morel, "La Réception du Droit Criminel Anglais au Québec," *Revue Juridique Thèmis* 13 (1978): 449–541; Brian Young, "'The Business of Law' in Missisquoi and the District of Bedford before 1861," *Proceedings of the Missisquoi Historical Society* 20 (1990): 10–24.

40. John Lambert, *Travels through Canada and the United States of North America*, vol. 1 (London: Baldwin, Cradock, and Joy, 1816), 251–253; Stewart, *A Short View*, 13; Harvey Strum, "Smuggling in the War of 1812," *History Today* 29 (1979): 532–537; Chilton Williamson, *Vermont in Quandary: 1763–1825* (Montpelier: Vermont Historical Society, 1949), 242–257. On borderlands, see Jeremy Adelman and Stephen Aron, "From Borderlands to Borders: Empires, Nation-States, and the Peoples in Between in North American History," *American Historical Review* 104 (1999): 814–841; Stephen Mihm, "Making Money, Creating Confidence: Counterfeiting and Capitalism in the United States, 1789–1877," Ph.D. diss., New York University, 2003, p. 59, n. 41.

41. B. F. Hubbard and John Lawrence, *Forests and Clearings: The History of Stanstead County, Province of Quebec* (Montreal: Lovel Printing & Publishing, 1874), 27; *Green Mountain Patriot*, 17 September 1805, 3; *Northern Post*, 7 November 1805, 2; Kenneth Scott, "Counterfeiting in Early Vermont," *Vermont History* 33 (1965): 297–307.

42. *American Mercury*, 19 June 1806, 3; Burroughs, *A View of Practical Justice*, 8, emphasis in original. On private law-enforcement initiatives, see David R. Johnson, *Policing the Urban Underworld: The Impact of Crime on the Development of the American Police, 1800–1887* (Philadelphia: Temple University Press, 1979), 45–46; Craig B. Little and Christopher P. Sheffield, "Frontiers and Criminal Justice: English Private Prosecution Societies and American Vigilantism in the Eighteenth and Nineteenth Centuries," *American Sociological Review* 48 (1983): 796–808.

43. Quoted in the *Providence Gazette*, 3 January 1807, 2. See also *Farmers' Cabinet*, 17 June 1806, 3; *Green Mountain Patriot*, 15 July 1806, 3; *Northern Post*, 31 July 1806, 2; Burroughs, *A View of Practical Justice*, 7–9; and Sheldon Carrol, "Currency of Lower Canada," *Journal of the Stanstead County Historical Society* 2 (1967): 29–40. On conflicting attitudes toward banks in the United States, see *New-Hampshire Gazette*, 28 October 1806, 2.

44. *NYEP,* 1/ January 1807, 3, emphasis in original; *Connecticut Herald,* 27 January 1807, 3, emphasis in original.

45. "The Juvenile Traveler . . . No. 3," *Omnium Gatherum* (1810): 404; Hubbard and Lawrence, *Forests and Clearings,* 74; *Weekly Wanderer,* 6 April 1807, quoted in Scott, "Counterfeiting in Early Vermont," 304; *Providence Phoenix,* 18 April 1807, 2–3; *Massachusetts Spy,* 22 April 1807, 3; Petition of Oliver Barker, 1 November 1809, vol. 74, p. 14, Vermont State Papers, VSA; Edward Cleveland, *A Sketch of the Early Settlement and History of Shipton* (1858; Sherbrooke, Quebec: Page-Sangster, 1964), 59–60.

46. McCaw, "United Empire Loyalists," 29–35; United Empire Loyalists Association of Canada, *The Loyalists of the Eastern Townships of Quebec* (Stanbridge East, Quebec: Sir John Johnson Centennial Branch, U.E.L., 1984); Burroughs, *A View of Practical Justice,* 9; Petition of Oliver Barker, VSA; Petition of Patrick Conroy et al. to the Honorable Thomas Dunn, 23 June 1807, in folder F1T1, "Burroughs, Stephen," Stanstead Historical Society, Stanstead, Quebec. Burroughs's petition for redress fell on deaf ears. See Arthur G. Doughty, ed., *Dominion of Canada: Report of the Public Archives for the Year 1831* (Ottawa: F. A. Acland, 1932), 415.

47. *Burlington Gazette,* 10 August 1807, and *Burlington Centinel,* 6 January 1808, cited in Scott, "Counterfeiting in Early Vermont," 304–305; *Connecticut Courant,* 26 August 1807, 3; *Columbian Centinel,* 7 October 1807, 2; *New Bedford Mercury,* 9 October 1807, 3; *New-Hampshire Gazette,* 13 October 1807, 2; *American Mercury,* 15 October 1807, 3; *New-Hampshire Gazette,* 20 October 1807, 2; *St. Albans Adviser,* 23 June 1808, 3; Petition of Oliver Barker, VSA; *American Watchman,* 19 June 1811, 1; Stephen Burroughs, *Sketch of the Life of the Notorious Stephen Burroughs: Containing the Most Interesting Events of His Life, as Given by Himself* (Hudson, N.Y.: H. & L. Steele, 1809), 104–105; "The Juvenile Traveler . . . No. 3," *Omnium Gatherum* (1810): 404; Gwilym R. Roberts, "Elijah Remington, the Castleton Counterfeiter," *Vermont History* 34 (1966): 66–69.

48. *Columbian Centinel,* 22 October 1806, 1; *New-Hampshire Gazette,* 28 October 1806, 2; *Massachusetts Spy,* 10 December 1806, 2; Petition of John Niles, 17 October 1810, vol. 48, p. 245, Vermont State Papers, VSA.

49. Hammond, *Banks and Politics,* 172–178; Bowers, *Obsolete Paper Money,* 59–62; Jane Kamensky, *The Exchange Artist: A Story of Paper, Bricks, and Ash in Early National America* (New York: Viking, forthcoming 2008).

50. *Windham Herald,* 20 April 1809, 4; Burroughs, *Sketch of the Life of the Notorious Stephen Burroughs,* 105–106, emphasis in original. On Gilbert and Dean, see *The Only Sure Guide to Bank Bills* (Boston: Columbian Centinel, 1806); and William H. Dillistin, *Bank Note Reporters and Counterfeit Detectors, 1826–1866* (New York: American Numismatic Society, 1949), 25–27.

51. Cleveland, *Sketch of the Early Settlement and History of Shipton,* 59–60; *New Hampshire Gazette,* 20 October 1807, 2; Petition of Oliver Barker, VSA. On Burroughs's fictional reputation, see, e.g., *Ladies' Port Folio,* 22 January 1820, 26.

52. *New-Hampshire Sentinel,* 22 September 1804, 3; *Farmers' Cabinet,* 7 October 1806,

2; Burroughs, *Memoirs*, 3. On democratization, see Joyce Appleby, *Capitalism and a New Social Order* (New York: New York University Press, 1984); Wood, *Radicalism of the American Revolution*, 229–369; Joyce Appleby, *Inheriting the Revolution: The First Generation of Americans* (Cambridge: Harvard University Press, 2000).

53. On counterfeiting and the federal government, see *The Public Statutes at Large of the United States of America*, vol. 2 (Boston: Charles C. Little and James Brown, 1845), 494–495; James Willard Hurst, *A Legal History of Money in the United States, 1774–1970* (Lincoln: University of Nebraska Press, 1973), 5, 13, 36, 39, 71, 134–135; and Dwight F. Henderson, *Congress, Courts, and Criminals: The Development of Federal Criminal Law, 1801–1829* (Westport, Conn.: Greenwood Press, 1985), 3–36. On the overture to Lower Canada, see *Records of the Governor and Council of the State of Vermont*, vol. 5 (Montpelier, Vt.: J. and J. M. Poland, 1877), 236; Williamson, *Vermont in Quandary*, 262–264; Lewis Cass Aldrich, ed., *History of Franklin and Grand Isle Counties, Vermont* . . . (Syracuse, N.Y.: D. Mason, 1891), 140–141; *Rutland Herald*, 29 August 1810, 2. On the debate in Lower Canada, see *Journals of the House of Assembly of Lower-Canada* (Quebec: House of Assembly, 1810), 34, 60, 62, 126, 200, 208; *Journals of the House of Assembly of Lower Canada* (Quebec: House of Assembly, 1811), 84, 264, 628; and *Montreal Gazette*, 1 April 1811, 3.

54. Petition of Stephen Burroughs, 6 April 1810, pp. 1045–1049, Lower Canada Petitions and Recommendations for Clemency, vol. 2, RG 4, B 20, NAC.

55. *New Bedford Mercury*, 20 April 1810, 4; *Spooners' Vermont Journal*, 23 July 1810, 3; *Quebec Gazette*, 9 August 1810, 2; *PADA*, 8 May 1811, 3; *American Watchman*, 19 June 1811, 1; Petition of Oliver Barker, VSA; Burroughs, *A View of Practical Justice*, 17–19, 26–27; Philéas Gagnon, *Essai de Bibliographie Canadienne* (Quebec: Philéas Gagnon, 1895), 80–81; J. I. Little, "American Sinner/Canadian Saint? The Further (Mis)adventures of the Notorious Stephen Burroughs, 1799–1840," unpublished paper in author's possession.

56. Burroughs, *View of Practical Justice*, 20–21; *New-Hampshire Gazette*, 13 October 1807, 2; *Quebec Gazette*, 20 June 1811, 1; *Quebec Gazette*, 9 January 1812, 3; *Quebec Gazette*, 28 May 1812, 1; *Knickerbocker* 51 (1858): 391–393; Gagnon, *Essai de Bibliographie Canadienne*, 80–81; *British Colonist and St. Francis Gazette*, 10 July 1823, 3; *Brattleboro Messenger*, 3 August 1833, 1; Little, "American Sinner/Canadian Saint?"

57. *Columbian Centinel*, 23 July 1817, 2; Burroughs, *Sketch of the Life of the Notorious Stephen Burroughs*, 104–105; *Les Ursulines des Trois-Rivières* (Trois-Rivières, Quebec: P. V. Ayotte, 1892), 93–95, 269–279, 482; *American Advocate and Kennebec Advertiser*, 6 May 1815, 4.

58. *Knickerbocker* 51 (1858): 391–392. On Burroughs's piety in Trois-Rivières, see *Alexandria Gazette and Daily Advertiser*, 10 October 1818, 2; Letter from Edmund Bailey O'Callaghan to Louis Joseph Papineau, 4 June 1838, in vol. 2, Correspondence 1833–1838, p. 2977, in Papers of Louis Joseph Papineau and Family, MG 24, B2, NAC. On Burroughs's death and literary afterlife, see *New Bedford Mercury*, 14 February 1840, 1; *NPG*, 9 September 1848, 1.

59. A Citizen, *An Appeal to the Public on the Conduct of the Banks in the City of New-York* (New York: Office of the *New-York Courier,* 1815), 6.

2. Cogniac Street Capitalism

1. Herbert Williams Denio, "Inscriptions in the Town Cemetery at the Village of Bakersfield, Vt.," *The New England Historical and Genealogical Register* 75 (1921): 16.

2. Folder V-107, MiHS; Philip Stansbury, *A Pedestrian Tour; or, Two Thousand Three Hundred Miles in North America* (New York: J. D. Myers & W. Smith, 1822), 250.

3. Howard Jones, *To the Webster-Ashburton Treaty: A Study in Anglo-American Relations, 1783–1843* (Chapel Hill: University of North Carolina Press, 1977); Francis M. Carroll, *A Good and Wise Measure: The Search for the Canadian-American Boundary, 1783–1842* (Toronto: University of Toronto Press, 2001).

4. William A. Coffey, *Inside Out; or, An Anterior View of the New-York State Prison* . . . (New York: James Costigan, 1823), 107–108, emphasis in original. *Cogniac* may be a sly reference to the French presence in Lower Canada or a portmanteau of several other words: *cog,* to cheat; also *cony* or *coney,* a dupe, or victim of a *cony catcher,* a swindler. See George Matsell, The *Secret Language of Crime* . . . (1859; Springfield, Ill.: Templegate, 1997), 29, 77; *The Oxford English Dictionary,* vol. 3 (Oxford, Eng.: Clarendon Press, 1989), 442–443, 884–886. For a map identifying Cogniac Street, see Charles Gore, *Plan of the Frontier of Canada East, from St. Regis to Canaan Surveyed in the Year 1839* (Montreal: Topographical Department of the War Office, 1863), on deposit at the Bibliothèque Nationale du Québec, Montreal.

5. John Carroll, *Case and His Contemporaries; or, The Canadian Itinerants' Memorial,* vol. 2 (Toronto: Wesleyan Conference Office, 1869), 263–264; John S. Dye, *The Government Blue Book: A Complete History of the Lives of All the Great Counterfeiters* . . . (Philadelphia: John S. Dye, 1880), 5.

6. *NWR,* 11 January 1812, 1; *Gospel Palladium,* 22 August 1823, 48. On Paige in the townships, see folders V-41, V-107, V-155, MiHS.

7. *PADA,* 1 September 1809, 3; *Geneva Gazette,* 13 September 1809, 3; *People v. Seneca Paige and Phinehas Whitney* (13 April 1811), NYCIP; draft indictment against Seneca Paige and John Wallace, Case Files for the Court of King's Bench, Montreal, box 128, TL19, S1, SS1 (hereafter "Case Files"), ANQ; Minutes of the Proceedings of the Court of King's Bench, Montreal, 10 March 1812, box 100, TL19, S1, SS1, Registres de procés (hereafter "Minutes"), ANQ.

8. *People v. John Connor* (12 November 1811), and *People v. Allen Gilman* (6 February 1812), NYCIP; *NWR,* 11 January 1812, 1; *American Watchman,* 14 April 1812, 3; Deposition of Seneca Paige, 13 May 1812, folder "Turner Wing," box 5, General Records of the Department of State, Petitions for Pardon, RG 5, NARA; *People v. Lucy Weatherby* (4 May 1813), NYCIP.

9. Complaint of William Spring against Thomas Adams Lewis, and Depositions of Abraham Welch and Ebenezer Gleason, box 129, Case Files, ANQ.

10. Deposition of Daniel Blasdell, box 129, Case Files, ANQ. Fine penmanship remained a rare commodity until later in the nineteenth century. See Tamara Plakins Thornton, *Handwriting in America: A Cultural History* (New Haven, Conn.: Yale University Press, 1996), 3–41.

11. Depositions of Thomas Adams Lewis, Daniel Blasdell, Valentine Bullard, and Joel Hill, box 129, and Depositions of Alexander McCormick and Wolcot A. Morse, box 134, both in Case Files, ANQ. See also *"Dominus Rex v. William Ross, Ward Bigelow, Thos. Adams Lewis,"* 9 March 1826, Criminal Cases, vol. 5, James Reid Papers, MG24, B173, NAC.

12. Thomas Adams Lewis to Thomas McCord, box 129, Case Files, ANQ.

13. Petition of Oliver Barker, 1 November 1809, vol. 74, Vermont State Papers, VSA; Thomas Adams Lewis to Thomas McCord, box 129, Case Files, ANQ; Petition of Patrick Conroy et al. to Thomas Dunn, 23 June 1807, in folder F1T1, "Burroughs, Stephen," Stanstead Historical Society, Stanstead, Quebec. For a contemporary account of this practice, see William Going, *Memoir of William Going, Formerly Keeper of the State Prison, Charlestown, Mass.* (Boston: William Going, 1841), 6.

14. Thomas Adams Lewis to Thomas McCord, box 129, Case Files, ANQ.

15. Charles Francis Adams, ed., *Works of John Adams*, vol. 9 (Boston: Little, Brown, 1856), 610, quoted in Bray Hammond, *Banks and Politics in America from the Revolution to the Civil War* (Princeton, N.J.: Princeton University Press, 1957), 196; Seventy-Six, *Cause of, and Cure for, Hard Times . . .* (New York: n.p., 1818), 23–24. On the explosion in the 1810s, see Hammond, *Banks and Politics,* 197–250; Warren E. Weber, "Early State Banks in the United States: How Many Were There and When Did They Exist?" working paper 634 (2005), Research Department, Federal Reserve Bank of Minneapolis.

16. Deposition of Thomas Adams Lewis, box 130, Case Files, ANQ, emphasis added.

17. Brian Young, "The Business of Law in Missisquoi and the District of Bedford before 1861," *Proceedings of the Missisquoi Historical Society* 20 (1990): 10–24; J. I. Little, *State and Society in Transition: The Politics of Institutional Reform in the Eastern Townships, 1838–1852* (Montreal: McGill-Queen's University Press, 1997), 48–59. On the presence of fugitives, see Deposition of Valentine Bullard, box 129, Case Files, ANQ; Charles Stewart, *A Short View of the Present State of the Eastern Townships in the Province of Lower Canada . . .* (London: J. Hatchard, 1817), 14; and Mrs. C. M. Day, *Pioneers of the Eastern Townships* (Montreal: John Lovell, 1863), 114–117.

18. Petition of Jacob Ruiter, quoted in "They Made American Money in Canada," *McDonald Farm Journal,* January 1962, in vertical file "Cogniac Street," MiHS; *Journals of the House of Assembly of Lower Canada from the 11th December 1821, to the 18th February 1822,* vol. 31 (Quebec: John Neilson, 1822), 99–100.

19. Deposition of Ephraim Knight, box 134, and Deposition of Abner Bickford, box 135, both in Case Files, ANQ.

20. Deposition of David Abbot Parker, box 136, Case Files, ANQ.

21. Deposition of John Weare, box 135, Case Files, ANQ; William B. Felton to

Charles Marshall, box 136, Case Files, ANQ; *Dominus Rex v. Hiram Gleason*, 6 March 1825, and *Dominus Rex v. Joab Smith, Turner Wing the Elder, Turner Wing the Younger,* 7 March 1826, Criminal Cases, vol. 5, James Reid Papers, NAC.

22. For evidence on the abuse of bail and other legal maneuvers, see 10 March 1812, 10 March 1818, 9 September 1818, box 100; 25 February 1824, 10 March 1824, box 101; 5 March 1825, 3 September 1825, 7 March 1826, 9 March 1826, 10 March 1826, box 102—all in Minutes, ANQ.

23. See, for example, the case against Elijah Hurd: 9 March 1825, 10 September 1825, box 102, Minutes, ANQ; *Montreal Gazette,* April 1830, 3. Hurd managed to escape execution and eventually win a full pardon, only to begin counterfeiting anew. See James Reid et al. to Liet. Col. Glegg, 3 December 1830, box 109, TL19, S1, SS777, "Documents administratifs," ANQ; *Baltimore Patriot,* 20 June 1834, 2; *BRCD,* 24 June 1834, 2; and Schuyler Hubbard to Governor Joseph Vance, 3 September 1838, Governors' Papers, OHS.

24. *Litchfield Gazette,* 10 May 1809, 3; 10 March 1818, 7 September 1818, 9 September 1818, box 100, Minutes, ANQ; Deposition of Henry Buys, box 133, and Depositions of Alexander McCormick & Wolcott A. Morse, James Stewart, and John Runyon, box 134, Case Files, ANQ. On competition, see Morton J. Horwitz, *The Transformation of American Law, 1780–1860* (Cambridge: Harvard University Press, 1977), 109–139.

25. Leon Lalanne to J. M. Mondelet, and Depositions of James Stewart, Thomas Adams Lewis, and John Runyon, box 134, Case Files, ANQ.

26. Leon Lalanne to J. M. Mondelet, and Thomas McCord to Leon Lalanne, box 134, Case Files, ANQ.

27. Deposition of Benjamin F. Waring, 17 September 1824, box 8, Council Pardon Files, 1784–1991, Massachusetts Governor's Council, MSA; *NPG,* 24 January 1846, 177. On William Crane's continuing troubles in 1819, see 10 March 1819, box 100, Minutes, ANQ; and Thomas Adams Lewis to Abiathas Boyce, box 134, Case Files, ANQ.

28. *American Repertory,* 6 May 1824, 3. Senega or seneca was the name given to the drug obtained from the root of the plant *Polygola Senega.* See *The Oxford English Dictionary,* vol. 14 (Oxford, Eng.: Clarendon Press, 1989), 970–971.

29. *NPG,* 24 January 1846, 177–178.

30. Ibid.; *NPG,* 31 January 1846, 185.

31. Sile Doty, *The Life of Sile Doty . . . ,* comp. J. G. W. Colburn (1880; Detroit: Alved of Detroit, 1948), 73, 94–95.

32. "Lyman Parkes," Commitment Register, 10 January 1818–30 September 1840, Charleston State Prison Records, MSA; *NPG,* 31 January 1845, 185. On Parkes's burgeoning reputation and his ties to Smith Davis, see *People v. Smith Davis* (10 April 1829), NYCIP.

33. *American Repertory,* 27 May 1824, 4.

34. Ibid.; *American Repertory,* 8 July 1824, 3. Seneca Paige's father, Foster Paige, was punningly identified in the *American Repertory* as "a Mr. P___, from Bakersfield, Vt, who Foster-s all coniac establishments." On visits to Cogniac Street, see *Peo-*

ple v. Peter La Rue (5 October 1830), and *People v. Francis Carlisle* (14 November 1832), NYCIP.

35. Seventy-Six, *Cause of, and Cure for, Hard Times,* 50, emphasis added.

36. Charles Z. Lincoln ed., *State of New York: Messages from the Governors . . .*, vol. 2: *1777–1822* (Albany, N.Y.: J. B. Lyon, 1909), 983–984.

37. William Stuart, *Sketches of the Life of William Stuart: The First and Most Celebrated Counterfeiter of Connecticut* (Bridgeport, Conn.: William Stuart, 1854), 39–40. See also Seth Wyman, *The Life and Adventures of Seth Wyman . . .* (Manchester, N.H.: J. H. Cate, 1843), 257–258.

38. *NYEP,* 2 September 1816, 2; *NYEP,* 13 July 1818, 2; *NYEP,* 7 September 1820, 2; *People v. Joseph Gay Stinson* (10 August 1814) and *People v. Ralph Van Syckle* (9 September 1824), NYCIP. See also Charles Williams to Joseph Watson, 16 December 1824, folder "2—1824," JWP-HSP; Philip F. Gura, ed., *Buried from the World: Inside the Massachusetts State Prison, 1829–1831; The Memorandum Books of the Rev. Jared Curtis* (Boston: Massachusetts Historical Society, 2001), 232–233.

39. *Hampden Journal,* 1 February 1826, 1. On Seneca Paige's dealings, see "Cogniac Street," vertical file at MiHS; "Extract from the 1825 Census of Lower Canada," p. 830, MiHS; Folder V-491, MiHS; *Seneca Page v. Joel Smith* (14 May 1825), vol. 51, file 5, Quebec and Lower Canada: Lawsuits, 1762–1839, RG4, B17, NAC.

40. *People v. Daniel Bailey* (18 November 1814), NYCIP; Deposition of Valentine Bullard, box 129, Case Files, ANQ.

41. Depositions of Joseph Brace and Henry Buys, box 133, Case Files, ANQ; Society for the Prevention of Pauperism, *Report on the Penitentiary System in the United States . . .* (New York: Mahlon Day, 1822), 98; *BRCD,* 24 June 1833, 2; *Christian Secretary,* 6 July 1833, 99; *NPG,* 8 August 1846, 402; *VCCD,* 1 July 1856, 3; Richard Maxwell Brown, "Vigilante Policing," in Carl B. Klockars and Stephen D. Mastrofski, eds., *Thinking about Police: Contemporary Readings* (New York: McGraw-Hill, 1991), 61–62.

42. Stuart, *Sketches of the Life of William Stuart,* 42–43, emphasis added. On "Slab City" as slang for sawmill towns like Frelighsburg, see Thomas B. Mott to Joseph Watson, 27 October 1824, JWP-HSP; James Reid, *The Diary of a Country Clergyman, 1848–1851,* ed. M. E. Reisner (Montreal: McGill-Queen's University Press, 2000), 275, n. 75.

43. Depositions of Alexander M. McCormick and Wolcott A. Morse, box 134, Case Files, ANQ. On supply and demand, see John Burnham to Joseph Watson, 5 June 1826, JWP-HSP.

44. *New-York Commercial Advertiser,* 27 October 1809, 2; *NYEP,* 2 September 1816, 2; *NYEP,* 10 July 1820, 2; *NYC,* 16 August 1820, 2, emphasis in original; *NPG,* 8 August 1846, 402.

45. *People v. Louis Sampier* (5 January 1821), ANA; *Providence Gazette,* 14 August 1824, 2. On Timothy Connor's arrest, see *NYC,* 30 November 1820, 2. On searches of counterfeiters in Vermont, see Stuart, *Sketches of the Life of William Stuart,* 118. On boodle carriers and account books, see *People v. Francis Carlisle,* 14 November 1832, NYCIP.

46. H. Craig, Civil Secretary of Lower Canada to the Governor of Ohio, 28 September 1833, OHS. On canals and economic development, see Ronald E. Shaw, *Canals for a Nation: The Canal Era in the United States, 1790–1860* (Lexington: University Press of Kentucky, 1990).

47. David Johnson, *Illegal Tender: Counterfeiting and the Secret Service in Nineteenth-Century America* (Washington, D.C.: Smithsonian Institution Press, 1995), 1–64; James Inciardi, "The Nature and Historical Roots of Professional Crime," in Frank R. Scarpitti and Amie L. Nielsen, *Crime and Criminals: Contemporary and Classic Readings* (Los Angeles: Roxbury, 1999), 390–404; Naomi R. Lamoreaux, *Insider Lending: Banks, Personal Connections, and Economic Development in Industrial New England* (New York: Cambridge University Press, 1994); Howard Bodenhorn, *State Banking in Early America: A New Economic History* (New York: Oxford University Press, 2003), 72–94.

48. *People v. Seneca Paige and Phinehas Whitney* (13 April 1811), *People v. Robert W. Cunningham* (6 November 1811), and *People v. John Connor* (12 November 1811), all in NYCIP; *NYEP,* 19 August 1818, 2; *People v. Charles and Mary Davis* (5 September 1815), ANA; *NYEP,* 16 July 1821, 2; *Providence Patriot,* 21 July 1821, 3.

49. *NYEP,* 4 October 1816, 2; *People v. Isaac Dunsmore* (3 June 1818), NYCIP. See also Depositions of James Connor, Abraham McCormick, and Wolcott A. Morse, box 134, Case Files, ANQ; *People v. John Connor* (12 November 1811), *People v. John Smith Burroughs* (10 March 1817), and *People v. John Strickland* (13 September 1820), NYCIP; as well as *People v. Louis Sampier* (5 January 1821), ANA.

50. *People v. Guy Fuller* (10 July 1821), ANA; *People v. Isaac Dunsmore* (3 June 1818) and *People v. Zebulon Ketcham* (9 August 1825), NYCIP.

51. *People v. Henry Hoare* (14 May 1816), *People v. Catherine Bedell* (10 February 1819), NYCIP; *People v. Elizabeth Connor* (7 September 1820), ANA; *People v. Timothy Connor* (4 September 1821), *People v. Rufus Severance* (11 March 1822), *People v. William Goldsby* (5 December 1823), and *People v. Guy Fuller* (4 September 1821), NYCIP. See also *NYC,* 16 August 1820, 2; *New-York American,* 8 February 1822, 2.

52. On Davis's career as a mail robber, see *NWR,* 1 April 1820, 81–82; *Ladies' Port Folio,* 1 April 1820, 111; *Hampden Patriot,* 5 April 1820, 2. His pardon is in folder "Case 565," box 9, "Monroe Administration, 1817–1825, Nos. 525–579," Petitions for Pardons, 1789–1860, General Records of the Department of State, RG 59, NARA. On his life in New York City, see *Longworth's American Almanac* (New York: Thomas Longworth, 1824), 146; and *Longworth's American Almanac* (New York: Thomas Longworth, 1826), 157.

53. Deposition of Benjamin F. Waring, 17 September 1824, box 8, Council Pardon Files, 1784–1991, Massachusetts Governor's Council, MSA; *People v. Leonard Lockwood* (12 May 1826), NYCIP; H. Craig, Civil Secretary of Lower Canada to the Governor of Ohio, 28 September 1833, OHS; *NPG,* 29 November 1851, 1.

54. Rev. John Luckey, *Life in Sing Sing Prison, as Seen in Twelve Years' Chaplaincy* (New York: N. Tibbals, 1860), 202–207; J. Owen Grundy, "Bergen Reformed Church Records, 1789–1877," *Genealogical Magazine of New Jersey* 47 (1972): 56.

See also *Baltimore Patriot*, 20 June 1834, 2; *BRCD*, 24 June 1834, 2; *People v. Mary Shepherd* (15 February 1843), NYCIP; *Rural Repository*, 6 May 1846, 69.

55. *Longworth's American Almanac* (New York: Thomas Longworth, 1823), 396; *Longworth's American Almanac* (New York: Thomas Longworth, 1824), 387; *People v. Jane Dorsey* (6 July 1825) and *People v. Philander Worden* (13 June 1837), NYCIP. On the transformation of the shoe industry, see Sean Wilentz, *Chants Democratic: New York City and the Rise of the American Working Class, 1788–1850* (New York: Oxford University Press, 1984), 124–127. On Shepherd's new neighborhood, see Tyler Anbinder, *Five Points: The Nineteenth-Century New York City Neighborhood that Invented Tap Dance, Stole Elections, and Became the World's Most Notorious Slum* (New York: Free Press, 2001), 14–37.

56. Luckey, *Life in Sing Sing Prison*, 208–214; *People v. Francis Carlisle* (14 November 1832) and *People v. Mary Shepherd* (15 February 1843), NYCIP.

57. Family history based on *NYH*, 14 January 1843, 2; *NYH*, 7 March 1843, 3; *NPG*, 28 March 1846, 245; *NPG*, 25 July 1846, 388; *NPG*, 12 September 1846, 5; Luckey, *Life in Sing Sing Prison*, 202–217; *NPG*, 14 May 1859, 4; and *NPG*, 26 November 1864, 2. On rivalry, see *People v. Smith Davis* (6 March 1830), NYCIP.

58. *People v. John Strickland* (7 December 1811), NYCIP; *People v. Charles and Mary Davis* (5 September 1815), ANA; *People v. Charlotte Hickman* (14 February 1822), *People v. Mary Allen* (9 October 1822), and *People v. Jane Dorsey* (6 July 1825), all in NYCIP. See also *People v. Elizabeth Connor* (7 September 1820) and *People v. Abigail Hickson* (9 August 1824), ANA.

59. *New-York American*, 4 October 1822, 2. On women's dependency on men in the working-class communities of New York City, see Christine Stansell, *City of Women: Sex and Class in New York, 1789–1860* (Urbana: University of Illinois Press, 1987), 19–30, 36–37, 76–83.

60. *People v. Smith Davis* (6 March 1830), *People v. Mary Shepherd alias Mary Manning* (6 July 1838), and *People v. Mary Shepherd* (15 February 1843), all in NYCIP.

3. The Bank Wars

1. *Morning Chronicle*, 11 July 1837, quoted in Russell F. Weigley, ed., *Philadelphia: A Three-Hundred-Year History* (New York: W. W. Norton, 1982), 253.

2. Bray Hammond, *Banks and Politics in America from the Revolution to the Civil War* (Princeton, N.J.: Princeton University Press, 1957), 114–143, 197–226; Richard H. Timberlake, *Monetary Policy in the United States: An Intellectual and Institutional History* (Chicago: University of Chicago Press, 1978), 1–12; David Jack Cowen, *The Origins and Economic Impact of the First Bank of the United States, 1791–1797* (New York: Garland, 2000).

3. Don Taxay, *The U.S. Mint and Coinage: An Illustrated History from 1776 to the Present* (New York: Arco, 1966), 119–126; David A. Martin, "The Changing Role of Foreign Money in the United States, 1782–1857," *JEH* 37 (1977): 1009–1027.

4. Hammond, *Banks and Politics*, 65–67, 144–171; Fritz Redlich, *The Molding of American Banking: Men and Ideas*, vol. 1 (New York: Johnson Reprint, 1968), 5–23.

5. Hammond, *Banks and Politics*, 114–143, 197–226; Timberlake, *Monetary Policy*, 10–12; Susan Hoffman, *Politics and Banking: Ideas, Public Policy, and the Creation of Financial Institutions* (Baltimore: Johns Hopkins University Press, 2001), 21–43.

6. M. St. Clair Clarke and D. A. Hall, *Legislative and Documentary History of the Bank of the United States* (Washington, D.C.: Gales and Seaton, 1832), 164–165, 207, 213, 254, 402, 625; Dwight F. Henderson, *Congress, Courts, and Criminals: The Development of Federal Criminal Law, 1801–1829* (Westport, Conn.: Greenwood, 1985), 12–13; Louis P. Masur, "The Revision of the Criminal Law in Post-Revolutionary America," *Criminal Justice History* 8 (1987): 21–36.

7. Hammond, *Banks and Politics*, 227–230; Eric P. Newman, "New York City Small Change Bills of 1814–1816," in *America's Currency, 1789–1866: Coinage of the Americas Conference* (New York: American Numismatic Society, 1985), 95–114; Richard Doty, *America's Money, America's Story* (Iola, Wis.: Krause, 1998), 107; James Kirk Paulding, *The History of a Little Frenchman and His Bank Notes . . .* (Philadelphia: Edward Earle, 1815), 5–6.

8. Clay quoted in Clarke and Hall, *Legislative and Documentary History*, 672; Ralph C. H. Catterall, *The Second Bank of the United States* (Chicago: University of Chicago Press, 1902), 1–21; Niles quoted in *NWR*, 26 June 1819, 289, emphasis in original; Hammond, *Banks and Politics*, 230–241; Hoffman, *Politics and Banking*, 43–49.

9. *NWR*, 14 March 1818, 36, emphasis in original. See also Catterall, *Second Bank of the United States*, 22–50; Hammond, *Banks and Politics*, 251–285; Murray N. Rothbard, *The Panic of 1819: Reactions and Policies* (New York: Columbia University Press, 1962), 1–23; Edwin J. Perkins, "Langdon Cheves and the Panic of 1819: A Reassessment," *JEH* 44 (1984): 455–461.

10. Nicholas Biddle to Peter Paul Francis Degrand, 27 April 1826, quoted in Hammond, *Banks and Politics*, 307; Walter Buckingham Smith, *Economic Aspects of the Second Bank of the United States* (Cambridge: Harvard University Press, 1953), 134; Redlich, *Molding of American Banking*, 110–161; "Banks, &c," *NWR*, quoted in *Connecticut Courant*, 1 November 1825, 3, emphasis in original.

11. William Smith to Joseph Watson, 22 August 1825, Charles Mitchell to Joseph Watson, 5 August 1827, and Charles Mitchell to Joseph Watson, 3 October 1827, all in JWP-HSP; Sentence Docket, vol. 6, "1825–1835," p. 131, RG 38.36, Philadelphia County Prison, Philadelphia City Archives; *Republican Star and General Advertiser*, 18 September 1827, 3.

12. Boxes 101–102, Minutes of the Proceedings of the Court of King's Bench, Montreal, TL19, S1, SS1, ANQ; David R. Johnson, *Policing the Urban Underworld: The Impact of Crime on the Development of the American Police, 1800–1887* (Philadelphia: Temple University Press, 1979), 3–11; David R. Johnson, *Illegal Tender: Counterfeiting and the Secret Service in Nineteenth-Century America* (Washington, D.C.: Smithsonian Institution Press, 1995), 5–7.

13. On Craig and his wife, see *Baltimore Patriot and Mercantile Advertiser*, 28 November 1818, 2; *Newport Mercury*, 5 December 1818, 3; Montreal Calendar, 1 October 1824, vol. 4, RG 4, B 21, Lower Canada and Canada East, Gaol Calendars and Prison Returns, NAC; Charles Mitchell to Joseph Watson, 6 Novem-

ber 1827, JWP-HSP. On the Moses brothers, see Montreal Calendar, 1 September 1812, vol. 2, RG 4, B 21, Lower Canada and Canada East, Gaol Calendars and Prison Returns, NAC; "Moses, Reuben," in Jacob Hays Ledger, Museum of the City of New York; *Commercial Advertiser*, 10 July 1816, 2; *NYEP*, 19 February 1821, 2; and Charles Mitchell to Joseph Watson, 5 August 1827, JWP-HSP. On Mitchell, see *PADA*, 14 August 1818, 3; *Westchester Herald*, 25 August 1818, 3; William Smith to Joseph Watson, 22 August 1825, JWP-HSP; *NPG*, 4 April 1846, 261; and *NPG*, 24 January 1846, 177–178.

14. *Salem Gazette*, 13 May 1825, 3; *Gazette & Patriot*, 14 May 1825, 2; A. Porter to Joseph Watson, 20 October 1825, Charles Mitchell to Joseph Watson, 5 August 1827, and Joseph Watson to Governor Shulze, 13 November 1827, all in JWP-HSP.

15. Smith, *Economic Aspects of the Second Bank*, 37–63; J. Van Fenstermaker, *The Development of American Commercial Banking, 1782–1837* (Kent, Ohio: Kent State University Press, 1965), 34–35, 111; Milton Friedman and Anna Jacobson Schwartz, *Monetary Statistics of the United States: Estimates, Sources, Methods* (New York: Columbia University Press, 1970), 216–221. For a contemporary comparison of the potential for counterfeiting notes of the Second Bank of the United States versus those of a typical state bank, see *NPG*, 28 February 1846, 217.

16. Peter Linebaugh, *The London Hanged: Crime and Civil Society in the Eighteenth Century* (New York: Penguin, 1991), 55–57; Carl Wennerlind, "The Death Penalty as Monetary Policy: The Practice and Punishment of Monetary Crime, 1690–1830," *HPE* 36 (2004): 131–161; Lawrence W. Friedman, *Crime and Punishment in American History* (New York: Basic Books, 1993), 65–66.

17. Henderson, *Congress, Courts, and Criminals*, 3–53; James Willard Hurst, *A Legal History of Money in the United States, 1774–1970* (Lincoln: University of Nebraska Press, 1973), 38–39; Kathryn Preyer, "Jurisdiction to Punish: Federal Authority, Federalism, and the Common Law of Crimes in the Early Republic," *Law and History Review* 4 (1986): 223–265; Frederick S. Calhoun, *The Lawmen: United States Marshals and Their Deputies, 1789–1989* (New York: Penguin, 1991), 52–63.

18. On the scope, limits, and contradictions of policing in the early republic, see Johnson, *Illegal Tender*, 39–40; William J. Novak, *The People's Welfare: Law and Regulation in Nineteenth-Century America* (Chapel Hill: University of North Carolina Press, 1996); Markus Dirk Dubber, *The Police Power: Patriarchy and the Foundations of American Government* (New York: Columbia University Press, 2005), 81–119.

19. Seth Wyman, *The Life and Adventures of Seth Wyman* (Manchester, N.H.: J. H. Cate, Printer, 1843), 206, 290–291; William Stuart, *Sketches of the Life of William Stuart* (Bridgeport, Conn.: William Stuart, 1854), 118–138, 169; David Lewis, *The Life and Adventures of David Lewis, the Robber and Counterfeiter*, ed. C. D. Rishel (Newville, Pa.: C. D. Rishel, 1890), 32; *First Annual Report of the Board of Managers of the Prison Discipline Society* (Boston: Perkins and Marvin, 1830), 15, 46; *Second Annual Report of the Board of Managers of the Prison Discipline Society* (Boston: Perkins and Marvin, 1829), 56, 62; Roger Lane, *Policing the City: Boston, 1822–1885* (New York: Athenaeum, 1971), 3–13; David R. Johnson, *American Law*

Enforcement: A History (Arlington Heights, Ill.: Forum, 1981), 73–81; Johnson, *Policing the Urban Underworld*, 3–11.

20. *NPG*, 31 January 1846, 185–186.

21. Commitment Register, 10 January 1818–30 September 1840, Charlestown State Prison Records, MSA; Folder "Convicts in Mass. State Prison," box 4, Henry Herbert Edes Papers, MHS; Charles Mitchell to Charles Coxe, 30 September 1825, and Charles Mitchell to Joseph Watson, 16 July 1827, both in JWP-HSP; *Newport Mercury*, 25 August 1827, 3.

22. *Democratic Press*, 1 June 1827, 2; *New-Hampshire Gazette*, 7 August 1827, 3; *Eastern Argus*, 10 August 1827, 2; *Pittsfield Sun*, 20 September 1827, 1; Charles Mitchell to Joseph Watson, 20 September 1827, JWP-HSP; *PADA*, 25 September 1827, 2.

23. Benneville Keim to Joseph Watson, 20 July 1827, 28 July 1827, and 11 August 1827, and Charles Mitchell to Joseph Watson, 5 August 1827, all in JWP-HSP; *United States v. Moses*, 27 Federal Cases 5 (1827); *PADA*, 31 July 1827, 3; *PADA*, 17 August 1827, 3; *Republican Star and General Advertiser*, 21 August 1827, 3; *Newport Mercury*, 25 August 1827, 3; *PADA*, 25 September 1827, 2; *Republican Star and General Advertiser*, 6 November 1827, 2; *Globe*, 1 October 1833, 3; *National Gazette*, 8 October 1833, 1.

24. *Newport Mercury*, 25 August 1827, 3; *Newport Mercury*, 1 September 1827, 2; *Pittsfield Sun*, 20 September 1827, 1; *PADA*, 22 September 1827, 3; *PADA*, 25 September 1827, 2; *Newport Mercury*, 29 December 1827, 2; *Connecticut Courant*, 31 December 1827, 3.

25. See *United States v. John W. Craig, Reuben Moses, Benjamin Moses, and Ebenezer Gleason*, in "October Sessions 1827," and *United States v. Benjamin Moses and Ebenezer Gleason* in "April Sessions 1828," Criminal Case Files of the U.S. Circuit Court for the Eastern District of Pennsylvania, NARA, Mid-Atlantic Region, Philadelphia; *Republican Star and General Advertiser*, 18 September 1827, 3; *New-Hampshire Gazette*, 16 October 1827, 2; *Democratic Press*, 5 November 1827, 2; *Republican Star and General Advertiser*, 15 July 1828, 3.

26. *Baltimore Patriot*, 8 September 1828, 1; Statement of B. W. Lear, in folder "John Snyder," box 26, "Jackson Administration, 1829–1837, Unnumbered Cases," Petitions for Pardon, RG 59, General Records of the Department of State, NARA; *United States v. Elijah Hurd*, box 130, "Ended Cases (Unrestored), 1830," Virginia District, U.S. Circuit Court Records, Library of Virginia, Richmond. On Hurd's banishment, see James Reid to Liet. Col. Glegg, 3 December 1830, box 109, TL19, S1, SS777, "Correspondence des juges de la Cour du banc du roi, matières criminelles, 1830–1839," ANQ.

27. *Norristown Register*, 24 November 1830, 3; *Working Man's Advocate*, 27 November 1830, 3; *Eastern Argus*, 30 November 1830, 2; Edward Livingston to Lord Alymer, Governor of Canada, 1 August 1831, p. 413, vol. 4, "Notes from the Department of State to Foreign Ministers and Consuls in the United States, 1793–1834," RG 59, General Records of the Department of State, NARA.

28. Charles Mitchell to Joseph Watson, 3 October 1827, emphasis in original, JWP-HSP; Nicholas Biddle to Edward Livingston, 27 July 1831, Letter Books, Nicholas Biddle Papers, LoC.

29. Nicholas Biddle to Daniel Webster, 28 June 1831, Biddle Papers, LoC. On extra-

dition, see George M. Dallas to Edward Livingston, 1 December 1831, "Miscellaneous Letters of the Department of State," RG 59, General Records of the Department of State, NARA.

30. Amos Kendall, *Autobiography of Amos Kendall* (New York: Peter Smith, 1949), quoted in Hammond, *Banks and Politics,* 334; James D. Richardson, *Messages and Papers of the Presidents,* vol. 2 (Washington, D.C.: Government Printing Office, 1897), 1224–1238, quoted in Robert V. Remini, *Andrew Jackson and the Bank War* (New York: W. W. Norton, 1967), 44; Hoffman, *Politics and Banking,* 59. On Jackson's entrepreneurial allies, see Hammond, *Banks and Politics,* 329–339. The Bank War remains one of the most debated events of Jackson's presidency. For a nuanced and sophisticated account of the factions in the Bank War, as well as a discussion of the relevant historiography, see Sean Wilentz, *The Rise of American Democracy: Jefferson to Lincoln* (New York: Norton, 2005), 360–374, 392–403, 436–446.

31. Nicholas Biddle to Richard Smith, 8 April 1833, Biddle Papers, LoC; Hammond, *Banks and Politics,* 286–325; Thomas Payne Govan, *Nicholas Biddle: Nationalist and Public Banker, 1786–1844* (Chicago: University of Chicago Press, 1959), 49–111.

32. Nicholas Biddle to Peter Paul Francis Degrand, 27 April 1826, Biddle Papers, LoC; *Globe,* 14 December 1830, 2, emphasis in original; *Globe,* 19 January 1831, 3.

33. Nicholas Biddle to Daniel Webster, 28 June 1831, and Nicholas Biddle to Horace Binney, 27 January 1832, both in Biddle Papers, LoC; Hammond, *Banks and Politics,* 286–325, 403; Redlich, *Molding of American Banking,* 128–129; Arthur Fraas, "The Second Bank of the United States: An Instrument for an Interregional Monetary Union," *JEH* 34 (1974): 447–467.

34. Speech of Thomas Hart Benton, 2 February 1831, quoted in William Nesbit Chambers, *Old Bullion Benton: Senator from the New West* (Boston: Little, Brown, 1956), 174; Paul K. Conkin, *Prophets of Prosperity: America's First Political Economists* (Bloomington: Indiana University Press, 1980), 207–215; Wilentz, *Rise of American Democracy,* 438–439. On the complicated allegiances of the urban working class during the Bank War, see chapter 3 of Joshua R. Greenberg, *Advocating the Man: Masculinity, Organized Labor, and the Household in New York, 1800–1840* (New York: Columbia University Press and Gutenberg-e, 2006).

35. *Portsmouth Journal and Rockingham Gazette,* 8 October 1831, 1; *Globe,* 12 October 1831, 2; *Farmers' Cabinet,* 22 October 1831, 3, emphasis in original; *Baltimore Patriot,* 24 October 1831, 2. On the branch drafts, see Nicholas Biddle to Daniel Webster and Horace Binney, 22 March 1827, quoted in Catterall, *Second Bank of the United States,* 118; Hammond, *Banks and Politics,* 397–404.

36. *Globe,* 28 October 1831, 2; *Globe,* 12 November 1831, 2, emphasis in original.

37. *United States v. Shellmire,* 27 Federal Cases 1051 (1831); *National Gazette,* 8 November 1831, 2; *Globe,* 9 November 1831, 2, emphasis in original; *Baltimore Patriot,* 10 November 1831, 2; *Globe,* 15 November 1831, 3; *Hazard's Register of Pennsylvania,* 3 December 1831, 1; *Abridgment of the Debates of Congress from 1789 to 1856,* vol. 11 (New York: D. Appleton, 1860), 364–380; Chambers, *Old Bullion Benton,* 180.

38. Govan, *Nicholas Biddle*, 169–180, 212; Remini, *Andrew Jackson and the Bank War*, 72–76.

39. Jean Alexander Wilburn, *Biddle's Bank: The Crucial Years* (New York: Columbia University Press, 1967), 5–16; Hammond, *Banks and Politics*, 326–329; Nicholas Biddle to Francis Lieber, 10 April 1833, Biddle Papers, LoC.

40. Remini, *Andrew Jackson and the Bank War*, 80–83; Robert V. Remini, *Andrew Jackson and the Course of American Freedom, 1822–1832*, vol. 2 (New York: Harper & Row, 1981), 366. On Biddle's characterization, see Nicholas Biddle to Henry May, 14 August 1832, Biddle Papers, LoC.

41. William Phillips to Andrew Jackson, 26 July 1832, Alex Trumbull to Andrew Jackson, 18 October 1832, Reuben Moses to Andrew Jackson, 12 December 1832, and Reuben Moses to Andrew Jackson, n.d., all in folder 1186, box 22, "Petitions for Pardons," RG 59, General Records of the Department of State, NARA.

42. Reuben Moses to Andrew Jackson, n.d., folder 1186, box 22, "Petitions for Pardons," RG 59, General Records of the Department of State, NARA; Pardon 1186, vol. 4, p. 362, "General Pardon Records, Pardons and Remissions, 1793–1893," RG 59, General Records of the Department of State, NARA. On Jefferson's record, see vol. 1, pp. 47, 118, 126, 131, 133, 141, 147, 153, 154, 160, and 167, "Register and Indexes for Pardons, 1793–1871," General Pardon Records, RG 59, General Records of the Department of State, NARA.

43. Norbert Scott Brien Gras, *The Massachusetts First National Bank of Boston, 1784–1934* (Cambridge: Harvard University Press, 1937), 372–373, 385–385; Letter to John T. Apthorp, 25 August 1811, Boston Bank Papers, MHS; Minutes of the New England Association against Counterfeiters, in carton 11, "Banks, Trust Companies," manuscript 781, Vertical Files Collection, BL-HBS; Suffolk Bank Directors Records, vol. 5, 24 November 1832, Suffolk Bank Collection, BL-HBS. On the cooperative relationships of the financial community of New England and the stability they engendered, see Naomi R. Lamoreaux, *Insider Lending: Banks, Personal Connections, and Economic Development in Industrial New England* (New York: Cambridge University Press, 1994); Howard Bodenhorn, *State Banking in Early America: A New Economic History* (New York: Oxford University Press, 2003), 72–94. For more on the Association against Counterfeiters, see Ann-Marie Szymanski and Loren Gatch, "The Propriety of Property? Legal Culture and Economic Rights in Early America," presented at the American Political Science Association Annual Meeting, September 2001.

44. "Notice of Benjamin R. Nichols," *Proceedings of the Massachusetts Historical Society, Boston*, vol. 2, 1835–1855 (Boston: Massachusetts Historical Society, 1880), 427; David R. Whitney, *The Suffolk Bank* (Cambridge: Riverside, 1878), 1–25; Hammond, *Banks and Politics*, 549–556; Redlich, *Molding of American Banking*, 67–78; Charles W. Calomiris and Charles Kahn, "The Efficiency of Self-Regulated Payment Systems: Learning from the Suffolk System," *JMCB* 28 (1996): 766–797; Bruce D. Smith and Warren E. Weber, "Private Money Creation and the Suffolk Banking System," *JMCB* 31 (1999): 624–659; Bodenhorn, *State Banking*, 95–122.

45. Minutes of the New England Association against Counterfeiters, BL-HBS; Hammond, *Banks and Politics*, 338–339, 408–409.

46. Minutes of the New England Association against Counterfeiters, BL-HBS; circulars dated 3 December 1832 and 23 January 1833 and undated receipt, folders 2, 6, 11, box 1, Records of the Phoenix Bank, 1832–1857 (Charlestown, Mass.), MHS; handwritten report dated 27 November 1833 and printed circular dated 10 December 1833, "Papers Relating to the Association of Boston Banks against Counterfeiters," Bostonian Society, Boston.

47. Minutes of the New England Association against Counterfeiters, BL-HBS; Levi Lincoln to William L. Marcy, 10 June 1833, Gratz Collection, Historical Society of Pennsylvania, Philadelphia; circular dated 10 December 1833 in folder "Oriental Bank Counterfeiters, 1832–1836," box 3, Baker Library Currency Collection (exhibit 2), BL-HBS.

48. Handwritten report dated 27 November 1833 and printed circular dated 10 December 1833, "Papers Relating to the Association of Boston Banks against Counterfeiters," Bostonian Society; Minutes of the New England Association against Counterfeiters, BL-HBS.

49. *Daily Chronicle*, 21 August 1833, 2; *Repertory*, 22 August 1833, 2; *Daily Evening Transcript*, 22 August 1833, 2; *Daily Evening Transcript*, 24 August 1833, 2; *Farmers' Cabinet*, 31 August 1833, 2; *Brattleboro Messenger*, 31 August 1833, 2; *NWR*, 7 September 1833, 29–30; *Supplement to the Montreal Gazette*, 12 September 1833, 2; *Daily Evening Transcript*, 21 September 1833, 2; *Repertory*, 3 October 1833, 3; *Dominus Rex v. Benjamin Dudley Wing et al.*, 5 September 1833, *Dominus Rex v. Ebenezer Gleason et al.*, 5 September 1833 and 6 September 1833, Criminal Cases, vol. 7, James Reid Papers, MG 24, B 173, NAC.

50. *Dominus Rex v. Ebenezer Gleason et al.*, 5 September 1833 and 6 September 1833, Criminal Cases, vol. 7, James Reid Papers, NAC; Confession of Ebenezer Gleason, attached to J. Craig to Levi Lincoln, 28 September 1833, in folder "Sec. of Comm. Correspondence, Executive 1833–1854, Counterfeiters Arrested in Canada," box 3, Executive Correspondence, 1801–1859, Massachusetts Office of the Secretary of the State, MSA; *Supplement to the Montreal Gazette*, 12 September 1833, 2.

51. *Dominus Rex v. Ebenezer Gleason et al.*, 5 September 1833 and 6 September 1833, Criminal Cases, vol. 7, James Reid Papers, NAC; *Supplement to the Montreal Gazette*, 12 September 1833, 2; *Montreal Gazette*, 14 September 1833, 2; *NWR*, 21 September 1833, 59; *Repertory*, 3 October 1833, 3; *Burlington Sentinel*, 11 October 1833, 2; Registers for the Prison at Montreal, 16 August 1833, box 50, E17, SA, SS1, ANQ.

52. James L. Crouthamel, "Did the Second Bank of the United States Bribe the Press?" *Journalism Quarterly* 36 (1959): 35–44; Catterall, *Second Bank of the United States*, 171, 248–251; Hammond, *Banks and Politics*, 412–423; Remini, *Andrew Jackson and the Bank War*, 88–153; Frank O. Gatell, "Spoils of the Bank War: Political Bias in the Selection of Pet Banks," *American Historical Review* 70 (1964): 35–58.

53. *National Gazette*, 26 September 1833, 3; *Portsmouth Journal of Literature and Politics*, 21 December 1833, 1.

54. *Globe*, 30 September 1833, 2; *Globe*, 1 October 1833, 3; *National Gazette*, 8 October 1833, 1; *BRCD*, 13 February 1834, 2; *Saturday Courier*, 22 February 1834, 3.

55. *Globe*, 30 September 1833, 2; *Globe*, 4 October 1833, 2; *Globe*, 5 October 1833, 2;

National Gazette, 8 October 1833, 1; *Globe,* 18 October 1833, 2. On private prosecutions, see Robert M. Ireland, "Privately Funded Prosecution of Crime in the Nineteenth-Century United States," *American Journal of Legal History* 39 (1995): 43–58; Szymanski and Gatch, "Propriety of Property?"

56. Nicholas Biddle to Joseph Hopkinson, 21 February 1834, Biddle Papers, LoC; Remini, *Andrew Jackson and the Bank War,* 153. On the negative consequences of the demise of the Bank of the United States, see Rose Razaghian, "Establishing Financial Credibility in the United States, 1789–1860," Ph.D. diss., Columbia University, 2003.

57. *NPG,* 14 February 1846, 201–202; *NPG,* 21 February 1846, 209–210; *NPG,* 21 October 1848, 2.

58. *People v. Smith Davis* (10 April 1829), NYCIP; *NPG,* 14 February 1846, 201–202; *NPG,* 21 February 1846, 209–210; *NPG,* 28 February 1846, 217–218; *NPG,* 25 November 1848, 2.

59. *BRCD,* 10 March 1835, 2; *United States Gazette,* 24 April 1835, 3; *Atkinson's Saturday Evening Post,* 25 April 1835, 3; *BRCD,* 28 April 1835, 2; *NPG,* 28 February 1846, 217–218; *NPG,* 7 March 1846, 225–226; *NPG,* 14 March 1846, 233–234; *NPG,* 21 March 1846, 241–242.

60. *Inquirer and Daily Courier,* 10 March 1835, 2; *BRCD,* 10 March 1835, 2; Willis Blayney to Parker Pierce, 4 March 1835, "Papers Relating to the Association of Boston Banks against Counterfeiters," Bostonian Society.

61. *United States v. Lyman Parkes,* "April Sessions 1835," Criminal Case Files of the U.S. Circuit Court for the Eastern District of Pennsylvania, NARA–Mid Atlantic Region; *Atkinson's Saturday Evening Post,* 11 April 1835, 3; *Inquirer and Daily Courier,* 23 April 1835, 2; *United States Gazette,* 24 April 1835, 3; *Atkinson's Saturday Evening Post,* 25 April 1835, 3; *BRCD,* 28 April 1835, 2; *Saturday Courier,* 23 May 1835, 3; *NPG,* 21 March 1846, 241–242.

62. *NPG,* 21 March 1846, 241–242. On Blayney's negotiations, see Nichols to Blayney, 7 March 1835, Blayney to Nichols, 11 March 1835, Nichols to Blayney, 14 March 1835, and Blayney to Nichols, 22 March 1835, all in "Papers Relating to the Association of Boston Banks against Counterfeiters."

63. *BRCD,* 10 March 1835, 2; *NPG,* 14 March 1846, 233–234; *NPG,* 21 March 1846, 241–242; *NPG,* 25 November 1848, 2, emphasis in original.

64. *Young America,* 28 February 1846, 2; Hammond, *Banks and Politics,* 438–439, 451–454; Reginald Charles McGrane, *The Panic of 1837: Some Financial Problems of the Jacksonian Era* (Chicago: University of Chicago Press, 1924), 1–69; and Marie Elizabeth Sushka, *An Economic Model of the Money Market in the United States, 1823–1859* (New York: Arno, 1978), 5–7. More sympathetic to Jackson are Peter Temin, *The Jacksonian Economy* (New York: Norton, 1969), and Hugh Rockoff, "Money, Prices, and Banks in the Jacksonian Era," in Robert Fogel and Stanley Engerman, eds., *The Reinterpretation of American Economic History* (New York: Harper & Row, 1971), 448–458.

65. Chambers, *Old Bullion Benton,* 174, 212; Theophilus Fisk, *The Banking Bubble Burst; or, The Mammoth Corruptions of the Paper Money System Relieved by Bleeding* (Charleston, S.C.: Theophilus Fisk, 1837), 76. On the evolution of

the Jacksonians' views on money, see Sister M. Grace Madeleine, *Monetary and Banking Theories of Jacksonian Democracy* (1943; Port Washington, N.Y.: Kennikat Press, 1970).

66. Chambers, *Old Bullion Benton*, 210–213; Remini, *Andrew Jackson and the Bank War*, 169–173; Francis Newton Thorpe, ed., *The Statesmanship of Andrew Jackson* (New York: Tandy-Thomas, 1909), 506–507. On the growing schism in the ranks of the Jacksonians, see Wilentz, *Rise of American Democracy*, 438–446.

67. Hurst, *A Legal History of Money*, 137–145; Hammond, *Banks and Politics*, 563–571.

68. Peter L. Rousseau, "Jacksonian Monetary Policy, Specie Flows, and the Panic of 1837," *JEH* 62 (2002): 457–488. See also McGrane, *Panic of 1837*; Temin, *Jacksonian Economy*; Richard H. Timberlake Jr., "The Specie Circular and the Distribution of the Surplus," *JPE* 68 (1960): 109–117.

69. *Saturday Courier*, 20 May 1837, 2, 3; *NYH*, 20 June 1837, 2; *New-Yorker*, 24 June 1837, 218; *NYH*, 5 October 1837, 2; *NYH*, 12 October 1837, 2; Fisk, *Banking Bubble Burst*, 81; Doty, *America's Money*, 105; Richard H. Timberlake Jr., "The Significance of Unaccounted Currencies," *JEH* 41 (1981): 853–866; Q. David Bowers, *Obsolete Paper Money Issued by Banks in the United States, 1782–1866* (Atlanta: Whitman, 2006), 229–232.

70. *NYH*, 5 October 1837, 2; Fisk, *Banking Bubble Burst*, 41–42; *New-Yorker*, 7 October 1837, 459. On free banking, see Hugh Rockoff, "The Free Banking Era: A Reexamination," *JMCB* 6 (1974): 141–167; and Bodenhorn, *State Banking*, 183–218.

71. Suffolk Bank Directors' Minutes, 4 October 1837 and Massachusetts Senate Document 69 (1847): 5, both quoted in Szymanski and Gatch, "Propriety of Property?"; J. I. Little, *State and Society in Transition: The Politics of Institutional Reform in the Eastern Townships, 1838–1852* (Montreal: McGill-Queen's University Press, 1997), 57.

72. Warden's Daily Journals, 21 May 1835, vol. 1, ser. 15.50, RG 15, Eastern State Penitentiary, Department of Justice, Pennsylvania State Archives; Miscellaneous Descriptive Books, p. 66, vol. 1, ser. 15.62, RG 15, Eastern State Penitentiary, Department of Justice; Samuel D. Patterson to John Forsyth, 19 May 1839, and Henry Baldwin and Joseph Hopkinson to Martin Van Buren, 6 May 1839, both in folder 73, box 28, "Van Buren Administration, 1837–1841, nos. 51–100," Petitions for Pardons, 1789–1860, RG 59, General Records of the Department of State, NARA; Elizabeth T. Pike, W. J. Frisbie, E. Edic, and E. H. Conant, *Pioneer History of Camden, Oneida County, New York* (Utica, N.Y.: T. J. Griffiths, 1897), 135.

4. The Western Bankers

1. William D. Ellis, *The Cuyahoga* (Dayton, Ohio: Landfall Press, 1998), 52–59; Larry L. Miller, *Ohio Place Names* (Bloomington: Indiana University Press, 1996), 60.

2. Samuel A. Lane, *Fifty Years and Over of Akron and Summit County* (Akron: Beacon Job Department, 1892), 57; David R. Johnson, "A Sinful Business: The Ori-

gins of Gambling Syndicates in the United States, 1840–1887," in David H. Bayley, ed., *Police and Society* (Beverly Hills, Calif.: Sage, 1977), 18.

3. Jonathan H. Green, *Secret Band of Brothers* (1847; Philadelphia: T. B. Peterson, 1858); Philip D. Jordan, *Frontier Law and Order: Ten Essays* (Lincoln: University of Nebraska Press, 1970), 23–37.

4. Daniel Mevis, *Pioneer Recollections: Semi-Historic Side Lights on the Early Days of Lansing* (Lansing, Mich.: Robert Smith Printing, 1911), 33–34.

5. This reconstruction is based on visits to Boston, Ohio, as well as Lane, *Fifty Years,* 877; Randolph S. Bergdorf, *Life along the Canal: The 1849 Journal of Robert Andrew* (Peninsula, Ohio: Peninsula Library and Historical Society, 1990), 14. On the approximate date of the lightning strike, see William G. Taylor to James Brown, 29 September 1829, case 3102, *United States v. W. G. Taylor,* Criminal Case Files of the U.S. District Court for the Eastern District of Louisiana, NARA Southwest, Fort Worth, Texas (hereafter "case 3102, NARA Southwest").

6. Taylor to Brown, 29 September 1829, case 3102, NARA Southwest; Lane, *Fifty Years,* 877–878.

7. *NPG,* 3 October 1846, 30; Lane, *Fifty Years,* 877–878; Execution Docket, vol. B, p. 280, and vol. F, p. 62, PCCR.

8. Jonathan H. Green, *Gambling Unmasked!* (Philadelphia: G. B. Zieber, 1847), 65; Green, *Secret Band of Brothers,* 26; Lane, *Fifty Years,* 878. On James and Daniel's correspondence, see case 3102, NARA Southwest. On Green, see Ann Fabian, *Card Sharps, Dream Books, and Bucket Shops: Gambling in Nineteenth-Century America* (Ithaca, N.Y.: Cornell University Press, 1990), 59–107.

9. Lane, *Fifty Years,* 876–877; *American Balance,* 21 September 1837, 5; *History of Dearborn and Ohio Counties, Indiana* (Chicago: F. E. Weakley, 1885), 368. On the Brown family, see Arthur James Brown, "Pedigree Chart," as well as the research notes of Priscilla Graham, both in the author's possession.

10. Green, *Secret Band of Brothers,* 36; *People v. Joel Sturdivant,* 4 June 1816, NYCIP; Deposition of Martin D. Lewis, 12 July 1816, folder 1, container 3, George Tod Papers, MSS 3203, WRHS; *Vermont Mirror,* 12 June 1816, 3; Elisha Haven to William Little, 7 July 1818, in folder "MSS 655/1/2," ser. 655, William Little Papers, OHS; *Baltimore Patriot,* 29 August 1822, 1; *Saturday Evening Post,* 7 June 1823, 2; Letter to Gabriel Tichenor, 20 August 1821, in folder "Counterfeiting and Other Bank Crime Activities, Correspondence, 1819–1834," box 2E974, Bank of the State of Mississippi Records, Center for American History, University of Texas at Austin; James Hall, *Sketches of History, Life and Manners, in the West,* vol. 2 (Philadelphia: Harrison Hall, 1835), 86–91; Randall Parrish, *Historic Illinois: The Romance of the Earlier Days* (Chicago: A. C. McClurg, 1919), 400–405; Otto A. Rothert, *The Outlaws of Cave-in-Rock* (Cleveland: Arthur H. Clark, 1924), 271–281; Ron Nelson, "The Raid on Sturdivant's Fort," *Springhouse Magazine* 15 (April 1998): 25–32.

11. *History of Dearborn and Ohio Counties,* 368; Lane, *Fifty Years,* 877. On horse theft, see Parrish, *Historic Illinois,* 405–406.

12. *Independent Chronicle and Boston Patriot,* 12 January 1822, 4; *American Mercury,* 14 January 1822, 3; *Providence Patriot,* 19 January 1822, 2.

13. *American Repertory*, 8 April 1824, 3; "Minutes of the Proceedings of the Court of King's Bench, Montreal," 2 March 1825, 7 March 1826, 7 September 1826, 9 September 1826, and 7 March 1827, boxes 102 and 103, TL19, S1, SS1, Registres des procés, ANQ; *Northern Sentinel*, 14 July 1826, 3; H. Craig, Civil Secretary of Lower Canada to the Governor of Ohio, 28 September 1833, OHS; Lucius V. Bierce, *Historical Reminiscences of Summit County* (Akron, Ohio: T. & H. G. Canfield, 1854), 44–45; Lane, *Fifty Years*, 878. On Taylor's relationship with Brown, see their correspondence from the 1820s in case 3102, NARA Southwest. On Crane, see Ellery Bicknell Crane, *Geneaology of the Crane Family*, vol. 1 (Worcester, Mass.: Press of Charles Hamilton, 1895), 93, as well as microfilm 138, p. 251, "Shalersville, Portage, Ohio," in *Fifth Census of the United States, 1830*, NARA.

14. Bierce, *Historical Reminiscences*, 44; *Chillocothe Supporter*, 4 February 1817, quoted in William T. Utter, *The History of the State of Ohio*, vol. 2: *The Frontier State, 1803–1825* (Columbus: Ohio State Archaeological and Historical Society, 1942), 276; C. C. Huntington, "A History of Banking and Currency in Ohio before the Civil War," in *Ohio Archaeological and Historical Publications*, vol. 24 (Columbus: Ohio State Archaeological and Historical Society, 1915), 255–291; Q. David Bowers, *Obsolete Paper Money Issued by Banks in the United States, 1782–1866* (Atlanta: Whitman, 2006), 113–122, 540–541.

15. *Ohio Watchman*, 3 December 1818, quoted in Huntington, "A History of Banking and Currency," 294; Logan Esary, "The First Indiana Banks," *Indiana Magazine of History* 6 (1910): 144–158; Utter, *History of the State of Ohio*, 276–295.

16. *Baltimore Patriot*, 30 June 1826, 2, emphasis in original; *Middlesex Gazette*, 5 July 1826, 3; *Northern Sentinel*, 14 July 1826, 3; Execution Docket, vol. D, pp. 163–165, PCCR; *Buzzard*, 30 June 1838, 2; Charles Whittlesey, "The Boston Bankers," in folder 169, subseries C, ser. 5, mss. 1, "Manuscripts Relating to the Early History of the Western Reserve, 1795–1869," WRHS; Lane, *Fifty Years*, 57.

17. Execution Docket, vol. D, pp. 163–165, PCCR; Common Pleas Journal, vol. 4, p. 320, and vol. 5, p. 149, PCCR; Whittlesey, "Boston Bankers"; Deposition of George Farr, 7 September 1827, case 3102, NARA Southwest.

18. *Northern Sentinel*, 14 July 1826, 3; David Hudson to Allen Trimble, 27 November 1827, and Petition of the Residents of Hudson, Ohio, 14 April 1828, both in folder 3, "George Darrow," BV5765, Pardon Papers, Office of the Governor, OSA; Whittlesey, "Boston Bankers."

19. *Newport Mercury*, 7 April 1827, 3; Execution Docket, vol. D, p. 164, PCCR; Common Pleas Journal, vol. 4, pp. 348, 359, and vol. 5, p. 149, PCCR; David Hudson to Allen Trimble, 27 November 1827, folder 3, "George Darrow," BV5765, Pardon Papers, Office of the Governor, OSA; Whittlesey, "Boston Bankers." On law enforcement, see *Painesville Telegraph*, 15 June 1827, 3, *Painesville Telegraph*, 2 November 1827, 3; and *Cleveland Herald*, 29 January 1829, 3.

20. *Painesville Telegraph*, 27 April 1827, 3; *Cleveland Herald*, 4 May 1827, 3; *Painesville Telegraph*, 4 May 1827, 3; *Painesville Telegraph*, 8 June 1827, 3; *Painesville Telegraph*, 15 June 1827, 3; *Painesville Telegraph*, 2 November 1827, 3; *Cleveland Herald*, 29 January 1829, 3; Bierce, *Historical Reminiscences*, 125–126; Nick Scrattish, *His-*

toric Resource Study: Cuyahoga Valley National Recreation Area, Ohio (Denver: National Park Service, 1985), 198, 210–211.

21. H. Craig, Civil Secretary of Lower Canada to the Governor of Ohio, 28 September 1833, OHS; Lane, *Fifty Years,* 649–652, 878. On Latta's marriage, see the postings in branch 46 of the Latta Family Genealogy available online at www.latta.org.

22. Oliver Clark to Allen Trimble, 19 May 1828, box 1, folder 8, Allen Trimble Papers, OHS. On the canal, see Harry N. Scheiber, *Ohio Canal Era: A Case Study of Government and the Economy, 1820–1861* (Athens: Ohio University Press, 1968).

23. William G. Taylor to James Brown, 3 May 1830, case 3102, NARA Southwest.

24. *New Orleans Courier,* 31 January 1831, 3; *New Orleans Courier,* 3 February 1831, 3; *Farmers' Cabinet,* 26 February 1831, 2; *NWR,* 26 February 1831, 463.

25. Lane, *Fifty Years,* 878–879.

26. Lucius Bierce to Duncan McArthur, 4 May 1831, folder 4, "John B. Foote," BV5766, Pardon Papers, Office of the Governor, OSA; Lane, *Fifty Years,* 878–879; Bierce, *Historical Reminiscences,* 45; *BRCD,* 20 February 1838, 3.

27. Deposition of James Brown, 2 May 1831; Deposition of Lucy Brown, 2 May 1831; Deposition of Daniel Brown, 2 May 1831; Deposition of William G. Taylor, 3 May 1831; Deposition of James Brown, 4 May 1831; Deposition of Daniel Brown, 4 May 1831, Deposition of Unidentified Witness, 13 March 1832; and Deposition of Rufus Whitlock, n.d., all in case 3102, NARA Southwest; Lane, *Fifty Years,* 880–881.

28. Deposition of William G. Taylor, 3 May 1831, case no. 3102, NARA Southwest; William G. Taylor, *A Synopsis of the Trial of Col. William G. Taylor* (New Orleans: A. T. Penniman Jr., 1832), 4–6, emphasis in original.

29. Green, *Gambling Unmasked,* 61–67; Green, *Secret Band of Brothers,* 18–21; Deposition of David Cunningham, 21 November 1831, and Deposition of D. W. Walling, 11 April 1832, case 3102, NARA Southwest.

30. William G. Taylor to James Brown, 29 September 1829 and 3 May 1830; Daniel Brown alias Cashell to Susan Turner, 23 May 1831 and 1 July 1831; Daniel Brown to Orange M. Stevens, 23 September 1831; Daniel Brown to Silas Walsworth, 14 October 1831; Daniel Brown to D. Cunningham, n.d.; and Daniel Brown to Mayor of New Orleans, n.d., all in case 3102, NARA Southwest.

31. Daniel Brown to Orange M. Stevens, 23 September 1831, Deposition of James Armstrong, 24 February 1832, and Deposition of Unidentified Witness, 13 March 1832, all in case 3102, NARA Southwest.

32. Deposition of William Taylor, 3 May 1831; Daniel Brown to Orange M. Stevens, 23 September 1831; Deposition of Rufus Whitlock, 15 February 1832, case 3102, NARA Southwest; Taylor, *Synopsis of the Trial,* 15.

33. Deposition of David Cunningham, n.d.; Deposition of Jonathan Green, 30 March 1832; Deposition of Samuel Strayer, 20 April 1832; and Deposition of James King, 20 April 1832, all in case 3102, NARA Southwest; Green, *Gambling Unmasked,* 63–79; *NWR,* 21 April 1832, 148; *Portsmouth Journal and Rockingham Gazette,* 26 May 1832, 1; Taylor, *Synopsis of the Trial,* 16. Green would later con-

tradict his earlier testimony, claiming in his memoirs that it was James Brown, not Taylor, who orchestrated the burglary.

34. *Saturday Courier,* 14 July 1832, 2; *Saturday Courier,* 15 December 1832, 3; Green, *Gambling Unmasked,* 71; Green, *Secret Band of Brothers,* 61; Lane, *Fifty Years,* 880.

35. Sile Doty, *The Life of Sile Doty . . .* (1880; Detroit: Alved of Detroit, 1948), 198–201; Green, *Secret Band of Brothers,* 17–18; Fabian, *Card Sharps,* 84–85. For Green's account—as told to him by Daniel Brown—see *Secret Band of Brothers,* 50–138.

36. Doty, *Life of Sile Doty,* 216.

37. Lane, *Fifty Years,* 881. On Brown's tenure as justice of the peace, see, e.g., Summons, 12 January 1835 and Certification, 21 March 1837, both in file "James Brown," Peninsula Library and Historical Society, Peninsula, Ohio.

38. Lane, *Fifty Years,* 649, 878, 882, 885, 922.

39. Bray Hammond, *Banks and Politics in America: From the Revolution to the Civil War* (Princeton, N.J.: Princeton University Press, 1957), 326–499; Warren E. Weber, "Early State Banks in the United States: How Many Were There and When Did They Exist?" working paper 634 (2005), Research Department, Federal Reserve Bank of Minneapolis. On free banking, see Kevin Dowd, "U.S. Banking in the 'Free Banking' Period," in Dowd, ed., *The Experience of Free Banking* (London: Routledge, 1992), 206–240.

40. Huntington, "A History of Banking and Currency in Ohio before the Civil War," 365–378; James A. Haxby, *Standard Catalog of United States Obsolete Bank Notes, 1782–1866,* vol. 3 (Iola, Wis.: Krause, 1988), 1909–2006. On the Kirtland, see Dean A. Dudley, "Bank Born of Revelation: The Kirtland Safety Society Anti-Banking Company," *JEH* 30 (1970): 848–853; Dale W. Adams, "Chartering the Kirtland Bank," *BYU Studies* 23 (1983): 467–482; Bowers, *Obsolete Paper Money,* 237–240. On Lane's opinion of the Kirtland, see *Buzzard,* 2 December 1837, 2.

41. Huntington, "A History of Banking and Currency in Ohio before the Civil War," 352–409; Jane Knodell, "The Demise of Central Banking and the Domestic Exchanges: Evidence from Antebellum Ohio," *JEH* 58 (1998): 714–730; Bowers, *Obsolete Paper Money,* 540–543.

42. H. M. Utley, "The Wild Cat Banking System of Michigan," *Pioneer Collections: Report of the Pioneer Society of the State of Michigan,* vol. 5 (Lansing, Mich.: W. S. George, 1884), 209–222; Hugh Rockoff, *The Free Banking Era: A Re-Examination* (New York: Arno, 1975), 94–97; Gerald P. Dwyer, "Wildcat Banking, Banking Panics, and Free Banking in the United States," *Federal Reserve Bank of Atlanta Economic Review* 81 (December 1996): 6–7.

43. On the origins of the term "wildcat," see *American Balance,* 2 August 1838, 2; Breckinridge Jones, "One Hundred Years of Banking in Missouri, 1820–1920," *Missouri Historical Review* 15 (1921): 359; Bowers, *Obsolete Paper Money,* 244–253, 522–523. On the actual importance of wildcat banking, see Rockoff, *The Free Banking Era;* Arthur J. Rolnick and Warren E. Weber, "Free Banking, Wildcat Banking, and Shinplasters," *Federal Reserve Bank of Minneapolis Quarterly Review* 6 (Fall 1982): 10–19; Dowd, "The Experience of Free Banking," 217–219; and Dwyer, "Wildcat Banking," 1–20.

44. *Cleveland Herald and Gazette,* 4 August 1837, 2; *New-Yorker,* 19 August 1837, 351; *American Balance,* 19 August 1837, 4; *Newport Mercury,* 26 August 1837; Execution Docket, vol. I, pp. 80–82, PCCR.

45. *Buzzard,* 23 September 1837, 3; *Saturday Courier,* 3 February 1838, 3; *American Balance,* 8 February 1838, 2, 3; Lane, *Fifty Years,* 882; Haxby, *Standard Catalog,* vol. I, 345–346.

46. *NYH,* 19 January 1838, 4; *NYH,* 27 January 1838, 2; *NYH,* 29 January 1838, 2; *Saturday Courier,* 3 February 1838, 3; *American Balance,* 8 February 1838, 2, 3; *People v. Abraham Pitcher, Charles Stearn, and James Brown* (12 March 1838), NYCIP; Lane, *Fifty Years,* 882.

47. *Buzzard,* 7 September 1837, 3; Lane, *Fifty Years,* 10–11, 217–218; Fabian, *Card Sharps,* 28–30.

48. Execution Docket, vol. I, pp. 80–82, PCCR; *Buzzard,* 7 October 1837, 1; *Buzzard,* 2 December 1837, 2; *Buzzard,* 1 January 1838, 3; *American Balance,* 1 March 1838, 2; Lane, *Fifty Years,* 11–17.

49. *Literary Inquirer,* 23 April 1834, 125; *Cleveland Herald and Gazette,* 22 February 1838, 1; *American Balance,* 1 March 1838, 2; *Saturday Courier,* 3 March 1838, 2; *Buzzard,* 10 March 1838, 2, 3; Execution Docket, vol. F, pp. 222, PCCR; Common Pleas Journal, vol. 6, pp. 216, 307, PCCR; Lane, *Fifty Years,* 891–892.

50. Criminal Records, vol. 1, "March Term 1835 to May Term 1839," pp. 347–349, 398–399, PCCR; *American Balance,* 1 March 1838, 2; *American Balance,* 8 March 1838, 2; *Buzzard,* 10 March 1838, 3, emphasis in original; *American Balance,* 12 April 1838, 2; *Buzzard,* 17 April 1838, 3, emphasis in original; *American Balance,* 26 April 1838, 2; Prisoner Register no. 1, pp. 17a–17f, March 1834–May 1849, Ohio State Penitentiary, GR 3627, ser. 1536, OSA; Lane, *Fifty Years,* 667–668.

51. *American Balance,* 2 November 1837, 3; William Henry Smith, *The History of the State of Indiana . . . ,* vol. 2 (Indianapolis: B. L. Blair, 1897), 610–611; Russell Rulau, *Standard Catalog of Hard Times Tokens, 1832–1844* (Iola, Wis.: Krause, 2001). On the vexed history and historiography of the panic, see Peter L. Rousseau, "Jacksonian Monetary Policy, Specie Flows, and the Panic of 1837," *JEH* 62 (2002): 457–488.

52. *American Balance,* 12 April 1838, 2; *Buzzard,* 21 April 1838, 2; *Buzzard,* 30 June 1838, 3, emphasis in original; William Henry Perrin, ed., *History of Summit County . . .* (Chicago: Baskin & Battey, 1881), 538.

53. *American Balance,* 19 April 1838, 2; *Buzzard,* 21 April 1838, 2; *Buzzard,* 30 June 1838, 3; *American Balance,* 11 October 1838, 2–3; *American Balance,* 25 October 1838, 2; Lane, *Fifty Years,* 882–885.

54. *Buzzard,* 14 July 1838, 4; *American Balance,* 23 August 1838, 2; *Buzzard,* 25 August 1838, 3; Execution Docket, vol. M, pp. 108–109, PCCR; Lane, *Fifty Years,* 651–652, 882–885.

55. *New-Yorker,* 1 May 1841, 111; *NPG,* 3 October 1846, 30; *Summit County Beacon,* 5 May 1841, 2; Lane, *Fifty Years,* 18, 885; Jeffrey J. Richner, *Archaeological Inventory at Two Historic Farms at Cuyahoga Valley National Recreation Area, Bath and Northampton Townships, Summit County, Ohio, 1994* (Lincoln, Neb.: U.S. Department of the Interior, 1997). On Brown's residence in Akron, see the research notes of Priscilla Graham, in the author's possession.

56. Gaol Calenders and Prison Returns for Lower Canada and Canada East, vol. 5, p. 2628, and vol. 6, pp. 2646, 2740, 2771, RG 4, B 21, NAC; Henry L. Boies, *History of Dekalb County, Illinois* (Chicago: O. P. Bassett, 1868), 450–452; Lewis M. Gross, *Past and Present in DeKalb County, Illinois*, vol. 1 (Chicago: Pioneer, 1907), 65–66, 184–185. Turner Wing was another emigrant to Dekalb County. See microfilm 104, p. 299, "Mayfield, De Kalb, Illinois," in *Seventh Census of the United States, 1850*, NARA.

57. Statement of Expense, 4 December 1838, and Indictment, *People of the State of Illinois v. William Taylor*, October Term 1838, in "Papers from the County Commissioners' Files Found in Court House Basement," on deposit at the Joiner History Room, Sycamore Public Library, Sycamore, Ill.; Boies, *History of Dekalb County*, 377–378; Gross, *Past and Present*, 65; Howard Jones, *To the Webster-Ashburton Treaty: A Study in Anglo-American Relations, 1783–1843* (Chapel Hill: University of North Carolina Press, 1977), 149; J. I. Little, *State and Society in Transition: The Politics of Institutional Reform in the Eastern Townships, 1838–1852* (Montreal: McGill-Queen's University Press, 1997), 55–58; Francis M. Carroll, *A Good and Wise Measure: The Search for the Canadian-American Boundary, 1783–1842* (Toronto: University of Toronto Press, 2001), 284–285; James E. Davis, *Frontier Illinois* (Bloomington: Indiana University Press, 1998), 320–352. The frontier was not always as lawless as some historians have argued, particularly when it came to violent crime. See David J. Bodenhamer, "Law and Disorder on the Early Frontier: Marion County, Indiana, 1823–1850," *Western Historical Quarterly* 10 (1979): 323–336; and Davis, *Frontier Illinois*, 287–289.

58. Boies, *History of Dekalb County*, 376, 451–455; Gross, *Past and Present in Dekalb County*, 184.

59. *History of the Regulators of Northern Indiana* (Indianapolis: Indianapolis Journal Company, 1859), 5; "Frank Gleason," vol. 4, p. 109, DIC-USSS, NARA; Allan Pinkerton, *Criminal Reminiscences and Detective Sketches* (1878; Freeport, N.Y.: Books for Libraries Press, 1970), 9–51, emphasis in original; Correspondence from Howard Gleason to Stephen Mihm, 1 September 2002, in the author's possession. On Crane's location, see microfilm 704, p. 97, "Unknown Townships, Lake, Illinois," in *Sixth Census of the United States*, 1840; and microfilm 432, p. 43, "Libertyville, Lake, Illinois," *Seventh Census of the United States*, 1850, NARA. See also Bartholomew C. Yates to John C. Clark, 30 August 1851, in box 7, "Central & Southern Pacific-Copper Rock," Closed Cases (Miscellaneous), RG 206, Solicitor of the Treasury of the United States, NARA.

60. *NPG*, 10 May 1851, 2; *History of the Regulators*, 6–8, 21; *Counties of Warren, Benton, Jasper and Newton, Indiana* (Chicago: F. A. Battey, 1883), 457–458; Elmore Barce, *Beaver Lake, Land of Enchantment* (Kentland, Ind.: Kentland Democrat, 1938), 101–116; Burt E. Burroughs, *Tales of an Old 'Border Town' and along the Kankakee* (Fowler, Ind.: Benton Review Shop, 1925), 138–153; Jordan, *Frontier Law and Order*, 23–37; John J. Yost, "Bogus Island History, Newton County Indiana," unpublished manuscript in the author's possession.

61. *New-Yorker*, 17 July 1841, 288; *New World*, 28 August 1841, 144; *New-Yorker*, 28 August 1841, 380; James W. Bragg, "Captain Slick, Arbiter of Early Alabama Morals," *Alabama Review* 11 (1958): 125–134; Malcolm J. Rohrbough, *The Trans-*

Appalachian Frontier: People, Societies, and Institutions, 1775–1850 (Belmont, Calif.: Wadsworth, 1990), 233, 248–249; Dennis C. Rousey, *Policing the Southern City: New Orleans, 1805–1889* (Baton Rouge: Louisiana State University Press, 1996), 1–10. Florida may have been an exception to the rule. See James M. Denham, *"A Rogue's Paradise": Crime and Punishment in Antebellum Florida, 1821–1861* (Tuscaloosa: University of Alabama Press, 1997).

62. B. H. Roberts, *A Comprehensive History of the Church of Jesus Christ of Latter-day Saints* (Provo, Utah: Brigham Young University Press, 1965), vol. 2, 532–534, and vol. 3, 56–57; *History of the Church of Jesus Christ of Latter-Day Saints: Period II . . .* , vol. 7 (Salt Lake City: Desert Book Company, 1973), 350, 491, 574, 608–609; John L. Brooke, *The Refiner's Fire: The Making of Mormon Cosmology, 1644–1844* (Cambridge, Eng.: Cambridge University Press, 1994), 268–271; Susan Sessions Rugh, *Our Common Country: Family Farming, Culture, and Community in the Nineteenth-Century Midwest* (Bloomington: Indiana University Press, 2001), 31–53.

63. D. A. Robert to R. H. Gillet, 4 November 1848, in box 7, "Central & Southern Pacific—Copper Rock," Closed Cases (Miscellaneous), RG 206, Solicitor of the Treasury of the United States, NARA; Huntington, "History of Banking and Currency," 413–432; Hammond, *Banks and Politics,* 605–630; Erling A. Erickson, *Banking in Frontier Iowa, 1836–1865* (Ames: Iowa State University Press, 1971); William Gerald Shade, *Banks or No Banks: The Money Issue in Western Politics, 1832–1865* (Detroit: Wayne State University Press, 1972), 60–144; Dowd, "U.S. Banking in the 'Free Banking' Period," 206–240.

64. Lane, *Fifty Years,* 892–893; Martin R. Kaatz, "The Black Swamp: A Study in Historical Geography," *Annals of the Association of American Geographers* 45 (1955): 1–13.

65. Lane, *Fifty Years,* 892–893.

66. *NPG,* 7 March 1846, 227; *Cleveland Herald,* 12 August 1846, 2; *NPG,* 15 August 1846, 412; T. W. Bartly to James Polk, 29 August 1846 and 19 October 1846, in folder 30, box 2, "Petitions for Pardon and Related Briefs, 1800–1849, Nos. 15–57," RG 59, General Records of the Department of State, NARA; Lane, *Fifty Years,* 885–887.

67. Prisoner Register no. 1, pp. 69a–69f, March 1834–May 1849, Ohio State Penitentiary, GR 3627, ser. 1536, OSA; James B. Finley, *Memorials of Prison Life* (Cincinnati: L. Swormstedt and J. H. Power, 1850), 205–206; Lane, *Fifty Years,* 887.

68. Lane, *Fifty Years,* 893–895.

69. *State of Missouri v. Joseph Dows and Timothy Lacey,* September Term 1848, case 40, Criminal Case Files, St. Louis County Circuit Court, microfilm 447, Missouri State Archives, Jefferson City; Lane, *Fifty Years,* 895–896.

70. Lane, *Fifty Years,* 895–896; J. Ray Cable, "The Bank of the State of Missouri," in *Studies in History, Economics, and Public Law,* vol. 102 (New York: Columbia University Press, 1923), 179–199; Lynne Pierson Doti and Larry Schweikart, *Banking in the American West: From the Gold Rush to Deregulation* (Norman: University of Oklahoma Press, 1991), 7–14.

71. *Summit County Beacon,* 11 July 1849, 3; Lane, *Fifty Years,* 887–888. Brown's pardon file is missing, though it seems most likely that it was Fillmore, not Taylor, who

signed it. See vol. 1, p. 348, "Abstracts from State Department Records, 1793–1853," RG 204, Records of the Office of the Pardon Attorney, NARA.

72. *BMSR,* December 1850, 508; *United States Biographical Dictionary and Portrait Gallery of Eminent and Self-Made Men: Missouri Volume* (New York: U.S. Biographical Publishing, 1878), 764; Lane, *Fifty Years,* 896; William Lewis Manly, *Death Valley in '49* (San Jose, Calif.: Pacific Tree and Vine, 1894), 472; Cable, "Bank of the State of Missouri," 191–192; Malcolm J. Rohrbough, *Days of Gold: The California Gold Rush and the American Nation* (Berkeley: University of California Press, 1997), 218–220.

73. *NPG,* 16 November 1850, 2–3; *NPG,* 23 November 1850, 2; *People v. Alvarado C. Ford* (6 December 1850), NYCIP; Lane, *Fifty Years,* 896.

74. *NPG,* 16 November 1850, 2–3; *NPG,* 23 November 1850, 2; Lane, *Fifty Years,* 897; William Franklin Fleming, *America's Match King: Ohio Columbus Barber, 1841–1920* (Barberton, Ohio: Barberton Historical Society, 1981), 13–15.

75. *Summit County Beacon,* 14 February 1855, 3; *NPG,* 17 February 1855, 2; *NPG,* 24 February 1855, 4; *Summit County Beacon,* 16 December 1857, 3; Whittlesey, "Boston Bankers," WRHS; Lane, *Fifty Years,* 888–889.

76. On crime in western cities, see *NPG,* 23 March 1850, 2; *NPG,* 10 July 1852, 2; Jeffrey S. Adler, *Yankee Merchants and the Making of the Urban West: The Rise and Fall of Antebellum St. Louis* (Cambridge, Eng.: Cambridge University Press, 1991), 100–101, 169–170.

5. Passing and Detecting

1. Reconstruction based on *People v. Mary Condon* (14 February 1854), NYCIP; Tyler Anbinder, *Five Points: The Nineteenth-Century New York City Neighborhood That Invented Tap Dance, Stole Elections, and Became the World's Most Notorious Slum* (New York: Plume, 2002), 14–37. The slang for someone who passed counterfeits was a "passer" or "utterer" until the 1840s, when the term "shover" first came into use. Throughout this chapter, I have used "passer" in connection with cases before this period, and "passer" and "shover" interchangeably in reference to cases from the 1840s onward. For an early example of the term "shover," see *NPG,* 26 June 1847, 332.

2. *NWR,* 26 June 1819, 289, emphasis in original; *Abridgment of the Debates of Congress, from 1789 to 1856,* vol. 11 (New York: D. Appleton, 1860), 375.

3. Sile Doty, *The Life of Sile Doty . . .* (1880; Detroit: Alved of Detroit, 1948), 52–53; *People v. Andrew Graham and Peter G. Young* (7 July 1825), NYCIP. See also *People v. Avery Read* (16 August 1820), ANA; Langdon W. Moore, *Langdon W. Moore: His Own Story of His Eventful Life* (1893; Freeport, N.Y.: Books for Libraries, 1971), 32.

4. *NYH,* 14 January 1843, 1; *NYDT,* 16 January 1843, 1; *NYH,* 17 January 1843, 3; *NYDT,* 18 January 1843, 3; *NYH,* 12 February 1843, 2; *NYH,* 14 February 1843, 2; *NPG,* 25 July 1846, 388; *Harbinger,* 5 February 1848, 6; *Boston Cultivator,* 1 April 1848, 107; Charles Sutton, *The New York Tombs: Its Secrets and Its Mysteries* (New York: United States Publishing Company, 1874), 597.

5. *NYH*, 14 February 1843, 1; *Second Report of the Prison Association of New York* (New York: Prison Association of New York, 1846), 51–52; *NYH*, 22 January 1848, 2; *NPG*, 29 January 1848, 82; *NPG*, 5 February 1848, 86; *Harbinger*, 5 February 1848, 108; *Harbinger*, 10 June 1848, 43.

6. Christine Stansell, *City of Women: Sex and Class in New York, 1789–1860* (Urbana: University of Illinois Press, 1987); Sean Wilentz, *Chants Democratic: New York City and the Rise of the American Working Class, 1788–1850* (New York: Oxford University Press, 1984).

7. *People v. Henry Green* (11 May 1818), *People v. Whitney Hendrickson* (9 November 1821), *People v. Henry Pemberton* (13 April 1832), *People v. George Patten* (13 April 1832), *People v. Ebenezer Cave* (12 July 1842), and *People v. James Murray* (14 December 1842), all in NYCIP. See also *NYC*, 16 August 1820, 2; *People v. William Waterman* (9 July 1827), ANA; William A. Coffey, *Inside Out; or, An Anterior View of the New-York State Prison* (New York: James Costigan, 1823), 107, 115.

8. *NYEP*, 4 September 1820, 2; *People v. Philip Selover* (8 September 1837), and *People v. Elisha Sanders* (11 September 1837), all in NYCIP; *Eastern Argus*, 30 March 1832, 2.

9. *People v. Philip Selover* (8 September 1837), and *People v. Case McAlister* (14 November 1844), both in NYCIP; John Burnham to Joseph Watson, 5 June 1826, JWP-HSP. On the Bonney twins, see *NPG*, 18 September 1847, 7; *NPG*, 30 August 1851, 3.

10. *People v. Samuel Baker* (5 October 1813), *People v. Henry Burnett* (13 April 1818), *People v. Horace Latimer* (16 June 1825), *People v. Quimby Baker* (7 March 1827), and *People v. Smith Davis* (11 December 1838), all in NYCIP.

11. *People v. Henry Burnett* (13 April 1818), *People v. John Strickland* (13 September 1820), *People v. Isaac Dermott* (8 January 1827), *People v. Archibald McMullen* (5 May 1831), and *People v. Silas Dean* (16 February 1832), all in NYCIP; *Eastern Argus*, 30 March 1832, 2, emphasis in original.

12. Doty, *Life of Sile Doty*, 16; *People v. Isaac Dunsmore* (3 June 1818), *People v. Garret Bergen* (9 August 1821), *People v. William McMenomy* (8 November 1823), *People v. Abby Bennett* (11 August 1831), *People v. Smith Davis* (11 December 1838), and *People v. Mary Fry* (16 January 1852), all in NYCIP. See also *NYC*, 16 August 1820, 2; *People v. Daniel Fulum* (9 July 1827) and *People v. Hiram Brown and Robert Brown* (14 February 1837), ANA; and *Second Annual Report of the House of Refuge of Philadelphia* (Philadelphia: Jesper Harding, 1830), 26–27.

13. *NYC*, 16 August 1820, 2; *NYC*, 14 September 1820, 2; *NYEP*, 15 September 1820, 2; *NYEP*, 16 September 1820, 2; *NYEP*, 31 August 1821, 2; *NPG*, 7 March 1846, 228; *NPG*, 23 November 1850, 2.

14. Henry C. Foote, *Universal Counterfeit and Altered Bank Note Detector* (New York: Oliver & Brothers, 1851), v, 24–25, 28–29, emphasis added. On handwriting and character, see Tamara Plakins Thornton, *Handwriting in America: A Cultural History* (New Haven: Yale University Press, 1996), 73–107.

15. Allan Pinkerton, *Thirty Years a Detective* (New York: G. W. Carleton, 1884), 518.

16. Seth Wyman, *The Life and Adventures of Seth Wyman* (Manchester, N.H.: J. H. Cate, 1843), 260; William Stuart, *Sketches of the Life of William Stuart* (Bridge-

port, Conn.: William Stuart, 1854), 41; *People v. Samuel Baker* (5 October 1813), *People v. Lewis J. Morrison* (7 July 1842), and *People v. William Lapham and Louisa H. Brockway* (15 May 1850), all in NYCIP; *NYH,* 14 January 1843, 1. On pin holes, see William H. Dillistin, *Bank Note Reporters and Counterfeit Detectors, 1826–1866* (New York: American Numismatic Society, 1949), 46; W. A. Philpott Jr., "Pin Holes in Paper Money," *Numismatist* 65 (1952): 876–877.

17. J. S. Gibbons, *The Banks of New-York . . .* (New York: D. Appleton, 1858), 175–176; Stephen Mihm, "Making Money, Creating Confidence: Counterfeiting and Capitalism in the United States, 1789–1877," Ph.D. diss., New York University, 2003, 156, n. 44.

18. Thomas David Beal, "Selling Gotham: The Retail Trade in New York City from the Public Market to Alexander T. Stewart's Marble Palace, 1625–1860," Ph.D. diss., State University of New York at Stony Brook, 1998, 304–506; *People v. Honora Shepherd* (22 January 1848), NYCIP.

19. *NYC,* 16 August 1820, 2; *People v. Dennis Dougherty* (13 July 1818) and *People v. Leonard House* (22 October 1844), NYCIP; *NPG,* 16 January 1847, 149.

20. *NPG,* 6 May 1846, 305. See also *Daily Evening Transcript,* 31 July 1833, 2; *NPG,* 23 March 1850, 3; as well as *People v. William Gilmer and John Osborn* (10 April 1828), *People v. Thomas Morton and Mary McKeon* (14 April 1852), and *People v. Charles Stratton* (13 September 1853), all in NYCIP.

21. *People v. Thomas and Maria Dodd* (11 October 1832) and *People v. Case McAlister* (14 November 1844), NYCIP. Detailed accounts of this tactic can be found in *Literary Inquirer,* 14 May 1834, 150; *NPG,* 25 January 1851, 3; *NPG,* 28 August 1852, 3; and *VCCD,* September 1857, 3.

22. Doty, *Life of Sile Doty,* 17; Stuart, *Sketches of the Life of William Stuart,* 65. See also David Lewis, *The Life and Adventures of David Lewis, the Robber and Counterfeiter* (Newville, Pa: C. D. Rishel, 1890), 39–62; Wyman, *Life of Seth Wyman,* 260–289; *Subterranean,* 19 October 1844, 3; *NPG,* 7 November 1846, 65. On canals and river boats, see *People v. Oliver H. Maxwell and Otis Allen* (5 May 1842), NYCIP; *NPG,* 19 February 1848, 94; *NPG,* 18 August 1849, 3; *NPG,* 17 June 1852, 3; as well as *People v. Mansfield Wood* (7 February 1851) and *People v. Lewis R. Morgan* (12 January 1854), NYCIP.

23. *NYC,* 7 September 1820, 2; *People v. Horace Carp* (9 January 1849), NYCIP.

24. *NYC,* 16 August 1820, 2, emphasis in original; *NYEP,* 16 September 1820, 2. This became a common refrain in the succeeding decades. See *Daily Evening Transcript,* 31 July 1833, 2; and *Pennsylvania Journal of Prison Discipline and Philanthropy* 9 (1854): 95.

25. *People v. Isaac Dunsmore* (3 June 1818), *People v. Mary Payne* (4 January 1827), *People v. Abby Bennett* (13 August 1831), *People v. Julia Ann Hunt* (8 January 1836), and *People v. Elizabeth Case* (9 February 1843), all in NYCIP. See also *NPG,* 25 January 1851, 3; and *VCCD,* July 1851, 3. On the urban legend, see *BRCD,* 20 August 1844, 2, emphasis in original; and *VCCD,* September 1844, 36.

26. *People v. John Cantar* (17 April 1846) and *People v. Peter O'Brien* (17 April 1846), NYCIP; *NPG,* 13 June 1846, 340; *NPG,* 14 July 1849, 2; *NPG,* 23 March 1850, 3; Sutton, *New York Tombs,* 258–260.

27. *Crayon*, June 1860, 172; *Illustrated Times*, 23 July 1859, 57; *Living Age*, 3 September 1859, 624.

28. Ann Carson, *The Memoirs of the Celebrated and Beautiful Mrs. Ann Carson*, vol. 2 (1838; New York: Arno, 1980), 147–148.

29. *NPG*, 17 October 1846, 45; *NPG*, 21 July 1849, 3; *People v. Thomas Bramhall* (4 November 1846) and *People v. William Schoolcraft* (17 April 1849), NYCIP; *NPG*, 6 May 1860, 4; *NPG*, 6 July 1861, 2.

30. *People v. James Clark* (14 January 1820), ANA; *NPG*, 30 October 1852, 2; *People v. Perthenia Bockover* (11 January 1823), *People v. John Murgoe* (6 February 1812), and *People v. Thomas Standish* (18 December 1840), all in NYCIP. See also *People v. John Lewis* (14 July 1838), ANA; *Second Annual Report of the House of Refuge*, 26–27.

31. *People v. Elizabeth Day* (17 December 1836), *People v. Eliza Campbell* (13 March 1843), and *People v. José Rios* (10 January 1851), all in NYCIP; *People v. Peter Crawbuck* (8 April 1815), ANA; Patricia Cline Cohen, *The Murder of Helen Jewett: The Life and Death of a Prostitute in Nineteenth-Century New York* (New York: Vintage, 1999), 130; *NPG*, 26 June 1852, 3.

32. Coffey, *Inside Out*, 110; *People v. Bartow Underhill* (3 June 1807), *People v. James Kelly* (5 April 1820), *People v. Bridget Murphy* (8 May 1822), *People v. James Erven* (16 March 1838), *People v. Eugene Foliot* (12 November 1845), *People v. George W. Niles* (26 June 1847), and *People v. Phidela Wirth* (4 April 1850), all in NYCIP; Petition of Stephen M. Sinnott, 29 May 1822, box 3, folder 60, and Petition of Jonathan Mann, 20 May 1824, box 4, folder 15, in Petitions to the Court of Pardons, New Jersey State Archives, Trenton. See also *People v. Mass Lloyd* (12 February 1835), ANA.

33. *BRCD*, 23 September 1834, 2; John Neal, *Wandering Recollections of a Somewhat Busy Life* (Boston: Roberts Brothers, 1869), 124–125, emphasis in original; *Weekly Pantagraph*, 10 June 1857, 3; W. A. Coffey, *Inside Out*, 107; *Lady's Home Magazine*, 9 (1857): 303; *Godey's Lady's Book*, 66 (1863): 197; *NPG*, 7 March 1846, 228; *VCCD*, May 1858, 3.

34. *VCCD*, February 1853, 2; *NYT*, 4 February 1860, 2; *People v. Leonard Tufts* (12 August 1840), NYCIP.

35. *NPG*, 25 December 1852, 2; *VCCD*, October 1854, 1; *NYT*, 4 February 1860, 2.

36. Dillistin, *Bank Note Reporters*, 154–160; David P. Forsyth, *The Business Press in America, 1750–1865* (Philadelphia: Chilton Books, 1964), 102; Mihm, "Making Money," 240–281.

37. *BRCD*, 31 July 1830, 1; *BRCD*, 23 December 1833, 3. On Bicknell, see Dillistin, *Bank Note Reporters*, 125–129. On lotteries, see Dillistin, *Bank Note Reporters*, 2–3, 109; and John Samuel Ezell, *Fortune's Merry Wheel: The Lottery in America* (Cambridge: Harvard University Press, 1960), 82–85.

38. *NYH*, 25 September 1840, 2; *People v. Sylvester J. Sylvester, Frederick J. Sylvester, and Lewis Morrison*, 19 October 1840, NYCIP; *BRCD*, 14 May 1839, 2.

39. *BRCD*, 2 April 1836, 3; *NWR*, 16 April 1836, 124–125; *NYDT*, 20 April 1891, 7; *NYT*, 20 April 1891, 5; John Thompson, "New York City—Early Days of John Thompson," *Banker's Magazine* 45 (1891): 989; Dillistin, *Bank Note Reporters*, 81–82; Ezell, *Fortune's Merry Wheel*, 84; Hugh G. J. Aitken, "Yates and McIntyre:

Lottery Managers," *JEH* 13 (1953): 36–57. For more on Thompson, see Mihm, "Making Money," 246–250.

40. H. H. Camp, "Reminiscences of Banking in Wisconsin in Early Days," *American Banker,* 2 December 1896, 2480; Hoyt Sherman, "Early Banking in Iowa," *Annals of Iowa* 5 (1901): 9–10. Both are quoted in Dillistin, *Bank Note Reporters,* 52.

41. *TBNR,* 17 March 1849, 11.

42. Ibid., 19; *TBNR,* 26 March 1844, 6.

43. Foote, *Universal Counterfeit and Altered Bank Note Detector,* 14, 24–27, 35; Wheeler M. Gillet, *The Infallible Bank Note Expositor and Detector* (New York: Wheeler M. Gillet, 1849), 13–14. On the equation of outward appearance with inner character, see Karen Halttunen, *Confidence Men and Painted Women: A Study of Middle-Class Culture in America, 1830–1870* (New Haven: Yale University Press, 1982), 33–55; John F. Kasson, *Rudeness and Civility: Manners in Nineteenth-Century Urban America* (New York: Hill and Wang, 1990), 70–111.

44. Gillet, *Infallible Bank Note Expositor and Detector,* 15; Foote, *Universal Counterfeit,* 28, emphasis in original; John Thompson, *The Autographical Counterfeit Detector . . .* (New York: Wm. W. Lee, 1851); Daniel T. Ames, quoted in Thornton, *Handwriting in America,* 103. For a contemporary refutation of these beliefs, see *VCCD,* July 1858, 3.

45. John Thompson, *Bank Note Descriptive List* (New York: Platt Adams, 1859); John Thompson, *The Coin Chart Manual* (New York: W. W. Lee, 1849); David A. Martin, "The Changing Role of Foreign Money in the United States, 1782–1857," *JEH* 37 (1977): 1009–1027.

46. John S. Dye, *Dye's Bank Mirror and Illustrated Counterfeit Detector* (Cincinnati: Ben Franklin Mammoth Steam Job and Book Printing House, 1852); John Tyler Hodges, *Hodges' American Bank Note Safe-Guard* (New York: John Tyler Hodges, 1857), 1; Dillistin, *Bank Note Reporters,* 145–148.

47. *BRCD,* 24 June 1833, 2; *BRCD,* 26 May 1840, 3; *VCCD,* February 1853, 2.

48. Gillet, *Infallible Bank Note Expositor,* 4; *TBNR,* 26 March 1844, 15; *TBNR,* 17 March 1849, 8; Thompson, *Bank Note Descriptive List,* 2, emphasis in original; *TBNR,* 11 July 1857, 1.

49. See "The Shoe and Leather Bank agt. John Thompson," in *Howard's Practice Reports,* vol. 23 (Albany: Joel Munsell, 1862), 253–256; "Shoe and Leather Bank a. Thompson," in *Abbott's Practice Reports,* vol. 18 (New York: J. S. Voorhies, 1865), 413–419; *WCCD,* November 1844, 1; Letter of A. J. Tyler, published in *CFBD,* October 1861, 1.

50. *TBNR,* 24 September 1842, 1; *TBNR,* 17 March 1849, 11–13; Thompson, *Autographical Counterfeit Detector,* 1. For a more positive view of these evaluations, see Gary Gorton, "Reputation Formation in Early Bank Note Markets," *JPE* 104 (1996): 346–397.

51. *VCCD,* December 1855, 3; *VCCD,* October 1857, 3; "Thompson, John," New York, vol. 341, p. 157, R. G. Dun & Co. Collection, BL-HBS; Notes of William Dillistin, in folder entitled "John Thompson—Biographical. Officers and Directors. R. G. #2—CNB," Chase Manhattan Archives, New York.

52. "Thompson, John," New York, vol. 341, p. 157, R. G. Dun & Co. Collection, BL-

HBS; *WCCD*, February 1851, 23; *WCCD*, October 1854, 1; *TBNR*, 1 December 1855, 1. See also the accusations against Thompson republished in *Dye's Bank Mirror, and Illustrated Counterfeit Detector*, 15 October 1853, 6–7. On Thompson's reputation, see Mihm, "Making Money," 266, n. 38.

53. *NYH*, 21 October 1837, 2; *NYH*, 6 November 1841, quoted in Dillistin, *Bank Note Reporters*, 47–48; *BMSR*, October 1850, 346. On "puffing," see *VCCD*, March 1853, 3; *VCCD*, October 1853, 2; *VCCD*, April 1855, 1, 3; *BMSR* 9 (1859): 153.

54. *VCCD*, October 1857, 2; *VCCD*, July 1858, 3; *BMSR*, October 1859, 294. See also *VCCD*, June 1856, 3.

55. *NPG*, 7 May 1859, 1, 3; "Hodges, John Tyler," New York, vol. 344, p. 494, emphasis in original, and "Hodges, Daniel M.," New York, vol. 378, p. 304, both in R. G. Dun & Co. Collection, BL-HBS; *NPG*, 25 April 1857, 2; *VCCD*, September 1858, 47.

56. *VCCD*, January 1850, 3; *VCCD*, August 1853, 1; *CFBD*, March 1859, 1; *VCCD*, October 1850, 3.

57. *TBNR*, 29 August 1857, 1; *Lord's Detector and Bank Note Vignette Describer*, 15 September 1857, quoted in Dillistin, *Bank Note Reporters*, 88; *VCCD*, October 1857, 3. See also *CFBD*, September 1857, 2.

58. *People v. Dominick Lavin* (7 August 1835), NYCIP; *NPG*, 17 May 1851, 3.

59. *NYH*, 7 January 1843, 2; *NPG*, 15 September 1849, 2. See also the discussions in *BRCD*, 1 July 1834, 2; *WCCD*, December 1845, 1; *People v. Thomas Moore* (6 July 1855), *People v. George Edward Davis* (11 April 1854), NYCIP; *NPG*, 16 November 1861, 2.

60. Foote, *Universal Counterfeit*, x–xi; Wheeler, *Infallible Bank Note Expositor*, 5; *People v. George Lomes* (17 March 1842), NYCIP; *NYH*, 25 January 1843, 2; *NPG*, 15 September 1849, 2; *NPG*, 25 May 1861, 2.

61. *Clark's New-England Bank Note List, and Counterfeit Bill Detector*, 1 March 1838, 8; *TBNR*, 26 March 1844, 15; *TBNR*, 17 March 1849, 20, 24. Thompson quoted in Waterman Ormsby, *A Description of the Present System of Bank Note Engraving* . . . (New York: W. Willoughby, 1852), 64.

62. Ormsby, *Description of the Present System of Bank Note Engraving*, 63–65; *TBNR*, 26 March 1844, 15; *Saturday Courier*, 22 April 1837, 3; *NPG*, 25 May 1861, 2; *Scientific American* 13 (1865): 280.

63. *NPG*, 6 October 1849, 2; *NPG*, 17 January 1852, 1; *WCCD*, November 1852, 24. See also *People v. Hiram Johnson* (28 December 1843) and *People v. William Schoolcraft* (17 April 1849), NYCIP.

64. *Saturday Courier*, 18 November 1837, 3; *BRCD*, 8 September 1840, 2, emphasis in original; *Saturday Evening Post*, 29 December 1860; Gerald Muhl, "Counterfeiting: A Rochester Way to Wealth," *Crooked Lake Review* (Spring 2002): 13–23; *NPG*, 15 September 1849, 2; Mihm, "Making Money," 279, n. 52.

65. *NPG*, 15 September 1849, 2; *Godey's Lady's Book* 56 (1863): 197.

6. Ghosts in the Machine

1. Reconstruction based on "W. L. Ormsby," New York, vol. 374, p. 5, R. G. Dun & Co. Collection, BL-HBS; *Abbotts' Reports of Practice Cases* . . . , vol. 2 (New

York: John S. Voorhies, 1856), 407–409; John Duer, *Reports of Cases Argued and Determined in the Superior Court of the City of New York,* vol. 5 (Albany: W. C. Little, 1858), 665–667; *NYT,* 23 March 1858, 2; *NYT,* 26 March 1858, 2; Joel Tiffany, *Reports of Cases Argued and Determined in the Court of Appeals of the State of New York,* vol. 37 (Albany: Weare C. Little, 1868), 477–486; *Records and Briefs of the Supreme Court of the United States,* pt. 2 (1861–1870), vol. 154 (Wilmington, Del.: Scholarly Resources, n.d.), 67–73 (hereafter *Records and Briefs of the Supreme Court*). Thanks to Scott Sandage for providing this last source.

2. On Ormsby, see Gene Hessler, "The Inventive, Controversial Ormsby," *Numismatist* 113 (2000): 1166; Robert McCabe, "Waterman Lilly Ormsby and the Continental Bank Note Co.," *Paper Money* 40 (2001): 163–170; Stephen Mihm, "Making Money, Creating Confidence: Counterfeiting and Capitalism in the United States, 1789–1877," Ph.D. diss., New York University, 2003, 285–334; Q. David Bowers, *Obsolete Paper Money Issued by Banks in the United States, 1782–1866* (Atlanta: Whitman, 2006), 275–305.

3. Waterman Ormsby, *Description of the Present System of Bank Note Engraving, Showing Its Tendency to Facilitate Counterfeiting . . .* (New York: W. L. Ormsby, 1852), 39; Waterman Ormsby, *Cycloidal Configurations; or, The Harvest of Counterfeiters* (New York: Waterman Ormsby, 1862), 6–8, 13; Joseph Hume Francis, *History of the Bank of England, Its Times and Traditions,* vol. 1 (London: Willoughby & Co., 1848), 170–171.

4. Greville Bathe and Dorothy Bathe, *Jacob Perkins: His Inventions, His Times, and His Contemporaries* (Philadelphia: Historical Society of Pennsylvania, 1943), 24; Jacob Perkins, *The Permanent Stereotype Steel Plate* (Boston: C. Stebbins, 1806), 5. See also Bowers, *Obsolete Paper Money,* 50–77.

5. Jacob Perkins, "Prevention of Forgery," *Transactions of the Society, Instituted at London, for the Encouragement of Arts, Manufactures, and Commerce* 38 (1821): 52–56; *Boston Monthly Magazine,* 1 (1826): 480; Bathe and Bathe, *Jacob Perkins,* 24.

6. Perkins, "Prevention of Forgery," 48; William Spohn Baker, *American Engravers and Their Works* (Philadelphia: Gebbie & Barrie, 1875), 131–132; Bathe and Bathe, *Jacob Perkins,* 25 n. 39, 182; "Original Banknotes samples, etc.; Original Letters, 1795–1828," folder 3, Jacob Perkins Papers, 1795–1934, American Antiquarian Society, Worcester, Mass.

7. Bowers, *Obsolete Paper Money,* 73–76; Jacob Perkins and Gideon Fairman, *Opinion and Remarks upon the Means of Preventing Forgeries* (London, 1819), reproduced in Bathe and Bathe, *Jacob Perkins,* plate 18, emphasis in original.

8. Ibid., emphasis in original; William H. Griffiths, *The Story of the American Bank Note Company* (New York: American Bank Note Company, 1959), 24–28.

9. Sol Altmann, "U.S. Designers and Engravers of Bank Notes and Stamps," typescript, Print Room, Humanities Division, New York Public Library, 13A, 15, 99, 188–189; Arthur Tobias, "Everything You Always Wanted to Know about the Stagecoach Holdup Scene," unpublished paper in author's possession. See also Bowers, *Obsolete Paper Money,* 275–280, 350–354.

10. *BMSR* 7 (1852): 253–257; *WCCD,* October 1852, 24; *NPG,* 2 October 1852, 2; *VCCD,* November 1852, 3.

11. Ormsby, *Description of the Present System,* vii, 2, 13.

12. Ibid., 61, 73–75; *NYT,* 21 January 1856, 1.

13. *NYT,* 21 January 1856, 1; *NYT,* 1 February 1856, 3; Perkins and Fairman, *Opinion and Remarks.* See also *WCCD,* October 1852, 1; *VCCD,* June 1853, 3; *Dye's Bank Mirror,* 1 July 1853, 1; *WCCD,* July 1853, 1; *VCCD,* July 1855, 3; *NPG,* 26 January 1856, 2; *NPG,* 25 May 1861, 2.

14. Ormsby, *Description of the Present System,* 68–70. See also *New-Yorker,* 1 August 1840, 319; *WCCD,* September 1844, 1; *NYT,* 19 October 1852, 2; and *NYT,* 22 January 1856, 3. On the instability of the bank-note engraving business, see Griffiths, *Story of the American Bank Note Company,* 27–35; C. John Ferreri, "American Bank Note Engravers of the State Bank Note Era," *Paper Money* 23 (1984): 22–26.

15. *NPG,* 25 October 1845, 75; *WCCD,* October 1845, 20; *NPG,* 3 January 1846, 156; *NPG,* 9 May 1846, 299; *NPG,* 29 January 1848, 82; *Dye's Bank Mirror,* 1 June 1853, 7.

16. On these and similar frauds, see *New-Yorker,* 11 November 1837, 542; *People v. Charles Tozer* (14 November 1837), *People v. Abraham Pitcher, Charles Stearn, and James Brown* (12 March 1838), and *People v. Harris Smith alias Charles K. Ashton* (19 October 1848), all in NYCIP; *NYH,* 19 January 1838, 4; *NYH,* 29 January 1838, 2; *American Balance,* 8 February 1838, 2; *NPG,* 30 September 1848, 2; *BMSR* 4 (1849): 261–262; *NPG,* 15 June 1850, 3; *BMSR* 5 (1850): 169.

17. Ormsby, *Description of the Present System,* 19–20; *People v. John T. Masters* (9 October 1840), NYCIP; *NYH,* 29 December 1840, 2; *NYH,* 30 December 1840, 1–2; *NYH,* 31 December 1840, 1; Robert A. Vlack, *An Illustrated Catalogue of Early North American Advertising Notes* (New York: R. M. Smythe, 2001).

18. *People v. Charles E. Ely,* 25 September 1840, NYCIP.

19. Ibid.

20. *NYT,* 23 March 1858, 2; *NYT,* 26 March 1858, 2; *Abbotts' Reports of Practice Cases,* 407–409; Duer, *Reports of Cases,* 665–666; Tiffany, *Reports of Cases,* 477–486; *Records and Briefs of the Supreme Court,* 62–67. On the practice of supplying customers with denominations, state locations, and other bank note plate components, see Bowers, *Obsolete Paper Money,* 298–299.

21. *NPG,* 21 November 1846, 84; David R. Johnson, *Illegal Tender: Counterfeiting and the Secret Service in Nineteenth-Century America* (Washington, D.C.: Smithsonian Institution Press, 1995), 43–48.

22. *NPG,* 23 December 1848, 3; *NPG,* 10 March 1849, 2; *NPG,* 18 August 1849, 3; *NPG,* 22 December 1849, 3; *NPG,* 7 January 1854, 2; *NPG,* 12 March 1859, 3, 4; Sherman Grant Bonney, *Calvin Fairbanks Bonney and Harriott Cheney Bonney* (Concord, N.H.: Rumford, 1930), 53–54; James F. Richardson, *The New York Police, Colonial Times to 1901* (New York: Oxford University Press, 1970), 51–108; David R. Johnson, *American Law Enforcement: A History* (Arlington Heights, Ill.: Forum, 1981), 25–28, 59–61.

23. *NYEP,* 15 September 1820, 2; *NPG,* 7 March 1846, 228; *NPG,* 28 March 1846, 246; *NPG,* 1 August 1846, 397; *NPG,* 15 December 1849, 2; *NPG,* 22 December 1849, 3; *Pennsylvania Journal of Prison Discipline and Philanthropy* 8 (1853): 198–205.

24. *Working Man's Advocate,* 23 August 1834, 2, emphasis in original; *Rural Repository,* 14 October 1846, 161. See also *Pennsylvania Journal of Prison Discipline and Philanthropy* 10 (1845): 1–27.

25. *Records and Briefs of the Supreme Court,* 66, emphasis in original.

26. *People v. John A. Packer and Thomas Jones alias Ames* (14 November 1837) and *People v. William Smith* (16 November 1837), NYCIP.

27. *People v. Isaac C. Baker* (26 January 1841), NYCIP.

28. *People v. Daniel O'Connor* (22 January 1840), NYCIP.

29. *People v. Joseph Rosencrans* (14 July 1851), NYCIP.

30. *New-Yorker,* 30 November 1839, 174; *BRCD,* 15 October 1844, 1; *Laws of the State of New York Passed at the Sixty-sixth Session of the Legislature* (Albany: C. Van Benthuysen, 1843), 299–300; *VCCD,* June 1853, 3; *NPG,* 10 September 1853, 4; *NPG,* 31 December 1853, 4; *VCCD,* July 1855, 3.

31. Ormsby, *Description of the Present System,* 75.

32. *BMSR* 4 (1849): 490; *NPG,* 13 April 1850, 3; *BMSR* 5 (1850): 30; Ormsby, *Description of the Present System,* 44–46, 57–62; *Overland Monthly and Out West Magazine* 8 (1872): 524–529; Brent Hughes, "Long Bill Brockway, King of the Counterfeiters," *Paper Money* 33 (1994): 191–193.

33. *People v. Peter O'Brien* (17 April 1846), NYCIP; *NPG,* 13 June 1846, 340; *VCCD,* December 1854, 3.

34. Quoted in Ormsby, *Description of the Present System,* 50.

35. Deposition of John Runyon, 16 November 1818, box 134, Case Files for the Court of King's Bench, Montreal, ANQ; *People v. Allen Gilman* (6 February 1812), *People v. Thomas A. Standish* (18 December 1840), *People v. William Schoolcraft* (17 April 1849), and *People v. Samuel Drury and Samuel Drury Jr.* (25 January 1850), all in NYCIP.

36. Ormsby, *Description of the Present System,* 49; *Clark's New-England Bank Note List, and Counterfeit Bill Detector,* November 1839, 1; *People v. Alexander A. Watts* (19 November 1841), NYCIP.

37. *NYDT,* 20 December 1844, 2; *BRCD,* 24 December 1844, 2; *People v. Michael O'Brien and Peter Van Pelt* (15 January 1845), NYCIP.

38. Milton Friedman and Anna Jacobson Schwartz, *Monetary Statistics of the United States: Estimates, Sources, Methods* (New York: National Bureau of Economic Research, 1970), 214–259; Bray Hammond, *Banks and Politics in America from the Revolution to the Civil War* (Princeton, N.J.: Princeton University Press, 1957), 326–548; Warren E. Weber, "Early State Banks in the United States: How Many Were There and When Did They Exist?" working paper 634 (2005), Research Department, Federal Reserve Bank of Minneapolis; Richard G. Anderson, table Cj54-69, "Currency in Circulation, by Kind: 1800–1999," in *Historical Statistics of the United States, Millennial Edition On Line,* ed. Susan B. Carter, Scott Sigmund Gartner, Michael R. Haines, Alan L. Olmstead, Richard Sutch, and Gavin Wright (Cambridge, Eng.: Cambridge University Press, 2006).

39. *NYDT,* 23 April 1842, 2; *People v. Oliver H. Maxwell and Otis Allen* (5 May 1842) and *People v. Benjamin D. Adams* (17 May 1842), NYCIP; *NYDT,* 14 September 1842, 3; *NYDT,* 16 September 1842, 4.

40. *NPG,* 18 September 1847, 7; *NPG,* 16 October 1847, 22. On brokers as intermediaries in the counterfeit economy, see *BRCD,* 27 August 1839, 2; *People v. Chauncey C. Larkin* (26 January 1841), and *People v. George Lomes* (17 March 1842), all in NYCIP; *VCCD,* October 1853, 2; and *NPG,* 1 October 1859, 3.

41. Langdon W. Moore, *His Own Story of His Eventful Life* (1893; Freeport, N.Y.: Books for Libraries, 1971), 46–48. On the prevalence of altered notes, see *VCCD*, October 1857, 1; *NYT*, 30 July 1862, 1–2; Edward M. Hodges, *Hodges' American Bank Note Safe-Guard* (New York: Edward M. Hodges, 1862), 10; Waterman Ormsby Jr., "On the Statistics of Counterfeiting; Defects in Our Paper Currency," *Papers of the American Geographical and Statistical Society* 1 (1863): 43–58.

42. Ormsby, *Description of the Present System*, 50; *People v. William Smith* (16 November 1837), NYCIP; *VCCD*, June 1858, 3.

43. *VCCD*, February 1855, 2; *VCCD*, July 1855, 3; *Third Annual Report of the Board of Managers of the Association of Banks for the Suppression of Counterfeiting* (Boston: William A. Hall, 1856), 25–26.

44. *People v. Daniel Kane* (16 October 1845), NYCIP.

45. Ormsby, *Cycloidal Configurations*, 42.

46. On the unit system, see Ormsby, *Description of the Present System*, 71, 79–100; Waterman Ormsby, "The Rapid Increase of the Crime of Counterfeiting Bank Notes," 1853, Broadside Collection (BDSDS), American Antiquarian Society, Worcester, Mass.; Ormsby, *Cycloidal Configurations*, 35–39.

47. Ormsby, *Cycloidal Configurations*, 37; McCabe, "Waterman Lilly Ormsby," 163–170. On Ormsby's work for the Carroll County Bank, see Bowers, *Obsolete Bank Notes*, 351–354.

48. *NYT*, 22 January 1856, 3, emphasis in original; Altmann, "U.S. Designers and Engravers of Bank Notes and Stamps," 60–80; Griffiths, *Story of the American Bank Note Company*, 27–48.

49. *VCCD*, December 1851, 3; *NYT*, 21 January 1856, 1.

50. *WCCD*, September 1844, 1; *WCCD*, April 1845, 1; *VCCD*, December 1851, 3; *WCCD*, October 1852, 24.

51. *VCCD*, December 1854, 3; *CFBD*, June 1859, 1; *NYT*, 23 January 1860, 2, emphasis in original. On denomination-specific safeguards, see Mihm, "Making Money," 327, n. 52.

52. *Second Annual Report of the Board of Managers of the Association of Banks for the Suppression of Counterfeiting* (Boston: William A. Hall, 1855), 13–16; James G. Carney and H. M. Holbrook, *A Report upon the Subject of Bank Notes* (Boston: Prentiss & Sawyer, 1854), 20–21.

53. *Second Annual Report*, 9–10, emphasis in the original; *Fourth Annual Report of the Board of Managers of the Association for the Suppression of Counterfeiting* (Boston: William A. Hall, 1857), 9. On growing concern over photographic counterfeits, see *NPG*, 10 February 1855, 2; *BMSR* 9 (1855): 738–739, 812–813; *VCCD*, March 1855, 3; *BMSR* 11 (1856): 188–190; and *WCCD*, February 1856, 1.

54. *BMSR* 10 (1856): 723; *BMSR* 11 (1856): 134–137; *Subject-Matter Index of Patents for Inventions Issued by the United States Patent Office from 1790 to 1873, Inclusive*, vol. 1 (New York: Arno, 1976), 43; *Fourth Annual Report*, 9, 17.

55. *BMSR* 10 (1856): 923; *BMSR* 11 (1856): 134–141; *Fourth Annual Report*, 10–43; James G. Carney, *A Third Report upon the Subject of Mr. Seropyan's Patent* (Lowell, Mass.: Daily Courier Steam Press, 1856); *BMSR* 11 (1856): 402–403; *BMSR* 11 (1857): 587–589. On Seropyan's patent, see *Subject-Matter Index of Patents*, 43.

56. Ormsby, *Cycloidal Configurations*, 30; Altmann, "U.S. Designers and Engravers," 60–80; Griffiths, *Story of the American Bank Note Company*, 33–44; Gene Hessler, *The Engraver's Line: An Encyclopedia of Paper Money and Postage Stamp Art* (Port Clinton, Ohio: BNR Press, 1993), 19–33; Bowers, *Obsolete Paper Money*, 367–394. On Ormsby's worsening reputation, see *VCCD*, August 1858, 47; *BMSR* 10 (1861): 497.

57. *BMSR* 10 (1861): 723. The precocious integration of the bank note engraving industry has entirely escaped the attention of economic historians. Only numismatists have recognized the significance of the American Bank Note Company. See, e.g., Richard Doty, *America's Money, America's Story* (Iola, Wis.: Krause, 1998), 101; Bowers, *Obsolete Paper Money*, 367–394.

58. *NYT*, 30 July 1862, 1–2, 4.

7. Banking on the Nation

1. Report of the Secretary of the Treasury, 4 December 1854, quoted in Bray Hammond, *Sovereignty and an Empty Purse: Banks and Politics in the Civil War* (Princeton, N.J.: Princeton University Press, 1970), 21.

2. Hammond, *Sovereignty and an Empty Purse*, 33–34; Frederick J. Blue, *Salmon P. Chase: A Life in Politics* (Kent, Ohio: Kent State University Press, 1987), 130–162; Robert T. Patterson, "Government Finance on the Eve of the Civil War," *JEH* 12 (1952): 35–44. On monetary reform, see Heather Cox Richardson, *The Greatest Nation of the Earth: Republican Economic Policies during the Civil War* (Cambridge: Harvard University Press, 1997), 66–102.

3. Hammond, *Sovereignty and an Empty Purse*, 47, 73; Arthur L. Friedberg and Ira S. Friedberg, *Paper Money of the United States: A Complete Illustrated Guide with Valuations* (Clifton, N.J.: Coin & Currency Institute, 1998), 11–13; John Jay Knox, *United States Notes: A History of the Various Issues of Paper Money by the Government of the United States* (New York: Charles Scribner's Sons, 1884). On the shift to uniformity, see John Niven, ed., *The Salmon P. Chase Papers: Correspondence, 1858–March 1863*, vol. 3 (Kent, Ohio: Kent State University Press, 1996), 128.

4. Hammond, *Sovereignty and an Empty Purse*, 73–105; David M. Gische, "The New York City Banks and the Development of the National Banking System, 1860–1870," *American Journal of Legal History* 23 (1979): 21–67.

5. Quoted in Hammond, *Sovereignty and an Empty Purse*, 88. See also Richardson, *Greatest Nation*, 69–70.

6. *ACG*, 37th Cong., 2d sess., 9 December 1861, 25–26.

7. Hammond, *Sovereignty and an Empty Purse*, 93–95; *CG*, 37th Cong., 2d sess., 6 February 1862, 691.

8. Samuel Hooper, *Small Bills: An Appeal to the Legislature for an Ounce of Prevention* (Boston: J. S. Potter, 1855), 7; *CG*, 37th Cong., 2d sess., 6 February 1862, 691.

9. John Sherman, *Recollections of Forty Years in the House, Senate and Cabinet* (Chicago: Werner, 1895); John Joseph Patrick, "John Sherman: The Early Years, 1823–1865," Ph.D. diss., Kent State University, 1982; *ACG*, 37th Cong., 2d sess., 13 February 1862, 57; Richardson, *Greatest Nation*, 66–102.

10. *NYH*, 8 April 1862; *NYH*, 13 June 1862. Successive authorizations on 11 July

1862, 17 January 1863, and 3 March 1863 raised the aggregate value of the greenbacks issued to $450 million. Hammond, *Sovereignty and an Empty Purse*, 252.

11. Friedberg, *Paper Money*, 11–47. On this process generally, see Eric Helleiner, *The Making of National Money: Territorial Currencies in Historical Perspective* (Ithaca, N.Y.: Cornell University Press, 2003); Emily Gilbert and Eric Helleiner, eds., *Nation-States and Money: The Past, Present, and Future of National Currencies* (London: Routledge, 1999).

12. Hammond, *Sovereignty and an Empty Purse*, 254–258; Charles Robert Lee, *The Confederate Constitutions* (Chapel Hill: University of North Carolina Press, 1963), 185. For a different perspective, see Richard Bensel, "Southern Leviathan: The Development of Central State Authority in the Confederate States of America," *Studies in American Political Development* 2 (1987): 68–136.

13. Eugene M. Lerner, "The Monetary and Fiscal Programs of the Confederate Government, 1861–65," *JPE* 62 (1954): 507; Hammond, *Sovereignty and an Empty Purse*, 255.

14. Lerner, "Monetary and Fiscal Programs," 512–513; Richard C. K. Burdekin and Farrokh K. Langdana, "War Finance in the Southern Confederacy," *Explorations in Economic History* 30 (1993): 352–376.

15. Lerner, "Monetary and Fiscal Programs," 518–520; Richard Cecil Todd, *Confederate Finance* (Athens: University of Georgia Press, 1954), 85–120; James F. Morgan, *Graybacks and Gold: Confederate Monetary Policy* (Pensacola, Fla.: Perdido Bay Press, 1985), 23–41.

16. James D. Dénégré to Christopher Memminger, 18 May 1861, quoted in Todd, *Confederate Finance*, 92; William H. Griffiths, *The Story of the American Bank Note Company* (New York: American Bank Note Company, 1959), 39–40. On these difficulties generally, see Henry Dickson Capers, *The Life and Times of C. G. Memminger* (Richmond, Va.: Everett Waddey Co., 1893), 318–337; Todd, *Confederate Finance*, 90–102.

17. Capers, *Life and Times*, 337; Todd, *Confederate Finance*, 90–98; Judith Ann Benner, *Fraudulent Finance: Counterfeiting and the Confederate States: 1861–1865* (Hillsboro, Tex.: Hill Junior College, 1970), 5–12; Ted Schwarz, "Counterfeit Confederate," *Civil War Times* 16 (1977): 34–39. On Duncan, see Brent Hughes, "Counterfeits of the Type 20 Confederate Note," *Paper Money* 32 (1993): 179–183, 198.

18. *NYH*, 19 September 1864; William Howard Merrell, *Five Months in Rebeldom; or, Notes from the Diary of a Bull Run Prisoner, at Richmond* (Rochester, N.Y.: Adams and Dabney, 1862), 57; Brent Hughes, "Englishmen Printed Much Confederate Currency," *Paper Money* 45 (2006): 259–263.

19. *BMSR* 16 (1861): 395; Benner, *Fraudulent Finance*, 5–12; Arlie R. Slabaugh, *Confederate States Paper Money*, 10th ed. (Iola, Wis.: Krause, 2000), 95–120; George B. Tremmel, *Counterfeit Currency of the Confederate States of America* (Jefferson, N.C.: McFarland, 2003), 7–18. Memminger's warnings can be found in Raphael P. Thian, *Reports of the Secretary of the Treasury of the Confederate States of America, 1861–65 . . .* , appendix, pt. 3 (Washington, D.C.: Raphael P. Thian, 1878), 113.

20. "Civil War Envelope Collection, 1861–1865," Print Collection, Library Company of Philadelphia; *Harper's Weekly*, 1 April 1865, 206; Samuel C. Upham to Dr. William Lee, 12 October 1874, quoted in Schwarz, "Counterfeit Confederate," 38–39; Brent Hughes, "Sam Upham's Confederate Notes: The Saga of a Lawful Counterfeiter," *Paper Money* 15 (1976): 188–199; Henry M. McCarl, "An Introduction to Confederate and Southern States Counterfeit Currency," *Paper Money* 26 (1987): 149–155, 164; Henry M. McCarl, "Confederate Counterfeit Currency Observations," *Paper Money* 29 (1990): 37–41, 48; Robert J. Lindesmith, "Adrian Sharp, Xylographer," *Paper Money* 30 (1991): 157–161; Tremmel, *Counterfeit Currency*, 37–45. On Upham's business dealings, see "Upham, Samuel C.," Pennsylvania, vol. 140, p. 78, R. G. Dun & Co. Collection, BL-HBS.

21. "Mementos of the Rebellion," circular dated May 1862, reproduced in Hughes, "Sam Upham's Confederate Notes," 188–199; *NYH*, 30 July 1862; *Charleston Mercury*, 26 August 1862.

22. *NYH*, 17 April 1862; *Charleston Mercury*, 4 July 1862; *NYH*, 30 July 1862; William Thompson Lusk, *War Letters of William Thompson Lusk: Captain, Assistant Adjutant-General, United States Volunteers, 1861–1863* (New York: W. C. Lusk, 1911), 232; Kate Mason Rowland and Agnes E. Croxall, eds., *The Journal of Julia LeGrand, New Orleans, 1862–1863* (Richmond, Va.: Everett Waddey Co., 1911), 132; *Charleston Mercury*, 27 May 1863; Thian, *Reports of the Secretary of the Treasury*, appendix, pt. 3, p. 81; Raphael P. Thian, *Correspondence of the Treasury Department of the Confederate States of America, 1861–65* . . . , appendix, pt. 5 (Washington: Raphael P. Thian, 1879), 423; "Message of President Jefferson Davis," *Journal of the Congress of the Confederate States of America, 1861–1865*, vol. 2, 18 August 1862 (Washington, D.C.: Government Printing Office, 1904), 226–227.

23. *Charleston Mercury*, 25 August 1862; unidentified newspaper quoted in Hughes, "Sam Upham's Confederate Notes," 190; Brent Hughes, "Another Confederate Contract Printer?" *Paper Money* 32 (1993): 128, 130; Brent Hughes, "The Counterfeit Notes of Winthrop E. Hilton," *Paper Money* 33 (1994): 10–16, 18; Tremmel, *Counterfeit Currency*, 45–53. On Winthrop, see vol. 1, p. 211, DIC-USSS, NARA; vol. 1, pp. 293, 410, RR-USSS, NARA; and "Hilton, Winthrop," New York, vol. 194, p. 749, R. G. Dun & Co. Collection, BL-HBS.

24. Hughes, "Counterfeit Notes of Winthrop E. Hilton," 10–11; Thian, *Correspondence of the Treasury Department*, appendix, pt. 4 (Washington, D.C.: Raphael P. Thian, 1879), 570–571; Tremmel, *Counterfeit Currency*, 45–53.

25. Thian, *Reports of the Secretary of the Treasury*, appendix, pt. 3, pp. 30, 81, 113, and Thian, *Correspondence of the Treasury Department*, appendix, pt. 4, p. 186, quoted and cited in Lerner, "Monetary and Fiscal Programs," 520, n. 39, 520–521; Marc D. Weidenmier, "Bogus Money Matters: Sam Upham and His Confederate Counterfeiting Business," *Business and Economic History* 28 (1999): 313–324.

26. John Worrell Northrop, *Chronicles from the Diary of a War Prisoner in Andersonville and Other Military Prisons of the South in 1864* . . . (Wichita, Kans.: J. W. Northrop, 1904), 54; John Beauchamp Jones, *A Rebel War Clerk's Diary at the Confederate States Capital*, vol. 2 (Philadelphia: J. B. Lippincott, 1866), 91–92; *Journal of the Congress of the Confederate States of America, 1861–1865*, vol. 3 (Washington, D.C.: Government Printing Office, 1904), 180.

27. *NYH*, 17 July 1863; *War of the Rebellion: Official Records of the Union and Confederate Armies*, ser.1, vol. 34, pt. 2 (Washington, D.C.: Government Printing Office, 1899), 978; Everett K. Cooper, "Trading in the Enemy's Currency," *Paper Money* 28 (1989): 112–115, 129.

28. *Continental Monthly*, February 1863, 140, 143; Message of the President, 1 December 1862 and Secretary of the Treasury report, 4 December 1862, quoted in Hammond, *Sovereignty and an Empty Purse*, 290, 292; Hammond, *Sovereignty and an Empty Purse*, 263–282, 290–292, 294–295.

29. Ibid., 142; *NYT*, 24 June 1861, 3; *NYT*, 12 July 1861, 3; Benson J. Lossing, *History of New York City*, vol. 1 (New York: Perine Engraving and Publishing, 1884), 732–733; *Daily Graphic*, 1 February 1881.

30. *ACG*, 37th Cong., 3d sess., 8 January 1863, 47–50.

31. Ibid.; Hammond, *Sovereignty and an Empty Purse*, 296–297.

32. *Hunt's Merchants' Magazine* 48 (1863): 31–34; Hammond, *Sovereignty and an Empty Purse*, 322–323; *NYT*, 28 January 1863, 5; *NYT*, 31 January 1863, 4; *NYT*, 2 February 1863, 4; *NYT*, 3 February 1863, 4–5.

33. *CG*, 37th Cong., 3d sess., 10 February 1863, 843–844. On the growth of nationalism, see Richardson, *Greatest Nation of the Earth*, 66–102; and Melinda Lawson, *Patriot Fires: Forging a New American Nationalism in the Civil War North* (Lawrence: University Press of Kansas, 2002).

34. Hammond, *Sovereignty and an Empty Purse*, 321–351.

35. *Thompson's Bank Note and Commercial Reporter*, April 1863, quoted in John Hickman and Dean Oakes, *Standard Catalog of National Bank Notes*, 2d ed. (Iola, Wis.: Krause, 1990), 16.

36. Robert McCabe, "Waterman Lilly Ormsby and the Continental Bank Note Co.," *Paper Money* (2001): 163–170; Griffiths, *Story of the American Bank Note Company*, 39–44; Hickman and Oakes, *Standard Catalog of National Bank Notes*, 15–18; Friedberg and Friedberg, *Paper Money of the United States*, 75–86; Q. David Bowers, *Obsolete Paper Money Issued by Banks in the United States, 1782–1866* (Atlanta: Whitman, 2006), 407.

37. Friedberg and Friedberg, *Paper Money of the United States*, 75–86; Slabaugh, *Confederate States Paper Money*, 39, 50–51.

38. Hammond, *Sovereignty and an Empty Purse*, 345; John Thompson, "Sixty Years in Wall Street," quoted in *American Banker*, 25 April 1891, 14; Ellis Paxon Oberholtzer, *Jay Cooke: Financier of the Civil War*, vol. 1 (Philadelphia: George W. Jacobs, 1907), 344, 469; J. T. W. Hubbard, *For Each, the Strength of All: A History of Banking in the State of New York* (New York: New York University Press, 1995), 115–125.

39. Report of the Secretary of the Treasury, quoted in Hammond, *Sovereignty and an Empty Purse*, 346–347.

40. David R. Johnson, *Illegal Tender: Counterfeiting and the Secret Service in Nineteenth-Century America* (Washington, D.C.: Smithsonian Institution Press, 1995), 65–73; William Emile Doster, *Lincoln and Episodes of the Civil War* (New York: G. P. Putnam's Sons, 1915), 104. On Wood, see Curtis Carroll Davis: "The Craftiest of Men: William P. Wood and the Establishment of the United States

Secret Service," *Maryland Historical Magazine* 83 (1988): 111–126; and "The 'Old Capitol' and Its Keeper: How William P. Wood Ran a Civil War Prison," *Records of the Columbia Historical Society of Washington, D.C.* 52 (1989): 206–234.

41. Davis, "Craftiest of Men," 112–113, 123, n. 9; Davis, "The 'Old Capitol' and Its Keeper"; *WSG,* 16 September 1883; *WSG,* 23 September 1883; *WSG,* 14 December 1884; *WSG,* 21 November 1886; *WSG,* 5 December 1886; and *WSG,* 23 January 1887, all in WWS-SSA. See also Belle Boyd, *Belle Boyd in Camp and Prison,* ed. Curtis Carroll Davis (South Brunswick, N.J.: T. Yoseloff, 1968), 225, cited and quoted in Davis, "The 'Old Capitol' and Its Keeper," 219; Doster, *Lincoln and Episodes of the Civil War,* 128–129, quoted in Davis, "The 'Old Capitol' and Its Keeper," 221.

42. *WSG,* 21 December 1884; *WSG,* 30 January 1887; *WSG,* 6 February 1887; *WSG,* 13 February 1887; and *WSG,* 20 February 1887, all in WWS-SSA. See also *The War of the Rebellion: A Compilation of the Official Records of the Union and Confederate Armies* (Washington, D.C.: Government Printing Office, 1899), ser. 2, vol. 4, pp. 670, 934, 942–945; ser. 2, vol. 5, pp. 229, 251, 400–403; and ser. 2, vol. 6, pp. 40–41, 348, 430–433; Davis, "The 'Old Capitol' and Its Keeper," 221–233.

43. Only in 1863 did Congress did allocate a small sum of money ($25,000) to the Interior Department to subsidize the employment of private detectives to protect the new currency. See Johnson, *Illegal Tender,* 67–68.

44. On Baker, Wood, and the raids of 1864, see *NYT,* 11 August 1864, 2; *NYT,* 9 October 1864, 2; and *NYT,* 14 October 1864, 1. See also *WSG,* 14 September 1884; *WSG,* 19 December 1886; *WFP,* 14 August 1887; and *WFP,* 4 March 1888; all in WWS-SSA; as well as Davis, "Craftiest of Men," 113–114; and Johnson, *Illegal Tender,* 69–70.

45. *WFP,* 14 August 1887, WWS-SSA. On Baker, see Lafayette C. Baker, *History of the United States Secret Service,* ed. Ray A. Neff (1867; Bowie, Md.: Heritage Books, 1992), 8.

46. Order of Secretary of the Treasury Salmon P. Chase, 22 December 1863, in RG 206, "Letters Received from the United States Secret Service," Solicitor of the Treasury of the United States, NARA; Davis, "Craftiest of Men," 114–115; Johnson, *Illegal Tender,* 68–70.

47. Vol. 1, pp. 3, 6, 11, 17, 20–22, 24–25, 26–27, 47–50, RR-USSS, NARA. See also *WSG,* 14 September 1884; and *WFP,* 14 August 1887, both in WWS-SSA; Davis, "Craftiest of Men," 114–115; Johnson, *Illegal Tender,* 70–73; and W. Emerson Reck, *A. Lincoln: His Last Twenty-four Hours* (Columbia: University of South Carolina Press, 1987), 31–38.

48. Wood hired clerks and began official record keeping shortly after his official appointment. See the discussion of "clerical management" in vol. 1, p. 84, RR-USSS, NARA. For more on the Secret Service's transition to a formal bureaucracy, see Johnson, *Illegal Tender,* 65–115.

49. *The Rogues and Rogueries of New York* (New York: J. C. Haney, 1867), 117; Gustav Lening, *The Dark Side of New York and Its Criminal Classes* (New York: Fred'k Gerhard, 1873), 404.

50. Vol. 1, pp. 54, 57–58, 66–67, 71, 105, 110, 122, 135, 142, 153, 201, 291, 309, 371, 413, 423,

DIC-USSS, NARA. See also vol. 1, pp. 17, 32, 87, 272, 410; vol. 2, pp. 199, 242, 245; and vol. 4, p. 437, all in RR-USSS, NARA.

51. Lening, *Dark Side of New York*, 405; *Rogues and Rogueries of New York*, 116.

52. On Miner, see vol. 1, pp. 67, 464, 476, 536; and vol. 4, pp. 106, 216, 270, both in DIC-USSS, NARA; as well as vol. 3, pp. 387–388, and vol. 4, pp. 166–167, 362–363, RR-USSS, NARA. See also George P. Burnham, *Memoirs of the United States Secret Service* (Boston: Laban Heath, 1872), 421–436. On Gleason, see vol. 1, pp. 261, 309, 415, 419, 435, 439; and vol. 4, pp. 20, 49, 96, 109, 148, 216, 226, 300, 325, 390, 415; both in DIC, NARA. See also vol. 1, pp. 324, 410; vol. 2, p. 41; vol. 3, pp. 387–388; vol. 4, pp. 437–438; vol. 5, pp. 488–491, 494–497; vol. 6, pp. 208–211; and vol. 7, pp. 320–321; all in RR-USSS, NARA. I am indebted to Howard Gleason for sharing information on his family's genealogy.

53. On Brockway, see vol. 4, p. 227, DIC-USSS, and vol. 1, pp. 264–265, RR-USSS, both in NARA; *NYT*, 27 June 1867, 2; *NYT*, 2 July 1867, 2; George P. Burnham, *American Counterfeits: How Detected, and How Avoided* (Springfield, Mass.: W. J. Hollan, 1875), 112–121; Allan Pinkerton, *Thirty Years a Detective* (New York: G. W. Carleton, 1884), 459–484; Thomas Byrnes, *Professional Criminals of America* (1886; New York: Chelsea House, 1969), 97–98; "Brockway, Veteran Counterfeiter," *American Law Review* 38 (1904): 576–577; Brent Hughes, "Long Bill Brockway, King of the Counterfeiters," *Paper Money* 33 (1994): 191–195. See also William Wood's recollections of Brockway in *WSG*, 6 May 1883; *WSG*, 20 May 1883; *WSG*, 11 July 1886; *WFP*, 14 August 1887; and *WFP*, 21 August 1887; all in WWS-SSA.

54. *Rogues and Rogueries of New York*, 116. On Ormsby's work with counterfeiters, see vol. 1, pp. 415, 435, 464, 481, DIC-USSS, NARA. See also vol. 3, pp. 387–388; and vol. 4, pp. 166–167, 362–363, both in RR-USSS, NARA; as well as *WFP*, 14 August 1887, WWS-SSA.

55. Vol. 1, pp. 54, 57–58, 66, 70, 73, 109, 121, 253, 291, DIC-USSS, NARA; *Rogues and Rogueries of New York*, 115. See also vol. 1, p. 127, 192; and vol. 2, p. 22, 59, 242; both in RR-USSS, NARA. A representative cross-section of this national network can be found in the list of names in vol. 1, pp. 127–132, DIC-USSS, NARA.

56. Vol. 1, pp. 18, 19, 21, 32, 34, 37, 38, 42, 43, 57–58, 80, 83, 87, 89, 92, 127–132, 245, 251, 404, 440, 487; and vol. 4, pp. 137, 284, 371, 381, 398, 406, 413; both in DIC-USSS, NARA. See also vol. 1, pp. 28, 33, 120; RR-USSS, NARA; and John S. Dye, *Government Blue Book: A Complete History of the Lives of All the Great Counterfeiters* (Philadelphia: John S. Dye, 1880), 46, 87–98.

57. Vol. 1, pp. 58, 60, 66, 127–132, 232, DIC-USSS, NARA; and vol. 1, pp. 28, 33, 38, RR-USSS, NARA; *Daily Cleveland Herald*, 14 December 1865.

58. On arrests, interrogations, and convictions, see vol. 1, pp. 38, 42–43, 81, 170, 232, 310, 369, 397, 413, 480, 535; and vol. 4, pp. 21, 137, 157, 381; both in DIC-USSS, NARA. See also vol. 1, pp. 26–27, 33–38, 86, 477–479; RR-USSS, NARA; as well as *WFP*, 4 March 1888; *WFP*, 11 March 1888; and *WFP*, 18 March 1888; all in WWS-SSA. Wood arrested over two hundred suspects in the first year alone. See Johnson, *Illegal Tender*, 76.

59. Vol. 1, pp. 163, 310, 380, 553; and vol. 2, pp. 167–168; both in RR-USSS, NARA. See also vol. 1, pp. 358, 441–442, DIC-USSS, NARA. For Wood's later recollec-

tions of the fight against corruption, see *WSG,* 16 November 1884; *WFP,* 14 August 1887; and *WFP,* 11 March 1888; all in WWS-SSA. On police corruption, see David R. Johnson, *Policing the Urban Underworld: The Impact of Crime on the Development of the American Police, 1800–1887* (Philadelphia: Temple University Press, 1979), 170–178.

60. *WFP,* 4 March 1888; *WFP,* 11 March 1888; both in WWS-SSA; vol. 1, p. 310, RR-USSS, NARA. Though it appropriated money for its activities, Congress did not formally recognize the Secret Service until 1882. See Johnson, *Illegal Tender,* 76–77, 106–107.

61. *NYT,* 16 October 1866, 2; *NYT,* 23 June 1867, 4, emphasis in original; *NYT,* 2 July 1867, 2.

62. Vol. 1, p. 479; and vol. 2, pp. 32–33; both in RR-USSS, NARA.

63. On this contretemps, see the request issued by House Republicans on 26 November 1867, noted in the *Journal of the House of Representatives of the United States* (Washington, D.C.: Government Printing Office, 1867), 271, as well as the response: Ex. Doc. no. 179, House of Representatives, 40th Cong., 2d sess., *Message from the President of the United States.* On Johnson's pardons to counterfeiters (159 in all), see vol. 3, "Register and Indexes for Pardons," RG 59, General Pardon Records, General Records of the Department of State, NARA; and Brent Hughes, "Paper Money Counterfeiters and Mr. Stanton," *Paper Money* 33 (1994): 161–167.

64. *WFP,* 21 August 1887, and William P. Wood, *An Exposure of the Methods of Getting Up Spurious Issues of Bonds and Currency of the United States* (Washington, D.C.: William P. Wood, n.d.), WWS-SSA; Davis, "Craftiest of Men," 120–121; Chief Brooks, Secret Service, to McCormick, Rayner, and Raum, 17 September, 1877, WWS-SSA, quoted in Davis, "Craftiest of Men," 116. See also Johnson, *Illegal Tender,* 77.

65. William P. Wood, *Circular of Instructions to Operatives, Secret Service Division, Treasury Department . . .* (Washington, D.C.: Government Printing Office, 1868), 6, in "Letters Received from the United States Secret Service," Solicitor of the Treasury of the United States, NARA; Johnson, *Illegal Tender,* 77–78.

66. Emily E. Briggs, *The Olivia Letters: Being Some History of Washington City for Forty Years as Told by the Letters of a Newspaper Correspondent* (New York: Neale, 1906), 69, quoted in Davis, "Craftiest of Men," 121; Wood to Boutwell, 4 May 1869, WWS-SSA; William P. Wood, *Letter from Wm. P. Wood (Late Chief of the Secret Service Division, Treasury Department), to the Hon. George S. Boutwell, Secretary of the Treasury* (Washington, D.C.: William P. Wood, 1869), cited in Johnson, *Illegal Tender,* 78, n. 49.

67. Vol. 1, p. 32, 104; and vol. 4, p. 93, both in DIC-USSS, NARA.

68. *Veazie Bank v. Fenno,* 75 U.S. 533 (1869), 549; James Willard Hurst, *A Legal History of Money in the United States, 1774–1970* (Lincoln: University of Nebraska Press, 1973), 180–181.

Epilogue

1. William Graham Sumner, *A History of Banking in the United States* (New York: Journal of Commerce and Commercial Bulletin, 1896), 455.

2. Ibid., 464–465; Bray Hammond, *Banks and Politics in America from the Revolution to the Civil War* (Princeton, N.J.: Princeton University Press, 1957), 572. See also John A. James, *Money and Capital Markets in Postbellum America* (Princeton, N.J.: Princeton University Press, 1978). This is not to suggest that banks stopped creating money. Rather, the medium—deposits and checks—changed. See Fritz Redlich, *The Molding of American Banking: Men and Ideas,* vol. 2 (New York: Johnson Reprint Corporation, 1968), 175–222.

3. Sumner, *History of Banking,* 464.

4. *NYT,* 23 October 1867, 1; *NYT,* 22 June 1871, 5. On Sherman and Cooke, see Heather Cox Richardson, *The Greatest Nation of the Earth: Republican Economic Policies during the Civil War* (Cambridge: Harvard University Press, 1997), 37, 43, 78.

5. *NYT,* 7 May 1874, 4; Irwin Unger, *The Greenback Era: A Social and Political History of American Finance, 1865–1879* (Princeton, N.J.: Princeton University Press, 1964), 398–402; Gretchen Ritter, *Goldbugs and Greenbacks: The Antimonopoly Tradition and the Politics of Finance in America, 1865–1896* (Cambridge, Eng.: Cambridge University Press, 1997), 34–38.

6. *NYT,* 22 June 1871, 5; *NYT,* 24 September 1877, 4; *NYT,* 29 September 1877, 1; Laurence F. Schmeckebier, *The Bureau of Engraving and Printing: Its History, Activities, and Organization* (Baltimore: Johns Hopkins University Press, 1929), 1–6; U.S. Treasury Department, *History of the Bureau of Engraving and Printing, 1862–1962* (Washington, D.C.: Treasury Department, 1962), 1–59; Benny Bolin, "Spencer M. Clark, Cornerstone of the Bureau of Engraving and Printing," *Paper Money* 27 (1988): 77–80; Letter from Michael Scalia, Historical Resource Center, Bureau of Engraving and Printing, 7 November 2002, in author's possession.

7. Hiram Whitley, *In It* (Cambridge, Mass.: Riverside, 1894), 102–245; David R. Johnson, *Illegal Tender: Counterfeiting and the Secret Service in Nineteenth-Century America* (Washington, D.C.: Smithsonian Institution Press, 1995), 78–87.

8. George P. Burnham, *American Counterfeits: How Detected, and How Avoided* (Springfield Mass.: W. J. Hollan, 1875), 112–121; George P. Burnham, *Memoirs of the United States Secret Service* (Boston: Laban Heath, 1872), 63–77, 421–436; John S. Dye, *Government Blue Book* (Philadelphia: Dye's Government Counterfeit Detector, 1880), 94–98; Whitley, *In It,* 107, 211–243; Louis Bagger, "The 'Secret Service' of the United States," *Appletons' Journal,* 20 September 1873, 360–365.

9. Dye, *Government Blue Book,* 64–66, 90–93; Johnson, *Illegal Tender,* 88–96.

10. "Attempted Theft of President Lincoln's Body, Copied from Original Secret Service Records," typescript, Secret Service Archives, Washington, D.C.; Dye, *Government Blue Book,* 83–86; Deane Robertson and Peggy Robertson, "The Plot to Steal Lincoln's Body," *American Heritage* 33 (1982): 76–83; James T. Hickey, "Robert Todd Lincoln and His Father's Grave Robbers; or, Left in the Lurch by the Secret Service," *Illinois Historical Journal* 77 (1984): 295–300; Bonnie Stahlman Speer, *The Great Abraham Lincoln Hijack . . .* (Norman, Okla.: Reliance Press, 1997).

11. Andrew Drummond, 17 February 1886, quoted in Johnson, *Illegal Tender,* 176–

177; Alfred Frankenstein, *After the Hunt* (Berkeley: University of California Press, 1969), 56, quoted in Bruce W. Chambers, *Old Money: American Trompe L'Oeil Images of Currency* (New York: Berry Hill Galleries, 1988), 22–23; Marc Shell, *Art and Money* (Chicago: University of Chicago Press, 1995), 87–105. The prohibition continues today. See Lawrence Weschler, *Boggs: A Comedy of Values* (Chicago: University of Chicago Press, 1999). On so-called flash notes, see Robert A. Vlack, *An Illustrated Catalogue of Early North American Advertising Notes* (New York: R. M. Smythe, 2001).

12. On these instruments and their resonance in the culture of the times, see Ann Fabian, *Card Sharps, Dream Books, and Bucket Shops: Gambling in Nineteenth-Century America* (Ithaca: Cornell University Press, 1990), 153-202; William Cronon, *Nature's Metropolis: Chicago and the Great West* (New York: W. W. Norton, 1991), 120-147; Jackson Lears, *Something for Nothing: Luck in America* (New York: Viking, 2003), 151-155.

13. *NYT,* 7 August 1892, 6. On these battles, see Robert P. Sharkey, *Money, Class, and Party: An Economic Study of Civil War and Reconstruction* (Baltimore: Johns Hopkins, 1957); Unger, *Greenback Era;* Walter T. K. Nugent, *The Money Question during Reconstruction* (New York: Norton, 1967); Gretchen Ritter, *Goldbugs and Greenbacks,* 173-174. On the connection of these struggles to racial equality or inequality, see Michael O'Malley, "Specie and Species: Race and the Money Question in Nineteenth-Century America," *American Historical Review* 99 (1994): 369-395.

14. Richard H. Timberlake Jr., *The Origins of Central Banking in the United States* (Cambridge: Harvard University Press, 1978), 186–206; James Livingston, *Origins of the Federal Reserve System: Money, Class, and Corporate Capitalism, 1890–1913* (Ithaca, N.Y.: Cornell University Press, 1986).

15. Timberlake, *Origins of Central Banking,* 186–206; Livingston, *Origins of the Federal Reserve,* 188–234; Richard Doty, *America's Money, America's Story* (Iola, Wis.: Krause Publications, 1998), 195–197; Chester L. Krause and Robert F. Lemke, *Standard Catalog of United States Paper Money* (Iola, Wis.: Krause, 2002), 6.

16. *NYT,* 12 May 1901, 26; *NYT,* 15 November 1908, SM10; *NYT,* 29 January 1911, SM3.

17. Lester V. Chandler, *American Monetary Policy, 1928–1941* (New York: Harper & Row, 1971); Doty, *America's Money,* 202.

A NOTE ON SOURCES

R esearching the history of counterfeiting in the nineteenth-century United States posed a few unusual
challenges. Finding sources was not the problem, but
they turned out to be far more dispersed and fragmented than I had
anticipated. Counterfeiters moved frequently across city, county, state,
and national boundaries, and documenting their activities eventually
required research in multiple parts of the United States, as well as in
Canada. An added complication was self-imposed, in that I wished to
rely on a handful of individuals to propel the narrative and analysis forward. This proved difficult enough when dealing with the obscure detectives, bankers, publishers, and other figures who had dealings with
the counterfeit economy; it was far more challenging to track the counterfeiters themselves, most of whom sought to cover their tracks, not
mark them for posterity.

In order to circumvent this problem, I devised a system of binders in
which I filed copies of every newspaper clipping, pardon application,
memoir, and other source I came across. I arranged these in alphabeti-
cal order by the name of the counterfeiter cited in each text, and gradually assembled a "rogue's gallery" that spanned the years between the
1790s and 1860s. The volume and variety of sources reviewed—criminal
memoirs, prison records, newspapers, magazines, family genealogies,
legislative proceedings, local histories, court records, criminal indictments, pardon applications, credit reports, extradition requests, city di-

rectories, and census records, to name a few—enabled me to identify certain key players in the counterfeit economy of the United States. It soon became apparent that many of them gravitated toward one of several nodes in the counterfeit economy.

The first of these was the border region between Vermont and Canada, which became the focus of the first two chapters. The opening chapter on Stephen Burroughs proved easiest to research. I reviewed the various editions of Burroughs's *Memoirs,* several of which contained information on his later career in Canada. I supplemented this review with an extensive survey of newspapers from throughout New England between 1804 and 1810, the years when he enjoyed the greatest notoriety; pardon files from the Vermont State Archives yielded additional information. But the richest sources surfaced on the other side of the border, particularly in the National Archives of Canada in Ottawa. There I combed through land records, pardon applications, correspondence of the provincial secretary, and several smaller collections. The materials extracted from these records, when combined with comprehensive reviews of newspapers from Montreal, proved helpful in reconstructing Burroughs's career, as did records on deposit at the Stanstead Historical Society in Stanstead, Quebec.

Chapter 2, a community study of the "Cogniac Street" enclave, turned to many of these same materials. But the core of this particular chapter relied on the tremendous resources at the Archives Nationales du Québec. It was only recently that this institution opened the case files of the Court of King's Bench for the District of Montreal, and I reviewed every criminal case in this district that was tried between 1809 (when the records begin) and 1835, when the counterfeiting industry began its slow decline. These records contain letters and depositions of astonishing detail, not only on counterfeiting, but on other criminal activity in both Canada and the United States. I fleshed out these cases by consulting the bench books of James Reid, chief justice of the Court of King's Bench from 1825 to 1838. Extensive surveys of newspapers in Quebec, New York City, Boston, and Vermont helped round out the picture. So too did a review of almost every travel account published between 1800 and 1850 that described this region and its inhabitants.

While the federal government did not play a significant role in prosecuting counterfeiters before the Civil War, scattered records on deposit at the National Archives and Records Administration proved useful for fleshing out Chapter 3, on the Bank War. A collection of criminal case files from the Eastern District of Pennsylvania was invaluable for researching the exploits of Ebenezer Gleason, Lyman Parkes, and others, while applications for federal pardons filled in much of the picture here and throughout the book. Additional records from the Solicitor of the Treasury revealed the limits of federal prosecution of counterfeiters, as did State Department correspondence concerning extraditions. Sadly, the Second Bank of the United States, which took the lead in prosecuting counterfeiters prior to the 1830s, destroyed its files not long after it closed its doors. The papers of its president, Nicholas Biddle, do survive, and these became the next best thing for filling in the details of the campaigns described in this chapter.

Several other sources contributed to my understanding of local law enforcement during this period, particularly the records of the New England Association against Counterfeiters at both Harvard Business School's Baker Library and the Bostonian Society; the published reports of its successor, the New England Association for the Suppression of Counterfeiting; prison records from Sing Sing and Eastern State Penitentiary, available at the New York and Pennsylvania State Archives; published reports of prison reform associations; and banking records at Harvard Business School's Baker Library and the Massachusetts Historical Society. I supplemented these materials with the usual assortment of newspaper accounts, criminal memoirs, and autobiographies of prison keepers, sheriffs, and other officers of the law. I was not able to make use of municipal police records simply because so many of them were destroyed long ago: the New York City police department, for example, pulped most of its antebellum records early in the twentieth century. The records of other major cities—Boston and Philadelphia, for example—are equally disappointing.

The counterfeiters of the Middle West formed the focus of Chapter 4. Here, research centered on the career of the Brown family in the Cuyahoga River Valley. The various local historical societies proved invaluable, as did the Western Reserve Historical Society. When paired with a review of all the relevant court records and case files from the Portage County Records Center, a portrait of the region's counterfeiters began to emerge. I supplemented this data with manuscripts from the Ohio Historical Society, as well as local newspapers published between 1820 and 1850, particularly Samuel Lane's *Buzzard*. The fortuitous discovery of correspondence, depositions, and other material in the federal court files from New Orleans put flesh on the bones of the narrative, as did pardon applications and the correspondence of several governors at the Ohio State Archives. Most useful of all was Samuel Lane's history of the region, written in the late nineteenth century. Lane, who witnessed many of the counterfeiters' exploits, was a serious historian, interviewing contemporaries and doing extensive research into legal files and other sources. Local histories and newspapers from other states in the region gave insights into similar enclaves that emerged from the 1830s onward.

New York City was the principal entrepôt for bogus notes, and here I turned to the Municipal Archives in New York City. The key collection—and the heart of Chapter 5—proved to be the indictments of the district attorney for the Court of General Sessions. Thanks to the ef-

forts of former archivist Kenneth Cobb, these records have been saved
and microfilmed; they contain a tremendous wealth of detail on crime
in New York City in the nineteenth century. Rather than sample the
records, which would have given an incomplete view of the counterfeit
economy at this time, I reviewed every counterfeiting indictment between 1790 and 1860, a total of approximately one thousand cases. In
time, I identified a separate cache of counterfeiting indictments from
New York City at the American Numismatic Society in Colorado
Springs. Its unusual provenance notwithstanding, I made use of this
additional collection, supplementing the indictments with the extensive collection of prison records and inmate release registers at the New
York State Archives. Surveys of multiple New York City newspapers
(particularly the penny press) provided additional information on key
cases, trials, escapes, and other events that illuminated in detail the
manufacture, distribution, sale, and passing of counterfeit notes, as well
as the corruption of the bank-note engraving industry.

One newspaper in particular deserves special notice: the *National
Police Gazette*. This weekly, which began publication in 1845, provided a
wealth of material on counterfeiters and their adversaries. The editors
kept detailed dossiers on criminals throughout the United States, and
published documents, letters, and reports from far-flung correspondents, providing a useful overview of the criminal underworld. It is a
well-known source, though most historians have used the microfilm
edition available through UMI's American Periodical Series (now ac-
cessible and searchable online). Unfortunately, this collection is woe-
fully incomplete, and only covers the years between 1845 and 1846. A
twenty-year gap follows, with the microfilm beginning again in 1866.
In time, I located two additional runs of the periodical. The first, at the
American Antiquarian Society, covered the rest of the 1840s; the sec-

ond, a recently unearthed set of volumes at the Boston Public Library, covered the years through 1855, as well as scattered issues from the end of the decade. Articles from these issues provided invaluable information on counterfeiting as well as law enforcement.

Many counterfeit detectors have suffered the same fate as police records: unlike more conventional periodicals, libraries generally did not save counterfeit detectors, and few exist today outside of private collections. Using several secondary works in numismatics, I was able to locate a considerable number of these in several research libraries, most notably the American Antiquarian Society, the Library Company, the Free Library of Philadelphia, the New York Historical Society, and the American Numismatic Society. These provided a surfeit of information on counterfeits and counterfeiters, as well as on the different kinds of bogus bills: spurious, altered, raised, and so-called wildcat notes. Aside from a handful of economic historians and numismatists, few scholars have made use of these publications, even though they provide a tremendous amount of qualitative information on the workings of the antebellum economy.

Bank notes are another neglected source. For most people in the nineteenth century, paper money was the most tangible evidence of the market revolution, yet bank notes rarely merit a mention in the historiography on this transformation. Though an iconographic analysis of bank notes was outside the scope of the present project, I made use of them as evidence as much as possible, drawing on extensive collections at the American Numismatic Society, the National Numismatic Collection at the Smithsonian Institution, and the American Numismatic Association. I was assisted in this by the many collectors of obsolete bank notes who have published their own research in journals unknown outside of numismatic circles. This same research was very helpful when it came time to write Chapter 6, on bank note engraving. So too were the bank notes themselves, which bear evidence of the transformation of that industry.

Chapter 7 focuses on a very different kind of paper money: the greenbacks and national bank notes. Here I also drew on more conventional materials: legislative records, economic pamphlets, newspaper accounts, and the government records of the Confederacy. I also relied on the records of the U.S. Secret Service, which survive in two distinct collections. The first, at the National Archives and Records Administration, contains correspondence, agents' reports, descriptions of counterfeiters, and a host of other sources from the early years of the bureaucracy's existence. A second collection of documents on deposit at Secret Service Headquarters in Washington filled out the story. This cache contains materials relating to William Wood, including his extensive reminiscences published in the 1870s and 1880s in Washington, D.C., newspapers. I made use of these records as well as the many memoirs of detectives, police officers, and Secret Service operatives active in the 1860s and 1870s.

This book was largely researched and written before the advent of digital resources. Nonetheless, I was able to make use of some of these materials, beginning with a number of newspapers and diaries from the Civil War. Last-minute searches for selected counterfeiters in Proquest's digital American Periodical Series, Early American Newspapers Series, and its full text version of the *New York Times* yielded several serendipitous finds, as did several other online resources: the collection of legislative materials compiled by the Library of Congress; the "Making of America" project operated by Cornell University and the University of Michigan; Indiana University's "Wright American Fiction, 1851–1875"; and local histories digitized by Ancestry.com.

I hope that the range of sources used in this project will show that the story of counterfeiting—and more broadly, money—is just as much a social, political, and cultural history as a story of economics. It is very strange indeed that historians studying the "market revolution" or the "transition to capitalism" have failed to examine the curious transformations that the money supply underwent during the nineteenth century, even while they have written countless books and articles on changes in production and consumption. Money was the mysterious link between all these elements, a tangible incarnation of the sometimes elusive economic transformation taking place at that time.

ACKNOWLEDGMENTS

This book is all about money, but the obligations I have accumulated over the past decade are personal rather than financial. I have benefited from having a number of teachers, friends, and family members who have illuminated, encouraged, and prodded at all the right moments. What follows is a first installment in payment of the many debts I owe.

As an undergraduate at Haverford College, I studied with several professors who shaped my scholarship and my prose: the political scientist Carol Hager and the classicist Dan Gillis both influenced me greatly. So, too, did Brunilde Ridgway and James Wright of Bryn Mawr College's Classical and Near Eastern Archaeology Department, who supervised my honors thesis on Minoan glyptic art. I am especially indebted to Haverford history professor Roger Lane. His seminar on the history of Philadelphia that I took my senior year is responsible, more than anything else, for my decision to study history of a more recent vintage.

I found a similar set of mentors in the doctoral program in history at New York University. Patricia Bonomi instilled in me a love of New York City's colorful past, while Martha Hodes gave me a respect for the power of narrative history. Richard Sylla introduced me to economic history, and has been a good friend and a thoughtful reader of this book in its different incarnations. Walter Johnson was a remarkable intellectual mentor, and my classes and my conversations with him have informed this book. I owe the greatest debt to my doctoral adviser, Tom Bender. At a time when scholars are encouraged to burrow into their specialties and subspecialties, Tom has pursued an expansive vision of historical research in which the whole is greater than the sum of its parts. This project is very much the beneficiary of his unwavering support and cosmopolitan approach to the study of the past.

In addition to my academic mentors, a number of other people helped make this project happen. I have especially appreciated the advice of the members of Tom Bender's dissertation writing group, as well as that of many other colleagues and friends who read portions of the manuscript and otherwise offered thoughtful criticism: Louis Anthes, David Bowers, Kathleen Brown, Brian Carlson, Joanne Chaison, Kathleen Clark, Duane Corpis, Peter Dizikes, Richard Doty, Mark Elliot, Jim Folts, Walter Friedman, Jim Green, Joshua Greenberg, Shane Hamilton, Peter Hoffer, Roger Horowitz, Joshua Humphries, Geoff Jones, Nancy Koehn, Allan Kulikoff, Michael Kwass, Michael Lacombe, Michael Laskawy, Ari Levine, Mary Lewis, Brian Luskey, Bruce Mann, Laura Mason, Cathy Matson, Thomas McCraw, Michelle Craig McDonald, Roderick McDonald, Lillian Miller, Mary Panzer, Amy Richter, Daniel Richter, Seth Rockman, Reinaldo Román, Jack Rosenthal, David Sampliner, Claudio Saunt, George Selgin, Andy Shanken, Caroline Sloat, Paul Sutter, David Ward, Michael Winship, Wendy Woloson, Robert Wright, Michael Zakim, and Michael Zuckerman. I am grateful as well to the members of my reading group in Cambridge, who gave their thoughts on multiple chapters of the book: Jona Hansen, Mark Peterson, Steven Biel, Michael Willrich, and Jane Kamensky. Special thanks go to Jane: she has been a tremendous mentor and a true friend, and this book is far richer because of our conversations.

All books go through various versions, but this one probably went through more than most. Disappointed with the direction of the project while still in graduate school, I spent some time outside academia. Thanks to my work with editors Henry Grunwald and Sarah Lewis, I became a far better writer, and discovered a love of storytelling that I eventually brought back to my academic work. A subsequent stint working at the *New York Times Magazine* further honed my abilities, and I owe a great debt to the editors and writers there, especially Katherine Bouton, Stephen Dubner, Stephen Hall, Rob Hoerburger, Daniel Lewis, Gerry Marzorati, Adam Moss, Claudia Payne, Michael Pollan, Jamie Ryerson, David Shipley, Alex Star, Catherine St. Louis, Camille Sweeney, Pilar Viladas, and Daniel Zalewski. Special thanks go to Jack Rosenthal. I could not have asked for a better mentor during my stay at the *Times*. Jack gave me a second education in the arts of researching and writing, and I returned to the project a far more resourceful—and intelligible—historian.

I am especially grateful to the staff of the following archives and libraries: New York City's Municipal Archives; the American Antiquarian Society; the New York State Archives; Harvard Business School's Baker Library; the Library of Congress; the National Archives of Canada; the Archives Nationales du Québec; the Secret Service Archives; the National Archives and Records Administration; the Library Company of Philadelphia; the Missouri State Archives; the New York Historical Society; the Ohio Historical Society; the Ohio State Archives; the Portage County Records Center in Ohio; the Massachusetts State Archives; the Western Reserve Historical Society; the Massachusetts Historical Society; the New England Historic Genealogical Society; the American Numismatic Society; the Boston Public Library; the Peninsula Library and Historical Society in Peninsula, Ohio; the American Numismatic Association Money Museum; the Smithsonian Institution's National Numismatic Collection; Hagley Museum and

Library; the Winterthur Museum and Library; and the Historical Society of Pennsylvania. As this partial list might suggest, this book required considerable travel, and many thanks go to those friends who provided me with a place to stay—and some rather delicious meals—during my peregrinations: Tony Apesos, Natasha Seaman, Brian Floca, and Christopher Young. Three people in particular provided a home away from home while I did research in New York City: Michael Lacombe, Michael Laskawy, and David Sampliner. Thank you for the food, wine, and friendship—and a couch on which to sleep.

Many more people provided assistance in other ways. Some loaned copies of documents from archives that I did not have time to visit. John Brooke of Ohio State University lent copies of pardon applications from the Vermont State Archives, while Scott Sandage generously sent me his research notes on Waterman Ormsby; members of the Brown and Gleason families, too, shared genealogical material on their colorful ancestors. Special thanks go to Priscilla Graham, a local historian based in Hudson, Ohio. I met Priscilla while conducting research into the counterfeiters of the Cuyahoga River Valley. She kindly gave me her research notes on James and Dan Brown, took me on a guided tour of the key sites in the area, and even made me dinner. Last but not least, I want to thank the numerous numismatists who shared their considerable expertise, especially David Bowers, Richard Doty, Robert McCabe, and Mark Tomasko, all of whom generously spent time educating a historian in the esoteric subject of nineteenth-century bank notes.

A number of fellowships and grants enabled me to start and finish this project. These included a Henry Mitchell MacCracken Fellowship from NYU; a grant from the Roothbert Fund; a predoctoral fellowship at the Smithsonian Institution; a Grant-in-Aid from the Hagley Museum and Library, which also contributed toward an Arts and Industries Fellowship awarded in partnership with the Winterthur Museum and Library; a Kate B. and Hall J. Peterson Fellowship from the American Antiquarian Society; a Littleton-Griswold Research Grant from the American Historical Association; a grant from the Gilder-Lehrman Institute of American History; an Alfred D. Chandler Fellowship from Harvard Business School; and a Larry J. Hackman Fellowship from the New York State Archives. A predoctoral fellowship in the Program in Early American Economy and Society at the Library Company and a Charlotte W. Newcombe Fellowship from the Woodrow Wilson National Fellowship Foundation enabled me to finish the dissertation. The Newcomen Postdoctoral Fellowship in Business History at Harvard Business School helped me to finish researching and writing the book, as did a grant from the New England Regional Fellowship Consortium. So, too, did a course release from the history department at the University of Georgia.

My agent, Tina Bennett, deserves special credit: she expressed early enthusiasm for the project and introduced me to Joyce Seltzer at Harvard University Press. The rest, as the saying goes, is history. Joyce has been a tremendous editor and mentor, and this manuscript is far more refined and sophisticated on account of her keen eye, sound judgment, and love of language. The anonymous reviewers who gave comments helped immeasurably, as did several other members of Harvard University Press. Jennifer Banks fielded innumerable requests and queries; Maria Ascher oversaw production of the book and kept things running on time. Julie Carlson's editorial prowess refined the manuscript still further, and I deeply appreciated her patience, diligence, and good humor throughout the copyediting process. Last but not least, an eleventh-hour thanks to art director Tim Jones for his skill and sensitivity in designing this book.

Most valuable of all has been the support of my family. My father, an intellectual by inclination, cultivated my curiosity and my interest in history; my mother stood by and supported me, even in the most trying of times. Both also sacrificed a great deal to send me to college, and I am forever indebted to their careful frugality. Special thanks go to my sister as well; she made a much-needed financial contribution at a critical time. Finally, I would like to thank Akela Reason. I met Akela ten years ago, and with a few brief exceptions, we have been inseparable ever since. She has been my critic, my muse, my friend. As we have grown together, our mutual interest in the nineteenth century has immeasurably enriched one another's research and writing. This project could not have been completed without her—or without the aid and assistance of our extended family of four-legged, furry friends Gus, Lily, and Ernie—who have kept Akela warm in bed on those cold winter nights when her husband remained tethered to his desk.

This book is dedicated to the newest arrival in our family: Silas Ezra Mihm. He was born as I completed a draft of this book; he began walking as I commenced final preparations for its publication. He has given me tremendous joy, as well as an appreciation for all that really matters in life. Thank you.

INDEX

Numerals in italics refer to pages with illustrations.